The Lady of Hebrew and Her Lovers of Zion

Toby

Hillel Halkin

The Lady
of Hebrew
and
Her Lovers
of Zion

The Toby Press

The Lady of Hebrew and Her Lovers of Zion

First Toby Press Edition, 2020

The Toby Press LLC
POB 8531, New Milford, CT 06776-8531, USA
POB 2455, London W1A 5WY, England
POB 4044, Jerusalem 9104001, Israel
www.tobypress.com

ISBN 978-1-59264-524-4, *hardcover*

Printed and bound in the United States

Contents

Preface

This book contains twelve essays, ten of which appeared in *Mosaic* magazine in 2015–2018. They have two purposes. One is to introduce English readers having little or no familiarity with them to a number of major Hebrew authors of the nineteenth and early twentieth centuries whose work forms an important part of the literary response to the modern Jewish experience. The other is to explore the reciprocal relationship in this period between Hebrew literature, the evolution of the modern Hebrew language, and the emergence of Zionism as a historic force in Jewish life. The book's twelfth and final chapter reflects on the contemporary relevance of all this.

All the translations in this book are my own. Considerable space has been devoted to them. Besides providing textual illustrations of points made by me, I wished to give the reader a palpable sense of the prose and poetry of writers who have been mostly translated into English poorly or not at all. A poor translation, unfortunately, can be worse than none. The untranslated writer remains unknown outside of his own language. The poorly translated one becomes known to his detriment. I hope I have done something to rectify both injustices in regard to the writers discussed in these pages.

In transliterating Hebrew names, words, and titles in these essays, I have generally done so in terms of their contemporary Israeli pronunciation and its accepted English spelling rather than of the East-European pronunciation to which most of the authors I write about were accustomed. Thus, for example, the Hebrew title of Smolenskin's "A Donkey's Burial," pronounced by him "Kvuros Khamor," is spelled by me *K'vurat Hamor*. As is often done, the English "h," besides representing the Hebrew letter *heh*, has been used to represent – as it does in the case of Smolenskin's novel – the letter *het*, pronounced in Israeli Hebrew like the "ch" in Bach.

I wish to thank Neal Kozodoy, the editor of *Mosaic*, for commissioning these essays; Avner Holtzman of Tel Aviv University for his assistance with my essay on Berdichevsky; Steven Zipperstein of Stanford University for providing me with an advance copy of the chapter on Bialik in his *Pogrom: Kishinev and the Tilt of History*; Jeffrey Saks, Director of Research at the Agnon House in Jerusalem, for reading and commenting on my essay on Agnon and providing supplementary materials; Sara Henna Dahan and Ita Olesker of Toby Press for their careful and thoughtful copyediting; and Matthew Miller, Toby's publisher. This book is dedicated to the memory of Alan Mintz, a good friend and outstanding scholar of Hebrew literature who died in 2017, his life's work sadly uncompleted.

Chapter One

Josef Perl and His Merrie Hasidim

1

A little over two hundred years ago, in 1815, a Hebrew book called *Shivhei ha-Besht*, "The Praises of the Baal Shem Tov," was published in the Belarussian town of Kopys. The Baal Shem Tov, the legendary founder of Hasidism, had died in 1760, more than a half-century previously, and the book's author, Dov Ber of Linitz, was the son-in-law of a man who had been his secretary.

Shivhei ha-Besht, a collection of stories about the Baal Shem, some of them heard by Dov Ber from his father-in-law, quickly went through many editions. In more ways than one, it was a literary milestone. It was the first written life of a figure known until then to his followers and detractors alike only by word of mouth. It initiated a new Hebrew literary genre, the Hasidic tale, which would proliferate in the years to come. And though modeled on an earlier book, "The Praises of the Ari," a hagiography of the Safed kabbalist Yitzhak Luria Ashkenazi printed in 1629, it was written in prose never before seen in a published Hebrew work: simple, functional, and lively, yet riddled with grammatical errors, calque translations from Yiddish, and Yiddish and Slavic words whose

Hebrew equivalents Dov Ber did not know or bother to look for. He was a ritual slaughterer, not a rabbi, and the rabbinic language of his times, with its scholarly conventions, densely compressive style, heavy mixture of Aramaic, and erudite allusions to biblical and rabbinic texts did not interest him and may have been beyond his ken.

Hasidic writings existed before "The Praises of the Baal Shem Tov." Yet they were homiletic and theological rather than anecdotal and were themselves composed in rabbinic language. The great battle that broke out over Hasidism in late eighteenth-century Eastern Europe, a region in which half the world's Jews lived, was fought by rabbis. Both Hasidim and Misnagdim, as the anti-Hasidic forces were called (the Hebrew word means "opponents"), knew and revered the same texts and traditions and excoriated each other in their name.

The Misnagdim were the initial aggressors. As Hasidic teachings and congregations began to spread after the Baal Shem Tov's death, the rabbinic establishment of the day, headed by the renowned Gaon of Vilna, Eliyahu ben Shlomo Zalman Kramer, did its best to stamp them out. Hasidism's emphasis on emotional as opposed to cognitive experience; its downgrading of the life of study that was rabbinic Judaism's highest ideal; its putting faith and trust in God before observance of the details of His Law; the pantheistic implications of its teaching of God's presence in all things; the boisterousness of its communal rites and prayer, with their dancing, singing, shouting, hand-clapping, jumping up and down and other displays of enthusiasm; its cult of the wonder-working tsaddik, the rabbinical holy man believed to serve as an intermediary between God and the ordinary Jew – all were deemed highly dangerous. They threatened the stability of the old order and raised the specter of a renewed outbreak of the antinomian forces, unleashed in the last decades of the seventeenth century by the messianic movement of Sabbatianism, that reached an extreme in the libertinism of Frankism, a post-Sabbatian sect whose leader, the Polish Jew Jacob Frank, converted to Catholicism with his followers in the Baal Shem's lifetime.

The stronger they grew, the more forcefully the Hasidim struck back. By the eighteenth century's end, the two camps were in a state of outright war. Mutual book burnings, excommunications, economic boycotts, physical violence, and the hounding of Hasidic and

Misnagdic minorities by Misnagdic and Hasidic majorities were common. Neither party shrank from what had always been considered, even in the fiercest of Jewish disputes, to be beyond the pale: informing on one's fellow Jews to the Gentile authorities. In 1798, and again in 1800, Misnagdic complaints to the Russian government led to the arrest and imprisonment of Shneur Zalman of Liady, the father of the Habad school of Hasidism, on charges of sedition and illegal currency dealings. (On both occasions, he was questioned by the authorities and freed.) In 1799, Hasidim accused Misnagdic communal officials in Vilna of embezzling public funds, once again leading to police detentions and investigations.

At the same time, success changed Hasidism's character. While some tsaddikim, like the Baal Shem Tov's grandson Nachman of Bratslav, lived materially modest or even impoverished lives far removed from the desire to exercise anything but spiritual power, others took advantage of their followings to amass wealth and property. Such was another grandson of the Baal Shem, Baruch of Mezhibozh, who lived in royal splendor made possible by an ongoing flow of gifts and remittances from his followers. Called *pidyonot*, "redeemings," these offerings were held to be acts of piety that assured their giver of the tsaddik's blessings. The religious justification for them had already been provided by the first-generation Hasidic rabbi Elimelekh of Lizhensk, who stressed the religious duty of supporting the tsaddik lavishly so that, freed from all economic worries, he might concentrate on his spiritual mission.

By the time of *Shivhei ha-Besht*'s publication, Hasidism had developed an entrenched but internally squabbling order of its own. Geographically, it was strongest in the south of Eastern Europe, that is, in Austrian-ruled Galicia and Russian Volhynia and Podolia, all parts of the kingdom of Poland until the latter's late eighteenth-century dismemberment by its neighbors, and weakest in the north, particularly in Lithuania, which remained heavily Misnagdic. Politically, it was split between the Tsarist and Hapsburg empires. Religiously, it was divided into different "courts," each headed by its own tsaddik, some co-existing amicably while others, like those of Shneur Zalman of Liady and Baruch of Mezhibozh, were locked in conflict over principles, influence, and territory.

All of these Hasidic groups had a common enemy not only in Misnagdism but in a new trend, sharing some of Misnagdism's values but clashing with its conservative rabbis, which was rapidly becoming a third force in Jewish life: the Haskalah or Jewish enlightenment. A movement of intellectual and social modernization that arrived from the West, especially from the Berlin of the Jewish philosopher Moses Mendelssohn and his circle, the Haskalah had struck roots in Eastern Europe by the early 1800s. For two reasons, it first did so in Galicia. One was the development there, earlier than in Russia and Poland, of a Jewish middle class intent on social and economic advancement. The other was the official status in Galicia of the German language, adopted by this class at a time when Yiddish was still universally spoken by East-European Jewry. This exposed it to intellectual influences from Germany, among them the attempt of Mendelssohn and his school to bring Judaism into line with European thought and to claim equality for Europe's Jews as full citizens of their native lands who, though professing "the Mosaic faith," should be considered as German, French, or English as their fellow countrymen.

2

One of the Haskalah's foremost representatives in Galicia was Josef Perl (1773–1839). An educator and man of literary cultivation – among his accomplishments was a translation of Henry Fielding's *Tom Jones* into Hebrew from a German version of the English original – Perl, though he unjustly has had to vie for the title, was Hebrew literature's first novelist. His fiction, rarely paid the attention it deserves, ranks to this day among modern Hebrew's finest. Accorded little more than passing mention by the standard histories, it had to wait two hundred years for a full-length treatment, the Israeli scholar Yonatan Meir's six-hundred-page Hebrew study of Perl's major novel *Megaleh T'mirin*, "The Revealer of Secrets." Meir's three ground-breaking volumes, published together in 2013, include an annotated edition of the novel's long out-of-print Hebrew text; thoroughly researched analyses of its sources, conception, composition, encoded allusions, and reception; extensive comparisons with Perl's subsequent Yiddish version of it; a full bibliography; and a long essay by Dan Miron, the doyen of Israeli literary criticism. An outstanding achievement, it will merit no small part of the credit when Perl finally assumes his rightful place in the Hebrew pantheon.

Perl was a native and resident of Tarnopol, a middle-sized town southeast of Galicia's capital city of Lvov, the Austrian Lemberg. Far from Vienna and close to the Russian frontier, Lemberg was the first center of the Haskalah in Galicia, in part due to the determined, if not brutal, figure of Naphtali Herz Homberg. A member of Mendelssohn's circle in Berlin, Homberg was appointed by the Austrian government in 1787 to supervise German-language Jewish schooling in Galicia. Based in Lemberg, he worked tirelessly for the Germanization of the region's heavily Hasidic population – a goal he sought to accomplish by rigorous implementation of a compulsory system of semi-secular education and a variety of other reforms, such as compulsory military service for all Jews and official dress codes barring traditional Jewish garb. Well in advance of German Reform Judaism, whose first synagogue was opened in 1818, he called for a drastic simplification of Jewish prayer and a sweeping liberalization of rabbinic law. Although his success was limited (the Jewish public school system he instituted was shut down in 1806 because of Jewish resistance and small enrollments), Homberg managed to make himself anathema not only to the Hasidim, who loathed him as much as he loathed them, but to many of his fellow Maskilim, as adherents of the Haskalah were called – who, though sympathetic to his aims, objected to his coercive methods.

Perl both was and was not cast in Homberg's mold. Drawn to Hasidism in his youth, he turned violently against it upon embracing the Haskalah, came to consider it the main obstacle to the advancement of Galician Jewry, and agreed with Homberg on the need to enlist the Austrian government in the campaign to break its strength. Yet he remained an Orthodox, Misnagdic Jew all his life and never developed the animus toward rabbinic tradition, in which he was well-versed, that Homberg was driven by. As an educator who restarted a modern Jewish school in Tarnopol in 1813, he believed in combining Orthodoxy with a sense of civic duty and an openness to European culture and science; as an Austrian citizen, he argued for anti-Hasidic legislation, the case for which he made in a German book written in

1816 and entitled *Über das Wesen der Sekte Chassidim*, "On the Nature of the Sect of the Hasidim." An intended exposé of the obscurantism, bigotry, and moral and financial corruption of Hasidic life, the book, to Perl's great disappointment, was banned by the Austrian censor, who feared the stormy Hasidic reaction it might provoke. Undaunted, Perl proceeded to do the next best thing by turning his disappointment into a novel, a genre hitherto unknown in Hebrew. For Hebrew literature, this was a stroke of luck.

3

Published in Vienna in 1819, Perl's novel was declared by its title page to be "The Book Of The Revealer of Secrets, Which Is As It Is Named, For It Reveals That Which Has Hitherto Been Concealed From All Eyes, The Reason For Which Will Be Apparent To The Reader Of The Introduction, In Which All Is Explained At Length." This was followed by: "Wherewith is appended a Glossary of Words used by our fellow Jews in Poland that are found in this and other Books by the Tsaddikim of our Age, so that those of our People who hail from elsewhere may comprehend the Holy Books that our Tsaddikim have written in Poland – and may the Reader take pleasure in it all."

By "Poland" was meant Polish-ruled territory, the home of most Yiddish-speaking Jews before its eighteenth-century partition by Russia, Prussia, and Austria. Informing non-Yiddish-speaking Hebrew readers of the existence of a glossary, however, was only partly the point of this statement. Its aim was also to convey that the book's author, unmentioned on the title page, was a Hasid, since no one else would speak of "the Holy Books that our Tsaddikim have written." This is confirmed on a dedication page that comes next, on which various tsaddikim are acknowledged as having been the book's inspiration, starting with the Baal Shem Tov himself, "that Source and Conduit of Divine Wisdom, the Crown and Glory of Israel." And now the author's name is finally given: he is "the renowned Hasid, Ovadiah ben Petahiah, who resides with the Tsaddikim and Great Men of our Age."

Immediately after this announcement appears a "Public Notice" in which Ovadiah advises the reader that "wherever in this Book appear the titles Rabbi, True Rabbi, Tsaddik, True Tsaddik, Tsaddik of the Age, Perfect Tsaddik, Great Man, Great Man of the Age … and so on, I allude only to the Tsaddikim who worship God, may He be blessed, in Rapture and Ecstasy, not to the Book-Learners left in our Land on whom, alas, the Light has yet to shine." And having made clear that no Misnagdim (for whom "Book-learners" is his derogatory epithet) could merit such superlatives, he proceeds to his promised introduction, which explains how his book came to be written.

He was traveling, Ovadiah writes, on a lonely road one night when, descending from his wagon to reconnoiter, he lost his way and wandered for hours in a forest before encountering an old man. Turning out to be the ancient guardian of the hidden writings of the mysterious Rabbi Adam, mentioned in "The Praises of the Baal Shem Tov" as a source of the Baal Shem's esoteric knowledge, the old man handed Ovadiah a manuscript page and showed him how to make himself invisible by slipping it into his pocket. Upon returning home, Ovadiah tells us, he decided to visit, equipped with this magical charm, the homes of the famous tsaddikim in order to discover what secret virtues their modesty kept them from divulging. In the course of his sleuthing he came across some correspondences that he deemed of sufficient interest to copy, and it is these letters, supplemented by explanatory footnotes, that he is now offering to the public.

We are thus informed, before beginning the main body of Perl's novel, that it will be epistolary in nature and Hasidic in point of view. The more sophisticated reader will suspect from the start, however, that its Hasidic authorship is a ruse. After all, even a Hasid who believes in wonders might find an ordinary Jew's being made invisible by a piece of paper hard to credit, while "Ovadiah the son of Petahiah" is a biblical-sounding name that is likely to be the invention of a Maskil. (The practice of giving imaginary characters biblical names goes back to seventeenth- and eighteenth-century Hebrew dramatic works and was adopted from them by Haskalah authors.) And indeed, "The Revealer of Secrets" will prove to be a Maskilic satire, though not a few Hasidim who read it, contemporary sources relate, were gullible enough to take it at face value, at least for its first several pages. Perl could not have wished for a greater compliment.

4

The first of the 151 Hebrew letters in "The Revealer of Secrets" is "From Reb Zelig Letitchever in Zolin to Reb Zeynvl Verkhievker in Kripin." A part of it reads:

> Yesternight I lingered at our Holy Rabbis after the Evening Prayer & heard him say a few words. They were sweeter than honey & I was much pleased by his being in fine fetal & cozy as always with God. God be praised I learn more from his Stories & Sayings than I could from any other Tsaddik. I could have listened to his Holy Words for days without eating or drinking but he wanted to have a Smoak & go the Privee & so I fetched him his Pipe but before I could light it someone else brought a Coal. And when I saw it was not his pleasure to be walked to the Privee I went home in a merrie mood thanking God for my good fortune at being in our Holy Rabbis Inner Circle & hearing such Amazing Things. Arriving home my wife handed me a Letter brought by someone from your Town. This improved my State of Mind still further because I reckognized your Writing but reading your news of a rag of a Book thats come out against us & all the True Tsaddikim which was sent from Galicia to your Squire my hands began to shake. You say its full of ridickule & lies about the True Rabbis which I wouldnt have believed from anyone but you …. Believe me it might have put me in a Glumness if I hadnt been feeling so mellow. I had a wee dram after reading it that helped drive away bad thoughts but we still have to think of what to do about this Book. For two reasons I fear to break the news to our Holy Rabbi. One is it might cause him agravation God forbid. Not that he musnt have already heard about it in the Upper Worlds but it could upset him to be told in a Lower One. And two suppose he gets back at the writer of this Book he might have the Angel of the Torah burn him alive or the like & so deprive us of the pleasure of doing it ourselves or turning him into the Law.

Setting aside for the moment the question of Zelig Letitchever's language, we are told several things by this letter that set the stage for what is to come: (1) Zelig and Zeynvl, while living in different towns, are followers of the same Hasidic rabbi; (2) This rabbi lives in Zolin, as does Zelig, who (as we soon shall find out) is his secretary; (3) Zeynvl has written Zelig that a wealthy Christian landowner in his own town of Kripin, called by him "the Squire," has gotten hold of a copy of a worrisomely anti-Hasidic book; (4) this book has been sent from Galicia, which means that both Zolin and Kripin are across the border in Russia.

And in fact, "the Book" (in the Hebrew of Perl's Hasidim this is always referred to as *ha-bukh*, using the Hebrew definite article "*ha*" and the Yiddish word for a book of a non-religious and therefore suspect character) is none other than a thinly disguised *Über das Wesen der Sekte Chasidim*. Perl's real-life book on Hasidism is thus at the center of his novel's imaginary plot! And a wild and woolly plot it is, involving so many twists, turns, characters, predicaments, and zany mishaps related by such a large number of correspondents that even the most highly concentrated reader can at times lose the thread of it. I will make do with the briefest of synopses.

Zelig and Zeynvl, without informing the Rabbi of Zolin, resolve to get their hands on the Book, this being the only way to learn what is in it, ascertain how dangerous it is, discover the identity of its author, punish him for writing it, and destroy if necessary all copies of it by buying and burning them. The two men first scheme to get the landowner's Hasidic maid Freyde to steal the Book from the armoire he keeps it in. When this plan goes awry, they forge a letter to him from a colleague in Zolin asking to borrow the Book and have it delivered by a messenger, a young Hebrew tutor in their secret employ who will pass it on to them. The landowner, however, decides to present the Book to his colleague in person; the forgery is discovered; and the tutor, now wanted for fraud, is forced to go into hiding.

Things go from bad to worse. The landowner reads the Book and is convinced by it that the Hasidim are untrustworthy connivers. Calling on him to pay the annual rent for the flour mill he leases from him, Zeynvl encounters him in the company of Freyde. When the landowner refers, while conversing, to a story about the Baal Shem Tov, Freyde asks him how he knows of it and he answers, so Zeynvl writes, "I read it in the Book." Zeynvl's letter continues:

> And with that he went to his Arm War & took the Book & thummbed thro it & said the Story is from The Praises of the Baal Shem Tov. My bones rattled so that I dropped the Rentle Money & when I bent to pick it up some Holy Writings of Rabbi Nachman fell from my Pocket & I snatched them up & kissed them & put them back. Just then the Squires Secretary came to take the Money & the Squire looked in the Book & said what just fell must be the Writings of Rabbi Nachman the Baal Shems Grandson. That means your a Hasid too & I wont lease you the Mill because it says there your allowed to cheat Christians. God forbid I cried it says no such thing. He looked in the Book & said but it says exackly that on page 14 section 7. So I took the Writings from my pocket & found the place & said God forbid Milord it says we can cheat Heathen & Idolaters not you.

The landowner is not impressed by the distinction and seeks to turn the district against the Hasidim. In this he has an ally, a Misnaged named Mordekhai Gold, a successful businessman and newcomer to the area. Gold, who has a sense of humor, plays a prank on Zeynvl by hiding in a hollow tree trunk and pretending to be a devil imprisoned there by the Baal Shem Tov. The credulous Zeynvl tells the world about his supernatural adventure and is made a laughingstock when Gold reveals the truth. Zeynvl and Zelig retaliate by bribing a young Christian woman to accuse Gold of fathering her illegitimate child. (She has in fact had sexual relations with two Zoliner Hasidim.) When this deception, too, comes to light, the woman is spirited away to Galicia in the Rabbi of Zolin's carriage.

Meanwhile, Zeynvl comes to seek an audience with the landowner and discovers Freyde having sex with him. Tiptoeing from the sitting room he has been asked to wait in to the door of the bedroom, he writes Zelig, "I put my eye to the Keyhole & saw that wicked Strumpet in bed with the Squire (dont think I didnt spit on the Floor & wish her in Hell) with his Paintbrush smack in her Paintbox." When Freyde emerges,

> I was left alone with the Wench in the Sitting Room & couldnt but step up to her & say though I dursnt look her in her sawcy

eyes I seen & heard all what went on twixt you & the Squire in the next Room & I mean to write the Holy Rebbe & your Husband & your Kinfolk all about it & let the cat out of the bag. She quaked in her boots she did most specially pon hearing our Holy Rebbes name. For the love of God, she cried, what are you trying to do? You'll have me ruined you will.

Fearing Zeynvl will expose her, Freyde talks the landowner into restoring the mill to him. Soon afterwards she becomes pregnant, and Zeynvl and Zelig, assuming the father is the landowner, plot to blackmail him, too. Yet the culprit turns out to be the Rabbi of Zolin's ne'er-do-well son Hirtsli, who is engaged to the daughter of a wealthy family in the Romanian city of Galatz.

Interspersed with the letters between Zelig and Zeynvl are two additional sets of correspondence, each involving another Hasidic court. One concerns the Rabbi of Aklu and his campaign to win over the prominent Misnaged Moshe Fishl; the other, the Rabbi of Dishpol, a bitter rival of the Rabbi of Zolin. The Dishpoler and the Zoliner are battling over the appointment of a new rabbi in the town of Koven, each promoting his candidate – the Dishpoler's the ignorant son of a rich follower who is prepared to pay well for the favor, the Zoliner's a distinguished scholar and closet Misnaged who feigns allegiance to him in order to get the job. The machinations of the two courts; the scholar's double life; the Dishpoler's attempts to sabotage Hirtsli's engagement so that his own son can marry into the Galatz family's wealth; and the Dishpoler and Zoliner's competing charity networks, whose funds are siphoned off for their own use, comprise this subplot.

In the end, all collapses. The landowner and Mordekhai Gold, aided by the scholar (who, having won the post of rabbi in Koven, now shows his true Misnagdic colors), sway opinion against the Hasidim and cause mass defections from their ranks. The Hebrew tutor is caught and confesses. The Christian woman is apprehended in Galicia and extradited to Russia for trial. Freyde dies from a botched abortion forced on her by the Zoliners when they discover that Hirtsli is the father of her child, ending his engagement.

The debacle mounts. Zelig Letitchever dies suddenly too, believed by the Zoliner Hasidim to be the innocent victim of the Angel of the Torah, which has bungled the Rabbi of Zolin's mystical instructions to kill the author of the Book. The Zoliner, shaken by the incident, has a fatal heart attack while smoking his pipe in the outhouse, to which he has repaired after a strenuous session of drinking and dancing with his Hasidim. Moshe Fishl turns his back on the Aklu Hasidim. The Rabbi of Dishpol is discovered to be in possession of a precious heirloom given him as a "redeeming" by a new follower who filched it from his Misnagdic father. Faced with arrest for concealing stolen property, the Dishpoler and his court escape to Galatz, where they are joined by Zeynvl Verkhievker, whose house has been impounded for his unpaid debts to Mordekhai Gold. Along with other Zoliner Hasidim on the run, all set out from there for Palestine.

The final letter in "The Revealer of Secrets" comes from Zeynvl in Istanbul. After informing its recipient in Zolin that the down-and-out fugitives are in urgent need of financial aid, it concludes:

> One more thing I forgot to write. I recieved a Letter from Home that Mordekhai Gold drat his soul has deeded my House to my Sister & Children & adopted my Eldest Son because he has none of his own & I know the lowdown curr didnt do it out of kindness he just wants God forbid to make my Son a freethinker like hisself. And so Im asking you to talk to my Sister & tell her nothing doing less he pays for my Wife who took sick on the way to Stamboul so Im not left high & dry without her & can pray in the Holy Land for my Son that he wont go picking up any of that mans nasty habits.

It is all because of the Book. If it hadn't been written, it wouldn't have found its way to the landowner. If it hadn't found its way to the landowner, Zeynvl and Zelig wouldn't have schemed to get hold of it. If they hadn't schemed to get hold of it, the events leading up to their and the Hasidim's downfall would never have been set in motion.

Thus does Perl's *Über das Wesen der Sekte Chassidim*, a failure in reality, triumph in the world of the imagination.

5

Gold and pearls are both valuables, and Mordekhai Gold is an idealized self-portrait of Josef Perl. Level-headed, conscientious, and the soul of honor, yet liking a good laugh at whatever deserves it, he is a Jewish gentleman and all a perfect Misnaged should be. It is a sign of the Hasidim's moral degradation in Perl's novel that they are unable to recognize a single one of Gold's good qualities or to attribute any but the worst intentions to him.

But if Gold is a fictional stand-in for Perl, who are the other characters in "The Revealer of Secrets"? Efforts have been made to identify some of them, based on Perl's encrypting use of syllabic inversion and *gematria*, the ancient method of parsing Hebrew words by the numerical value of their letters. Zolin, for example, is Liozno, the Belarussian town that was Habad's center before it moved to Liady, while the numerical value of Dishpol, spelled *daled, yud, shin, peh, alef, lamed*, is 425, the same as that of Mezhibozh, spelled *mem, ayin, zayin, bet, vav, shin*.

Yet as Yonatan Meir observes, one mustn't make too much of such things. Although the rivalry between the Zoliner and the Dishpoler may resemble that between Shneur Zalman of Liady and Baruch of Mezhibozh, neither man is closely modeled on these figures, and Perl's Rabbi of Zolin and his court have none of the intellectuality and theological daring that characterized early Habad. All of the Hasidim in "The Revealer of Secrets" are equally venal and debauched, without the slightest redeeming feature. One would never guess from Perl's novel that Hasidism was a revolutionary movement that galvanized the Jewish masses of Eastern Europe with its faith, dynamism, and valorization of the ordinary Jew who felt overlooked by the text-driven legalism of Misnagdism and crushed by the class structure of East-European Jewish society. As portrayed by "The Revealer of Secrets," it is simply one huge swindle.

Perl was aware that he could be accused of gross distortions, and refuting such a charge is the purpose of Ovadiah's many footnotes in the book. Consisting of references to well-known Hasidic texts, these are meant to demonstrate that the beliefs and practices depicted in "The Revealer of Secrets," no matter how bizarre or unscrupulous, are attested to by Hasidism's canonical writings. Thus, for example, Zelig's fears, expressed in his first letter, of invoking the intervention of the Angel of the Torah are footnoted by Ovadiah: "See 'The Praises of the Baal Shem Tov,' p. 2." The cited passage reads:

> Once, the son of the [local] rabbi asked the Baal Shem Tov to make manifest the guardian Angel of the Torah so that it might be questioned about some matter, but the Baal Shem refused and said: "If we make, God forbid, the slightest mistake in our conjurations, it could be highly dangerous." ... But when he [the rabbi's son] persisted day after day, he [the Baal Shem] could no longer refuse him, and so they fasted [to purify themselves] from one Sabbath to the next and underwent the required ritual ablutions, and when the Sabbath was over, they performed the appropriate conjurations. All at once the Baal Shem Tov cried out, "Ai! Ai! We've made a mistake! The Angel of Fire is going to burn the town down! Everyone knows you're a good Jew – quick, go tell your father and the rest of the town to run for their lives, because it's going to burn." And so it did.

Ostensibly for the benefit of his supposed Hasidic readers, Ovadiah's footnotes are used by Perl to address his actual Misnagdic ones. To Ovadiah's mind, the citation from "The Praises of the Baal Shem Tov" comes to assure his fellow Hasidim: "You see? There is nothing outlandish about believing in a guardian Angel of the Torah or ascribing such powers to it, because the Baal Shem Tov did the same." As intended by Perl, they convey: "Don't imagine for a moment that any of these absurdities have been invented by me, because they've been part of Hasidism all along."

Although these references to Hasidic sources, his knowledge of which was extensive, were meticulously accurate, Perl knew that few readers would bother to check them. In a fictional sequel to his novel entitled *Bohen Tsaddik* or "Testing for a Righteous Man," several Hasidim are arguing about "The Revealer of Secrets," of whose satirical nature they are by now aware. Two of them have this exchange:

Avrom: Listen here! I heard there was some footnotes in his book. Well, I ask you: can you really believe that all that stuff comes from *our* books?

Mordekhai: And suppose it does. Who knows if what the tsaddikim were thinking when they wrote it is what that atheist says in his atheist book? We could live to be a thousand and not know what they were thinking, and that lowlife copies it and thinks he knows what it was.

In "Testing for a Righteous Man," "The Revealer of Secrets" is being talked about everywhere. Like the impact in "The Revealer of Secrets" of *Über das Wesen der Sekte Chasidim*, this was as much literary wish-fulfillment as it was a novelistic stratagem; in actual fact, "The Revealer of Secrets" sold poorly. Not many readers appreciated Perl's freewheeling mixture of fact and fiction, which seems almost post-modern today. Similar cases of self-referentiality, to be sure, can be found in previous European literature, such as in the well-known passage in *Don Quixote* in which two of its characters discuss Cervantes's verse novel *La Galatea*. There, however, this is a passing joke, whereas for Perl it is a central plot device. Precisely because he wrote *Über das Wesen der Sekte Chassidim* in the unrealistic hope of changing reality, the line between the real and the unreal was easily crossed by him.

6

Still, a device is only a device. Given the simplistically black-and-white contrast between "The Revealer of Secrets'" nefarious Hasidim and its upright Misnagdim, which precludes all psychological subtlety, it needs to be asked what the source of the novel's appeal is. The most obvious answer is the vibrancy of its language.

This language is a parody of the prose of "The Praises of the Baal Shem Tov" and other popular Hasidic works, such as the mystical stories of Nachman of Bratslav, a collection of which was published the same year that *Shivhei ha-Besht* was. The Hebrew of Perl's Hasidim is even more faulty, its grammar more atrocious, its Yiddishisms grosser. Moreover, they are proud of it. In his introduction to "The Revealer of Secrets," Ovadiah writes:

I've copied all these Letters exactly in the Language they were written … even though I've seen, alas, how often the Mockers of our Times make sport of the Faithful, saying they can't write the Holy Tongue properly, the which they garble like simple Ignoramuses. But I say: What's all their Mockery to me? Let those pretenders to being Jewish laugh all they like! I'll write in the Language of the Tsaddikim and the Faithful, that of the Holy Praises of the Baal Shem Tov and the Holy Writings of Rabbi Nachman and his Holy Stories most of all … for now everyone sees with his own eyes how the whole World, even if it doesn't keep the Faith, is so used to writing in the simple language of our Tsaddikim, which has spread with God's help to Jews everywhere, that whichever of our People writes what they call Pure Hebrew is known to be a Freethinker and a Freethinker is what I say he is.

The "freethinkers" were the Maskilim, whose high style the Zeynvls and Zeligs could never master. Hasidism made Hebrew available to ordinary Jews in a way it had not been before. No less than their Misnagdic opponents, the Hasidim of Perl's day considered Hebrew the written medium that a male Jew with any education was expected to use, Yiddish being an acceptable substitute for the unlettered alone. But because it did not seek and even disdained to reflect "book learning," or to adhere to traditional standards of correctness, Hasidic Hebrew was not only far easier to learn to read and write, it had a spontaneity and naturalness that Maskilic Hebrew lacked.

Compare, for example, Zeynvl Verkhievker's closing tirade against Mordekhai Gold with a passage in Avraham Mapu's "The Painted Vulture," published in installments between 1857 and 1869, in which there is also a biting description of a wealthy Misnaged. Named Ga'al, his detractor is not a Hasid but a young Maskil, who writes of him:

Such is Ga'al. His heart is crooked, yea, most abominably loathsome, for he would give his soul, his very soul, for money, and all of his money and fortune for public acclaim. When his hands stained with iniquity disperse funds to the poor, they always do so in the public eye, that he might be honored with due pomp and ceremony: he, the pious one in all his ways and the righteous one in all his works!

Such rhetoric has an elegance of its own, and Mapu's neoclassical pastiche of post-biblical and biblical Hebrew (the final phrase in the passage comes from the book of Psalms) set a standard for Hebrew prose fiction that lasted for years. Indeed, its dominance led not a few critics, disqualifying "The Revealer of Secrets" for its bastardized language, to award the palm of the first Hebrew novel to Mapu's 1853 "The Love of Zion." Even Perl, though he surely would have resented such a judgment, would have agreed that the Hebrew of "The Revealer of Secrets" was fit only for satire. And yet how much more forceful than Ahituv's "his hands stained with iniquity disperse funds to the poor…that he might be honored with due pomp and ceremony" is Zeynvl's "The lowdown curr didn't do it out of kindness!" Precisely because it is so Yiddish-inflected, the language of Perl's Hasidim has more of the feeling of real speech than anything written in Hebrew between its demise as an oral medium in ancient times and its twentieth-century spoken revival – a millennium-and-a-half in which it was the second language of every educated Jew and the mother tongue of none.

Translating "The Revealer of Secrets" is difficult. It has been tried once, by Dov Taylor, whose English rendition was published in 1997. In his preface to it, Taylor asks: "Is there a model that approximates in English the way Perl's Hasidic characters express themselves in Hebrew?" His answer is: "Today one can hear in New York, London, Jerusalem, and elsewhere, the English spoken by Jews whose mother tongues are Yiddish and Polish. It is they who provide the linguistic models for an English approximation to Perl's Hebrew-speaking characters, and I acknowledge my debt to them."

But while Taylor's use of Jewish immigrant English is ingenious, the analogy drawn by it is fallacious. Perl's Hasidim (who were actually more likely to know Ukrainian than Polish) are not immigrants. They are native sons of their region, and while their Hebrew is heavily Yiddishized, Yiddishizing it in English can only misrepresent their social and linguistic relationship to their environment. My own approach in the translated excerpts in this essay has been to opt for a native-sounding English such as might have been written by early nineteenth-century speakers with enough education to spell most if not all words correctly but with no interest in rules of punctuation, let alone in polished prose, and unaware that the capitalization of nouns is no longer in fashion. I think such language conveys something not only of the at-homeness of Perl's Hasidim in their world but of their rascally determination and grit. That they ultimately win our affections is the real secret of "The Revealer of Secrets"' charm and must be taken into account in any discussion of it.

7

"Milton was a true poet and of the Devil's party without knowing it," said William Blake about *Paradise Lost* in one of literary criticism's great one-liners. Blake meant, of course, that while Satan is the arch-villain of Milton's poem, Milton so identified with him subconsciously that he made him its most interesting and memorable character. He remains with us long after Adam, Eve, God, Jesus, and *Paradise Lost*'s many angels and archangels have faded from memory.

Something similar might be said of "The Revealer of Secrets." Although Zelig Letitchever and Zeynvl Vierkhevker were intended by Perl to be viewed as mentally benighted and morally depraved epitomes of the folly of Hasidism, they end up stealing the show. We laugh at their ignorance, are bemused by their credulity, shake our heads at their perversity, and enjoy them unreservedly. The uninhibited liveliness of their speech is matched by the shameless vitality of their actions.

In his essay on "The Revealer of Secrets" in Meir's critical trilogy, Dan Miron makes this same point. Perl's "conscious or unconscious identification" with his novel's language, Miron writes, "necessarily points to his unconscious and perhaps conscious identification with the world this language emerges from." Although as a rational Maskil, Perl considered Hasidism a disgrace, he was instinctively attracted to its

> pursuit of enjoyment, gratification, and uplifting and exalting emotional and physical experience. [Perl's Hasidim] break every rule not only because they crave money, power, and other

material things, though they do, but because of their erotic rela-tionship to reality, their wish to cast all its limitations aside.

Yet it is not an unrestrained libidinousness that makes us side with the likes of Zelig and Zeynvl. While both men are minor accomplices in the sexual infractions of others, neither is himself a sexually charged being; nor, although both like to eat and drink, are they gluttons or sots. They are hardly the Rabelaisian voluptuaries that Miron suggests they are.

What most attracts us to them, rather, is their sheer energy. They are indefatigable. Nothing gets in their way or gets them down. They recognize no obstacle, concede no defeat, bounce back with a new plan each time a previous one is thwarted – and always with the same inex-haustible good cheer. They do not grouse or complain; they are never self-pitying; they are always looking ahead for the next opportunity. When we identify with them, we identify with that part of ourselves that insists on believing, sometimes against all odds and appearances, that it is possible to persevere and come out on top.

Such essential optimism was a large part of Hasidism's attraction for East-European Jews, who objectively had little to be optimistic about. Misnagdism typically took a dim view of the human condition; life for it was a trial whose only hope for acquittal lay in one's personal piety and scrupulous ritual observance. The Haskalah thought in terms of gradual social and economic progress that would take decades. Hasidism preached the rewards of the here-and-now and the satisfaction of making the best of things. It made its followers feel empowered and able to cope.

It is this, I would say, that made Perl, who knew Hasidism from within, secretly envious of it. He *thought* Hasidism was nonsense; he *felt* its emotional buoyancy and power. Moreover, he knew that without a similar power to move masses of Jews, the Haskalah could never triumph in reality as it does fictionally in "The Revealer of Secrets." Herein lies the subtext of the novel.

8

"Testing for a Righteous Man," written in an epistolary form like "The Revealer of Secrets," was published twenty years after it in 1838, a year before Perl's death. History in those two decades had not gone as he had wished it to. Although the Haskalah had made further inroads in Galicia, it remained a small, elite movement, while Hasidism had grown even stronger and established ever more powerful dynasties. Its war with Misnagdism had ended in an undeclared but lasting truce, leaving the Maskilim to carry on the anti-Hasidic battle by themselves. In the reign of Franz II (1804–1835), the Austrian government gradually retreated from its forced Germanization policies, a trend accentuated during the lengthy period of reaction under Metternich that followed the 1815 Congress of Vienna. Wary of all forms of liberalism, the regime ceased to take the Haskalah's side against Galicia's Hasidim.

"Testing for a Righteous Man" reflects Perl's disillusionment with these developments. Yet the book's opening chapters are playful, consisting of a series of vignettes in which Ovadiah ben Petahiah, curious to know how "The Revealer of Secrets" has been received by his fellow Hasidim, publishes samples of their reactions. At first he uses his powers of invisibility to eavesdrop on their conversations about the book; soon, however, he realizes that he cannot write these down fast enough to produce accurate versions of them. Frustrated, he resorts to the Hasidic custom of a "dream question," praying for an answer to come to him in his sleep – and so it does when he dreams of the underground passage by which, according to "The Praises of the Baal Shem Tov," the Baal Shem once set out for the Land of Israel before being turned back by a giant frog that blocked his way. Upon waking, Ovadiah finds this route, encounters the same frog, and rescues it from its subterranean prison, whereupon it is restored to its normal size. In gratitude, it gives him a magical gift like the one received by him in "The Revealer of Secrets": a portable *Schreibtafel* – the German word means "writing slate" – that registers every word uttered in its vicinity. With it comes an instruction manual that tells him what to do when the slate is full: it needs only to be breathed on by a righteous man to be wiped clean and made ready for re-use.

This science-fiction instrument, imagined by Perl over two decades before the first phonograph recordings, enables Ovadiah to resume his project. Since the field work can now be done by others, he hires two assistants to make the rounds with the *Schreibtafel* and transcribes what they record. All goes well until the slate is full and is returned to him for erasure. Then, looking for a righteous man to breathe on it, he discovers that finding one is more difficult than he had thought it would be.

The search for such a person constitutes the second and longer half of Perl's book. At first, Ovadiah sticks to the confines of Hasidism. Sure of finding his quarry there, he sees no point in troubling "the Tsaddikim of the age," since any of their followers should be righteous enough to erase the *Schreibtafel*, too. Yet none of those asked to breathe on it can erase a single line written there, and when Ovadiah tries the new Rabbi of Dishpol, the successor of the Zoliner's old rival (at first, not wishing to bother him, by surreptitiously placing the slate before his mouth while he is in a drunken stupor), the results are the same. Other tsaddikim do no better, and spying on them while using his powers of invisibility to find out why this is so, Ovadiah discovers that each secretly reviles his competitors as fraudulent imposters. Since all can't be wrong, he concludes that all must be right and loses his faith in Hasidism.

Erasing the *Schreibtafel* no longer matters very much, but Ovadiah is now driven by a new concern: are there righteous men *anywhere* in the Jewish world – and if so, where? In pursuit of them, he wanders from place to place. Turning to the Misnagdim, he sees that all their learning and ritual piety are a sham, an outward display calculated to earn them the social status, recognition, and material comforts that they crave. Next, he approaches the Maskilim, again to be disappointed: they are simply aping the European culture they aspire to possess without meaningfully internalizing it. Perhaps he should look to the plain workaday Jew who is too busy earning a living to identify with any of these groups? But no, this, too, is an illusion. The Jewish commercial and working classes prove to be just as vice-ridden. They lie, cheat, pad their bills, produce and deal in shoddy goods, falsify their weights and measures, and renege on their commitments. The struggle for a livelihood has only degraded them even more.

Having searched in vain for a ray of light in all this gloom, Ovadiah writes to a friend (since his abandonment of Hasidism, his Hebrew has become more Maskilic):

Such is the behavior of the population I have seen as I have gone from town to town and land to land. It has all but made me ill and I can bear it no longer. All human endeavor has become tiresome to me. The world is not what I imagined. As long as I stayed home and paid no attention to its affairs, I thought our people had retained its ancient character. Yet ever since I have taken to scrutinizing its ways, I see that these are worlds apart from those of our ancestors. May God in His mercy take pity on us and rescue our people from its confounded state.

In his despair, Ovadiah decides to leave Eastern Europe. Had he done so ten or fifteen years later, he might have joined the growing number of Jews, mostly from Germany, heading for America. Yet when "Testing for a Righteous Man" was written, this emigration had hardly begun. And so, turning eastward rather than westward, Ovadiah sets out for the land of the fabled medieval Jewish kingdom of Khazaria, where he hopes to encounter the vanished glories of the Jewish past.

Although he doesn't find what he has hoped to, what he does find gives him new hope. The glories of Khazaria are gone without a trace, but while traveling in the vicinity of Crimea, Ovadiah is overtaken by a blizzard and takes shelter in a farmer's home. To his surprise, the man turns out to be a Jew. Not only that, he introduces Ovadiah to a community of Jewish farmers like himself, all inhabitants of the area. They live, Ovadiah writes, in a half-dozen villages, most having Hebrew names, along the Ingol River, on either side of which they work the land "industriously and in the best possible fashion, from every Sunday morning until Friday afternoon." They also tend cows, their dairy products being the best in the region, and "their homes, though small like all farmers', are spick-and-span as most farmers' are not." Moreover, "while all the peasants of the countryside are heavy drinkers, hardly a Jewish farmer whom I have met is fond of alcohol and a single tavern serves all."

On Sabbaths, all the farmers go to synagogue. On weekdays, they pray in their fields during the growing season and spend much of the long winter studying Jewish texts, of which every house has a bookshelf. Hospitable to a fault, Ovadiah writes, they "generously bestow with beaming faces what I haven't even asked for" and are "scrupulously honest in all their dealings." They live simply, subsist on the fruits of their labor, and are content with their lot. When he hands the *Schreibtafel* to the farmer he is staying with, the latter wipes it clean with one breath – an ordinary feat along the Ingol, where anyone can do the same.

Ovadiah's joy at what he sees knows no bounds. A changed man, he resolves to become a farmer himself. "I have made up my mind," he informs his friends, "to live here with my fellow Jewish tillers of the soil and be as one of them. Soon, God willing, I'll send for my wife and family to join me."

Perl's Jewish farmers were not figments of his imagination. The Ingol was a real river, joining the southern Bug on its way to the Black Sea north of Kherson, midway between Odessa and the Crimean peninsula; near it, seven Jewish agricultural colonies had been established in 1806 by the Tsarist government with the aim of encouraging Jews to work the lands of "New Russia," the area of southeastern Ukraine conquered from the Turks in the late eighteenth century. Several of these colonies were given Hebrew names, such as Nahar Tov ("Good River"), Har Shefer ("Mount Plenty"), and S'deh Menuhah ("Field of Rest"), and within a few years close to two thousand families had settled in them. Their fate, however, was less rosy than Ovadiah's description of it. The land proved unsuitable for small holdings and the colonists never received the initial financial assistance promised them. Many fell ill; many died; many, demoralized, gave up, sold their properties, and returned to where they had come from. In 1810, all government funding for the project was cut off, and while it was partially resumed in 1823, an 1845 census reported a total of 1,500 Jewish farming families in the entire Kherson region, less than there had been thirty years previously.

Perl never visited the New Russia project. His knowledge of it came from the reports and impressions of others, which were enough to make him realize that the utopia sketched by Ovadiah had no basis in reality. Yet utopias are best read as critiques of the present, not as blueprints for the future; by imagining what might be, they put what is to shame. While not credible horses, Jonathan Swift's Houyhnhnms in *Gulliver's Travels* are devastating critics of humanity, as Ovadiah's farmers are of their fellow Jews.

9

"I thought I was in a little Land of Israel," Ovadiah writes of his tour of the New Russia colonies. This does not make Perl an early Zionist. The trope of Zion away from Zion was commonplace in Jewish writings, to say nothing of Christian ones. In "The Revealer of Secrets," Palestine is no more than a cover for charity scams, a refuge for Hasidic scoundrels, and a mausoleum for sham saints. "The first thing we'll do when we get there," writes Zeynvl from Istanbul, "is go to the Graves of the True Tsaddikim from our Parts & tell them everything... & give them no rest until they take Vengeance on our Foes. With Gods help your sure to see Wonders soon amen selah."

Wonders, however, were not reasonably to be expected from the Jewish community of Palestine in the first half of the nineteenth century. Small in size, it was divided into feuding ethnic and religious factions united only by an extreme Orthodoxy and a dependence on philanthropy from abroad. The Ottoman empire, though fraying at the edges, was still largely intact and its rule in Palestine faced no foreseeable challenge. Large-scale Jewish settlement there was not part of Jewish or general discourse in Perl's lifetime. The first influential Jewish proponent of such an idea, the Sephardi rabbi Yehuda Alkalai, did not publicly promote it until the year of Perl's death; while in America, the Jewish politician and journalist Mordecai Manuel Noah, after having unsuccessfully sought to found a Jewish mini-state on an island near Buffalo, sounded a pioneer call for the massive return of Jews to Palestine five years later, in 1844. Christian Zionism, a largely British phenomenon, had its start in England at about the same time.

Perl's two novels, however, are not unrelated to Zionism. They depict an Eastern Europe whose Jewish society is fundamentally ill and in need of a radical cure. Its malady is both spiritual and economic – economic before spiritual, since its spiritual life has been corrupted by a greed that shuns honest work and seeks to turn religion into a money-making machine. It is noteworthy that anti-Semitism, though Perl was not blind to it, is marginal to both his novels. Not only is it not the real problem, it is treated – as it generally was by the Haskalah – as an understandable Christian reaction to the debased nature of Jewish existence. "Just as one cannot find the remedy for a disease if its cause remains unknown," Ovadiah writes in his next-to-last letter from New Russia,

> so no one can be helped to rise from misfortune without knowing what led to his fall. Thus, I have felt obliged to inquire into the reason for our people's decline and to inform it of what, to the best of my modest intellectual ability, I have found this to be. In all my travels, I have seen that we differ from our revered ancestors not only in matters of belief, but also in those of getting and spending. Our abandonment of agriculture and handicrafts are the root of all the evils that have overtaken us.

Perl was not the only Maskil to argue along these lines, although he was one of the first. Economic productivization and a return to the soil were an intrinsic part of the Haskalah's program for East-European Jewry. Typically Maskilic, too, is Ovadiah's conception of how this is to be brought about:

> It would be simple to purge ourselves [of this economic distortion] if only our leadership and upper class in every town were to agree to carry out the enormous reforms needed to distance ourselves from these vices, for the rest of our people would surely listen to them. I hope that our leaders in other countries will agree with me, too – and if any find fault with what I say, let them [think of other ways to] come to the rescue of our wretched people, whose gratitude they will earn.

The solution is to be introduced from above: a Jewish elite, fully converted to Haskalah ideals as Ovadiah has been, will impose it on the Jewish masses. That such change might come from the masses themselves is not conceivable to Ovadiah. Led astray by Hasidism, into whose exploitative clutches they have fallen, they will have to be freed by more independent and rational minds.

Zionism, when it would appear as a serious force in Eastern Europe toward the end of the nineteenth century, would adopt much of the Haskalah's analysis. It, too, would argue that East-European Jewry was economically and socially deformed; that drastic structural changes in Jewish life were called for; and that these included an embrace of physical and agricultural labor. A new start had to be made. Where Zionism would break with Haskalah thinking was in insisting that this start could be made only in a new land; that this land had to be Palestine; that anti-Semitism was more than a natural response to Jewish failings and would not disappear if and when they did; and that its own success depended on becoming the mass movement that the Haskalah never was.

For success to be possible, Zionism had to adopt not only the Haskalah's critical habits of thought but many of the features of Hasidism: its enthusiasm, its rebellion against established authority, its missionizing zeal, its anti-elitist character, its messianic impulses, its faith in miracles. It is told of the early Hasidic master Levi Yitzhak of Berdichev that once, on his way to synagogue on Yom Kippur, he glanced through the window of a house he was passing, saw a group of Jews playing cards with intense concentration, and exclaimed, "God, how wondrous are your people! Just think what they will be like when they serve You with the same devotion!" Zionism was to do the reverse and tap the religious energy of Hasidism for secular purposes. Although this was not what Josef Perl had in mind when he ended "The Revealer of Secrets" on the way to the Land of Israel, it might serve as the novel's last footnote.

Chapter Two

Avraham Mapu and the Lady of Hebrew

1

Avraham Mapu (1808–1867), the first Hebrew novelist.

Actually, not. That honor, we have seen, rightfully belongs to Josef Perl. Yet it has generally been accorded to Mapu. This is how he has been mentioned by the encyclopedias, treated by the literary histories, and read by his readers, many of whom had never opened a novel in any language before discovering him. Such was the Hebrew poet and literary critic Ya'akov Fichman, born in 1881. At the age of twelve, as a pupil in the heder, the Jewish schoolhouse of Eastern Europe, Fichman stole into the room of his teacher's absent son, reputed to be a reader of Hebrew literature, and found there a copy of Mapu's first volume of fiction, his 1853 biblical novel "The Love of Zion." In a memoir penned long afterwards in Tel Aviv, Fichman wrote:

> I looked at the book and was caught up from the first page in its bright, visionary net. I don't know whether I grasped everything I read intellectually or emotionally. I only remember a blissful, wondrous day. The light in the room was rose-colored, and rose

was the color that lit the pages of the book – the whole world was bathed in its freshness...I sat in the room holding my breath for fear someone might notice I was missing, devouring its pages one after another. I was like a man lost many days in a wilderness who suddenly comes across a pure mountain spring. My heart stopped beating; my eyes saw only the book; the sounds of the world no longer reached me....I read all day from morning to night, and when I stepped out of the room the sun was setting and the people around me were all strangers, as if I had returned from a distant land.

Novels can do that to one when one is twelve. They rarely have such an effect past early adulthood, even though – or rather, because – one has become a better, more experienced reader. Upon approaching "The Love of Zion" for the first time today, therefore, one can't expect to have Fichman's reaction, especially since today's Hebrew-reading twelve-year-olds don't have it, either. In fact, they don't read Mapu at all. Who does? Even more than other once widely read and now neglected nineteenth- and early twentieth-century Hebrew authors, he has become a literary antique. He isn't like such historical novelists of his times as Walter Scott or James Fenimore Cooper, who remain enjoyable even though they, too, no longer have much of an audience.

Reading Mapu today is tiresome. His dialogue is stilted. His descriptions are trite, his plots wearyingly intricate and improbable; each time one thinks one more unlikely event can't take place in them, it does. His many characters are rarely memorable. When they reappear in one of his novels after an absence, one often has to thumb backwards to remind oneself who they are.

On top of all this is his neo-biblical prose. High-flown in its day, it has become arcane in our own. Take "The Love of Zion"'s beginning, which might be rendered in contemporary English as:

> In the days of Ahaz the king of Judah, there was a man in Jerusalem named Yotam ben-Aviezer, a high official and military commander. He was a wealthy man who owned fields and vineyards in the Carmel and the Plain of Sharon, sheep and cattle in

Bethlehem, and fine, splendidly furnished mansions, and he had two wives, Hagit bat-Ira and Na'ama.

In terms of the information conveyed by these lines, Mapu's nineteenth-century readers would have read it no differently. Yet read literally, the words would have been (their biblical source or association is indicated in brackets):

A man there was [Job 1:1] in Jerusalem in the days of Ahaz king of Judah [Isaiah 7:1] and his name was Yoram son of Aviezer, a governor in Judah [Zechariah 9:7] and a captain over thousands [I Samuel 18:13], and he owned fields and vineyards in the Carmel and Sharon and flocks of sheep and cattle in Bethlehem of Judah, and he had silver and gold [Genesis 24:35], palaces of ivory [Psalms 45:19], and all manner of pleasant things [Isaiah 2:16], and two wives did he have, the name of one being Hagit the daughter of Ira and the name of the other Na'ama [I Samuel 1:2].

In translating such prose, there is no point in trying to reproduce its biblical diction or syntax. This would make it seem bizarre in a way that it was not for readers of its day, who were thoroughly conversant with the Bible and accustomed to Hebrew's long literary tradition of drawing on biblical language. It would only obscure Mapu's winning moments, of which there are some. One of these occurs early on in "The Love of Zion," in a scene in which its hero and heroine, the prenatally destined for each other, unhappily parted, and ultimately reunited Amnon and Tamar, meet for a second time. Tamar is the beautiful and plucky daughter of Yedidiah, a wealthy Jerusalem aristocrat and minister in the court of the Judean king Hezekiah, a contemporary of the prophet Isaiah. It is the late eighth century BCE; Judah and its northern rival Israel are enemies, and the armies of the expanding Assyrian empire are threatening both. Amnon, a rustic shepherd, is unbeknownst to himself and others the son of Yedidiah's best friend Yoram, who has gone missing in war and is presumed dead. Encountering Tamar vacationing in the countryside, he gives her a bouquet of wildflowers. The next day, wandering by a stream with flowers she has picked herself, she spies him with his flock on its far bank. "Like two fluttering doves," Mapu writes,

> their eyes, too shy to meet, skimmed the gladsome water, each glimpsing the other's fair form in its faithful mirror. First to speak, Tamar held out her flowers.
>
> "Here, dear sir," she said. "Permit me to pay back my debt to you."
>
> "You can see for yourself, miss," said the youth, "that I can't reach across the water."
>
> "If you can't reach me," Tamar said, "I'll reach you." And she cast her flowers into the current for it to carry them to his feet.

This is charming. But then,

> "Miss!" cried Amnon in a fright.
>
> Tamar looked and recoiled in mortal dread, for a fierce lion had stalked from the reeds along the stream. Of fearful mien, it had a mane whose hairs stood up like nails; a tail as thick as a cedar tree; eyes that flashed fiery sparks; a throat like an open sepulcher; a red flame of a tongue thirsting for the blood of victims. Swiftly and surely, it bounded with powerful stride toward the flock on the bank, then paused to spring on the human prey it feasted its eyes on. Faster than lightning, Amnon aimed his bow and a moment later the lion let out a single, terrible roar, its vitals pierced by an arrow. Lifeless, it fell ten paces from Tamar, who lay in a deathly swoon.

Amnon hastens to revive Tamar and says:

> "Be calm and have no fear, gracious maiden. The peril has passed; the danger of death is no more. The Lord gave your servant's arm strength and my arrow struck home and felled the beast that would have felled you."

And so,

Amnon restored Tamar to her senses and calmed her agitated spirits. At last she spoke and said: "O wondrous God! What man can look upon life and death in the balance and remain resolute? Tender young maid that I am, I have just seen both. How will I still the storm within me? The lion was right before me. How dreadful were its horrid teeth, its fangs as sharp as swords! It glared as though meaning to tear my heart apart and crunch my bones....and your right arm, brave lad, saved me from its clutches. You have been like a brother to me in danger; a good angel hastening to my aid. Great has been your kindness; no thanks can equal it."

"Salvation is from God," Amnon replied. "He it is who emboldened me to vanquish the king of beasts. Rise and bless your Savior."

This is turgid. No lion was ever more cartoonishly ferocious or dispatched with greater ease; no rescued damsel in distress more prolix in her gratitude; no young dragon slayer more demure in disclaiming credit. Long before the last page of "The Love of Zion" has been reached (by which Tamar and Amnon, his true identity revealed, are about to be wed at last; Yoram has returned from long captivity; the Assyrians have been repulsed from the gates of Jerusalem, and all good deeds have been rewarded and evil ones punished), one wishes one had arrived at it – and not to find out how the story ends. That much one already has guessed.

Although Mapu's novels were highly popular in his age with the small Hebrew readership for them that existed, they were criticized for their naiveté practically from the start. The prominent Haskalah author Moshe Leib Lilienblum relates in his autobiography how he excitedly devoured "The Love of Zion" in 1863 as a twenty-year-old yeshiva student after first combing religious texts for permission to read a work of secular fiction. Two years later he read its 1865 sequel, "The Guilt of Samaria," "with great enthusiasm," concealing it in a volume of the Talmud on his study lectern. Yet in 1873, his break with religious observance behind him, he published a respectful but frank attack on Mapu's "The Painted Vulture," whose five parts, dealing with the struggle of mid-nineteenth-century Jewish youth to free itself from the heavy hand of its tradition-bound elders, appeared (the last two volumes posthumously) between 1858 and 1869. In this critique, which Lilienblum called *Olam ha-Tohu* or "The In-Between World," he observed of the novel's main protagonists, Na'aman and Elisheva, who fall in love at first sight like Amnon and Tamar:

> The only world in which a Na'aman and Elisheva could be infatuated with each other after a few minutes of small talk is that of Mapu's imagination... I honestly don't know what to say about Mapu's conception of love. Was he given to such emotional ecstasies that he believed love of this sort was realistically possible, or did he have not the slightest experience of love, having acquired his entire knowledge of it from popular romances?

Lilienblum was thinking of such French potboilers as Eugène Sue's *The Mysteries of Paris*, by which Mapu's convoluted plots were said to have been influenced. Yet whatever Lilienblum's reservations concerning Mapu's fiction, it had been an emancipating force in his own life. Readers of a later period could no longer say this of it and were less forgiving of its shortcomings. Many would have agreed with the Lithuanian-born, French-educated scholar and critic Nahum Slouschz, whose 1902 *Renaissance de la littérature hébraique* was the first history of modern Hebrew literature. After describing Mapu's great impact on his contemporaries, Slouschz added that "if one were inclined to apply strictly aesthetic standards to Mapu's novels, their radical failure would be obvious." Mapu was so popular in his own age, he wrote, only because "[his] faults were not noticed by his simple, uncultivated readers."

There have been attempts to revive critical interest in Mapu. A particularly ambitious one was made in the early 1970s by Dan Miron, not yet then the preeminent Hebrew literary critic he was to become. In a lengthy essay written to refute the myth, as he saw it, of Mapu's artlessness, Miron argued that he was in fact a highly self-conscious author who, far from being indifferent to literary values, had rigorous ones of his own. If so, however, this only underlines his inability to implement them. To praise, as does Miron, the scene of Tamar's rescue for its attempted depiction of the "awesome embodiment of nature's essential beauty, discernible in the perfect rhythm of the marauding lion and the inner harmony of its body," is to equate an intention with an achievement. One can understand why a twelve-year-old might be carried away by such writing, just as one can understand why an ambitious young critic might seek to challenge the judgments of his elders by reviving a faded reputation. What, however, so enthralled the twenty-year-old Lilienblum?

2

"The success [of "The Love of Zion"] was impressive," writes Slouschz.

> The novel made its way everywhere, into the academies for rabbinical students, into the very synagogues. The young were amazed and entranced by [its] poetic flights ... Upon all minds the comparison between ancient grandeur and actually existing misery obtruded itself. The Lithuanian woods witnessed a startling spectacle. Rabbinical students, playing truant, resorted thither to read Mapu's novel in secret. Luxuriously they lived the ancient days over again.

Slouschz's "rabbinical academies" were the yeshivas of Yiddish-speaking Eastern Europe, heavily concentrated in Misnagdic Lithuania. They were by no means attended only by future rabbis. The Jewish high schools and colleges of their day, they were the institutions to which, having finished the heder at or before bar-mitzvah age, intellectually gifted youngsters were sent by religiously traditional parents and mentors to continue their education. This education, however, was as constricted as it was demanding. Already in the heder, after a few years of Hebrew and Bible studies, the advanced pupils proceeded to concentrate almost entirely on rabbinic law. By this stage, their poorer and less mentally agile peers had dropped out. The hours were long; the discipline harsh; the methods of instruction dull. Lilienblum wrote of his heder years:

> When I was four years and three months old, before any of my incipient faculties had developed, I was already yoked to the Torah and my heder teachers. From then on, I was imprisoned all day long in the schoolroom. I was given no chance to enjoy the pleasures of childhood; I had no free time for play or the

cultivation of my abilities; I was never taught to express myself as I yearned to do; I was deprived of all knowledge of anything that wasn't in the Talmud.... The reading and speaking of languages wasn't taught me, either, and if I knew the Russian and Polish alphabets, this was only because the name of every Hebrew book was printed in them on the title page.

Married off in his mid-teens, like many in his generation, to a girl his age whom he barely knew, Lilienblum went to live with her family. Now in a yeshiva, his formal studies began each morning at ten and ended at ten at night, after which he closeted himself with a volume of the Gemara and its commentators for two more hours. "You may laugh at me, dear reader," he continued,

and you have reason to, but how was I to blame? What else could I have done, put in the charge of foolish pedagogues when I was all of fifteen? Today I know that while I was driving myself to exhaustion over utter nonsense, other boys my age were learning important things in Russian lyceés and commercial and vocational schools. I know now, too, that many of them turned out to be happy individuals who led good and satisfying lives – not like myself, who was the most miserable person on earth.

These "happy individuals," some of whom studied enough Russian, Polish, German, or French to read Lermontov, Mickiewicz, Goethe, and Victor Hugo, did not learn enough Hebrew to read Mapu. Those who did were the yeshiva students or graduates – Slouschz's "simple, uncultivated readers" who, though able to unravel the logical complexities of a talmudic text that would have baffled anyone else, could not, prior to "The Love of Zion," have read a novel even had they wanted to. Perl's "The Revealer of Secrets" was no longer available; the first translation of a European work of fiction into Hebrew did not take place until the late 1850s; and the earliest Yiddish novels appeared only in the 1860s.

Read in defiance of their teachers' bans on it, "The Love of Zion" transported such students beyond the walls of the study hall to a world that was familiar but strange. It was that of the Bible but not of the Bible they knew, studied by them as a text whose sole purpose was to serve as the divine basis for rabbinic jurisprudence. The Torah should have begun not with the creation of the world but with the laws of Passover, writes Rashi in his commentary on the opening verse of Genesis, since these laws were "the first commandment given the Israelites, and the crux of the Torah is its commandments alone." This was the perspective from which biblical narrative was taught to the heder pupil.

For an experience-starved young Jew like Lilienblum, the encounter with "The Love of Zion" and "The Guilt of Samaria" was dramatic. Biblical law plays no part in them. God, though sometimes prayed to or thanked by their characters, is assigned no active role. The entire emphasis is on human activity: on the joys and sorrows of young lovers; on the conflicts of their elders; on loyalty and treachery, greed and self-sacrifice, marital devotion and infidelity; on the intricate ties of kinship amid which individuals make their way in life; on the aspirations of rulers and the ambitions of kingdoms; on the steadfastness and devotion that ultimately vanquish selfish scheming. All this opened new horizons. It raised the possibility of reading the Bible as a human and national epic rather than as divine history. It converted the biblical landscape from an abstraction into a reality.

In the Bible itself, nature is peripheral. References to it are brief and – apart from the ecstatic evocations of it in the Song of Songs – divisible into two categories. These treat it either as a source of illustrative metaphors, as in Isaiah's "The grass withereth, the flower fadeth ... surely the people is grass," or else as a testimony to its Creator's greatness, as in the Psalmist's "When I behold Thy handiwork the heavens, the moon and stars that Thou hast made, what is man that Thou shouldst remember him?" In Mapu's novels, nature exists for its own sake. Sometimes delightfully pastoral, sometimes awesome and wild, it is what it is, not what it stands for. "The Guilt of Samaria" begins:

> On the fringe of the mountains of Lebanon, where the northland of Naphtali and the peaks of Hermon conjoin, rises the crag of Omna. At its foot lies a wonderfully pleasant valley surrounded by chains of hills; from their rocky base gush springs that trickle down to a pool in the valley's midst; there, forcing

their way upward, their underground currents meet to form a rushing freshet, the River Jordan.

A blanket of dew still covered Mount Hermon, its downs and dells, its heather and heath, as dawn touched its summits and gilded with gold the splendor of Lebanon's mighty cedars that sank their roots deep into the earth and lifted their crowns to the clouds. These ancient, lordly trees were as old as the soil they grew in; their tangled boughs and branches, which cast their shade even at noon, were home to all manner of birds that sang the mountains' praises for God to hear. No ear tired of the dulcet majesty of their song; wild asses brayed from cliffs where lions and leopards had their lairs; this clamorous concord caused the soul to tremble with joy.

Into this scene – whose birds sing the praises not of God, but of nature "for God to hear" – is about to step Uziel, the crag of Omna's reclusive inhabitant who has fled Jerusalem to escape the machinations of the impious king Ahaz, Hezekiah's father and predecessor. (Though written after "The Love of Zion," "The Guilt of Samaria" is set in the years before it.) As unremarkable as such a passage would have been in a European novel of its age, there is nothing like it in the three thousand years of Hebrew literature preceding Mapu. The Lithuanian yeshiva student strolling outside the shtetl would have been struck immediately by "The Guilt of Samaria"'s mountainous landscape, with which the flat countryside around him had nothing to compare. But what mattered more was that this landscape was the Land of Israel's. What Jew before reading Mapu had even thought this land *had* a landscape? A sacredness, of course; a Temple that God had dwelt in – that, too; rules and regulations pertaining to the days in which this Temple had stood, naturally; but an actual terrain that could be walked through as one walked through the Lithuanian fields and woods, and that, unlike them, was one's own Jewish patrimony? This was something new and thrilling to contemplate.

In the same memoir in which he recalls first reading of "The Love of Zion," Ya'akov Fichman connects Mapu with the advent of modern Zionism:

Subsequently, a friend brought me "The Guilt of Samaria." In no time I was in the forests of Lebanon, misty with morning dew, its droplets falling from the branches with sweet birdsong…. The world shone with a different light after reading Mapu. Here was the feel of things to come, the future texture of my life. Whether strolling through a field or daydreaming in bed, I saw those ancient vistas not as relics of old but as intimations of redemption. I saw myself returning to my land and harvesting its bounty. There was my true mother lode, my ancestral home, where I would find the glory, so lacking around me, that my soul craved when walking slowly home from the heder on summer nights, my head full of poetic bits and snatches about a blessed land of mountains and valleys, date trees and springs. More and more have I come to realize what Mapu was to us, to our times, and to our national revival. How paltry Haskalah literature would be without him, how dreary our own childhoods would have been!

3

Europe, it can be said, departed the Near East in 1291, when the last Crusader sailed back to it from the Palestinian port of Acre, and returned in 1798 with Napoleon's unsuccessful siege of the same city after invading Egypt and marching up the Palestinian coast. In his wake came the British, followed by other European powers. European imperial ambitions, nourished by the weakness of an Ottoman empire that was beginning to disintegrate; the development of new disciplines like Oriental linguistics and archeology; the beginnings of mass tourism, greatly abetted, starting with the 1830s, by regular steamship service across the Mediterranean; inexpensive, often illustrated volumes describing journeys to the Holy Land and adjacent countries – all led to a steady growth of interest in and travel to Palestine, driven by a wish to see the holy sites of Christianity and explore exotic climes. By the mid-nineteenth century, such trips were being made by Jews as well. In "The Painted Vulture," Mapu, who never undertook the voyage himself, has one of its characters, a young Lithuanian Jew named Azriel, visit Jerusalem and write home about the throng of Jews in the city at Passover time. Not all were tourists. Between

1838 and 1864, Jerusalem's Jewish population, nearly all of it religiously Orthodox, practically tripled.

Most nineteenth-century travelers to Palestine reacted to what they saw with mixed emotions, the romance of the East and the wonder of walking on sacred ground tempered by disappointment, sometimes shock, at the neglect and abandonment they encountered. "Of the sadness of Jerusalem in which no chimney smoke rises and no sounds are heard," wrote the French author and traveler François-René de Chateaubriand in his 1811 *Itinéraire de Paris á Jerusalem*, one of the earliest of the new genre of travel books, "of the solitude of the mountains [around the city], where not a living soul can be seen, of the disarray of so many broken, smashed, half-open tombs, one can only be made to feel that the trumpet of the Last Judgment has already sounded and the dead are about to rise in the Valley of Jehoshaphat." Jewish first impressions were the same. In a letter from Jerusalem in 1838, Eliezer Halevi, an aide of the Anglo-Jewish philanthropist Moses Montefiore, wrote that "the road [to the city] is as waste as if no human foot had trodden it for years, so that I seemed to be approaching not an important town but a deserted one…The closer I came to it, the greater the desolation grew."

This was not simply, as is sometimes argued today, a condescendingly "Orientalist" view of a country that failed to meet European standards of scenery and decor. In part, it was a matter of climate. Tourism to Palestine was as a rule confined to the summer dry season when roads, often impassable in winter from the rains, were more easily traversed. Travelers accustomed to the mild heat and lush greenery of a European June or July could not but be dismayed by the sere, blistering vistas of a land in which vegetative growth began in late autumn, reached its acme in spring, and soon died off. Only when irrigated from wells and springs was Palestine's summer landscape verdant, too – a cheering sight some Europeans took note of. Yet the very fact that main roads were frequently useless in winter was testimony to the disrepair into which Palestine had fallen after centuries of inept and corrupt Ottoman rule. Even when traveled on, these roads were subject to brigandage by highwaymen and lawless Bedouin. Large tracts of countryside lay barren; undrained lowlands had turned into malarial swamps; woods were denuded by overgrazing and overcutting for firewood; cities languished commercially. A land that in ancient times had supported millions had, in the mid-nineteenth century, an estimated 300,000 inhabitants, a small fraction of them Jews. The dereliction reported by travelers was real.

Curiously, Mapu, though undoubtedly familiar with some of this travel writing, made little use of it in his work. His physical descriptions of Palestine, so stirring to readers like Fichman, depended almost entirely on information gleaned from the Bible and second-hand Hebrew literary sources. As a result, his biblical landscapes lack specificity. Their hills and dales could be anywhere; their leafy trees are rarely singled out by species; the birds that sing in them are of no particular variety. Not even their basic geography is always accurate. While the "crag of Omna" can be identified with a height, today occupied by the ruins of a medieval fortress, that overlooks the site of Tel Dan in northern Israel where the tributaries of the Jordan come together, the water into which Tamar casts her flowers was a pure figment of Mapu's imagination, no such stream existing in the vicinity of Jerusalem. It was simply a requirement of the Arcadian landscape that Mapu wished to portray and was not prepared to forego.

Such indifference to contemporary accounts of Palestine is perhaps understandable in Mapu's two biblical novels, which aimed to depict a flourishing ancient Land of Israel that did not correspond to nineteenth-century reality. It is less so in "The Painted Vulture." Azriel, who arrives in Palestine from Egypt, hardly notices his surroundings. On his ascent from the Mediterranean coast to Jerusalem, he is conscious only of the imagined land of the Bible, whose "pure breeze," he writes, "inhaled the perfume of the flowers of Sharon and of the lilies of the valleys and wafted them in its path, as my spirit imbibed the loveliness of yore from my enchanted senses." After spending several weeks in Jerusalem, of whose appearance he says not a word, he sets out for Tiberias. Yet of this journey, too, which would have required several days, he recounts only the following:

> As dawn rose on the eve of the Sabbath, we were not far [from Tiberias]. The Sea of Galilee lay on my right; dew from Mount Hermon wet my head; the morning star was reflected in the water in facets of diamond and sapphire; a clean mountain breeze whipped the rippling waves, whose silver runners were sliced by

the morning light. A multitude of native birds sang their matins from Hermon's heights, proudly warbling their heart-warming song. These pleasant sights and winged diapasons escorted us merrily to Tiberias.

A moment later Azriel spies a figure struggling in the water and leaps in to rescue a young lady he predictably falls in love with on the spot, causing us to forget that his description could just as well be of Lake Lucerne, let alone that Mount Hermon is dozens of kilometers from the Sea of Galilee, well beyond the range of dewdrops and birdsong. And when he reaches the once prosperous lakeshore city of Tiberias, described by European travelers as having declined into a sorry jumble of stone hovels, he has nothing to say about it, either. Never once does he reflect that the "loveliness of yore" might be restored to such drear scenes by a Jewish return to a depopulated Palestine.

Azriel does not do this because such a possibility was not mooted in the Jewish world in the years in which Mapu wrote his novels. When the oft-cited Zionist slogan of "a land without a people for a people without a land" was coined in the 1850s, its author was the British statesman Lord Shaftesbury – who, asking rhetorically whether there was anywhere "a country without a nation" and a "nation without a country," answered: "To be sure there is, [Palestine and] the ancient and rightful lords of its soil, the Jews!" His was not the first Christian voice to support a Jewish return to Palestine. As far back as the siege of Acre, Napoleon was said to have favored re-establishing Jewish rule there, and various European statesmen and writers, predominantly British, expressed themselves similarly throughout the first half of the nineteenth century. They justified their sentiments in terms of the past glory of biblical Israel; Palestine's degraded state; the distressed situation of Europe's Jews; the independence struggles of other ancient peoples like the Greeks and Italians; the impending collapse of the Ottoman Empire; and the imperial interests of their own countries.

With rare exceptions, most notably Moses Hess's 1862 "Rome and Jerusalem," written by a German-Jewish intellectual and one-time colleague of Karl Marx, Jews took no part in this discourse. It seemingly lay beyond their horizons and boldest dreams. "The Jews dare not think of possessing again the land of their fathers," wrote the Frenchman Ernest Laharanne in his 1860 *La Nouvelle Question d'Orient*. What kept them from entertaining the idea, Laharanne believed, was their assumption that the European powers would never permit such a development in a land sacred to Christianity and would react harshly to any expression of Jewish aspirations to it. This would not have been an unrealistic fear in an age in which Europe was nibbling away at the Ottoman Empire while exerting increasing influence in Palestine itself. Yet not even Christian Zionism, which preceded Jewish Zionism in Europe by several decades, is so much as hinted at in "The Painted Vulture." Educated and abreast of current events though some of the novel's characters are, they give no sign of having heard of it.

4

The total absence of Zionist motifs from his work is even more striking when one considers that, like Perl and other Haskalah writers, Mapu thought that an overconcentration in towns and cities was one of the ills of East-European Jewish society. The virtues of the agrarian life are a recurrent theme in "The Love of Zion." In it, confronting the novel's chief villain, the Jerusalemite Azrikam, who has just mocked "the peasants and shepherds who spend their time listening to the mewling of goats and are as ignorant of the knowledge of God as they are coarse of speech and devoid of wit," the farmer Sitri replies that, on the contrary, no one is more naturally pious. "Lodge in the villages," he tells Azrikam,

> and see how their inhabitants rise early in the morn, when night's silence still reigns and the hills and mountains slowly shed their veil of mist. It is then that the men go forth to labor in the fields and their hale and hearty wives set about spinning the wool and linen that clothe their households. By and by, the sky-supporting hilltops are cleared by the halo of the sun....The farmer chants his glad prayers to the God he delights in; heavenward they ascend like clouds of incense. Returning home, he is greeted joyfully by his fair hearth-mate, her winsome eyes shining; waking their brood, they breakfast together on the Lord's bounty. The day waxes as they delight in each other's company; meanwhile, the

denizen of Jerusalem turns over in bed like a cake turned in the oven. At long last the sloth rises and paces his room while waiting to be attended, like an idol without hands that can do nothing for itself, by the servant he has imperiously commanded to bring him soap, water, and fragrant unguents.

The motif of the happy rustic versus the effete urbanite is as old as Aesop's country mouse and city mouse and was not lacking in Hebrew literature before Mapu's time. Sitri's peasants are as romantically idealized as are Perl's utopian Jewish farmers. When he returned to the subject several years later in "The Painted Vulture," on the other hand, Mapu added a realistic note to it, though with a bow to "The Love of Zion" – by which Na'man, who has grown up in the 1850s in a poor family that has been defrauded of its wealth, is inspired to leave home and study agronomy at a university. (Mapu may have gotten the idea of inserting a real book of his into a fictional plot from "The Revealer of Secrets.") In a Hebrew letter to his friend Ahituv, Na'aman writes: "How overwhelmed I was by the words of Sitri the Carmelite, who speaks so winningly of rural life, the charms of which I long for, too." And in a more philosophical vein, he tells Elisheva, "From the day God expelled Adam from the Garden of Eden, the Tree of Knowledge no longer refreshes those who seek its shade. He that increaseth knowledge, increaseth sorrow, the Bible says, and God says to man, 'I have given you in recompense the earth, the mother of all life: there find your lifework and your wisdom.'"

Na'aman is no impractical dreamer. His doctoral thesis on soil cultivation, he hopes, "will bring me enough renown to assure that, instead of my having to go and look for work, work will come looking for me." His goal is a well-paying job with "someone of high station of whose estate I can be the steward" – that is, an aristocratic Lithuanian or Polish landowner like the "squire" of "The Revealer of Secrets." Such figures, who commonly employed Jewish overseers, bookkeepers, land managers, and commercial agents, played an important role in the Jewish economy of Eastern Europe and Na'aman's plan to land a position with one of them with the help of an academic degree, something that few East-European Jews of his time could boast of, reflects both personal ambition and the Haskalah creed of self-advancement through secular education.

And yet the thought of one day using his education to help bring life to the barren fields of Palestine never crosses Na'aman's mind. A modern young man with no strong attachment to religious tradition but with a powerful feeling of Jewish patriotism, he is a few years too early for this. It was only in 1862 that the German rabbi Zvi Hirsch Kalischer sounded the first public call of its kind for a Jewish society that would buy "as many towns, fields, and vineyards in the Holy Land as possible," to which "Jews from all parts of the world, and especially from Russia, Poland, and Germany, should be brought." Those with farming experience, Kalischer proposed, would be granted freeholds, while those without it would be instructed by "experienced teachers." In 1866 he established a Society for the Settlement of the Land of Israel, which led to the founding in 1870 of Mikveh Yisra'el, Palestine's first agricultural school.

Na'aman, though eminently qualified to take part in such a project, has no inkling that it is in the offing. Palestine is not on his personal map. His Jewish identity expresses itself above all in his love of Hebrew, in which he reads widely and corresponds with like-minded friends. Part of his bond with Elisheva is her having received a Hebrew education, a rare thing for a girl of her generation. "Your mind is a Hebrew one," he writes her in a letter after their first meeting, "and so is mine. And it is in Hebrew that I mean to tell you about myself and my path in life."

This is the meeting ridiculed by Lilienblum. Reminiscent of Tamar's streamside encounter with Amnon, it takes places at the opera. As Na'aman recalls it:

> I was watching the performance when I heard an educated young woman say in French to the person next to her, "Move to the back! You don't belong here, no matter how expensive or fancy your clothes are. Go sit with your friends!" I looked at the unfortunate object of these insults, who was quite beautiful, and seeing by her looks that she had a noble spirit, I turned angrily to her detractor and said in no uncertain terms, "As far as I can judge, this young lady would grace any place she sat in." The poor girl,

however, had already risen from her seat, and so I got up from mine and gave it to her. She sat and thanked me.

Between acts, I asked the young lady what her name was and why she had been treated so rudely. "It's my own fault," she said. "I'm Elisheva. My father is Eden, the son of Ovadiah of Atika, and I won't change my or my family's name, because they're precious to me. But who, sir, are you that you so graciously defended me and gave me your place?"

Elisheva's insistence on being called by her biblical Hebrew name rather than by its Russian form of Elizaveta has brought down on her the scorn of her assimilating Jewish acquaintances. As he chats with her during the intermission, Na'aman, who dislikes these young snobs with their French-speaking airs as much as she does, is stunned to discover that she is the granddaughter of the very man who defrauded his parents. He realizes this when she tells him that as a small girl she knew a boy who was also named Na'aman, and that while playing with him she heard the story of his family's downfall at her grandfather's hands and swore to one day make good the loss. "He was so struck by my magnanimity," she relates, not realizing she is talking to the same person, "that he began to caper and prance and promised to give me a songbird as my reward."

Na'aman chooses not to reveal his identity, thus adding another complication to an already overcomplicated plot. Is it any wonder, though, that he loses his heart to this beautiful, high-minded, and proudly Jewish young woman with a knowledge of Hebrew who pledged as a child to restore his family's plundered fortune? Lilienblum, one feels, was being unfair.

5

Hebrew was, for Mapu, the one great passion of an outwardly uneventful life, most of it lived in the Lithuanian city of Kaunas, the Jewish Kovno, where he was born. Except for brief excursions to Russia and Western Europe, his only other places of residence were Raseiniai, some fifty kilometers to Kovno's northwest, and Vilnius, the Jewish Vilna, a hundred kilometers to its southeast. After a standard heder and yeshiva education, which left him an observant but not especially devout Jew, he worked for long years as a Hebrew teacher while studying foreign languages on his own. (The first of these, Latin, was reportedly learned with the help of a church psalter and the Hebrew Psalms that he knew by heart.) Twice married, each time to a wife he lived with contentedly until her death, and the father of an only son whom he helped put through medical school, he was barely able to eke out a living from his books. Hebrew publishers made their money from religious texts and were not prepared, even after the success of "The Love of Zion," to print Mapu's novels at their own expense, thus requiring him to pay for their publication and market them himself, whether to dealers or individual buyers.

Many of his letters complain about this. In a typical one to a bookseller a year before his death, when in failing health, he wrote: "Of the 1,600 copies of 'The Guilt of Samaria' printed this year, I still have 500, and I would like to sell them in a single batch for my own and the buyer's benefit, so that I can afford the specialists I need to consult while exerting myself for the Lady of Hebrew and her place in our people's hearts...." There were, he suggested, three possibilities. He could let the bookseller have small numbers of the novel on consignment, the proceeds from their sale to be split half-and-half; he could send him 50 copies at a 33 percent discount in return for an advance of 50 rubles; or he could, as he preferred, ship all 500 copies for a larger advance at a discount of 50 percent.

"The Lady of Hebrew" is how I have translated Mapu's *ha-Ivriyya*, literally "the Hebrewess," a favorite term of his. This romantic personification of the language he loved reached rhapsodic heights in a letter to the literary scholar Shneur Sachs, an old friend and the first to urge him to attempt a novel in Hebrew despite its abandonment by increasing numbers of young Jews no longer wanting or able to read it:

> It was you, my friend and mentor, it was you who gave me the courage and inspired me to seal a pact with my Lady of Hebrew. I remember the day on which I removed the veil from her face: lo, there was the daughter of Zion in all her loveliness of yore! Bewitchment on her lips, she said: "Gaze upon me, thou champion of Zion, and tell me why the sons I raised have disdained me. Am I no longer comely in their eyes? They claim my breasts

are fallen so that they may revel in foreign bosoms, but am I so diminished, is my speech so mean, as my revilers falsely claim?" "Thou still art beauteous, my gentle one," I answered her, taking her lovingly in my arms. "Thou art still the delight of our people – my joy and my bliss – the playmate of our young and the comforter of our old. I have seen Latin and its ancient vigor; German with all its logic; the enticing charms of French; Russian in its first bloom. All wear the laurel crown. Yet whose is the voice that calls to me from their midst? Thine alone, my dove..."

Mapu next recalled in his letter to Sachs how he proposed to the Lady of Hebrew that she "elope" with him to the ancient Land of Israel – that is, that he set a Hebrew novel there. "Come away with me to Lebanon, my ravishing sister," he told her, paraphrasing the Song of Songs, "come away with me to Mount Carmel and the mountains of Zion."

Then my Lady of Hebrew took me and brought me to Mount Zion, to Jerusalem's heights. Donning her finest garments, she stood before me in glorious majesty and showed me all her bounty... "Write what thy Fancy has seen," she said, "that it be a reminder to the renegades who mock my holy mount." With that I seized a pen and wrote down that which I saw in my mind's eye in commemoration of the love of Zion.

Setting a Hebrew novel in ancient Palestine had the advantage of evoking a time and place in which Hebrew was actually spoken rather than merely used to represent the Yiddish-speaking world of Eastern Europe. (Perl had gotten around this dilemma by having his Yiddish-speaking characters correspond in Hebrew, a technique used by Mapu, too, in parts of "The Painted Vulture.") This need not have necessitated resorting to biblical times or a biblical manner. Mapu could equally well have written about the Palestine of the early rabbis, when Hebrew, though largely displaced by Aramaic and Greek, was still spoken on a regular basis. Indeed, the mishnaic language of this period might have been more suitable for modern fiction. It was more flexible, more everyday-like; it had a vocabulary whose core biblical lexicon had been enriched by thousands of new words; and it was considerably closer to the Hebrew written by both the rabbis and the Maskilim of Mapu's day.

Yet it did not have what Mapu was looking for. What this was is articulated by Na'aman in his letter to Ahituv. Alluding there to the well-known "Discourse on Style" of the eighteenth-century Comte de Buffon, the French author and naturalist Georges-Louis Leclerc, Na'man writes:

> Buffon says that the most supremely knowledgeable of books will never obtain lasting fame for its author unless written with grace, grandeur, fine style, and facility; otherwise it will perish and be forgotten, and its knowledge will be credited to whoever adorns and embellishes it properly. For the style is the man, and in it we see his mind and its form. Not so is knowledge, which belongs equally to everyone of intelligence.

And if this is true, Na'aman muses, of the books of other peoples

> whose styles and tastes change ceaselessly, what shall we say of the Hebrew tongue whose style, because fixed and preserved by Holy Scripture, is immutable and will remain for as long as light remains distinct from darkness? The mountains will move from their place and the hills topple before it changes, being eternal... And yet it may be reformulated and cast in a new light by an author's character, temperament, time, and place. Such is "The Love of Zion" that you sent me.

This literary credo did not mean that Mapu thought standards of Hebrew style had remained immutable since biblical times. No one knew better than he did what vast differences there were between the language of the Bible and of the Mishnah, between the Hebrew poetry of Byzantine Palestine and of Muslim Andalusia, between a medieval Hebrew rhymed-prose narrative and his own "Love of Zion." All varied greatly in grammar, morphology, syntax, vocabulary, and overall configuration.

Nevertheless, while literary Hebrew, lacking the baseline of a vernacular, did not so much evolve linearly in the course of its history as repeatedly change form under the influence of different linguistic and cultural environments, none of its forms was imaginable without the Bible. While English readers too, of course, may notice echoes, or even the systematic influence, of the King James Version in the style of this or that author, such cases stand out as exceptions; it is practically impossible, however, to read a single pre-nineteenth-century Hebrew poem or work of prose without the Bible's presence in the background being felt. "Fixed and preserved," as Na'aman says, in Jewish consciousness as holy scripture, it never ceased to serve the Hebrew writer as a point of reference and a model for what Na'aman, citing Buffon, calls "grandeur."

Such grandeur or "sublimity," to use a popular term in eighteenth-century European literary criticism, was commonly taken to be the mark of great literature. *Le style*, wrote Buffon, *s'il est élevé, noble, sublime... soit durable et même éternelle* – and it was an "elevated and noble" style of a "lasting and eternal" nature that, Mapu believed, was the essence of Hebrew alone, just as "vigor" was the essence of Latin and "charm" the essence of French. If Hebrew was to remain the language of the Jewish people, the glue that bound its separate parts even as the hold of religion was weakening, it had to have a power equal to the power of religion. For this it had to be, however, "reformulated and cast in a new light" by an author's "character, temperament, time and place," as Na'aman says of the language of "The Love of Zion": not just a biblically influenced Hebrew but a modernized version of biblical Hebrew itself.

This was not the first time in Jewish literary history that a decision to return to biblical diction had been made. This was the choice of the authors of the Dead Sea Scrolls and the Hebrew pseudepigrapha of the Second Temple period, though they were writing in an age when rabbinic Hebrew already existed; of the Hebrew poets of medieval Spain, who sought to "purify" Hebrew of its post-biblical elements; of eighteenth-century Hebrew dramatists like Moshe Chaim Luzzatto and Yosef Ha-Efrati. Yet in being faithful, as they thought they were, to Hebrew's true spirit, such writers restricted their linguistic options by skipping over centuries of Hebrew's development. All paid an expressive price for shackling themselves to Scripture.

Mapu paid one, too, a steeper one than he realized. It would have angered him to be told that the barbarous Hebrew written by Josef

Perl's Hasidim was more creative and interesting than his own. Nonetheless, while never doubting his choice of biblical language, he was aware of the problem of applying it to contemporary settings. Alluding to "The Painted Vulture," his letter to Sachs continued:

> Then I pleaded with my Lady of Hebrew, saying: "Thou hast kept faith with thy people from days of old; thou hast not ceased thy converse with them nor thy plaint at their breach of thy spirit; thou hast looked kindly and smiled upon me... Arise, then, my gentle lady! Descend from thy mountainous peaks; forsake thy domicile and come with me; leave thy ancient Eden for the present habitations of thy people; for thy ways are as the ways of the world and thy wings have spanned it from eon to eon as the sky spans the earth.

The Lady of Hebrew replies that she will comply with Mapu's wishes and permit him to use some post-biblical language:

> See thou, my dearest! Look and know what lies before thee. Thou wouldst bring me to the people for whose sake I was banished to Babylon [where the Talmud was composed in a mixture of Hebrew and Aramaic]. There I was befriended by the Babylonian damsel [*ha-Bavlit* – i.e., Aramaic], who stayed by my side as my people did by hers... Therefore, take her with thee in thy return to thine own times. Her speech has lived on through the generations; put it in the mouths of the persons thou wouldst create...

Mapu was referring not to Aramaic itself but to Hebrew as it changed under Aramaic's impact. And indeed, although the biblical element in it still predominates, the Hebrew of "The Painted Vulture" is freer and more eclectic than that of "The Love of Zion" and "The Guilt of Samaria." It is so only up to a point, though. Thus, when Mapu, describing Na'aman and Elisheva's encounter at the opera, needs a Hebrew word for "theater," he turns to the Bible and has Elisheva, accosted during the intermission by a young man named Emil who addresses her as Elizaveta, reply angrily: "What have I to do with you?

I'm Elisheva and you're Emil. Go find yourself an Emilia in this valley of vision [*gey hizayon*, Isaiah 22:1]!" What makes "valley of vision" so absurdly periphrastic is that the word *te'atron*, from Greek *theatron*, which is how one says "theater" in modern Hebrew too, occurs many times in rabbinic literature and was certainly known to Mapu and could have been used by him. Its foreign ancestry, however, no matter how ancient, disqualified it in his eyes.

6

Na'aman and Elisheva's falling in love was not the main target of Lilienblum's criticism of "The Painted Vulture." What preoccupied him more was the couple's failure, as he viewed it, to fight for its love against the forces that oppose it, led by the patriarchal Ovadiah, Elisheva's grandfather and de facto parent, whose plans to marry her off to someone of his own choosing she resists but does not openly defy. For all her charm and esprit, Lilienblum's "The In-Between World" argued, Elisheva is weak-willed for not walking out on her grandfather and his world at whatever risk to herself or others this might entail. (In this judgment, Lilienblum was projecting: he himself had deserted a young wife and child to devote himself to a literary career.) Moreover, in real life as opposed to romantic fiction, the weak do not win; they lose. Had Mapu been more courageous, Lilienblum wrote, he would not have ended "The Painted Vulture" as he did with Na'aman and Elisheva's happy marriage. Rather, he would have condemned them to a tragic separation,

> and this for two reasons. One is that he would have thereby fulfilled his obligation to portray ordinary reality as it is rather than as prettily dressed up…The second is that a tragic ending would have made a deeper impression upon readers, who would have gotten their comeuppance for their foolishness [in identifying with Elisheva's course of action] – a comeuppance that might conceivably have been beneficial to some of them.

"The In-Between World" was not merely an attack on "The Painted Vulture." It was aimed at the entire Haskalah, whose reformist approach,

Lilienblum had come to believe, had proved delusory. In fearing to go too far, the Maskilim had not gone far enough. "These dreamers," he wrote,

> think that if only all Jews were to start using Hebrew and desist from [such superstitious customs as] Tashlikh, Kapparot, prayers for the souls of the dead, and the observance of every last detail of each commandment; if only the Haskalah and religion could agree on a signed-and-sealed pact of collaboration between them; and if only we were to wear modern clothes, drink the national beverage, and call our children Johann, Ivan, and Gregory instead of Yochanan and Gershon, all our problems would be solved. If they weren't dreaming, they would understand that an entire people, or even just the greater part of it, can't write in a language [i.e., Hebrew] that has no place in the marketplace of daily life; that there is no such thing as religion without superstitious nonsense; that it is impossible to expect science and tradition to be always in agreement; and that no people can assimilate to another people on its own terms. Assimilation can only mean the total merger of two peoples by the acceptance by one of the other's customs, manners, and aspirations. And yet there are too many walls between [Jews and Gentiles] ever to allow such a merger to take place.

Apart from Mapu's aversion to Jews Russianizing their names, Lilienblum's description of the typical Maskil fits him well. Mapu *did* believe that Judaism could modernize successfully; *did* want Jews to read novels, go to the theater, and outwardly resemble others; *did* think a passionate attachment to Hebrew could take the place of religious fervor. And he clearly did *not* think, as did Lilienblum, that "whoever knows that life is more powerful than noble feelings also knows that the abandonment of Hebrew, along with the Talmud's prophecy that 'one day the Torah will be forgotten by Israel,' as saddening as they may be, are as inevitable as death itself as long as we do not have a country of our own to protect our national existence."

A country of our own to protect our national existence – and without which Hebrew and Hebrew culture had no future. This may be the earliest formulation of secular Zionism in modern Hebrew literature, though it was only a decade later that Lilienblum helped found the Hibat Tsiyon or "Love of Zion"[1] movement that was formed, in the wake of the unprecedented pogroms that swept southern Russia in 1881, to sponsor Jewish settlement in Palestine. In his 1873 essay he barely mentioned Mapu's biblical novels or their Palestinian setting, which he seems to have considered, if not outright escapist, of little relevance to East-European Jewish life.

And yet everything in Mapu's novels points to Zionism. His strong Jewish national feeling; his discontent with the conservatism and backwardness of East-European Jewish life; his grasp of the need for a new, post-religious basis for Jewish identity; his love of Hebrew, by which he believed such a basis could be provided; his advocacy of a Jewish return to the soil and to nature; his romantic attitude toward the biblical Land of Israel, accompanied by an admiration for physical bravery, military prowess, and the pomp and power of the ancient Judean state – all this, one would think, would have led him to arrive at Zionist conclusions before any other Hebrew writer.

All the elements were in place – all except Lilienblum's realization that, in the modern world, it was impossible to assimilate outwardly to non-Jewish society without a massive inward erosion of Jewish identity. For its early Christian supporters, Zionism was a grand idea; for the educated Jews of Europe, it was also the bitter admission of defeat that Lilienblum demanded of them. The Haskalah had put its trust in Europe. For the better part of a century, it had preached integration in European society, confident that Jews could become Europeans while remaining Jews. This belief began to founder in parts of western Europe before it did in the east because the west was further advanced in the process of Europeanization. Just as initial success occurred earlier there, so did initial intimations of failure. Yet when the consciousness of failure began to spread in the east, too, it was more devastating precisely because the

---

1. The title of Mapu's "The Love of Zion" is *Ahavat Tsiyon*. Although both *ahava* and *hiba* mean "love" in classical Hebrew, *hiba* has more the sense in modern Hebrew of "fondness" or "affection." Possibly, it was preferred by the movement's founders as a way of disambiguating its name from the novel's.

progress made up to that point had been so much smaller and the distance separating the Jew from full acceptance by his surroundings was still so much greater.

In the "The Painted Vulture," whose heroes were, Lilienblum wrote, "the small-town intellectuals and dreamers of an in-between world," the Haskalah's vision is still alive. 1881, the year in which it might be said to have died, or perhaps more accurately, to have been murdered, was also the year of Ya'akov Fichman's birth, and by the time Fichman was twelve, Zionism was a hotly debated issue in the East-European Jewish street. For members of his generation, it was natural to read the excitement of Zionism's emergence into the excitement of reading Mapu's novels. What is actually in these novels, however, is Zionism's stopping short of emerging, like an idea that trembles on the cusp of consciousness and falls back. One is left with a strong sense of almost.

Chapter Three

Smolenskin's Stagecoach

1

In Peretz Smolenskin's first Hebrew novel, *Simhat Hanef*, a title translatable as "The Humbug's Happiness,"[1] is an account, set in the 1850s or '60s, of a stagecoach journey from Berdichev, a heavily Jewish town in central Ukraine, to the Black Sea port of Odessa.[2] It starts with an introductory reflection of the kind Smolenskin was fond of, a brief discourse on the spread of Russian railroads, the demise of stagecoach travel, and the author's obligation to memorialize the old means of transportation, "so that posterity may recall the cumbersome ways of its ancestors." A prolific essayist as well as writer of fiction, Smolenskin liked to begin a chapter with a historical, philosophical, or psychological generalization and then zoom in on an illustrative episode. Once the technologically transformative nineteenth century has succeeded in changing everything, the narrator

---

1. The title comes from Job 20:5, "The triumphing of the wicked is short, and the joy of the hypocrite [*simhat hanef*] is but for the moment."
2. Like other East-European writers of Hebrew fiction, Smolenskin generally gave his Russian or Polish towns and cities imaginary and sometimes satirical Hebrew names, often by inverting or rearranging their letters. Thus, the Berdichev of "The Humbug's Happiness" is Toshavey-Ba'ar ("Inhabitants of Ignorance"), while Odessa is Ashadot ("Waterfalls").

of "The Humbug's Happiness" asks, who will believe that stagecoaches ever existed? "It's all a figment of your imaginations," future historians who unearth such relics from the darkness of the past will be told.

The Odessa coach is about to depart. Despite having promised his passengers a comfortable trip with plenty of leg room, the coachman has packed as many of them into his vehicle as can fit. In addition to a father and daughter returning from a visit to Berdichev, they are:

> Four or five Hasidim on their way to see their Rebbe; several Lithuanian Misnagdim in pursuit of the livelihood that had eluded them thus far; a merchant; an itinerant bookseller; a midwife; an abandoned wife roaming from town to town with her children in search of the cavalier who deserted her; a Polish Jew disguised by a red head cloth as a mendicant from Jerusalem collecting alms for its poor, which he would put to good use far from Zion, the proceeds being in any case insufficient to keep the wolf from all its many doors; a matchmaker; and a Hebrew author cradling his books as a beggar cradles her (or someone else's) sick child to stir the compassion of our merciful Children of Israel.

The sarcastic humor of this description is typical of Smolenskin. So is its motley assortment of Jews. The third of nineteenth-century Hebrew literature's major novelists, Smolenskin came a generation after Mapu, whom he considered his predecessor, and two after Perl, whom there is no evidence of his having read. Yet whereas Mapu's sedentary life limited his exposure to East-European Jewish society and his portrayal of it in "The Painted Vulture," Smolenskin, a semi-vagabond in his youth, knew it from top to bottom. He had ridden many a stagecoach himself and rubbed shoulders with each of the types he depicts setting out for Odessa and then some.

He was born in or about 1840, during the reign of Tsar Nikolai I, in a Belorussian village not far from the town of Smolensk that gave his family its name. A geographic extension of Lithuania, Belarus or "White Russia" was a flat land of numerous rivers feeding into the southward-flowing Dnieper, a predominantly Misnagdic region with a large minority of Habad Hasidim. Smolenskin's father, a Misnaged, kept a tavern that was gutted by fire when Peretz, the youngest of six children, was eight, forcing him to flee when accused of stealing church artifacts found in the ruins, which were in fact a surety for a loan he had made to a local priest.

Two years later, Peretz's father died. Without a breadwinner, the family lived in penury, and misfortune struck again when the eldest of its three boys was abducted and impressed into military service. Until abolished by the newly crowned Alexander II in 1856, such forced conscription, whose victims rarely returned from its twenty-five-year term, was a scourge of nineteenth-century Russian Jewish life; every Jewish community had its quota of conscripts to meet, and the victims, some not yet even in their teens, were commonly seized from the ranks of the poor and defenseless by bounty hunters working hand-in-glove with communal leaders. If Smolenskin, a bright, mischievous boy with a sharp tongue, was sent by his mother at an unusually young age to the well-known yeshiva of Shklov, a center of Misnagdic learning on the northern reaches of the Dnieper, this was not just to keep him out of trouble or to have one less mouth to feed. It was also because yeshiva students, no matter how poor, were safe from impressment.

He spent four years in Shklov, studying Talmud, independently learning Russian, a language most Yiddish-speaking Russian Jews did not know, and secretly reading Haskalah literature. He was not alone in this. It was via the yeshivas of Eastern Europe that the Haskalah and its ideas were disseminated most thoroughly; nowhere else was a good enough knowledge of the Hebrew needed to read its authors possessed by young minds eager to transcend the narrow confines of a traditional education, so that by mid-century, most yeshivas had their clandestine cells of budding Maskilim. They also, however, had their proctors tasked with rooting out such deviants, and Smolenskin was eventually caught and expelled. For a while, he found shelter in a local synagogue, occupying himself with religious texts by day and, when alone at night, with secular books read by candlelight before falling asleep on a bench. Soon, though, accused of stealing and selling the missing candles, he had to abandon this refuge.

Homeless, the seventeen-year-old outcast wandered through villages along the Dnieper, staying in synagogues or with charitable families until he decided to try his luck at the Habad court in the small town of Lubavitch. At first, his native intelligence and learning betokened a bright future in the service of the dynasty's third Rebbe, Menachem Mendel Schneerson, better known as the Tsemach Tsedek. Yet careless about concealing his Misnagdic views, he fell out with the Rebbe's followers and had to take to the road again. In Vitebsk, he found work with a Habad businessman, the Tsemach Tsedek's uncle, who was looking for a Russian-speaking assistant, and spent three years in his employ until a miscalculated embroilment in a Hasidic intrigue led to his dismissal.

Smolenskin now set out down the Dnieper for the Ukraine. At one point, he fell in with a traveling cantor and sang in his choir; at another he earned a living as an itinerant preacher. Only upon arriving in 1861 in Odessa, in Russia's far south, did he settle down. Founded in the late eighteenth century as the Tsarist empire's maritime gateway to the world, Odessa was the sole city in Russia proper without restrictions on Jewish residence; its Jewish population, the fastest-growing in the country, was also the freest and least traditional, and though its golden age as a hub of Jewish culture lay ahead of it, it was already a haven for young Maskilim like Moshe Leib Lilienblum who were seeking to escape the backward provinces. Progressive-minded tutors able to give the children of its Jewish nouveau riche a not too onerous Hebrew education were in demand, and Smolenskin stayed in the city until 1867, teaching the sons and daughters of the well-to-do, pursuing his autodidactic studies, and writing his first fiction.

Set in Odessa, "The Humbug's Happiness" has as its main characters two Maskilim, Shimon and David, the former a cultivated and honorable young man, the latter a pretender to intellectual and moral qualities he does not have. Much of the novel consists of their long conversations. They talk about the purpose of life; about the nature of happiness; about Shakespeare, Goethe, and the Bible; about Jewish and non-Jewish views of romance and marriage – about everything but their rivalry for Shifra, a religiously conservative businessman's daughter whom David has been actively wooing and Shimon, her former tutor, is secretly in love with. Convinced that she loves David back, Shimon encourages him to court her while keeping his true feelings to himself.

Enter the stagecoach. Returning in it from Berdichev, Shifra (for it is she who is the young lady traveling with her father) strikes up an acquaintance with the abandoned wife, who is robbed of her money by one of the Hasidim at an inn they stop at for the night. When discovered, the thief turns out to be not a Hasid but a wanted murderer playing the part of one. A more fateful dissemblance, however, is disclosed only toward the novel's end, when we learn that the runaway husband is none other than David, who has meanwhile proposed to Shifra and been accepted. He is about to take his place with her under the wedding canopy when his lawful wife, invited by Shifra to the ceremony, arrives and sees him. The wife screams, David takes to his heels, Shifra faints, and she and Shimon, following some further complications, are happily wed.

The aspiring author forced to peddle his own books is heard of no more once the coach reaches Odessa. Perhaps, continuing to view events from a hidden vantage point, he will write "The Humbug's Happiness."

2

Much fault can be found with "The Humbug's Happiness." Though not lengthy, it manages to be wordy. Its dialogues lapse into tiresome monologues. Its plot depends on too many unreasonable twists of fate. Its dramas are melodramas. These are weaknesses that Smolenskin inherited from Mapu, whom he admired more than he should have.

But "The Humbug's Happiness" is alive as Mapu's work rarely is. Shimon and David are well-rounded characters. Their long arguments about life and literature, while appearing naive and digressive at first, are integral to the tale and psychologically revealing, since neither man realizes what the author knows all along and the reader grows gradually aware of, namely, that they are really arguing about Shifra and their claims on her. Being Hebrew tutors rather than Christian gentlemen, they duel with ideas, not pistols, but their lives are no less at stake.

Smolenskin's second novel, written in Odessa too, was more ambitious. A long, sprawling, first-person narrative in four parts (the last added at a later date), to which he gave the name *Ha-To'eh b'Darkei he-Hayim* or "Lost On Life's Way," it tells the story of Yosef, a boy born in the White Russian shtetl of Azuva. (The name in Hebrew means "Deserted.") Yosef's father has vanished, presumed a suicide, after being defrauded of his wealth by a brother, and soon afterward, Yosef's mother dies, too. At first, the orphan lives with the nefarious uncle and his wife, by whom he is mistreated; then, with the small amount of money given him by his mother on her deathbed, all that is left of the family fortune, he runs away. He joins a band of professional beggars masquerading as paupers and invalids, parts company with them, and falls in with a *balshem*, a seemingly pious purveyor of amulets, charms, fortunes, and magical cures who takes him to Odessa, trains him to be his shill, and appropriates his money, so he claims, for safekeeping. Although not unkind to the boy, the man is, as Yosef quickly discovers, a scoundrel and a mountebank. This makes him decide to retrieve his money, which is kept under lock and key in his master's room. Already schooled in the ways of deceit, he soon finds a way of laying his hands on it:

> In our neighborhood lived an attractive but sickly woman in her mid-twenties who came to my master for healing….When she returned the next evening, he sent me to an acquaintance of his at the far end of town and told me to lock the front door when I left. Had this happened several weeks earlier, I wouldn't have disobeyed him, but now all I had seen had made me a different person. And so I said, "I'm on my way," hid under my bed, and crawled out and peeked through the keyhole into his room as soon as he shut its door.

Yosef sees the *balshem* give the woman a glass of brandy and embrace her. When she protests, he tries convincing her to submit. "I glanced at her face," Yosef relates, "and saw that his words had an effect. Although she kept murmuring objections, she didn't raise her voice when he hugged her again and kissed her on the mouth. Did she let him do it for love or for money? The reader can ask her himself. She knows and I don't, never having been a woman. I only know that I thought: here's my chance!"

Yosef runs outside, bangs on the front door, and blurts when his master opens it: "Her husband! The woman's husband!" The *balshem* exclaims:

"What are you talking about, boy? What woman? What husband? Explain yourself!"

"The woman who was just here," I gasped as haltingly as I could. "Her husband...."

"What did he do? Tell me, quick!"

"Drat him, he...." I spoke as though befuddled while enjoying his distress. "The skunk!"

"Speak to the point!" My master urged worriedly. "What did he do? Where did you see him?"

"He looked in the window, and when I came to the door he tried forcing his way into the house. I blocked it and wouldn't let him in. We wrestled and he saw he couldn't get past me, so he ran off saying he was going to the police."

The ruse works flawlessly. The *balshem* tells Yosef to harness his carriage, transfers his and Yosef's money to his jacket pocket, and runs to pack his bags. Years later, Yosef, who makes off with the money when the *balshem* falls asleep at their first rest stop, reflects:

> At the time, I was amazed how such a swindler failed to see I was conning him. The same man who had fooled so many people, virtuous women too, had fallen like a fool into a trap set by a thirteen-year-old.... Today, though, this doesn't surprise me, because I've learned how easy it is to outwit the clever wits who think everyone but themselves can be duped.

Although many of the episodes in "Lost On Life's Way" are autobiographical, such as Yosef's yeshiva years in the town of Shkhula (a scrambling of Shklov meaning "bereaved") and his experiences at the Hasidic court of Tsvuel ("God's Hypocrite": a play on the letters of Lubavitch), others are not. Contemporary readers saw in them the influence of Dickens, particularly of *Oliver Twist*, available to Smolenskin in a Russian translation. Yet while Dickens's interest in the London demiworld may have encouraged Smolenskin to write about the shady side of East-European Jewish society, Yosef and Oliver are not alike. Oliver's experience of human depravity never causes him to lose his innocence;

his resistance to infection by the vice that surrounds him is his distinguishing, almost saint-like mark. Yosef, on the other hand, internalizes the world's ways quickly; from the moment he sets out into it, he learns to lie, cheat, and justify doing so. Though, like Oliver, he meets kind people who help him to survive, such as his yeshiva friend Gidon, a hidden Maskil who is like an older brother to him, he is never able to reciprocate their trust fully. Sooner or later he lets them down or betrays them, not because he is conscienceless, but because he has learned that the world is a place in which a conscience can be a disadvantage. His life is a struggle against the cynicism that is the natural conclusion from all he has seen, and while he is never totally defeated in this struggle, neither can he ever win it, because a part of him has been permanently damaged. This theme is sounded from the novel's opening paragraph:

> I have been lost, lost like a lamb from the flock – not for a month or a year or several years, but for my entire life on this planet. "But why have you been?" the reader may ask. "Why, if you saw you were on the wrong path, did you stay on it?" To which I reply: I have been lost because I've kept telling myself that I *was* lost. Had I been wise enough to say "I *am* lost," I might have caught my mistakes in time, but I've always realized them too late, and each time I've tried to make amends I've only made things worse, because I could never bring myself to acknowledge that some things are beyond repair.

Above all, it is through his love for a girl, again named Shifra, that Yosef seeks to redeem himself. He first meets her during his yeshiva years in Shkhula, when he takes his meals with her family. He is sixteen or seventeen, she several years younger; they are mutually attracted; yet too shy to exchange more than a few words over the dinner table, they live in an adolescent turmoil of unexpressed emotion until Yosef is made to leave the school and town. Regretful that he never mustered the courage to bare his feelings to her, he thinks and dreams of her during his subsequent wanderings until, four years later and now a grown man, he returns to Shkhula in hope and trepidation, afraid to discover she has in the meantime been wed.

She has not been. Yosef, taken on as a junior partner in her father's business, declares his love for her. They grow closer when he is asked to escort her and her ailing mother to a health spa on the North Sea island of Heligoland. Passing through St. Petersburg on their way, they see a chain gang of convicts, and Shifra, to her horror, recognizes a long-lost, ne'er-do-well brother among them. Although she keeps this from her mother, she reveals it to Yosef and relates her family history – and now it is his turn to be horrified, for her innocent disclosure that her father is in fact her stepfather, married to her widowed mother whose first husband died in the town of Azuva, leads him to the realization that she is his cousin, the daughter of the uncle who robbed his father, and that her mother is the woman who abused him as a child.

Yosef is thunderstruck. He never wants to see Shifra's mother again. He is just not ready to leave Shifra. And yet, he tells himself, "She's the daughter of a murderess! How can I love a woman stained with blood?" His parents, he feels sure, will pursue him from the grave if he marries her.

Yosef gets a grip on himself and the three of them sail on for the Swedish port of Malmö. At sea, their ship is caught in a violent storm. The deck pitches wildly. Yosef ties himself to Shifra with his belt while her mother clings to a railing and prays. Consumed by the anger that has been building up in him, he shouts: "Why don't you pray to the Devil you've made a pact with! I hope you sink to the bottom of the sea for what you've done!" "Are you the Devil, then?" cries Shifra's mother, suddenly recognizing him. "Or are you Yosef, come back to haunt me?"

"I'm Yosef!" I raged at the top of my voice.

She clapped her hands and cried, "Ah, me!" As she took them from the railing, a wave swept her overboard and she was gone forever, not a sailor having the pluck to come to her rescue.

The ship reaches port safely. Shifra, however, badly traumatized, has a severe breakdown. The doctors in Malmö tell Yosef that she is suffering from an incurable psychosis. And he tells us:

In vain, I tried talking to her and comforting her. She wouldn't look at me and didn't recognize me. My heart broke. I felt sick for what I had done. I knew her pitiable state was my doing. It was maddening to think I couldn't take any of it back. In a moment of fury, I had wreaked vengeance on an enemy and destroyed the innocent woman I loved.

3

Yosef's story doesn't end in Malmö, which from a purely literary point of view is unfortunate. What remains – the last third of Part III of "Lost On Life's Way" and all of Part IV – still has a long way to go. It takes Yosef to Hamburg, to London, to Paris, to Brussels, to Berlin, to Bucharest, and back to Odessa, and has him fall in love again, this time with a beautiful Anglo-Jewish heiress. Yet just as she is about to fall into his arms, she is revealed to be a half-sister of whose existence he was unaware and he flees. In the last of the many letters that he sends her from Russia, dying and tormented by his unfulfillable incestuous longings, he writes that he wants the inscription on his tombstone to read: "Here lies one lost on life's way."

Highly successful with Smolenskin's readers, "Lost On Life's Way" could have used an editor. Still, it is a gripping book, the story of a young man of great promise who is his own worst nemesis. Even its outrageous improbabilities, exceeding those in the novels of Mapu, are no greater than similar ones in European novels of the time. *Oliver Twist* is one of these. Ever since Sophocles's *Oedipus*, far-fetched coincidence has served Western literature as a symbol of the fateful interconnectedness of all things.

But the web of connections in "Lost On Life's Way" serves a more specific purpose. Nowhere previously in the Jewish literature of the nineteenth century, in Hebrew or any other language, does one encounter so broad a social canvas with such a wide range of types. It was of "Lost On Life's Way," more than of any other novel by Smolenskin, that his early twentieth-century biographer, the Hebrew literary critic Re'uven Brainin, was thinking when he wrote:

> If a future author should wish to describe the first Hebrew Maskilim, their lives, battles, and ideals; the heder teachers and the yeshiva students; the Hasidim and their Rebbes; the amulet

writers and snake doctors; the jobbers and parasites; the Misnagdic communal leaders and powers-that-be; the rabbis, the can-
tors, the intellectuals, the informers – in a word, should such an
author come to describe the life of our people in the Russian Pale
of Settlement in the first decades of the seventh century of the
sixth millennium [i.e., the epoch starting with the Hebrew year
5600 or 1840], he will find much of his material in Smolenskin.

Brainin's list could be expanded considerably, on the basis of "Lost
On Life's Way" alone, to include Jewish lawyers, doctors, businessmen,
coachmen, tradesmen, rustic villagers, wealthy contractors, klezmer
musicians, criminals, fallen women, kidnapped conscripts, cabaret
singers, apostates, missionaries, philanthropists, authors, Hebrew poets,
concert pianists, university professors, feminists, nihilists, assimilation-
ists, London socialites, French Bonapartists, German Reform temple-
goers, Romanian pogrom victims, and Russian revolutionaries – and
then, too, it would be far from complete. There is a Jew in the novel for
every occasion, and yet never, despite all their differences and antago-
nisms, does Yosef fail to feel a kinship with them all or to doubt that
all are Jews; nor do most of them, even those who would prefer to be
something else, doubt it themselves.

What do they have in common, apart from figuring, to a greater
or lesser degree, in Yosef's life? Some have more, some less. Smolenskin's
Hasidim and Misnagdim, for all their mutual disdain, share a great deal:
a habitat, Eastern Europe; a language, Yiddish; a religious tradition which,
despite their different understandings of it, shapes their daily lives in
similar ways. But what does either share with a Reform Jew in Berlin, a
Jewish French patriot in Paris, or a well-bred and wealthy London Jewish socialite? Seemingly, very little.

It is here that the role of coincidence in "Lost On Life's Way"
takes on a greater significance. When Yosef discovers that Shifra is his
cousin; or learns that his father, far from having killed himself, has fled
to America, recouped his fortune there, moved to London, married a
Jewish woman, and raised an aristocratically bred daughter whom he,
Yosef, has fallen tragically in love with; or reads in this daughter's letters
to him that she has become engaged to his old yeshiva friend Gidon,

long given up by him for dead but now a renowned professor in Switzerland; or stumbles in his adventures on other strange nexuses of fate, we are being told something about the Jewish world as surely as we are told something about England when the ex-waif Oliver turns out to be a wealthy heir, the nephew of the finely mannered but illegitimately born Rose Maylie and the half-brother of the criminal Monks. In both cases, we are dealing with a large but not limitless realm in which such coincidences are possible because everyone within its circumference is potentially linked to everyone else, as he or she is not to those outside it, by strands of circumstance capable of bringing together persons of vastly different social and economic backgrounds and geographic locations.

One such realm is a people. That there was, in the nineteenth century, an English people would have been contested by no one. That there was *still*, geographically dispersed and centrifugalized as it was by the weakening hold of traditional religion and the pull of the different languages and cultures of the European countries it lived in, a Jewish people was questioned by many – not least by the growing number of Jews who thought of themselves as the members of the "Mosaic faith" that Mendelssohn had said they were, no more linked to each other across the national boundaries of Europe than were English to German Protestants or French to Irish Catholics. If Jewish peoplehood still existed, it had to be conceived of in post-religious terms, and Smolenskin, who was to make this peoplehood the grand cause of his life and battle programmatically for it in his non-fictional writing, needed fiction to command an imaginative view of it. This he achieved in "Lost On Life's Way."

4

In 1868, Smolenskin moved to Vienna, where he made his home until his death in 1884. He arrived there, so legend has it, with seven Russian kopecks in his pocket and the ambition to found and edit a monthly Hebrew literary review. Vienna was a logical place for this. It had a large Jewish population, much of it East-European in origin, that was comparable in size and growth rate to Odessa's (40,000 strong when Smolenskin came to Vienna, it doubled during his years there); a lively Jewish intellectual life; and a relatively free press unhindered by an intrusive censorship like Tsarist Russia's. With the help of a job landed in a

Hebrew print shop, whose owner agreed to let him set the type for it at no cost, Smolenskin's review, called *Ha-Shahar*, "The Dawn," made its first appearance the following year.

Ha-Shahar continued to come out for the rest of Smolenskin's lifetime, sometimes sticking to its monthly schedule, sometimes falling behind, sometimes temporarily ceasing publication and renewing it. The struggle to keep it solvent while recruiting talent and material for its pages was never-ending. Yet though estimated to have had barely one thousand subscribers at its height, its actual readership was far larger, and it quickly became an influential Hebrew periodical alongside such older rivals as the Warsaw *Ha-Tsefira*, the St. Petersburg *Ha-Melitz*, and the Berlin *Ha-Maggid*.

Ha-Shahar ran essays and informative articles on a wide range of subjects, published poetry and fiction, and serialized Smolenskin's own novels, starting with "The Humbug's Happiness" and "Lost On Life's Way." A typical issue was Number 1 of 1878, which came off the press in April rather than in January as it should have. In it was an editorial by Smolenskin on German rabbinical schools; part two of an explication of obscure terms in the Bible by the Haskalah author Avraham Dov Ber Lebensohn; a survey of Jewish education in southern Russia by the bibliographer and historian Ephraim Deinard; an article on recent developments in the field of molecular chemistry, accompanied by illustrative diagrams; a short story signed by "Bar Drora" ("Son of Freedom"), the pen name of the revolutionary Aharon Shmuel Lieberman, who had started the world's first Hebrew socialist periodical a year previously; a contribution from Yehuda Leib Gordon, the most celebrated Hebrew poet of the age; and a travel journal from Palestine by Shlomo Mandelkern, the future compiler of a widely used biblical concordance. Annual subscriptions, as noted on the masthead, cost 6 florins in Austria, 4 thalers in Germany, 22 francs in France, 5 rubles in Russia, and 4 gold dollars in the United States.

During the 1870s, Smolenskin published a series of essays in *Ha-Shahar* that were collected in three books: *Am Olam*, "An Eternal People"; *Et La'asot*, "A Time To Act"; and *Et Lata'at*, "A Time To Plant." All three dealt with "the Jewish question," a term introduced into European discourse by the German historian Bruno Bauer in his 1843 book *Die Judenfrage*. The existence of such a question was increasingly acknowledged by Jews and Gentiles alike in the course of the nineteenth century. In Western Europe, legal and political emancipation, completed everywhere by the century's end, had led to widespread Jewish bourgeoisification and assimilation but also to an upsurge of anti-Semitism. In the East, where emancipation lagged behind and anti-Semitism was fiercer to begin with, a far larger Jewish population – rapidly increasing due to high birth rates and lowered mortality rates; economically displaced as industrialization and government policies drove it out of its traditional trades and commercial niches; and severely restricted by residential laws and quotas in its geographic mobility and educational opportunities – was progressively pauperized and reduced to desperation. The Haskalah's vision of the successful integration of the Jews in a European society to which they would adapt their ways and manners while having their religion legitimized and their collective existence assured had begun, as was argued by Moshe Leib Lilienblum, to founder.

Like Lilienblum, Smolenskin was a product of the Haskalah. It had opened new vistas for him, given him the tools and mental freedom to explore European thought and culture, and led him to abandon the ritual trappings of Jewish tradition. In his essays in *Ha-Shahar*, however, he now came to this tradition's defense. The Haskalah, he argued, had undermined Judaism without taking the consequences into account. It had made a double mistake, first, by promising Europe's Jews that they could blend into Christian society as Frenchmen or Germans of a non-Christian religious confession, and second, by encouraging the dilution of this religion to the point that renouncing it had become a mere formality. Why not, then, take the last step and be done once and for all with the burden of Jewishness, whether through conversion to Christianity or simply dropping out of the Jewish community entirely?

And yet, Smolenskin wrote, the Jews were not a confession like Protestants or Catholics. They were, by virtue of the ties that connected them, a separate people. Many of them who were not religious felt these ties, too, which was why the French would never accept them as fellow Frenchmen any more than they would accept Germans or Russians; worse, the French would revile them as they did not revile Germans or Russians because Germans and Russians did not pose as French. The

Jews were thus fated to go on being a separate people whether they wanted to be one or not. The problem was that, having lost their land and political independence in antiquity, they had come to express their peoplehood solely by means of their religion; take this away from them and they were, though still a people, a demoralized one no longer knowing who it was. This was now the situation of most of Western Europe's Jews. It would become that of Eastern Europe's, too, if they blindly discarded everything in Judaism that failed to conform to contemporary European standards of religious belief and behavior.

To be sure, the religiously conservative wing of the Haskalah had also warned against pruning Judaism excessively of its particularisms. But although Smolenskin published the writings of such Maskilim in *Ha-Shahar*, he did not share their sense of belonging to a Misnagdic Brahmin class that was the custodian of Judaism's eternal verities and high achievements. For all his sardonic descriptions of the chicanery of the Jewish street, he had a novelist's empathy with it. Apart from frequent but vague references to an ethical monotheism that he called "the spirit of Torah," he did not apologetically dwell in his *Ha-Shahar* essays on Judaism's values or merits; nor did he write as a *baal teshuva*, a lapsed Jew returned to the faith of his fathers. While he had never ceased to feel attached to this faith despite his abandonment of religious observance, his attachment was less to its content, let alone to its God, than to the people who upheld it. This people had always been a central pillar of the Jewish religion. And yet in conceiving of it as theoretically separable from its religion, even if he thought such a separation undesirable, Smolenskin laid the ground for a secular Jewish nationalism.

A Jewish people existed *objectively*, whether it practiced Judaism or not. "It is not the laws of our religion that unite us," Smolenskin wrote. "They will not live forever, but our people will. Jews who do not observe them or who never possessed them, like those of India or China, are our brothers, too." The problem lay in translating the objective fact of this people's existence into the subjective desire to belong to it – and here, it must be said, Smolenskin was putting the effect before the cause by blaming the Haskalah alone for weakening Jewish national feeling. More than an outcome of the Haskalah, assimilation was a reaction to the same social and political forces that had produced the Haskalah, such as the spread of science and religious skepticism, and the ascendance of the secular European state that extended equal rights and duties to all its citizens. If the unifying force of religion was failing, attacking the Haskalah would not strengthen it. Yet what could replace it?

Ultimately, Smolenskin fell back on the same thing that had sustained Mapu: a belief in the power of Hebrew. Although Jews did not have their own land, they had their own language. It may not have been spoken by them, but it remained the principal vehicle of reading and writing for many of them, particularly in Eastern Europe, and a vital medium of literature, scholarship, and communication. If a deep devotion to it was needed to maintain Hebrew's primacy vis-a-vis the European languages that were making swift inroads on its territory, such a feeling, acquired from a veneration for the Bible, the prayer book, and the great texts of Judaism, and from emotions going back to the earliest years of one's childhood, was still common. "A single language unites us," Smolenskin wrote in "A Time To Plant." "It puts words in our mouths with which to speak to one another to the farthest isles and ends of the earth... Hebrew has been the cord that binds us. We must strengthen and empower it for our own power to grow."

How get Jews to read Hebrew in a post-religious age? By addressing them in it in the forms they craved to be addressed in – and in an age of Dickens, Thackeray, Balzac, Stendhal, Turgenev, and Dostoyevsky, no form was more popular than the novel. If it was through the novel that Smolenskin best imagined Jewish unity, it was in the name of Jewish unity that he wrote novels, as ill-suited to the medium as Hebrew may have been.

5

The novel, it has been said (probably inaccurately) was given its name because it brings us the news. It tells us, better than do the daily papers, what is happening. Yet this can be difficult to do in a language so old that it hasn't been spoken for thousands years, so that we can't even be sure what a key word in a crucial scene means.

The scene is in Smolenskin's novel *K'vurat Hamor*, "A Donkey's Burial," serialized in *Ha-Shahar* in 1874. It takes place early in the story, in the White Russian town of Kshula, which is none other than Shklov again, this time as an anagram of the Hebrew verb *kashal*, fail. The time is the week before Hanukkah – the nineteenth of Kislev to be exact, a date many of Smolenskin's readers would have recognized as a Habad holiday commemorating the release from Tsarist imprisonment of the movement's founder, Shneur Zalman of Liady. The local Hevra Kadisha or burial society, the most powerful of the town's fraternal lodges, is holding its annual banquet. A grand event brimming with food and drink and eagerly awaited all year long, its crowning glory is its final course of luscious, pan-fried *tufinim* that are the pride of all Kshula.

The moment for them has arrived. A waiter sets a large skillet on a table, removes the domed lid that covers it – and runs in a fright to tell Reb Getsl-Shmaryeh, the head of the Hevra Kadisha, that the pan is empty.

"That's a good one!" said Getsl-Shmaryeh to the waiter, who was standing at attention. "That's a good one! You'd better look again. I can see you're blind drunk."

"But Reb Getsl, I swear by all that's holy that I looked in the skillet and nothing was there. By my wife and children, I swear! There was nothing under the lid. The *tufinim* have been stolen for sure."

"Who would have stolen them? Me? One of the Hevra Kadisha?"

"How would I know?" asked the waiter.

"There hasn't been a scandal like this since the day our lodge was founded!"

"There are thieves among us!"

"The *tufinim* have been filched from under our noses!"

"A banquet without *tufinim*!"

"We'll have *tufinim* or someone will swing for it!"

"This will go down in history!"

Everyone had an opinion.

How did Smolenskin, decades before the revival of spoken Hebrew in Palestine, manage to write such racy dialogue? One might answer that he didn't. "You're blind drunk" in the original is "You've drunk to satiety and your eyes have deceived you." "Have been stolen for sure" is *ganov nignevu*, literally, "stealing they were stolen," an emphatic biblical construction rarely used in post-biblical Hebrew. "Or someone will swing for it" is "If mountains must be uprooted with fingernails," a talmudic idiom meaning "Whatever lengths must be gone to." Smolenskin's characters speak a Hebrew, crafted eclectically from biblical, rabbinic, and Haskalah sources, that is far more erudite and elevated than the Yiddish they would have spoken in real life.

My translation takes liberties with this Hebrew. But the fact that taking them produces such lively results testifies to its smooth flow. Though its language is artificial, its clever phrasing and rapid pacing make up for this. Without resorting to gross Yiddishisms like Perl, Smolenskin creates the illusion that we are listening to speech that is spontaneous, not bookish like Mapu's.

But what is a *tufin*? The word occurs once in the Bible, in the book of Leviticus, where the high priest Aaron and his sons are enjoined to bring an offering of "*tufinim* made with oil in a pan." Apart from its method of preparation, however, neither the ancient rabbis nor the Bible's medieval commentators had any idea what manner of dish this was, and Smolenskin's readers would have had to guess, too. Were the Hevra Kadisha members looking forward to a last course of pre-Hanukkah *latkes*? Jam-filled *blini*? Russian *pierogi* or Ukrainian *varenyky*? After a lengthy discussion of *tufin*'s etymology in his ground-breaking sixteen-volume Hebrew dictionary that appeared in the early 1900s, the linguist and lexicographer Eliezer Ben-Yehuda could only conclude that the word was "of uncertain meaning."

Smolenskin could, of course, have written *latkes*, *blini*, *pierogi*, or *varenyky*, using the Yiddish, Russian, or Ukrainian word. Perl's Hasidim would not have hesitated to do so. But when it came to Hebrew, Smolenskin, like Mapu and other Haskalah writers, was determined to prove that it had the resources to do everything on its own. When, for instance, he made mention in his fiction of that nineteenth-century invention the photograph, he didn't borrow French *photographie* or Russian *fotografiya*; rather, he wrote *tsel tselem ish*, "the shadow of a man's image," using the word found in the biblical story of man's creation in the image of God. (Twentieth-century Hebrew would take *tselem*, and coin from it the verb *l'tsalem*, to photograph, and the nouns *tsilum*, a photo, and *matslema*, a camera.) For a railroad train, Smolenskin could have resorted to Yiddish *ban* or *tsug*; instead, he chose *merkevet esh*, "a chariot of fire." If Haskalah Hebrew was a hobbled tongue lacking the vocabulary for innumerable features of modern life, a vernacular to write dialogue in, and clear standards of usage, such purism was like a lame man who insists on going everywhere without crutches. No one knew what a *tufin* was? Better not to know than to lean on a non-Hebrew word!

For all his ardor for Hebrew, however, Smolenskin was no more able to explain how it could survive in a modern world in which better novels could be written in other languages than he could explain how Jewish tradition might prosper in a secular age. This point was made by Ben-Yehuda, then a twenty-one-year-old medical student in Paris. Impressed by the recent success of the Bulgarian struggle for independence from Turkey, he declared in an article published in *Ha-Shahar* in 1879 that missing from Smolenskin's analysis was a call for a territorial base where a Jewish majority could read, write, and speak Hebrew as its native tongue. Without such a place, Hebrew would never be more than the occupation of a dedicated and dwindling band of loyalists – and this place could only be Palestine. "Let the Land of Israel be our center," Ben-Yehuda wrote five years after Lilienblum had stressed the need for "a country of our own to protect our national existence," and "the world's Jews will know that they have their own land and their own language." Whereas Mapu had stopped short of linking Hebrew's future to a Jewish return to Palestine, and Lilienblum had come a step closer, Ben-Yehuda now went the rest of the way, making him the first in the world of Hebrew letters to do so.

Smolenskin answered with an open letter to Ben-Yehuda in which he wrote that he did not believe in the revival of spoken Hebrew and that Jewish normalcy was not his goal. "I've never said," he stated, "that the Jews are a people like all others. On the contrary: ever since first discussing the subject, I've held that they are *not* like others." The Jews were a "people of the spirit," and Hebrew would survive among them as that spirit's written expression, not as a language of daily life. He was not interested in Palestine, Smolenskin said, if it meant surrendering Jewish uniqueness. "Suppose we were told," he asked,

"Palestine is yours. Take it and do as you wish with it...but on the condition that you exchange your beliefs for different ones." What would you say to that, Ben-Yehuda, my friend? Should we accept this great gift with the strings attached to it? By your lights, it would be an act of treason to turn it down. What need have we for our beliefs and the Torah and the spirit of Israel if we have our own land? But I tell you that the traitor is he who would agree.

Ben-Yehuda, an unabashed secularist, replied in a letter of his own in which he declared that Smolenskin was contradicting himself and ignoring the historical processes his thinking was based on. "Because it was said by the Berlin Maskilim," Ben-Yehuda wrote, "that no people can exist without a land and we who live in the lands of others are therefore not a people, you now answer: 'Not so! The Jews are different! Other peoples have earthly kingdoms and we have a spiritual one!'" But if it was not part of a lived religion, such a "spirit of Israel" was a mere abstraction. And as an expression of an abstraction rather than of daily life, Hebrew was doomed. Who needed it? Why bother to study it and read its literature when Jewish thought and history could just as well be read and written about in German, Russian, French, or English? Everything of value in it, from the Bible on, could be translated, and a small coterie of Hebrew-reading scholars would suffice to make such works available to whoever cared to be acquainted with them. "Permit me to ask you, sir," Ben-Yehuda wrote, "what can Hebrew mean to the person who is no longer Hebraic?" He himself was a more consistent Smolenskinian than Smolenskin, because he was drawing the logical conclusions from Smolenskin's writings that Smolenskin refused to draw:

This is why I say, sir, that you have strayed from the path [you set out on]. It is useless to proclaim: We must cling to Hebrew or die! Only if we give our people life by returning it to the soil of its homeland will Hebrew live too...In all that I am saying, sir, it is you who speak in me. You were the first of our intellectuals to raise the banner of *national* redemption and to have the courage to do so without fear of being called a zealot or a madman. You have not labored in vain, sir.

6

Let us return to the *tufinim*. They have been pilfered – and the culprit is Yakov-Hayim, the protagonist of "A Donkey's Burial" and along with Yosef in "Lost On Life's Way" the most memorable of Smolenskin's fictional characters. He and Yosef have much in common: both excel as students at the same Kshula-Shkhula-Shklov yeshiva and both are intelligent, self-confident, impulsive, and quick to give and take offense. The adolescent Yakov-Hayim, though, is also a prankster. High-spirited and scornful of authority, he steals the *pièce de résistance* of the Hevra Kadisha's banquet as a practical joke. In return, the irate banqueters swear that if they discover the thief's identity, he will be punished when he dies with a "donkey's burial," an unmarked grave outside the Jewish cemetery.

At the time of the banquet, Yakov-Hayim, chosen by Getsl-Shmaryeh as one of the yeshiva's outstanding students, is affianced to the latter's orphaned granddaughter, the beautiful Esther. Soon after, the wedding is held. Yet finding out the next day that his new grandson-in-law has proven to be the *tufinim's* thief, Getsl-Shmaryeh insists on an immediate divorce and offers to pay Yakov-Hayim to grant it. Yakov-Hayim, secretly intending to use the money to run away with Esther and start a new life with her elsewhere, agrees. As the writ of divorce is being penned by the town rabbi, however, a quarrel breaks out over the size of the sum. Yakov-Hayim balks at the last moment and threatens to abscond without signing.

> "Speak up!" exclaimed Reb Getsl in a fury. "Are you going to grant the divorce right this minute or not?"
>
> "You'll get your divorce when I get my money," the young husband answered coolly.
>
> "You'll see the back of your ears before you see the money!"
>
> "And you'll see the top of your head before you see me again! Your granddaughter will never be able to remarry."
>
> "My granddaughter a grass widow?" cried Esther's grandmother. "Lord have mercy! You murderer! How can you be so godless as to leave a poor orphan high and dry? You wicked, scurvy, bloody thief!"

"I'm neither wicked nor a thief. I love my wife and don't want to leave her."

"Thief! You're a thief! Where do you get the gall to say you aren't? Did you hear him, brothers?" the old woman appealed to the onlookers. "Did you hear what this shameless fellow said? He said he loves the wife he married yesterday. They haven't been married a day and he's already telling the whole world he loves her! What Jew ever loved his wife the day after their wedding?"

Perhaps only the Jew for whom the sexual consummation of the wedding night, an awkward mortification for most young shtetl couples, was a positive experience. Soon, though, the novel's semi-comical beginnings turn somber. To the chagrin of Zvadia, Kshula's wealthiest Jew who covets a divorced Esther for himself, she and Yakov-Hayim remain together. Befriended by the provincial governor for his winning personality and good knowledge of Russian, Yakov-Hayim finds lucrative work as an intermediary between the authorities and the town's Jews, many of them smugglers needing protection from the law. Eventually, though, his indiscreetly shown contempt for them leads to their rejection of his services. In retaliation, he becomes a paid police spy until, his activities revealed, he is excommunicated by the Kshula community.

Esther, who loves her husband but has a strong sense of Jewish loyalty, persuades him to give up his informer's life. Yet with a small child and no means of support, they sink into indigence. The only solution, Esther convinces Yakov-Hayim, is to beg the leaders of the community for forgiveness and ask to rejoin it. Yakov-Hayim swallows his pride and does so. His overtures are rejected. Enraged and despairing of a normal existence, he throws in his lot with a gang of criminals. On his way to a midnight rendezvous with them, he is murdered by an assassin hired by Zvadia. His body, cast into a river and washed ashore, is given the burial promised the thief of the *tufinim*.

The novel nears its end. The governor takes Esther under his protective wing and is enchanted by her. Thoroughly alienated by now from Kshula's Jews, she agrees to marry him and is baptized. The wedding is held to the peals of church bells. Zvadia, whose role in Yakov-Hayim's death has meanwhile come to light, uses his wealth and influence to escape punishment, and "A Donkey's Burial" ends on that note.

Although a synopsis can make any book sound silly, "A Donkey's Burial," despite some clumsy plotting, is Smolenskin's most accomplished fictional work. Yakov-Hayim's fate is genuinely tragic, for many of the qualities that are his undoing – his imaginativeness, his enthusiasm, his courage, his capacity for love and sacrifice – could have made him an asset to Kshula if it weren't so hidebound that it drives him to a life of crime. This is *its* tragedy.

And yet "A Donkey's Burial" is far from being a blanket indictment of East-European Jewry as represented by Kshula's inhabitants. Not only is Yakov-Hayim, like Yosef, partly to blame for his own misfortune, but apart from the villainous Zvadia, Smolenskin's depiction of Kshula's Jews is not unsympathetic. His most outspoken defense of them is put in the mouth of a well-off member of the community at a meeting of its prominent citizens, held to decide whether to raise bribe money for the release of smugglers arrested on a tip from Yakov-Hayim:

> Fifteen thousand Jews live in this town with no other way of earning a living, and we're supposed to tell them, "Go home, obey the law, and die of hunger with your families?" We rich Jews are told we should help the less fortunate. We do and we will. No other town in this country gives more to charity. Just look at our yeshivas, our Talmud Torahs, our orphanages, our aid societies, our poor funds and our sick funds, our dowry donations for brides, and all the rest. But how much good can any of this do so large a population?...The fifty rich Jews of Kshula can't support fifteen thousand others. How will they manage if they don't deal in contraband? You say they should learn a trade? Where would they find work? Every last tailor, shoemaker, woodcutter, and smith in this town is a Jew, and they're all glad if there's food on the table at the end of the day...The first, sacred duty of us all is to keep ourselves and our families alive. If we can't do it honestly, we'll have to do it by bribery.

Kshula is narrow-minded but not cold-hearted. There is just no place in it for a Yakov-Hayim. Like "Lost On Life's Way," "A Donkey's Burial" is about social and national boundaries. Whom do they and don't they include? They can embrace, as they do in "Lost On Life's Way," a people's farthest-flung progeny while ejecting, as in "A Donkey's Burial," its homegrown sons and daughters. No one could be more Jewish than Esther.

But not even apostasy need irreparably breach the circumference of Jewish interconnectedness. There is another case of it in Smolenskin's novel *G'mul Yesharim*, "Virtue's Reward," published in *Ha-Shahar* in 1875–76. This one, too, involves a young woman from a traditional home, located in the Polish shtetl of Shtika (Hebrew for "silence"). Gotten pregnant by a Pole, she is cast into the street by her parents and finds asylum in a convent, where she gives birth and goes to the baptismal fount. In the novel's final pages, now a single mother eking out a living for herself and her small son as a washerwoman in Warsaw, she is recognized as the daughter of a family he knew in Shtika by a brilliant young Jewish lawyer, who represents her in court against a physically abusive employer, wins the trial against all odds, and rescues her from poverty by hiring her to be his well-paid housekeeper. Although she is terrified at having her Jewishness exposed and begs him to reveal it to no one, the novel's ending strongly implies that she and her son will be restored to their people.

One more unlikely coincidence? No doubt. But it is to a big city like Warsaw that such a woman must repair if she wishes to conceal a past both Jewish and sinful; the lawyer is yet another of Smolenskin's ex-yeshiva students, inclined by his talmudic training to a profession to which only the brightest Jewish candidates gain admission; the place to study and practice it is the nation's capital; and who but an idealistic Jewish lawyer would volunteer to fight in court for a poor Jewish laundress who cannot afford to pay for legal help? Once more we find a people defined as the largest possible group whose members, though drawn from the most varied walks of life, have fewer degrees of separation between them than they would have if chosen at random. The Jews are, as it were, a stagecoach to Odessa multiplied by many magnitudes.

Moreover, changing religion can be a two-way street. Another character in "Virtue's Reward" is Emil, born Immanuel. The son of a wealthy Maskil, he drifts away when young from a Jewish world he feels stifled by, spends his days and nights in the company of Shtika's young Polish nobility, and joins the anti-Russian Polish rebellion of 1863, fighting heroically as an officer in its ranks. From a Jewish point of view, Emil seems lost. And yet in the end, no longer able to ignore the Poles' ingrained anti-Semitism or to suppress his own Jewish feelings, he returns to the Jewish fold – and when he does, he brings with him the brave and charming Polish aristocrat Elżbieta, who converts to marry him. Borders with exits also have entry points.

7

Centered in the Ukraine, the unprecedented wave of pogroms that swept Russia from April 1881 to May 1882 inflicted widespread injury and property damage, though little loss of life. While triggered by the assassination of Alexander II, for which Jewish conspirators were widely blamed (in fact, only one Jew was involved), the riots had been preceded by decades of anti-Semitic agitation. Deicide, revolutionary activity, economic exploitation of the masses, pro-Polish sympathies, religious fanaticism, supremacist doctrines, draft dodging, ritual murder, avaricious greed, plots against Christianity, control of international finance, a drive for world domination – there was nothing Russian Jews weren't accused of.

The response of the new regime of Alexander III to the pogroms was hardly reassuring. In many places, the police and army did little or nothing to stop them. Much of the press and public opinion held Russian Jewry responsible for its plight, and the government, in the name of reducing friction between it and the general population, enacted new anti-Jewish legislation, tightening Jewish residency restrictions and educational quotas. The liberalization policies of Alexander II, already rolled back during his lifetime, were officially abandoned.

Increasingly, it seemed that the only alternatives for the Jews of Russia were to opt for mass flight, hope for a revolution, or accept a long, slow death under Tsardom. Their spontaneous reaction was to quicken the pace of an emigration that had been a trickle until then. In the 1860s and '70s, a few thousand Jews had left Russia every year. In the first months after the pogroms broke out, an estimated 10,000 departed for the United States alone.

In late 1881, Eliezer Ben-Yehuda chose a different destination and sailed for Palestine with the intention of settling there. Before setting out, he traveled to Vienna to see Smolenskin, who had just returned from a trip to Russia. Ben-Yehuda's memoirs relate:

> He [Smolenskin] invited me to lunch with him at home and received me with a cordiality that signaled that he was in the highest of spirits. Ushering me into his study, he spent the time before we were called to the table telling me about his trip, about the dramatic growth in Russia of Jewish national feeling, and about the honors accorded him there....
>
> "By the way," he said genially, "do you know that your 'Letter From Ben-Yehuda' was published in the last issue of *Ha-Shahar* before I left on my trip?"
>
> "Many thanks for that, sir. I'm quite pleased by it."
>
> "Don't rush to be pleased. I answered you and rebutted all your arguments."
>
> "On that score, I'm not pleased at all. But let's wait and see. Perhaps I'll be able to defend myself and prove – "
>
> "There's no need for that," Smolenskin interrupted. "You needn't bother, because your work has already been done for you by others....namely, by me. You see, I've replied to my rebuttal of your views by adopting them and even stating them more strongly. You're wondering how I could come out against my own self? It's simple... I'm not ashamed to admit that I've changed my mind. When your letter [to *Ha-Shahar*] arrived, the world was still the same world and I was still of the opinion that we Jews could live as a people even in the Diaspora as long as we told ourselves that we *were* a people...but the terrible events in Russia have shaken me and my thinking to the core. They've made me feel that our national existence needs something more tangible, a ground beneath our feet – yes, our own land and [spoken] language.... After spending two months in Russia and seeing the national- ist fervor kindled in its Jews and the desire of many of them to

settle in Palestine, I now believe with all my heart that the Land of Israel is the hope of the Jewish people. I believe it's possible, if only our people back it to the full....

"If we say," wrote Smolenskin in this rebuttal of his rebuttal, "that we all belong to one people, then our first duty as a people is to seek our unity in a land [of our own]." From then until his death four years later, he put *Ha-Shahar* solidly behind Zionism – or rather, "Zionism" being a term coined only in 1890, behind the Hibat Tsiyon movement. Many of the editorials run by him in the remaining years of *Ha-Shahar*'s publication dealt with this movement's activities, which included the founding in the early 1880s of Palestine's first Jewish agricultural settlements by Jews from Romania and Russia. Smolenskin also lent his name as a sponsor to Kadimah, a Viennese student association established in 1882 that became a focal point of Zionist thought and activity. In this he was joined by the Odessa physician Leo Pinsker, whose influential essay "Autoemancipation" was published that same year. Inasmuch as the anti-Semitism manifested in "the [recent] bloody atrocities," Pinsker wrote there, was not a mere prejudice that could be overcome by education and progressive politics, but the natural reaction of any people to a foreign body in its midst, a "psychic aberration" that was "hereditary, and as a disease transmitted for two thousand years, incurable," the only solution to the Jewish question was a land that Jews could call their own.

As usual, Smolenskin turned to fiction to give imaginative expression to his views. The result was a short work, more a novella than a novel, entitled *Brit Nakam*, "A Pact of Vengeance." Its tripartite division similar to a play's three acts, it begins with its young hero, Ephraim Hahagri, taking part in a meeting convened by his fellow Jewish university students in St. Petersburg to debate attending a talk by a nationalist Hebrew author – clearly Smolenskin himself – who is on a visit from Vienna. Ephraim, though esteemed by his Jewish confreres for having defended their honor by slapping a Russian student for an anti-Semitic remark, espouses the anti-nationalist, assimilationist creed that he has been brought up by his parents to believe in. Yet he raises no objection to hearing the author out and the group votes to honor the visitor with its attendance.

Ephraim returns from this meeting to his rented room – thus begins Part II – to find two letters waiting for him. One, from his father, is an anguished account of a bloody pogrom that has hit their family's provincial town. The family's home, Ephraim learns, has been looted and his sister, her gold locket torn from her throat, nearly raped. Even worse than the physical damage has been the shattering of his father's dreams of Christian-Jewish brotherhood, now realized to have been a chimera.

The second letter, from Ephraim's mother, takes the opposite tack. Begging him not to be influenced by his father's depression, which she is sure will prove temporary, she insists that the pogrom was the work of unrepresentative riffraff, a mere blip on the nineteenth century's upward curve of progress. "Be strong, my son," she writes. "Don't be swayed by reactionary thoughts. Crabs go backwards, not human beings." Though shocked and disturbed by his father's letter, Ephraim is heartened by his mother's and decides to boycott the Hebrew author's talk after all.

The story's third part takes place several weeks later in Ephraim's native town, to which he has gone for his summer vacation. Visiting a Russian family he has been friendly with since childhood, he spends time with its only daughter, a girl his age, and basks in their warm feelings for each other. Just as her older brothers arrive home with a friend, however, he notices to his consternation that she is wearing his sister's locket. Telling her it was stolen from its Jewish owner, he pleads with her to remove it. She sees no reason to. "What do I care about some Yi….some Jewish girl?" she asks. "This was given me by a person of honor." "It was given you by a thief!" retorts Ephraim – and is promptly slapped by the brothers' friend, the very "person of honor," it turns out, who was his sister's attacker. A moment later he is thrown down the stairs and out of the house to a peal of laughter. "If that's not payment enough for the locket, Yid, you can have more," comes a shout from the window.

Although tempted to take vengeance with the revolver he habitually carries in his pocket, Ephraim refrains. In an agitated state, he wanders through the streets of the town; finds himself outside a synagogue; enters it; and sees the congregation seated on the floor in observance of the fast of Tisha B'Av, the day of mourning for the destruction of the Temple. Joining the service, he announces at its end that he is leaving Russia for Palestine. "Our flag of vengeance is Jerusalem!" he proclaims. "We'll even the score not with blood but by standing together as brothers. Hurrah for our people! Hurrah for the land of our fathers!"

Like Emil in "Virtue's Reward," Ephraim, whose Hebrew last name of Hahagri means "the wanderer" or "the emigrant," is forced back on his Jewishness by a combination of outer and inner forces. Unlike Emil, though, who had no such option in his day, Ephraim's conclusion is a Zionist one. The story ends:

> Only one person was still in mourning as the day drew to a close: Ephraim's mother. Gone, gone was the nineteenth century, and no one could bring it back.

These well-wrought lines are not enough to save "A Pact of Vengeance" from being a tendentious and overly schematic work. But the Hebrew author from Vienna who wrote it was dying of tuberculosis and can be excused for having been in a hurry.

8

Although Smolenskin is remembered today as an early Zionist, he would be thought of differently had he died a few years earlier, or had the pogroms of 1881 broken out a few years later. His reputation would then have been that of a Diaspora nationalist with little or no interest in Palestine.

And yet in the last years of his life, nothing fundamental changed in his thinking. What had changed was the situation he was required to think about. An alternative not worth considering because it had not appeared to be remotely practical was now on the Jewish agenda. In the ongoing interplay of ideas and events that moves history forward, events had taken the lead. The Jewish people was suddenly on the move. Why let it be stampeded to America, one more diaspora in which, for better or for worse, one more diasporic fate awaited it? Why not steer it to Palestine, where it might become, as Ben-Yehuda had insisted it must, a Hebrew-speaking majority in control of its own destiny?

More even than was the case with Mapu, everything Smolenskin wrote had pointed to Zionism all along. Ben-Yehuda understood this before Smolenskin did. But because Smolenskin's conversion to Zionism came so early in its development, though so late in his own brief life, one can only guess what sort of Zionist he would have been. The Zionist goal of a Jewish return to the soil left him skeptical. "Just because our ancestors were farmers three thousand years ago," he asked in "A Time To Plant," "does that mean we have to be farmers today?" The Jews were an entrepreneurial people, not the agrarian one they had been in antiquity. There was no turning back the clock on what they had become.

He was unlikely to have been attracted, either, to any of the versions of Zionism, soon to appear, that envisioned a perfected Jewish society in Palestine as a justification of the national effort that Zionism entailed. He was too aware of the recalcitrance of life and the contrarian nature of human impulses to be tempted by utopian thinking. Nor would he have been, like Herzl, in favor of concentrating in a Jewish state all the Jews who wished to live there while writing off the rest. Diaspora life, admired by him for its diversity, did not strike him as a misfortune or pathology that called for its elimination.

In the end, Smolenskin's novels, with their rough-and-tumble human arena that is the site of innumerable contending wills, some far-seeing and some blind, some mutually reconcilable and some not, are the best guide to how he might have envisioned a Jewish state. A tolerator of difference whose pluralism was less an ideology than an intuitive sense of the incalculable complexity of things, he had a conservative's belief that life cannot be planned or engineered and must be left to work itself out – that it *will* work itself out, left to do so or not, in its own unpredictable ways. At the heart of much of what he wrote is the conflict between legitimate self-interest and a necessary concern for others that all societies, like all individuals, must learn to navigate. Both Yosef and Yakov-Hayim are made to realize from a young age that whoever does not aggressively stand up for himself goes down to defeat, and Smolenskin, with his disdain for the universalist liberalism of the Jew who is ashamed to put Jewish needs first, thought the same of national interests: the Jews had to look out for themselves because nobody else would do it for them. It is harder, however, for Smolenskin's characters to understand that they are not the only ones who must be accommodated and that a refusal to compromise can be a sign of weakness rather than of strength. Negotiating the space between these two poles was to be Zionism's perennial dilemma.

Chapter Four

The Poet's Toil of Yehuda Leib Gordon

1

On March 10, 1883, according to the Julian calendar in use in Tsarist Russia, the St. Petersburg Hebrew semi-weekly *Ha-Melitz* published a special Purim literary supplement. In it was a poem, "My Sister Ruhama," by the newspaper's editor Yehuda Leib Gordon.

The title of Gordon's poem would have been recognized by his readers as an allusion to the book of Hosea, in which the prophet is commanded to wed a sexually dissolute woman as a symbol of God's relationship with an idolatrous Israel. His new wife, he is told, will bear him a daughter whom he is to name Lo Ruhama, "The Unpitied One," because of the retribution God will wreak, and a son to be called Lo Ami, "Not My People." Yet all will end well: Lo Ruhama and Lo Ami will persuade their mother to repent and Israel's marriage to God will be renewed. "Then," concludes Hosea's prophecy, "you will call your brother Ami ["My People"] and your sister Ruhama [The Pitied One]."

Gordon's poem had a biblical subtitle, too: "In honor of the daughter of Jacob, abused by the son of Hamor." Puzzling at first glance, this dedication to Jacob's daughter Dina – raped by Shechem ben Hamor,

87

the book of Genesis relates, when she "went out to see the daughters of the land" – would quickly have been understood by the poem's readers to be a concession to the Russian censor, a pretext for overlooking the poem's real subject, which was the pogroms that had swept southern Russia in 1881–82. The fifty-three-year-old Gordon had been a staunch believer in the successful entry of Jews into Russian life; its slow pace had been blamed by him more on Jewish social insularity and religious obscurantism than on Russian anti-Semitism, which an increasingly liberal Russian ruling class and intelligentsia, he held, had renounced. Now, however, he wrote:

> Why weep you, my sister Ruhama?
> Why is your heart sore and your spirit not calm,
> And why has the rose of your cheeks grown wan?
> Have despoilers sullied your honor?
> If hard is the fist of the foe who has harmed you,
> Fault not yourself, my sister Ruhama.

> "But the disgrace!" Where is the disgrace?
> Your heart never faltered nor failed to keep faith.
> Come, look away from your injured place,
> For the stain is not yours! It belongs to the stainer.
> The pure are not fouled by their profaner.
> You are blameless, my sister Ruhama.

> As Abel's blood marked the brow of Cain,
> So yours forever will be a sign,
> Seen by all and never dimmer
> On the brows of your base assassins.
> Let the world know to its far horizons
> Of your torments, my sister Ruhama.

> Yea, I am glad of them. My soul has withstood
> Every trial and travail that a soul could.
> I have worked for this land; my hopes have been here
> Despite each vile act and violent drama.

Now, though, the insult is too much to bear.
Let us go, my sister Ruhama!

Come, let us go – not to the warm
And natively loving home of the mother
We no longer have, but to yet another
Lodge for the night. There we will wander
Until our Father has mercy. Yea, yonder
Shall we wait, my sister Ruhama.

Let us go where liberty's beacon
Shines its bright light on each single being
Born in God's image and no creed or color
Has an ill name! There no enemies clamor
And there you shall know neither stigma nor shame.
Let us go, my sister Ruhama!

Had a subscriber to *Ha-Melitz* fallen asleep at the end of the 1870s and suddenly awoken, he would not have known what to be surprised by more: the poet who had repeatedly criticized Russian Jews for their lack of openness to Russian society reassuring them that they were blameless for its hostility; his urging them to abandon the country he had adamantly insisted they could live happily in; or his telling them to do so not for Palestine, "the natively loving home of the mother we no longer have," but for America, the land of "liberty's beacon." Even readers who had kept abreast of Gordon, had read his pro-emigration poem "With Our Young and Our Old, Let Us Go," written within months of the pogroms' first outbreak, and had followed his *Ha-Melitz* editorials regularly enough to know of his changed attitude toward Russia and skepticism regarding the prospects for Jewish colonization in Palestine, would have been taken aback by his unqualified endorsement of the United States as the sole desirable destination for Jewish emigrants. Although "My Sister Ruhama" referred to America as a "lodge for the night," a temporary asylum such as other countries had been in the past for a people still awaiting the day of its ultimate redemption, that day was clearly considered far off.

Of course, "My Sister Ruhama" was not, in 1883, proclaiming anything that Russian Jews were not already saying with steamship tickets. Jewish emigration from the Tsarist empire to the United States, which soared in the immediate aftermath of the pogroms, more than doubled again in the next few years, reaching nearly 20,000 annually by 1884. In the same four-year period, no more than a few thousand Jews left Russia for Ottoman-governed Palestine. Such figures spoke louder than any Hebrew poem could do.

They did not, though, tell the whole story. Among the many Jews contemplating emigration, if only as a future possibility, interest in Palestine was great. Following the pogroms, numerous Love of Zion societies had sprung up throughout Russia for the purpose of encouraging agricultural settlement in the Land of Israel. What kept the numbers of actual settlers low was a combination of economic and political factors. While tilling the soil of an ancestral homeland may have been a romantic ideal, few Jews wanted, as Smolenskin had predicted, to be farmers, let alone possessed the necessary skills; arable land in Palestine was expensive; and reports from the new colonies of physical hardship, malaria, crop failure, and hunger were discouraging. Moreover, in the spring of 1882, alarmed by the prospect of a large influx of Russian Jews to Palestine, the Turkish government had issued an edict barring their entry; though never strictly enforced and eventually rescinded, this served as a deterrent to potential Jewish colonists throughout the 1880s. And if five Palestinian Lovers of Zion colonies, populated by several hundred families, had nevertheless been established by March 1883, so had Jewish farming communities in Louisiana, South Dakota, and Oregon, sponsored by an Odessa-based organization. One could live on the land in America, too.

Yet even as emigration to Palestine languished, Zionism was hotly debated in the Hebrew press of Eastern Europe. Temporary setbacks, its advocates argued, were to be expected; what mattered was fighting the intellectual war on Zionism's behalf, so that when conditions for its implementation ripened, Jews would be prepared to take advantage of them. "The idea [of Zionism]...has gotten off to a bad start for acknowledged reasons," wrote the publicist Yehuda Leib Levin in the pro-Zionist Hebrew weekly *Ha-Maggid* two weeks after *Ha-Melitz's*

Purim supplement. "Since it is an incontrovertibly just one, however, we mustn't be daunted by short-term obstacles....[or by] those of us who, in the face of the confusion and reversals inflicted on [Zionism] by non-intrinsic causes, have basely rushed to decry its essential beauty." Levin was not thinking only of Gordon when he wrote these words. They were directed at other intellectuals within the Jewish nationalist camp, too, such as the future historian Simon Dubnov, who had published articles calling Zionism unrealistic. Still, for any supporter of the movement, "My Sister Ruhama" could only have been taken as a particularly cruel stab in the back.

Zionism had lost the short-lived momentum given it by the pogroms. Fresh adherent of it though he was, Smolenskin, writing in the July 1883 issue of *Ha-Shahar*, observed that the chance to capitalize quickly on Russian Jewry's initial enthusiasm for settlement in Palestine "is now gone forever." Funds raised to support emigration by organizations like the French-based Alliance Israélite Universelle and the American-run Hebrew Immigrant Aid Society were being used to direct Russian Jews westward rather than eastward. "The word is now out," Smolenskin lamented, "that Jews have their hearts set only on America and no longer want to hear about Palestine." And in the same issue of *Ha-Shahar*, which had published many of Gordon's poems in the past, he printed a riposte to "My Sister Ruhama" in the form of a parody.

The author of this spoof, Yisachar Ber Hurvitz, a businessman and part-time poet, was both a Lover of Zion and an Orthodox Jew. Substituting *ne'eshama*, "the Guilty One," for Ruhama, he attacked Gordon not only for turning his back on Palestine but for his lifelong support of Haskalah ideals. Russia's Jews, Hurvitz proclaimed, *were* in part to blame for the pogroms. Under the Haskalah's influence, they had taken to aping the ways of their Russian neighbors with doubly deleterious results. On the one hand, they had antagonized Russians by pretending to be no different from them when every Russian knew this wasn't so. On the other hand, they had, by losing confidence in their own traditions, lost their natural resilience in the face of disaster. Playing on Gordon's dedication to "My Sister Ruhama," the first of Hurvitz's seventeen stanzas went:

> Why complain, my sister Ne'eshama?
> Why is your heart pained and your mood grown glum?
> Were you, far from home, abused while you slummed?
> Has Jacob's sole daughter been robbed of her honor
> By a brute's cruel hand laid upon her?
> The fault is yours, too, my sister Ne'eshama!

Line 3 of this stanza was a special taunt, because Hurvitz's word for "home," *ohel*, literally "tent," was the same word used by Gordon twenty years previously in his verse declaration that became a Haskalah rallying cry, "Be a Jew at home [*b'ohalekha*] and a citizen abroad." The Jews, Hurvitz was saying, had followed Gordon's advice and gotten their due comeuppance. The poem's fifth stanza drove this point home:

> You went to stroll among the country's belles
> And hoped to be one of its demoiselles;
> You called their holy days your own and quite forgot
> Your father, your religion, and your God.
> Their acceptance, so you thought, would be your armor.
> How wrong you were, my sister Ne'eshama!

The final stanza of "My Sister Ne'eshama" was aimed at the view that Zionism was unfeasible because the world powers would never countenance it. On the contrary, Hurvitz's poem argued: they would be only too glad to sponsor a Jewish exodus from their countries. The Jews themselves had only to want it:

> Look back, come home to your inheritance
> Bequeathed to your progenitors by Providence!
> The monarchs of the nations will support you
> And wholeheartedly transport you
> From your exile to the land of God's old promise.
> Then will your name be – my sister Ruhama's!

Gordon did not reply to "My Sister Ne'eshama," though it was he who, in a gentlemanly gesture, had sent Hurvitz's parody to Smolenskin after turning it down for *Ha-Melitz*. When Hurvitz wrote him in May 1883 to ask if he knew whether Smolenskin intended to print the poem, Gordon replied in a dig at Smolenskin's taste: "Of course he will, because it's better than most of the poems that appear in *Ha-Shahar.*" And in a swipe at the likelihood of Zionism's fulfillment, he added in a paraphrase of Maimonides's formulation of the Messianic credo: "After all, you're a good Jew and will get used to waiting for it all your days, even though it lingers."

2

The Hebrew press in 1883 had an influence far beyond the paid circulation of its four leading publications: *Ha-Melitz*, with some 2,000 subscribers; the weekly Warsaw *Ha-Tsefira* with 2,500; *Ha-Maggid*, published in Germany, with 1,800; and *Ha-Shahar*, which averaged close to a thousand. Actual readership was far greater, as subscriptions were often shared by several persons, who lent their copies to still others when they were done with them, and numerous towns in Eastern and Central Europe had Jewish public libraries in which Hebrew periodicals were available and in demand. An educated guess might be that these had, in the early 1880s, well over 100,000 readers in Russia alone – far more than did the two Russian-language Jewish publications of the times, the weekly *Razsviet* and monthly *Voskhod*, and the one Yiddish weekly, the *Yiddishes Folksblat*.

For Eastern Europe's Jews, the great majority of whom who could not read Russian, Polish, Lithuanian, or other languages spoken in the Tsarist empire, the Hebrew press was their main window on the world. Besides serving as a platform for the Jewish debates of the day and publishing feuilletons, poetry, fiction in installments, and articles on various subjects, it also ran numerous news items. The March 10 *Ha-Melitz* in which "My Sister Ruhama" appeared included, in addition to a long editorial by Gordon, an article on turtles as house pets and sources of food; a letter from Constantinople defending colonists in Palestine from accusations of anti-religious behavior; an item on anti-Semitic agitation in Poland and a Catholic priest who was bravely combating it; a report on a new rabbinical school in Budapest; and political dispatches from Austria, Romania, Paris, Ireland, and Turkey. There were also stories of Jewish interest from all over Russia. Near Vitebsk, a beheaded Jew was found on a road beside a wagon and its murdered coachman. In Plotsk, a Jew presumed dead had regained consciousness while members of the Burial Society argued with his family over their pay. In Verzhbolove, a returned Jewish emigrant who had abandoned a wife in Glasgow was exposed by her unexpected arrival in pursuit of him as he was bigamously about to remarry. (This last item, similar to the ending of Smolenskin's "The Humbug's Happiness," was a classic case of life imitating art.)

Gordon's Purim editorial played on the name Haman and the Hebrew verb *hama*, "to be noisy," in order to observe – somewhat at variance with how he had stood up for them in "My Sister Ruhama" – that the Jews were a loud and know-it-all people who made enemies with their brashness. They talked too much and did too little. For example: an entire year had gone by since the Odessan Dr. Pinsker had published his excellent treatise "Autoemancipation," in which he counseled Jews to look for a country they could make their own – yet even though, Gordon wrote, "the Holy Land, it seems, is barred to us forever," had anyone acted on Pinsker's advice and looked elsewhere? All Russian Jewry had done was argue about it.

Gordon published occasionally in the Russian Jewish press, too. Yet only in Hebrew, he prided himself, did he allow himself to be critical of Russia's Jews, whom he consistently defended when writing in Russian – and indeed, in an age of great inner division and uncertainty, Hebrew provided Jews with a protected private space of their own. Their secrets were safe in it. In Hebrew, they could argue, shout, call each other names and wash their dirty linen without fear of being overheard. Not even Yiddish, which not a few Russians had some knowledge of, was as hermetic. When Yiddish speakers in the shtetl, the village or small town in which most of Eastern Europe's Jews still lived in the late nineteenth century, had something to say to each other in public that they wished to be sure no Gentile understood, they mixed as much Hebrew into their Yiddish as possible.

As the vernacular of the shtetl, Yiddish in the 1880s was still taking its first strides toward becoming a vehicle for serious literary and intellectual life. For Gordon, as for other Maskilim, it remained a symbol of Jewish backwardness, the language of a mental ghetto whose walls were waiting to be torn down. Moreover, it was a language that half the world's Jews, the millions of them living in central, western, and southern Europe, North Africa, and the Middle East, did not speak. Throughout Jewish history, Hebrew had been the sole means of communication (and sometimes the oral lingua franca) between Jews who spoke different languages. In the late nineteenth century, when French (which few East-European Jews knew anyway) had lost the international status that English had yet to gain, Hebrew alone held the Jewish world together.

It was also, linguistically, all that linked Jews to their past. Yiddish was a relative newcomer to Jewish history, a language with less than a thousand years behind it and almost no written monuments to speak of. Hebrew had an immense literature, starting with the Bible and representing millennia of Jewish history, creativity, and thought. Being able to pun on Haman and *hama*, to make a recognizable allusion to Hosea, or to tease an opponent with the help of Maimonides were minor debating advantages, but they proclaimed a familiarity with a literary terrain that only an intensive Jewish schooling could provide. For a people that had lost its land in antiquity and was now faced with losing – or so the nineteenth century appeared to be heralding – the religious faith that had sustained it ever since, Hebrew stood to remain, as Mapu and Smolenskin had argued, the only territory it still possessed. Yet it was as vast a territory in its way as any country's and as capable of arousing patriotic emotions.

It has been said that Hebrew was the *patria*, the linguistic fatherland, of East-European Jewry, the language of a religious education and practice that were male domains, and that Yiddish was the motherland, the language of home and hearth. There is some truth in this. Although Yiddish was also the language of the Jewish street, used by men and women alike for all aspects of everyday life, only men, with rare exceptions, knew some Hebrew, and only advanced students knew it well. Yet just as the Torah was sometimes imagined by Jewish tradition in feminine terms as an alluring object of masculine scrutiny and longing, so Hebrew could be, too. Mapu had his "Lady of Hebrew," and he was not alone in his age in depicting the Hebrew language as a loving and beloved maternal presence – not a cozily domestic one but a regal queen who continued to command her subjects' allegiance after they had cast off the kingly authority of religion.

Such a personification of Hebrew can be found in Gordon as well, especially in an elegiac masque published by him in 1853 on the first anniversary of the death of his friend Micha Yosef Lebensohn. Lebensohn was a rising star in the world of Hebrew poetry when his life was cut short by tuberculosis at the age of twenty-four, and in this dramatic threnody Gordon pictured him ascending heavenward to a Madonna-like figure addressed as "Goddess" by the archangel Michael. Wiping away her tears of mourning, she says to the risen poet:

> Do you not know me, my dear boy?
> Do you not know me?
> I am your mother, the Hebrew tongue.
> All your life, you delighted in my lap.
> I was your aspiration and your passion,
> And invisible to you, I nursed you
> With the milk of consolation.
> The mother of your brothers I am, too,
> And of all the exiles of Zion and Jerusalem.
> Whene'er the foe's hard hand caused you to groan,
> Or life's burdens were too much for you,
> You turned to me and I gave you strength.

These lines testify to the filial love of Hebrew felt by readers and writers of Gordon's generation. From infancy, it had put them to sleep with the words of the *Sh'ma*, the "Hear O Israel" prayer they were taught to whisper in bed, and woken them in the morning with the *Modeh ani*, the thank-you for having slept safely through the night. "Mother of all that is holy!" Hebrew was called by the dying Lebensohn at the same time that he was writing in a letter to Shneur Sachs: "I'm under no illusion that I would go to the stake for my people or for God.... I have no religion! My brothers [are] all mankind!" And Gordon's bereaved goddess exclaims to the prophets and poets of Jewish tradition: "O great fathers of the Hebrews who were a mouth to me in ancient times, rise and weep together with me!" Ordinarily, one thinks of a language serving its users. Here, it is the other way around: Hebrew speaks through the greatest of her speakers. They are her ranking attendants, her knights and chevaliers.

East-European Zionism evolved from a pre-Zionist Jewish nationalism. But this nationalism, in turn, grew out of a pre-nationalist loyalism
to Hebrew. As was true of other national movements in nineteenth-
century Europe, such as the Gaelic revival in Ireland and the Czech
renaissance in Bohemia and Moravia, the initial banner raised was that
of language. Ultimately, it led Gordon to Jewish nationalism, too. Why,
then, did he not, like Smolenskin, continue from there to Zionism?

3

He was born in 1830 in Vilna, a city renowned for its rabbinic learning
that had been a stronghold of Misnagdic resistance to Hasidism. But
Vilna was also, starting with the 1840s, a center of Haskalah activity with
a progressive, state-run rabbinical seminary and several modern Jewish schools. Living there in Gordon's youth were figures like Sachs; the
writer Avraham Ber Lebensohn, Micha Yosef Lebensohn's father; the
Hebrew memoirist Mordekhai Ginzburg; and the author and translator
Kalman Shulman, best known for his pioneer renditions into Hebrew
of European novels. Yet while he met and befriended such older men
as he grew up, the greatest influence on Gordon as a budding poet was
the young Lebensohn, cloaked by his early death in the tragic aura of a
Hebrew Novalis or Keats.

Lebensohn had great but largely unfulfilled talent. Nineteenth-
century Hebrew poetry's first and perhaps only true romantic, he was
shackled by the classical diction of a language that he had more mas-
tery of than freedom from. Had Hebrew had a spoken form, he might
have been more able to find his own voice in it; as it was, he did so only
fitfully in some of his short lyric poems and longer historical ballads.
The latter, mostly on biblical themes, were a favorite genre of his, and
Gordon's first major poetic effort, an epic in twelve cantos called "The
Love of David and Michal," was an attempt to emulate and outdo them.

Completed in 1857, "The Love of David and Michal" tells the
story of the flowering and decline of the relationship, described in the
Bible with extreme brevity, of the Israelite shepherd boy who became a
poet-king and his first wife, King Saul's daughter. Beginning with their
youthful romance and marriage, the poem ends decades later with a
lonely, life-weary, and sex-sated David and a noble Michal who still

loves him though long since discarded and forgotten by him. Its sympathy for women, and for their unequal position in love no less than in worldly affairs, was to reappear in Gordon's later poetry, too; he himself, however, the future poet-king of nineteenth-century Hebrew literature, was no David in his private life. Married in his early twenties to a wife described by his biographer Michael Stanislawski as a "kind, if simple" person who "barely knew Russian, understood no Hebrew, and remained cut off from and slightly befuddled by the literary, intellectual, and political interests of her husband," he had two daughters and a son with her and never seems to have sought other female companionship.

At its best, "The Love of David and Michal" holds the reader's attention only intermittently. Suffering from the same shopworn phrasing that had held Lebensohn back, the poem moves a step sideways for every stride forward, pausing to moralize about its plot each time it advances it. David, for example, summoned for the first time to Saul's court, is introduced by the lines:

> And so David the shepherd, Bethlehem's son,
> A redheaded lad with a staff in his hand
> And a pack on his back, proceeded anon
> To the king's palace, for so had God planned.
>
> God's wisdom! It towers on high!
> It is deep as the seas that girdle earth's sphere.
> Yet many an eye is unable to spy
> What many an ear is unable to hear.

But while agonizingly slow-paced and without Lebensohn's emotional urgency, "The Love of David and Michal" had something that Lebensohn lacked – namely, wit and a capacity for trenchant, cleverly phrased social and psychological judgments. When it proved a commercial failure, Gordon turned to a new project that might exploit these gifts better, a series of versified animal fables that he hoped would be used as a textbook for teaching Hebrew. Borrowing freely from Ivan Krylov, La Fontaine, and Aesop, the book was published as *Mishlei Yehuda*, "The Fables of Judah," in 1859. Although the only school to adopt it was a Karaite institution in Crimea, and Gordon complained that he spent more money mailing copies of it to friends than he received in royalties, the form suited him well. Played off satirically against its animal characters, its classical language is amusing. A typical tale about a donkey and a horse goes:

> Beware, my friends! Assist your fellow man
> Before he's made to bear more than he can
> And you end up by carrying his load.
>
> Cudgeled by its master cruelly,
> A donkey staggered down a road
> Beneath some heavy bags of grain
> When a noble steed came prancing by,
> Burdened only by its bit and rein.

Asked by the donkey to relieve him of part of the weight, the steed haughtily replies "Are horses to be asses? / Are grandees like the masses?" and disdains to help. Whereupon,

> The party hadn't reached the nearest town
> When the donkey stumbled, fell, lay down,
> Gave up the ghost, and died.
> And so its load was transferred to the steed,
> Which now also had to bear an ass's hide.

The social message was clear: if wealthier Jews refused to help the Jewish poor, they would be saddled with a collapse of their communities that would cost them far more. The virtues upheld by Gordon's fables – thrift, hard work, honesty, responsibility, a willingness to help others – were those of the genre in general. They were also the values of the bourgeois family life that, his hopes of earning a living from his writing dashed, he now attempted to lead as a schoolmaster in the Lithuanian provinces. The schools he administered and in part founded – one of them, unusually for the times, for girls – were in the spirit of the Haskalah. Their hours were shorter than those of the traditional heder and they taught, besides Jewish subjects, European languages, literature, mathematics, and history. A radical departure from accepted Jewish pedagogy, they embroiled Gordon in a series of running controversies with local rabbis and religious conservatives that gradually turned him into one of the most radically anti-religious of Haskalah writers. He was one of the few Maskilim to regard German Reform Judaism as a model for Eastern Europe, whose rabbinical establishment he considered benighted and corrupt.

Yet the times were a cause for optimism. Not only was the Haskalah gaining ground in Jewish society but Russia itself, with the ascent to the throne of Alexander II in 1855, had entered a period of economic and social reform, most dramatically manifested by the emancipation of the serfs in 1861, that heralded a new age. In the running battle between the country's Westernizing liberals and its advocates of Russian autarky and Tsarist autocracy, a final victory for the former appeared to be in sight. One of Alexander's first edicts was the abolition of Jewish juvenile conscription, which was followed in 1856 by an imperial order calling for the revision of all anti-Jewish legislation in favor of a policy of "fusing" Russia's Jews with its general population. In the next several years, the Tsarist regime relaxed residential restrictions limiting Jews to the Pale of Settlement, the southwestern corner of Russia to which they had been confined, cut back on its encouragement of missionary activity, and took steps to strengthen the government-supported Jewish educational system of which Gordon's schools were a part.

The Haskalah's faith in integration had seemingly been vindicated. In 1863, Gordon published a poem trumpeting the new day:

> Wake my people! Sleep no more!
> Night is over. The sun shines.
> Open wide your eyes, explore
> New surroundings and new times!
>
> Has time stood still with drooping wings
> Since, shorn of freedom, your exiles
> Began their worldwide wanderings
> And two thousand years of trials?

Attitudes toward Jews had changed. Russian writers and intellectuals like Turgenev and Chernyshevsky were speaking out against anti-Semitism. Now was the turn of Russian Jewry to reciprocate:

This country of your domicile and birth
Belongs to Europe, whose expanse,
Though a small part of the globe's girth,
In spirit is the most advanced.

Its paradise can now be yours.
Its sons and daughters call you "Brother."
Why go on being sojourners
Who insist on being other?

Their yoke upon your neck has eased
Its heavy burden. They extend –
Their ancient hatred of you ceased –
Their hand in greeting like a friend.

Raise your head high! Stand tall!
Look around with approbation.
Educate yourself! Learn all!
Speak the language of the nation!

Your students to the university!
Your workmen to their crafts and trades!
The bravest of your sons to the army!
Your farmers to their plows and spades!

Make a contribution of your own!
Be a brother to your countrymen;
A servant of the king and crown;
A Jew at home – abroad a citizen.

Heyei adam b'tsetkha v'yehudi b'ohalekha: "Be a *man* abroad and a Jew at home" is how Gordon's Hebrew has generally – and technically speaking, correctly – been translated. But Gordon did not intend to suggest a dichotomy between Jewishness and humanness. What he had in mind was the difference between the Russian Jew who felt the same sense of belonging and civic responsibility to his country felt by the non-Jew and the Russian Jew who did not. It is ironic that a well-turned phrase from a propagandistic, tritely worded poem should have become his single most famous line. Yet Gordon was a propagandist for the Haskalah even when more than trite. Dominating the Russian literary culture of his day were critics like Chernyshevsky and Dobrolyubov who held that art had value only if socially useful, and this was a view that he, too, shared with his Maskilic readers. His cleverness, verbal agility, and skill at handling rhyme and meter were inseparable in their minds from his criticisms of the rabbis, of the moneyed Jews who colluded with them, and of the ordinary shtetl dweller who went on leading a semi-medieval life as if it were his foreordained lot. Now was the time to cast all that aside.

4

Gordon went on writing fables, of which he eventually put out a second book, throughout the 1860s. This was a decade in which it became clear that the incorporation of Russian Jewry into Russian life would be at best slower and more difficult than was envisioned in Alexander's first years. Many individual Jews, particularly in urban centers, had responded enthusiastically to the call to Russianize. But in the small towns and villages of the Pale of Settlement, Jews went on clinging to their isolation, speaking and often understanding only Yiddish, practicing all the stringencies of their religion, looking and dressing differently from their non-Jewish neighbors, and having little or nothing to do with them. A government "Committee for the Amelioration of the Condition of the Jews," appointed in 1870 to determine why shtetl Jewry was continuing to form "a secluded religious and civil caste…a state within a state," reported back a year later that the "communal cohesion" of Jewish society ruled out further progress. The government, losing confidence in its earlier measures, backtracked. Some of Alexander's reforms were modified; others were never implemented. The walls of the Pale rose higher again.

Gordon reacted by accusing Russia's Jews of failing to rise to the challenge of Russification. He also reverted to the form of the verse narrative while trimming it and focusing it more sharply. On two such poems, "In the Lion's Teeth" and "The Tip of a Yud," much of his reputation ultimately came to rest. The first, written in the early 1860s, had a historical setting: the great Jewish revolt against Rome and its disastrous defeat, attributed by Gordon to a religious culture whose mixture of blind faith and talmudic scholasticism precluded rational thought and action. Who but the Jews, the poem asked, would have taken up arms against the world's greatest military power on the sole basis of messianic prophecies and a belief in the superiority of their endlessly cogitated divine laws?

> Your ruin, Israel, was never being taught
> How wars were waged and battles fought.
> What good was all your strength and desperation
> Without a strategy or organization?
> What did you learn from your instructors in
> The study house in every century?
> To store the chaff – to bottle wind –
> To plow the rock – to sieve the sea.

The protagonists of "In the Lion's Teeth" are the rebel leader Shimon bar Giora and his wife Martha, who are taken captive, separated, and brought to Rome, she to be sold into slavery, he to do battle as a gladiator. Waiting his turn in the arena of the Coliseum, Bar Giora catches sight of Martha sitting with the Roman matron she now serves and exchanges a last, loving glance with her. A lion is released and bounds toward him. He,

> ....springing forward with the cry
> "Where is the God of Samson?" strove to pry
> The beast apart and tear it limb from limb.

Alas, he is able to do no such thing. And the poet addresses him caustically:

> Doomed gallant! You could look long and hard
> And not find a single sign of Him.
> The God of Gods, your God and Samson's God,
> Has lost interest in His people and its heroes
> And joined forces with the Tituses and Neros.
> You'll have the luck with Him your people had!

Bar Giora, standing no more chance against the lion than did the revolt he led against the might of Rome, is quickly clawed to death. Although the God they call upon is either non-existent or indifferent to their fate, the Jews keep putting their trust in Him instead of relying on their own resources. In reverting to the time of the earliest rabbis to make such a point, Gordon was attacking not this or that perceived excess or distortion of rabbinic Judaism in later ages, as the Haskalah generally limited itself to doing, but rabbinic Judaism itself. If "In the Lion's Teeth" did not arouse a public furor among his Maskilic readers, this was only because he took pains to veil its radical statement with a plot set in antiquity.

He almost never again phrased his anti-religious views quite so extremely. But the smooth weave of pathos and biting commentary that he achieved in "In the Lion's Teeth" while managing to keep its story briskly progressing as he had not done in "The Love of David and Michal" was now to become his trademark. Nowhere was it better displayed than in "The Tip of a Yud," published in Smolenskin's *Ha-Shahar* in 1875. By then Gordon had moved to St. Petersburg, having accepted a dual post there as secretary of both the city's well-to-do Jewish community and its Society for the Promotion of Enlightenment Among the Jews of Russia, an organization dedicated to Jewish acculturation.

The printed letter Yud, the smallest in the Hebrew alphabet, has a tiny upward extension without which it cannot be considered to be formed correctly, so that *kotso shel yod*, "the tip of a Yud," is a Hebrew expression for a trivial detail that becomes a bone of contention. In Gordon's poem, however, the Yud is a real one – the optional second letter of the Hebrew name Hillel, which can be spelled either with it, used as an auxiliary vowel sign, or without it. The Hillel of the poem is the husband of the beautiful and sterling-souled Bat-Shua. Wed to her in a loveless arranged match while both were in their teens, he has gone abroad in search of a living and disappeared without a trace, leaving her unable to remarry according to Jewish law unless he is found and persuaded to divorce her. (Such *agunot* or "chained women" were not rare in a society in which, as in Smolenskin's "The Humbug's Happiness," men often absconded from unhappy marriages that had not been of their choosing.) Bat-Shua is forced to open a small provisions store in which she labors drearily day and night to support herself and her children, and Gordon began his poem with a proto-feminist invocation of her plight:

> O Jewish woman! The story of your life, who knows?
>   You come in darkness and in darkness you depart.
> Your joy and sadness, your wishes and your woes,
>   are born and die with you in your own heart.
> The goodness of this land, its plenitude,
>   are for the daughters of another folk.
> A Jewish woman's life is servitude;
>   the little shop she tends is her grim yoke.
> Thus she proceeds to bear, to nurse, to wean, again to breed,
>   to cook, to bake, and quickly go to seed

Bat-Shua's fortunes improve when a decent, sensitive man, a railroad contractor named Fabi who has come to work in her town, falls in love with her and she with him. Things look even brighter when the missing Hillel is located in Liverpool and sends Bat-Shua a writ of divorce shortly before perishing in a shipwrecked ocean liner bound for America. At last, she and Fabi can be happily wed. Yet Hillel's name, it turns out, has been written in the document without a Yud. When a rabbinical court of three judges, presided over by the town's rabbi, Vofsi, convenes to consider the matter,

> The judge who read the writ aloud, a Kabbalist,
>   found esoteric reasons to approve of it.
> The second judge, a learned Talmudist,
>   proved by logic that the writ was fit.
> But Vofsi, citing the Shulhan Arukh,

insisted that Hillel must have a vowel,
And on the say-so of that august book,
    he faced the other judges with a scowl.
Like a tree that can't be moved by any force,
    he cried sternly, "There is no divorce!"

Vofsi is appealed to. He refuses to budge. The Shulhan Arukh, the definitive code of Jewish law, demands that a writ of divorce be written correctly, and since he is convinced that it isn't and the court can only confirm the divorce by a unanimous decision, Bat-Shua can never remarry, there being no surviving witnesses to her husband's death. And so the heartbroken Fabi finishes his work in town and departs, and Bat-Shua, crushed, resumes her former life, from which there is now no hope of release. The letter of the law has triumphed over common sense and human happiness.

There were readers of "The Tip of a Yud" who, while conceding its literary merits, complained that its portrayal of the Orthodox world of Eastern Europe was an unfair caricature. As strict as some rabbis might be, they argued, few were as heartless as Vofsi, and had the situation been a real one, Bat-Shua and Fabi could easily have found another, more lenient authority to grant the divorce. Gordon, for his part, while conceding the point, quite rightly pointed out that satire works by exaggeration and that the thrust of "The Tip of a Yud" was in any case a limited one – a call for religious reform, not revolution.

On the whole, it was the reformer's rather than the revolutionary's mantle that Gordon preferred to wear. However he may have questioned its theological or practical premises, Judaism remained inseparable for him from Jewish identity and needed, he thought, to be ameliorated, not abandoned. This was what enabled him to remain popular with readers who, though exasperated by Orthodoxy's rigidity, did not wish to burn their bridges to tradition. They appreciated Gordon's caution no less than his combativeness; together, they placed him in the middle of the same road that they, too, were struggling to travel on. He was now widely known as Yalag, the initials of Yehuda Leib Gordon, an accolade in a world of Hebrew letters that reserved such acronymic titles for its famed figures. By the end of the 1870s he was being called by critics "the Jewish national poet," the living embodiment of the Haskalah's finest ideals.

5

In late October 1881, half a year after the outbreak of that year's pogroms, the cream of St. Petersburg's Jewish society, relates Michael Stanislawki, gathered at a festive banquet in Gordon's honor. It was the twenty-fifth anniversary of the publication of "The Love of David and Michal," and besides being toasted, lauded, and presented with a gold pen, Gordon was publicly informed of the community's decision to raise subscriptions for a four-volume collection of his verse. He was gratified. "You have honored me," he wrote to his readers in *Ha-Melitz*, of which he had become editor the previous year, "as no Hebrew author has been honored before." Yet two years later he was to write wryly of the event:

> When all of my friends and my well-wishers saw
> That my soul was depleted and I had no more
> In my pantry or purse, they consulted and then
> In their kindness they gave me – a golden pen.

The empty pantry and purse were metaphorical: he was at the time receiving a handsome salary from *Ha-Melitz*'s wealthy publisher Alexander Zederbaum and was at the height of his literary power and prestige. But he was also tired. Still traumatized by several nightmarish months in 1879 in which he and his wife had been arrested and exiled from St. Petersburg by the Tsarist police in what proved to be a case of mistaken identity, he was deeply shaken by the pogroms and pessimistic about the future of Hebrew. The same wry poem spoke not of one pen but two: that given him at the banquet and that he wrote with. The former would be bequeathed to his heirs when he died, the latter to….but what use, the poem ended with a sigh, would anyone have for a Hebrew-writing pen?

His concern for Hebrew was not new. As far back as 1871 he had published a poem whose title of "For Whom Do I Toil?" came to be another of his signature phrases:

Even as my muse sings shyly
Lines of poetry penned by me
In a language almost now forgotten,
I ask: for whom do I toil?
What was the purpose of it all?
Has my whole life been misbegotten?

Did I labor for our parents,
With their God and his commandments
And their hatred of all science and all art?
"Poetry is heresy!
Literature is deviltry!"
They pilloried those like me from the start.

Was it for my fellow intellectual?
He thinks Hebrew ineffectual,
An old maid spinning last year's yarn.
"Really, now, it's so passé!
No one uses it today.
Let Europe's languages be ours from now on!"

Might you, my Jewish sisters,
Hearken to my muse's whispers
With a taste and grace that are God-given?
Alas, you lack all Hebrew schooling,
For (such is our rabbis' ruling)
"The girl who studies Torah studies sin."

And our children, that progressive generation?
Taught naught but alienation,
They pierce my wounded heart most to the core.
Yes, they progress from year to year.
Who knows how far? Who knows to where?
Perhaps to where there's no returning any more.

For whom then do I toil?
For the few who don't recoil
From the song of Zion's goodly bounty?
Scant pickings! If I counted
To how many they amounted,
Would I find one in every town, two in each county?

And yet you are my brothers, wherever
You may be! Our fathers' tongue,
Our pitied sister, you refuse to scorn.
Let others wander where they would;
You alone have understood
The thoughts to which my verse has given form.

For you I've sacrificed my years
And the libation of my tears.
I send you a thousand kisses and embraces.
Ah, who can foreknow it?
Am I Hebrew's last poet,
And you the last of all its readers in our places?

On the face of it, "For Whom Do I Toil?" was overstated and self-pitying. Gordon's depiction of Hebrew letters as condemned by an older generation, ignored by a younger one, and having no female readers was far from the reality in an age which Mapu's novels were popular, young new writers like Smolenskin and Lilienblum were avidly read, and the Hebrew press was growing and developing. Nor did the poem's plaint have any basis in Gordon's personal life. Far from "pillorying him" for writing Hebrew poetry, his father, a traditionally pious Jew, had been supportive of his efforts, and he did not lack the company of fellow Hebrew-reading-and-writing intellectuals. One of them, Zev Kaplan, his best friend since adolescence, was the father-in-law of his daughter Minna, with whom Gordon's relations were warm and close, as they were with his other two children. And while it was true that few girls in the 1860s and '70s received a Hebrew education, Gordon himself had taught many of those who did and had corresponded in Hebrew with more than one woman. His fears of being "Hebrew's last poet" were hardly justified.

But he saw the writing on the wall. Hebrew would not be for the next generation, let alone for those that came after it, what it was for his own. And the bitter irony was that this was due to the Russification he had fought so hard for! Granted, in the shtetls of the Pale of Settlement the Russian language and its culture had yet to make serious inroads. But social and cultural trends started in the cities and spread outward – and once Gordon moved to St. Petersburg, he could see even more clearly what the trend was, not least of all in his own family. In a heartfelt letter written to Kaplan in 1879, he began by recalling their Vilna youth in which they and their friends had actually tried speaking Hebrew to one another. No one had been more able to make it come alive than Kaplan. "I was a sixteen-year-old in my father's home when I first met you," Gordon wrote. "You were like a flag on a mountaintop that made me look upward and think: 'If only I could speak Hebrew like he can!'"

Kaplan, who knew Gordon was feeling despondent, had written to assure him that he would always be a "bright star in the future histories" of Hebrew literature. Gordon's reply went on to say:

> Ah, trusting soul to think that Hebrew has a future and not just a past – a past that will be followed by nothing! What makes you believe that the names of its authors will shine like stars instead of smoldering like swamp lights? Can't you see that only "trouble, darkness, and dim anguish" [the phrase is from Isaiah] cloud the sky above our poor language and its followers, who will vanish from beneath it? Who will write your histories? Your son? My son? Perhaps our grandson Iakob and his progeny? Can't you see where we are heading and what will happen to us in the end of days? The Sadducees will study Greek wisdom and the Pharisees will expound the laws of the bathroom: these are the two camps into which we Children of Israel will be divided.

Decoding the last sentence calls for knowing that "Greek wisdom" was a rabbinic term for the arts and sciences; "Sadducees," Gordon's way of alluding to the Jewish Russianizers; and "Pharisees," to the militantly

Orthodox and their rabbis, mocked by him for their obsessive regulation of life's smallest details. In time to come, he was saying to Kaplan, there would be only assimilated Jews with no Jewish knowledge on the one hand and parochially religious Jews on the other with no interest in anything but their faith, neither having the slightest use for Hebrew as a literary medium. The Haskalah Jew – modern yet attached to tradition; at home both in the world and in the ways of his people; acquainted with the languages of Europe but committed to his own ancestral tongue – was a transitional phenomenon. Just look at Gordon and Kaplan's own children! Minna and her husband Maxim, a successful St. Petersburg lawyer, might still remember a bit of the Hebrew they had been taught when young and attend synagogue services once or twice a year, but they lived entirely in Russian and Russian culture. What hope was there that *their* child, little Iakob, whom Gordon was extremely fond of, would have even that much Jewishness, let alone Hebrew? What hope was there that *his* children would have any at all?

The Haskalah had failed to understand that its success would spell its downfall. "We thought," Gordon wrote in *Ha-Melitz* in March 1882,

> that we could heal our fractured people with the balm of the Haskalah and its educational reforms. For a generation – one single generation – our people ate of the tree of knowledge and digested its fruit … Alas, our celebration was short-lived.

The Haskalah was compared by Gordon to a bigamous marriage. Whereas its husband had thought he was taking European culture as a second wife alongside his Jewish one, his children now regarded her as their sole mother. Although Hebrew might not yet be the "almost forgotten" language that "For Whom Do I Toil?" called it, it soon would be.

6

Hebrew-writing intellectuals like Smolenskin and Lilienblum had warned all along that the Haskalah was a self-destructing enterprise salvageable only by a nationalism that would reinforce the sense of Jewish identity undermined by Europeanization. Now, Gordon had come to agree with them. Why then, to return to our opening question, did he write "My Sister Ruhama" instead of turning to Zionism as they had done? And why, especially, did he write it when the dream of reviving Hebrew as a spoken language in Palestine, first put forth by Ben-Yehuda and now endorsed by others, seemed the only way to save it from oblivion?

It was a question that he asked of himself – and that in 1887, five years before his death, he answered in a letter to Lilienblum, with whom he had become reconciled after years of estrangement. The rift between them had had two causes. One was Lilienblum's anger at Gordon's failure to be supportive of Zionism in his poetry and *Ha-Melitz* editorials. The other was Gordon's resentment of a critical review Lilienblum had written of the four volumes of his verse when they appeared in 1884. Now that all that was behind them, Gordon wrote:

> I wasn't angry at you for thinking my poems had their shortcomings, many of which I could have pointed out myself, but for failing to understand me, accusing me of being who I wasn't, and vilifying me in front of the Jewish people as the traitor and hater of Zion that I never was. If I didn't write editorials and poems about the dream of settling the Land of Israel, this wasn't because I was against it but because I didn't believe it was possible. Having no faith in it, I wasn't inspired by it – how then could I have written poetry about it? And yet I wanted it even more than you did, wanted a complete redemption, not a small-time rescue mission. And because I wanted it all, there was nothing for me to take hold of.

What Gordon meant by a "complete redemption" rather than a "small-time rescue mission" had been explained by him in March 1883, in one of the *Ha-Melitz* editorials that Lilienblum took umbrage at. Published on the eve of Passover under the heading "Our Redemption and Our Spiritual Emancipation," it began with a review of the bitter year of pogroms that had gone by and stated:

> If we all agree on one thing, it is that we have no choice but to leave the vale of tears that is this country. The only argument is over which direction to choose and whether to end this year's Seder with "Next year in Jerusalem!" or "Next year in America!"

America, Gordon said, was the easier alternative. "Whoever heads for it arrives in a developed country, one thriving in the bloom of its youth...which isn't the case with Palestine." True, from a Jewish point of view, "there can be no doubt that the ascent [*aliya*] to the Land of Israel takes precedence over the descent to America – but only on the clearly understood condition that this *aliya* be considered not just one more option for displaced and downtrodden Jews in search of a better life, for whom America really is the better choice, but a national duty." If Jews were emigrating from Russia solely to save their necks and improve their material condition, "why be dreamers and fantasize about memories of an ancient homeland?" The only justification for choosing Palestine was the "unambiguous determination to stake our [national] claim there and live the life of a people...like all the families of man."

Up to this point, Gordon's editorial was all any Zionist could desire. Now, however, it took a sharp turn. Since he was writing in Hebrew, Gordon told his readers, "with no strangers around to eavesdrop," he could be honest with them. "We [East-European Jews] live in a swamp of superstition and mindlessness...Tolerance for other faiths and those who practice them is low among us; religious fanaticism and obstinacy prevail." The "physical fortress" in which Diaspora Jewry lived in Eastern Europe was accompanied by a "mental fortress" that was even more difficult to break out of.

His greatest fear, Gordon continued, was that if East-European Jews were to move en masse to a Turkish-ruled Palestine that would not expose them to the forces of progress they would be subject to in the West, they would simply reduplicate their degraded condition. "Before the Jews are redeemed from their geographical exile, they must be emancipated from the spiritual exile in which they are now bound hand and foot," he wrote. Settling the Land of Israel, though a "sacred goal," was "premature." At the present juncture, "we would do better to send our emigrants to America or some other enlightened country." Only when, after "two or three generations," these emigrants had become "a civilized, cultured, hard-working, professionally skilled population," should they be encouraged to settle in large numbers in Palestine. "Let our sojourn in America or elsewhere," the editorial concluded, "be what the desert was for the Israelites who left Egypt to receive the commandments of life, cast off the chains of slavery, and learn to be free men before entering the Land of Israel."

This editorial, in effect a gloss on the last two stanzas of "My Sister Ruhama," which had appeared that same month, was replied to by Lilienblum in *Ha-Melitz's* next issue. Gordon, Lilienblum wrote there, was conflating two separate issues. The need for a fundamental change in Jewish life was one thing, the need for a Jewish homeland in Palestine was another – and the second could not wait for the first to be addressed. Moreover, no amount of generations in America would produce the liberal, progressive Jewish consensus that Gordon believed it would. The notion of "complete redemption" was a chimera. "We have never been a unified people," wrote Lilienblum, "and we never will be; nor will you find such unity anywhere on earth." There wasn't an independent nation in Europe without its conservative and clerical parties alongside its liberal and progressive ones. The difference was that these contending forces were both required and enabled by a shared political system to find ways of resolving their conflicts, whereas the Jews, lacking such a framework, were not. Gordon was putting the cart before the horse. Rather than emancipate themselves psychologically and culturally before creating a Jewish society in Palestine, Jews had to create such a society in order to emancipate themselves. Genuine emancipation was unachievable in the Diaspora. "A [national] political life," Lilienblum declared, "is the answer to everything!"

For a while, in early 1888, Gordon thought he was borne out by events. A dispute had broken out in Palestine between its colonists and rabbis over the question of *shemita*, the biblical injunction to let the land lie fallow every seven years. The Jewish year 5649, due to begin in the autumn of 1888, was such a septennial, the first since the new colonies were founded, and a cessation of agricultural activity during it, the colonists argued, would be financially ruinous. Halakhically, there were ways of circumventing the law, such as nominally selling or leasing the land in the *shemita* year to non-Jews, as was traditionally done with forbidden food on Passover. Palestine's rabbis, however, like Vofsi in "The Tip of the Yud," refused to approve such a solution and were threatening to impose a ban on the colonies' produce. Gordon was incensed. "Didn't I tell you," he wrote Lilienblum, "that without spiritual emancipation – emancipation from these despots – there can be no redemption in the Land of Israel?"

7

In the end, the rabbis reversed themselves and a crisis was averted. But Gordon's problem with Judaism ran deeper than that. The reformer who repeatedly protested that he only wished to see Judaism rationalized and modernized was far from sure this could be done. His doubts about the Jews' ability to create a viable society in Palestine went beyond his animadversion toward the rabbis – beyond even his one-time criticism, in "In the Lion's Teeth," of the basic values and institutions of rabbinic Judaism. He had written one other poem that went even further – a poem of which Lilienblum, without bothering to explain himself, had said in his review, "better it were it had never been published." Called "Zedekiah in the Dungeon," it was composed in 1879 during Gordon's period of imprisonment and banishment from St. Petersburg, by which its setting was inspired.

Zedekiah, according to the book of Kings, was the last Judean king after the Babylonian conquest of Jerusalem in 586 BCE. A Babylonian puppet installed by the conqueror Nebuchadnezzar after two of his brothers were deposed, he eventually, in defiance of the counsel of the prophet Jeremiah, led a swiftly crushed rebellion that resulted in the Temple's destruction. Captured and forced to see his sons slaughtered before his eyes, he was then blinded and sent to live out his life as a prisoner in Babylonia. Supplementing the account in Kings are several verses in Chronicles that tell us: "Zedekiah was one-and-twenty years old when he began to reign and he reigned eleven years in Jerusalem. And he....would not yield to Jeremiah the prophet speaking from the mouth of the Lord."

Chronicles is referring to Zedekiah's refusal to call off the rebellion as Jeremiah demanded. Gordon's poem, however, introduces a second theme. As the Babylonian army, the book of Jeremiah tells us, was nearing Jerusalem to quell the uprising, the prophet, zealous for the observance of the Sabbath, stood in the gates of Jerusalem and proclaimed: "Take heed and bear no burden on the Sabbath day, nor bring it in the gates of Jerusalem ... And if you will not hearken to me to hallow the Sabbath day and not to bear a burden ....then will I kindle a fire in the gates thereof, and it shall devour the places of Jerusalem and it shall not be quenched." Gordon's poem, framed as a mental soliloquy in which the blind king recalls the rebellion's final days, connects the two texts:

> "Because you would not yield to Jeremiah!"
> What did that priest of Anatot [Jeremiah's birthplace] desire?
> "Carry no burden on the Sabbath day!"
> Was that a time for anyone to bray
> About the Sabbath, with the enemy all around,
> Our outlying towns razed to the ground,
> The foes' ramparts reaching to our capital,
> The kingdom tottering – and all
> He could speak of at the city gate,
> Where the people came to congregate,
> Was burdens on the Sabbath? There were folk
> Who even said, making of it a joke,
> "And what about the burden of God's word?"
> And yet I weighed it carefully. I conferred
> With Zepheniah and Seraiah;
> Neither fathomed Jeremiah.
> How could a city that would "stand forever"
> (For so he said) be saved by never
> Carrying one day a week?

Militarily, a day each week in which it is impossible to prepare for an impending siege is a serious handicap, so that Jeremiah is sabotaging the war effort. But Jeremiah does not care about the war effort. He cares only about the spiritual transformation that he has prophesied for "the house of Israel and the house of Judah" in which, God tells him, "I will put my law in their inward parts....and they shall all know me, from the least of them unto the greatest of them." In his prison cell, Zedekiah recalls bitterly:

> Not only that, he now began to speak
> Of a new covenant: all Judah,
> Young and old, would study Torah –
> From prince to peasant, all would be

Scribes and devotés of prophecy.
The plowman would put aside his plow;
The soldier would no longer practice how
To wield his spear and javelin;
The potter's wheel would cease to spin;
The smith would leave his forge, the shopkeeper his wares,
To wear haircloth and be soothsayers;
The carpenter's drills would be beaten into quills,
His chisels into priestly codicils.

If Jeremiah had his way, religious duty would be all that mattered. Even before the war was lost, civil society would cease to
function. Moreover, Zedekiah reflects, this sublime indifference to a
people's needs is not just Jeremiah's. It is endemic to the prophetic
calling. The conflict between the ruler who must govern a kingdom
of men and the prophet concerned only with the Kingdom of God
is never-ending. It already existed at the time of Israel's first king,
Saul, and first prophet, Samuel, who initially crowned Saul and then
disavowed him for ignoring a divine command that Saul thought it
impolitic to obey:

Since our nation first began to be,
The Law's upholders and the monarchy
Have been at war. Always the visionaries
Have sought to make the kings their tributaries,
As did, going back five hundred years,
The earliest of all our seers,
The son of Elkanah [Samuel]....
So every prophet in his hour
Has fought to get the king under his power.
What Samuel did to Saul is what
I met with from the man of Anatot,
And what awaits each ruler of our nation
Until the final generation.
I see how on that distant day
The son of Hilkiah [Jeremiah] will have his way.

> His dispensation will prevail;
> All governance will founder and then fail;
> Our people, erudite in chapter and in verse,
> Will go from woe to woe and bad to worse.
> I see … alas, I see!

Israel's prophets are not in Gordon's poem visionary figures whose grand theophanies were reduced by the rabbis to the tip of a Yud. They are – and in this, Gordon and rabbinic Judaism concurred – the rabbis' forerunners. The two stand for the same life-denying purism and are expressions of the same dysfunctional religious values infected by an uncompromising insistence on moral and/or ritual standards of perfection that defeat all attempts to come to terms with the real world.

In the entire history of Hebrew literature, no critique of Judaism had ever been more sweeping or more damning. It went to Judaism's most ancient roots – and when the roots are judged to be sickly, what hope can there be for the tree? Written long after "In the Lion's Teeth," "Zedekiah in the Dungeon" is its historical prelude. The Jewish people, it declares, could no more rule itself in the time of the Bible than it could rule itself in the time of the Roman Empire. It would be unable to rule itself, Gordon thought, in modern Palestine, too. Of what use to it would a "national political life" be when it cleaved to a religion so certain of its divine truths that it held them to be above the practical considerations of politics? "Woe is us," Gordon wrote in another *Ha-Melitz* editorial, if in a Jewish country, "every fanatic and wild-eyed zealot will be able to wreak havoc by blowing the ram's horns of excommunication and furiously turning on whoever's ideas and behavior do not accord with his own."

As Zionism groped its way toward the politics that Lilienblum believed it needed to adopt, Gordon grew more apprehensive that it *would* succeed than that it would not. A Jewish return to Palestine, he feared, would simply set one more national debacle in motion. One can understand why Lilienblum, who began his review of Gordon's collected poems with praise for their "style, wit, and formal structure," all qualities "Zedekiah in the Dungeon" excelled in, thought it should never have seen the light of day.

8

Gordon died of cancer in 1892. His last years were plagued by illness and discouragement. In 1888, he left *Ha-Melitz* after the last of many quarrels with Zederbaum over his editorial independence. Offers to back him as the head of a new Hebrew newspaper were spurned. "Isn't it enough for you," he asked the maker of one such proposal, "that I have warred for and over my people for forty years and come away from the battlefield bloodied and scarred? Must I now don armor once more and rejoin the fray?" To earn a living in an age in which there were no pensions, he took a job as editor of the Jewish section of a Russian encyclopedia. Although he cooperated in a new edition of his poetry and prose compiled by the young Odessan scholar Yehoshua Ravnitzky, he had given up writing. "You ask if I still dally with the muses," he wrote in 1891 to Nachman Syrkin, a future theoretician of socialist Zionism. "It has been three years since I laid down my Hebrew pen without picking it up again…What visions remain for us bards when every good thought we once had about our people now seems a distant memory?"

Distant, too, was the memory of a woman named Chana whom he had not seen since before his marriage. He had written a poem to her then lauding her youthful beauty. She need never fear growing old, he had assured her in it, because

> Cheeks' roses wilt
> And flesh decays;
> Teeth fall, eyes dim,
> Come winter days;
> But your spirit will, untouched,
> Flower till you lie in dust.

Yet in 1882, encountering her once more by chance, he wrote a second poem called "Chana (Thirty Years Later)" that began:

> Again I saw you, fair one of my youth,
> And fell as far as from the furthest star.
> Could this be you? Were these the looks
> I yearned and prayed for from afar?

Chana's cheeks are wrinkled. Her eyes are the color of "faded flax." She is toothless. The sight of her leaves the poet emotionally numb:

> Why, gazing on the ruins of your face,
> Old kisses frozen on my lips,
> Do I feel as would a block of ice,
> Unshaken by your memory's sacredness?

But he *is* shaken – shaken by the realization that, approaching old age himself, he has taken false comfort in the belief that it is possible to "age well."

> Chana! I thought you never had to fear
> The passage of the years or Time's sharp bite,
> Because, however bent your back,
> Your inner beauty still would cast its light.

No such beauty shines through Chana's decrepitude. One can only age badly, because

> The Father of Creation, who does dwell
> In the bright house of Venus, has ordained
> That youth and vigor suit the high-borne soul,
> And healthy bodies host the healthy mind.

Playing on astrology to conjoin the God of Genesis with the Greek goddess of love, the Hebrew poem ends on a Hellenic note. *Mens sana in corpore sano*! (Gordon actually provided the Latin maxim in a footnote.) The divine, un-Judaically, resides in the beautiful and all outward decay has its inward counterpart.

Another reflection on growing old was "The Root of My Soul." In the guise of addressing God, the poem looked back on the poet's life:

> Lord, this soul I have been given –
> Whence was it riven?

If new and introduced
Into me unused,
How came it to be so rife
With wounds in its brief life?
From the day that it was led
Into this world, it bled.
With each sensation, every thought,
New hurt was wrought.
Not one ideal for which I strived
Has survived:
Hopes blasted, love betrayed,
Faith destroyed;
All honesty, all human decency –
Spume upon the sea.
And when I look at my own people,
My spirits sink still deeper.
You have for seventy generations
Indulged its aberrations
Until all is rack and ruin
Without and within.
No one knows what must be done;
Solutions there are none.
There is only aggravation
At belonging to this nation.

The Jewish situation seemed to him hopeless. Gordon had, in 1886, while still at the helm of *Ha-Melitz*, run an editorial in praise of the Jewish farming colonies in Palestine and their resolve. Yet half a year before his death, writing to Ravnitzky, who had criticized as anti-Zionist a poem of his that contained the biblical phrase *mezareh yisra'el yekabtsenu*, "He that scattered Israel will gather it in," Gordon returned to the theme of "Our Redemption and Our Spiritual Emancipation" by punning on the verb *l'kabets*, "to gather in," and the noun *kabtsan*, "beggar":

You, apparently, consider a handful of colonists living like Bedouin in the hills of Palestine to be the complete redemption of our entire nation, whereas I see in them an ingathering of beggary and believe in something greater, the time of whose arrival is unknown.

Indeed, Zionism in the late 1880s had little more to show for its efforts in Palestine than this acid summation of them. It had enthusiasm, but no organization; a dim goal, but no strategy for reaching it; a following, but no effective leadership. Things had not progressed greatly beyond the state described by Gordon in an 1883 poem that he had dedicated to Pinsker and his newly published "Autoemancipation:"

Who are we? What are we?
All ask the same question:
A people or just a religious confession?
Speaking confidentially
(For I wouldn't want to be overheard),
We're neither. All we are is a herd.

There was no plan. It was every small group of Lovers of Zion for itself. In an editorial about the Love of Zion movement in *Ha-Melitz*'s year-end issue of 1885, Gordon began by recapitulating how, after the 1881 pogroms,

our people took to its heels in all directions to the globe's far ends, to America, and to Australia, and to South Africa ... at which point the Lovers of Zion societies convinced a handful of the Jews on the run to choose the soil of Judea.

Nothing substantial had come of this. And yet, Gordon asked, returning to the biblical story of Saul, who went in search of his father's donkeys and ended by being crowned king by Samuel,

suppose that what happened to Saul happens to us and sends us a prophet who crowns us with a redeeming project .... The difference between our past of false messiahs and our own times, and between the means employed by them and those employable today, is enormous. The false messiahs deceived our people with mystical promises and kabbalistic calculations that were never more than castles in the air, whereas a would-be contemporary benefactor must rely on natural processes that evolve as circumstances and possibilities permit, according to the principle of "God helps those who help themselves."

A prophet with a redeeming project! He might have been thinking of Herzl.

Chapter Five

Ahad Ha'am Writes a Book Review

1

It was to prove the most contentious Jewish book review of the century, although the century was but three years old when it appeared. Published in December 1902 in the prestigious Hebrew monthly *Ha-Shiloah*, Ahad Ha'am's long, cutting attack on Theodor Herzl's Zionist-utopian novel "Altneuland" touched off a furor that did not die down until the following summer, when an even fiercer controversy broke out at the Sixth Zionist Congress.

Ahad Ha'am, "One of the People" – the pen name of *Ha-Shiloah*'s founder and first editor Asher Ginzberg – had emerged in the 1890s as a foremost Hebrew essayist and Zionist thinker. Born in the Ukraine in 1856 and a resident of Odessa since the mid-1880s, he was at once a highly private and public figure, a naturally aloof man whose intellectual distinction and sense of Jewish mission propelled him to a prominence that he both basked in and was uncomfortable with. Not by chance was the only formal group he ever belonged to – he was the force behind its creation – a shadowy society, called B'nei Moshe or "the Sons of Moses," which sought like a secret lodge to work behind the scenes for the betterment of East-European Jewry. Short-lived and ineffective, it expressed his preference for being a discreet mover of events rather than an active participant in them. Just "one of the people," whether chosen ironically or not, was clearly not what he thought he was.

His Zionism was elitist, too. In an early essay written in 1889, "This Is Not the Way," he had argued against the idea of Palestine as a destination for the Jewish masses. The Love of Zion movement, he maintained, had erred by calling for speedy, large-scale settlement in the Land of Israel. Hoping to compete with America for the swelling wave of Jewish emigrants from Eastern Europe, it had made unrealistic promises of profitable homesteads in new agricultural colonies, lucrative business opportunities, thriving Jewish villages in which to raise a family, and so on, that could only lead to disillusionment and re-emigration. Zionism, the essay maintained, echoing Gordon's "Our Redemption and Spiritual Emancipation," could not succeed by appealing to the lowest common denominators of human motivation. Only by invoking an idealism dedicated to national revival rather than personal benefit could it attract settlers capable of withstanding the difficulties of Palestinian life. Their numbers might be small, but they would be a solid base that could be built on.

In 1891 and 1893, Ahad Ha'am made a pair of fact-finding trips to Palestine and published a two-part report on them entitled "The Truth from the Land of Israel." Devoted to the decade-old Jewish colonization enterprise, it confirmed the worst predictions of "This Is Not the Way." Wherever he looked, Ahad Ha'am wrote, he had found mismanagement, wasted opportunity, stagnation, and demoralization. The country was poor and without resources. Its tiny community of Zionist immigrants had ceased to grow. The Jewish agricultural colonies were surviving as wards of the Zionist philanthropist Edmond de Rothschild. Economically, they were failures, their one-crop policy of grape growing misguided, their farmers subsisting on subsidies and the exploitation of cheap Arab labor, their French overseers autocratic and incompetent – and with all that, Jewish land purchases had led to rampant real estate speculation that kept pushing up prices. The Turkish government, ill-disposed toward Zionism, was corrupt and barely functional; exorbitant taxes and cumbersome bureaucratic regulations made commercial ventures impractical. Jewish schools taught their children either in European languages that did nothing to foster Jewish culture, or in a Hebrew so crude that "the young pupil can only chafe in the artificial chains of the speech imposed on him." Without a thorough overhaul of its structure, no significant expansion of the Yishuv, the Zionist community of Palestine, was thinkable or even desirable.

"The Truth from the Land of Israel" was a harsh critique. It did not, however, cause Ahad Ha'am to consider himself less of a Zionist. Pessimism, he declared in several essays published in the first half of the 1890s, was justified only if one thought quantitatively. In sheer numbers, Palestine could never vie with America or have the economic capacity to absorb more than a small percentage of the world's millions of Jews. To the extent that the problem of these millions was anti-Semitism and the poverty to which they were condemned by it, Palestine could be of no help to them. They would have to cope in the Diaspora, where most of them would go on living.

Yet if the "problem of the Jews" could not be alleviated by Zionism, the "problem of Jewishness" was something else. This had to do not with anti-Semitism but with assimilation, which was most severe in Western Europe, where anti-Semitic strictures against Jews no longer existed. In an increasingly secular age, as Haskalah writers had noted, Jewish religious tradition was losing its hold. With nothing to replace it, Jews were being stripped of their cultural and national uniqueness. In the absence of a counter-force, this process would only accelerate, devastating the Jewish people from within.

And this was where Palestine could matter. Suppose, wrote Ahad Ha'am in an 1892 essay dedicated to the memory of Leon Pinsker, an association of high-minded Jews were to take responsibility for the reorganization of Palestinian Jewry. Suppose it were to reform Jewish agriculture, weaning it from its dependence on philanthropy, viticulture (itself a semi-philanthropic enterprise based on the export of inferior Palestinian wines to Jewish markets), and Arab labor, and turn its villagers into hard-working husbandmen. Suppose it were to rebuild Jewish education, bringing the best pedagogues and Hebrew teachers to raise a new generation of knowledgeable, fluently Hebrew-speaking youth. Suppose it were to found a Hebrew press and publishing industry to

meet this generation's intellectual and cultural needs. And suppose word
were to spread in the Diaspora that there were

> Hebrew farmers, real farmers, who plowed, sowed, and reaped
> with their own hands and came home at night from their fields
> to read and study....would it not be natural for many prominent
> Jews to come to the Land of Israel to see this wonder? And surely,
> when they came and saw it and the association's other achieve-
> ments, they would feel a deep love for their ancestral land and
> their brothers living in it, whose wholesome life has raised esteem
> for Jews throughout the world, [so that] many of them would
> soon become Lovers of Zion themselves and visit the Land of
> Israel with their families each time they went abroad on vacation.

One is reminded of Josef Perl's imagined Jewish peasants in the
Crimea, now also become a Jewish tourist attraction. Nor was that all:

> Moreover, suppose the Jewish youth educated in the associa-
> tion's schools traveled to the world's leading countries (for the
> association will send them to the best universities for advanced
> study) – and behold another wonder: educated young Jews who
> are not Germans, French, or anything but sons and daughters
> of the Land of Israel communicating with one another in the
> Hebrew language of yore!... Seeing the honor accorded it, the
> language of Scripture, by their Christian friends, Jews, too, will
> recognize that their ancient tongue has come gloriously back to
> life. Many will become aware of its grace and beauty and long to
> learn it themselves. And when they do, they will have teachers
> from Palestine, whom they will prefer to instructors from their
> own countries, just as one would always rather be taught by a
> native speaker.

In a word, Palestinian Jews could create a model Jewish society
whose influence would radiate to the Diaspora, giving it a sense of pride
and purpose. Obviously, this would not happen overnight. The association would not act impetuously or in the expectation of quick results. It

would guide events slowly and without attempted shortcuts, building
the Yishuv immigrant by immigrant and colony by colony until

> after several generations, it will have achieved its goal: the creation
> in the Land of Israel of a national spiritual center for Jewishness
> that is loved by the entire Jewish people and binds it together – a
> center of knowledge, of Torah study, of the Hebrew language and
> its literature, of the purest of bodies and souls – a true miniature
> of the Jewish people as it should be.

The resemblance between Ahad Ha'am's high-minded association and the B'nei Moshe, still active when he wrote these words, is
evident; most likely he conceived of the B'nei Moshe as the association's founding nucleus. Paradoxically, the elitism of his vision, with its
Palestine whose superior Jewish life would provide an inspiration but
not a physical home for most of the world's Jews, had a broad psychological appeal. It addressed an oppressive concern that "The Truth from
the Land of Israel" had helped aggravate; for if Zionist colonization in
Palestine was proceeding at a snail's pace at the same time that Jewish
emigration to America was growing by leaps and bounds, what could
be the point of it? And how, moreover, could one call oneself a Lover
of Zion if deterred from living in Zion by its difficulty?

Here was a comforting answer. One could be a good Zionist and
remain in Europe or emigrate to America. Palestine did not require large
amounts of settlers. Indeed, more than could be productively absorbed
would only be harmful. To the Land of Israel would come "first Jewishness and then Jews." This would not be the "complete redemption" for
less than which Gordon had refused to settle, but neither would it be
the "just one more option for Jews in search of a better life" that Gordon had dismissed as of no value. Zionism needed to be patient. And
if Ahad Ha'am's readers complained, "But the way is too long and the
realization of the hope is too distant," his reply to them was:

> Yes, my brothers. The shore we yearn for is exceedingly far-off.
> But a people that has wandered for thousands of years will not
> find even the longest road too long.

2

Though it had its critics like Moshe Leib Lilienblum, who considered it defeatist, Ahad Ha'am's brand of Zionism had, by the mid-1890s, gained wide acceptance in Eastern Europe. His trips to Palestine gave it credibility. Others merely argued about the country. *He* had been there. He had traveled widely, investigated, collected opinions and statistics, talked to the experts. He had a first-hand knowledge on which he brought to bear a sober realism and a long-range perspective that made him the leading Zionist spokesman of the age.

And then, in 1896, came Theodor Herzl and his book "The Jewish State."

The book was actually written in 1895, the year of the first Dreyfus trial, which Herzl, a well-known journalist and playwright, covered as the Paris correspondent of the mass-circulation Vienna *Neue Freie Presse;* its German publication, which he went ahead with despite the pleas of acquaintances who read it in manuscript and thought it deranged, took place early the following year. By any intellectual standard of the times, it *was* deranged: a slim volume, hardly more than a brochure, that consisted of two parts – a shorter one explaining why, faced with worsening anti-Semitism that would inevitably spread to the rest of the world, the Jews of Europe needed a country of their own, and a longer one detailing how a mass exodus to such a land could be carried out swiftly. It was this second part that must have struck those given a preview of it as particularly bizarre. Whereas a call for a Jewish state coming from a Jewish journalist with no known previous interest in the subject could be written off as a mere eccentricity, a step-by-step plan for achieving such a goal by means of international diplomatic agreements, well-capitalized stock companies, vast land purchases, coordinated networks of emigrant-bearing trains and steamships, and modern cities rising from the wilderness in record time to house the new arrivals could hardly be deemed the product of a rational mind.

It was Herzl's good luck, the same acquaintances must have thought, that "The Jewish State" went largely unnoticed when published. This was so not only in Germany and Austria, where the very idea of Zionism was still a curiosity, but also in Jewish Eastern Europe, where Zionism was now an everyday subject of discussion. Although it has been said that Herzl's book rocketed him to instant fame among East-European Jews, this was hardly the case. A cursory review of the Hebrew press suggests that little interest was taken in him until the weeks preceding the Zionist congress that he organized for the late summer of 1897. Even when his existence was acknowledged, as when an article of his translated from an Austrian weekly appeared in the Warsaw *Ha-Tsefira*, it was with no inkling of the role he was about to play. Introducing this article, *Ha-Tsefira*'s editor Nachum Sokolov described its author, for the benefit of readers who had never heard of him, as a figure "well-known in the literary world of Vienna" whose ideas, though "their practicality can be challenged," deserved a hearing.

Indeed, even as curiosity mounted with the approach of the congress's opening session on August 28, East-European Zionists, most of them disciples of Ahad Ha'am, remained skeptical. The advance notices struck them as pretentious. Herzl himself, it was felt, was an upstart, a Jew with no real knowledge of Judaism and a latecomer to a movement that had been promoting colonization in Palestine for years. His abrupt conversion to it demonstrated the difference between the Yiddish-speaking and Hebrew-reading Jews of Europe's East, with their deep rootedness in their people's culture and traditions, and the deracinated Jews of the West, who needed the shock of anti-Semitism to remind them of who they were. Irritating too was his belittlement of the Lovers of Zion colonies as a needless provocation of the Turks, from whom he hoped to buy or lease all Palestine by paying off, with the help of Jewish financiers, Turkey's large international debt – and more aggravating yet, his suggestion that, should this prove impossible, the Jews might establish a state in Argentina, where the Bavarian-born banker and railroad magnate Baron Maurice de Hirsch had been trying to settle them since the early 1890s. Nor did Herzl believe that the language of such a Jewish state should be Hebrew, in which there was no way, as he put it, of even asking for a railroad ticket.

To Ahad Ha'am's followers, Herzl's scheme seemed like a parody, a wild exaggeration of the fantasy-ridden Zionism of instant fulfillment that Ahad Ha'am had decried. They, the "Easterners," had no need of it. "To listen to [Herzl's] advocates," said an editorial in the August 8 *Ha-Melitz*, "one would think that a genius had suddenly discovered that the Jewish people was still alive without knowing it and needed to be informed that it was....and that there was such a place as the Land of Israel in which it could be reborn." So great was the ridicule that, writing in the same newspaper, the future literary historian Yosef Klausner, himself an "Easterner," felt called upon to rebuke it. "We can," he wrote,

> oppose Herzl's approach and are obliged to, as every Lover of Zion who attends the Basel congress is free to do if he thinks it will harm the steady growth of Jewish settlement in Palestine.... It may be that Herzl's political-diplomatic Zionism is dangerous, and that the Jewish people must be warned of this. But to laugh? One doesn't dismiss ideas [like Herzl's] with witticisms.

And yet when the congress actually convened in Basel, Herzl, with all the theatricality he had learned from the Viennese stage, brought it off with grand flair. From the huge blue-and-white bunting draped over the entrance of the casino rented for the occasion to the tails and white ties that the delegates were instructed to wear, all was calculated to impress with its festivity. "The opening of the congress was most magnificent," wrote the Hebrew author Re'uven Asher Braudes in *Ha-Maggid*. One-hundred-ninety-two delegates, he reported, attended from a large number of countries, plus numerous representatives of the Jewish and European press and literary dignitaries like Ahad Ha'am. Herzl's opening speech was "a fine one." Following it came a keynote address on the condition of world Jewry by the celebrated German Jewish author Max Nordau, "every word of which," Braudes wrote, "struck home like an arrow." Never before had there been such an international assembly of the Jewish people. In his final dispatch, though insisting that "we [East-European Zionists] know far better than the congress's organizers what Jewishness is," Braudes confessed:

> The congress was like a wonderful dream, a fabulous, divine spectacle....It was an extraordinary event, not because it arrived at any great decisions, witnessed any great debates, or produced any great insights, but in and of itself....It is enough for our people to

know that it now has something to hope for, that it still has the will to live, that it has taken its future into its own hands.

Herzl's speech was indeed a masterpiece of careful phrasing in which he made an effort to placate the East-European delegates, of whose views he was by now well-aware, without retreating from his own positions. In a rhetorical gesture to both the Ahad Ha'amists and the congress's religiously Orthodox attendees, he declared that Zionism must be "a return to Jewishness even before there is a return to the Jewish land," and he paid tribute to the Lovers of Zion colonies as deserving the "sincere gratitude" of the Jewish people for being "the first but not the last word of Zionism" – the success of which depended on the massive settlement that would follow recognition of the Jewish right to Palestine by Turkey and the world. The Easterners were won over by Herzl's charisma. ("He is tall and handsome," wrote Re'uven Brainin in *Ha-Melitz*, "the Hebrew type at its purest, with a rare charm, an Oriental grace, and two dark eyes, burning like coals, that lend majesty to his mild and pleasant mien.") They were swept away, too, by the congress's atmosphere of Jewish solidarity. "Every one of us [who was at the congress]," Brainin related, "feels that it lasted more than three days. It was as if we had known each other for ages. If we were to measure our lives by thoughts and feelings, we lived in Basel for years."

Everyone, that is, but Ahad Ha'am. He had felt in Basel, he wrote after returning to Odessa, "like a mourner at a wedding." True, he admitted, the call for a "national answer to the Jewish question" had been sounded loudly and clearly. Herzl, whom he met with briefly, was personally impressive. Had the congress convened for a single, symbolic day and dispersed, all hearts "brimming with the sacredness of the moment," there would be no cause for complaint. Alas, however, the moment had been wasted. Two more days were spent wrangling in committees about how Zionism's program should be formulated, about how the world should be asked to recognize it, about the Jewish bank that would underwrite it, and so on, as if these were imminent realities rather than the pipedreams they would surely prove to be. And even if they were more than dreams – even if Herzl's Jewish state were to come into being – what purpose could it serve without the Jewish content that Herzl had no interest in? What stood to be gained from the existence of one more small country that would be tossed back and forth between stronger neighbors like a ball, surviving by "the guiles of diplomacy" and groveling before the powers of the day? "There is no way," Ahad Ha'am wrote, "in which an ancient people that has been a light unto the nations can, in recompense for all its tribulations, make do with such a bare minimum."

3

There was undoubtedly an element of injured pride and even vanity in all this. Prior to Basel, Ahad Ha'am had been *the* voice of Zionism. Now, he was suddenly in the shadow of a man who was not only his opposite in many respects but had no appreciation of who he was.

It rankled. Although there were to be more Zionist congresses, one annually during Herzl's lifetime, Ahad Ha'am did not attend any of them. His followers who did formed an informal opposition to Herzl, one of whose organizers was the young Chaim Weizmann, that called itself "the Democratic Faction." Herzl paid it scant attention. He was frantically engaged in these years in the "guiles of diplomacy" that Ahad Ha'am had mocked: traveling repeatedly to Constantinople to tempt the Sultan with promises of money that he did not have at his disposal; vainly cajoling wealthy Jews to make it available; pulling every string to get an audience with the German Kaiser that, when finally granted him, led nowhere; and entering into negotiations with the British for a Jewish protectorate in the Sinai peninsula. "The great task," he had written soon after the First Congress, "is to set people in motion." His great fear was that what he had set in motion would stutter and stall. A poker player with the weakest hand at the table, he could only hope to win by bluffing. Ahad Ha'am, who never considered Herzl anything but an illusionist and referred to him as "the Zionist leader" only when being sarcastic, did not fail to comment on this. Nevertheless, his comments were restrained until the publication of "Altneuland."

Herzl had been thinking of writing such a fictional work for years. Its title of "Oldnewland" was taken from the Altneuschul or "Old New Synagogue" in Prague, originally the "New Synagogue" when built in the thirteenth century. Yet the novel itself was inspired by his own "The

Jewish State." Wishing to rebut the critics, Zionists and anti-Zionists alike, who called the book's blueprint for Jewish statehood far-fetched, he set out to show how it could in fact be the basis of a society more advanced than any envisioned by Ahad Ha'am, one capable of accommodating the millions of Jews that Ahad Ha'am thought Palestine had no room for.

"Altneuland" begins in 1902 with a prologue. Its central character, Friedrich Löwenberg, is a twenty-three-year-old Viennese Jew rejected in love, disdainful of the bourgeois Jewish society to which the woman who has spurned him belongs, and suffering from a bad case of Weltschmerz. Answering a newspaper ad for a "cultured and despairing young man willing to try a last experiment with his life," he meets one Mr. Kingscourt né Königshof, a wealthy German aristocrat who has left Europe for America and then, fed up with civilization, bought a small island in the South Pacific to which he intends permanently to retire. He is looking for a companion to share it with and Friedrich, feeling he has nothing to lose, agrees to join him.

The novel now jumps to 1922. Friedrich and Kingscourt, having spent a happy twenty years on their island, sail their yacht back to Europe, curious to see what has transpired in their absence. Passing through the Suez Canal, they decide to pay a visit to Palestine – a country that was poor and neglected when they stopped there on their outward-bound voyage. To their amazement, it has been transformed. Splendid cities with broad boulevards have replaced its wretched towns; green fields worked by tractors carpet former swamps and barren hills; trains and automobiles whiz across distances once traversed by donkeys and camels; power lines, their electricity produced by canal-borne water plunging from the Mediterranean to the Dead Sea, run to the horizons. There are silent, speedy trams, large, modern department stores, attractive apartment buildings, even theaters and opera houses. Friedrich and Kingscourt can hardly believe their eyes.

It is all, they learn, the work of the New Society for the Colonization of Palestine, the organization created by the Zionist movement upon chartering the country from the Turks soon after the two men sailed for the South Pacific. Financed by London bankers assured of a reasonable return on their investment, the organization managed swiftly and efficiently to transfer a majority of Europe's Jews, eager to escape anti-Semitism, to their new homeland. A board of experts used its commercial know-how to dispose of the emigrants' property at its true value, buy large tracts of land from Palestine's Arabs without driving up prices, make the necessary mass travel arrangements, have the needed infrastructure in place before the new arrivals disembarked, and provide them with immediate housing and work.

Successfully created with the help of the latest technology, the New Society, as the Altneulanders call it, is run on the basis of the most progressive political and economic principles. It is a full democracy in which universal suffrage prevails and the civil and religious rights of non-Jewish minorities are scrupulously respected. (Herzl chose to illustrate this by means of a lengthy scene, set at a town meeting in the village of Neudorf, at which, following an appeal by Altneuland's president David Litwak, the villagers vote overwhelmingly to reject the platform of the nationalist rabble-rouser Dr. Geyer, who would limit membership in the New Society to Jews.) Major enterprises are cooperatives run by their workers. Free education and health care are provided to all. Palestine has become a country any European would be envious of.

And precisely this, Ahad Ha'am scathingly wrote in his review of "Altneuland," was proof of everything he had said about Herzl all along. "The cat is out of the bag!" he began as if having caught Herzl red-handed. "The Zionist leader has finally revealed his conception of the Messianic Age that is around the corner." Herzl's Jewish utopia had nothing Jewish about it. It was simply a replica of Europe – Europe at its best, to be sure, but what of it? – transplanted to the Middle East.

One by one, Ahad Ha'am enumerated the New Society's features and institutions. Its better-educated inhabitants speak German; its common folk, Yiddish. Its theaters and opera houses, to which the Altneulanders wear white gloves as if in Paris, performs in these languages, too, as well as in French, English, Italian, and Spanish – in everything but Hebrew. If the many newspapers and magazine on the New Society's newsstands have any Jewish content, "we haven't been informed what it is." The curriculum of its schools, in which Hebrew is not the medium of instruction, includes sciences, European languages, and athletics, but not, it would seem, Jewish history or culture. The country's inhabitants pride themselves more on their good relations with their Muslim and Christian neighbors than on their own traditions. Although there is a "Jewish Academy" modeled on the Académie Française, its stated goal is to encourage work that will "benefit the human race"; Jews, presumably, as members of this race, will benefit, too. "And why is it called the Jewish Academy?" inquired Ahad Ha'am before answering his own question. "Perhaps because only Jews would treat their own language and literature in such a fashion."

Indeed, Ahad Ha'am asked, if one imagined "the Zionist leader" heading a movement not for the return of the world's Jews to Palestine, but for that of America's Negroes to Africa, and writing a novel about it,

> how would a Negro Altneuland be any different from a Zionist one? I believe it no exaggeration to say that a few superficial changes would suffice to Africanize [Herzl's] book completely. [His belief in] imitating others without the slightest originality; going to all lengths to avoid anything smacking of national chauvinism, even if this means obliterating a people's nationality, language, literature, and spiritual propensities; making oneself small to show how great, even revoltingly so, is one's tolerance ... all is a monkey-like aping of others with no show of national distinctiveness. The spirit of slavery within freedom, the spirit of the Western European Diaspora, is everywhere.... A Jewish renaissance that would truly be Jewish cannot be created overnight by stock companies and cooperatives. A historic ideal demands historic development, and historic development takes time.

"Slavery Within Freedom" was the title of an early essay of Ahad Ha'am's in which he had contrasted the Jews of Eastern Europe, who were inwardly free to be themselves despite outward oppression, with their emancipated Western European counterparts, who slavishly internalized the culture of their emancipators. Herzl was a mental and spiritual slave: such was the bottom line of the review in *Ha-Shiloah*. His Jewish state was just a program for Jewish assimilation in another form.

4

Simultaneously with its appearance in *Ha-Shiloah*, Ahad Ha'am's review ran in the Russian Jewish periodical *Voskhod* and was sent by him to the German Jewish monthly *Ost und West* with a request to translate and publish it. *Ost und West* did so, submitting an advance copy to Herzl for comment. Herzl was stung badly. From his point of view, he had made no small effort to stress his state's Jewish character. He had had Friedrich and Kingscourt attend a grand Passover Seder; experience a Sabbath in Jerusalem whose peaceful ambience affected them "like a spell"; visit that city's main synagogue, a facsimile of the ancient Temple, whose worshipers "intoned Hebrew words [that had] aroused nostalgic echoes for hundreds of years in the breasts of a people dispersed all over the globe"; hear from their guides of the New Society's adoption of the biblical Jubilee Year, in which all debts were cancelled as a unique instrument of social justice; and see a play at the National Theater about the Jewish messianic pretender Shabbetai Tsvi. (A sly choice of a subject on Herzl's part given the accusations that he himself was the latest of a long series of false Messiahs.) That Ahad Ha'am should have thought all this empty window-dressing was unfathomable to him. Fearing the damage the review might inflict on him and his movement but reluctant to be dragged into an undignified quarrel, Herzl asked Nordau, his confidant and closest Zionist colleague, to answer Ahad Ha'am for him.

Nordau was only too happy to comply. A cultural and political iconoclast with conservative leanings, he liked nothing better than a literary brawl. He began this one, in an article published in the German-language Zionist weekly *Die Welt* in March 1903, with a point-by-point rebuttal of Ahad Ha'am's review and then waded in. Ahad Ha'am, he wrote, was a nationalist fanatic. He was unable to shake off "the chains of the ghetto." The only freedom he recognized was that *of* the ghetto. He thought toleration of non-Jews was unbecoming for a Jewish state. He mocked Herzl for taking opera houses and white gloves from Europe because all he himself wished to take from it was the Inquisition. Although he wanted Zionism to proceed slowly, there was nothing slow about the spread of anti-Semitism, and what anti-Semitism would ultimately lead to if Jews did nothing about it, "any fool can guess." Ahad Ha'am was no Zionist. He is the opposite of one. It's a cheap trick to attack "political Zionism" as if there were some other, mysterious kind of Zionism, his own, to believe in. Zionism *must* be political. A Zionism that isn't political and doesn't strive to create a homeland for that part of the Jewish people that won't or can't adjust to life in the Diaspora is not Zionism at all, and the [true] illusionist is he who uses the word in a sense other than that of the Basel program. We have no choice but to make this clear to the Jews of Russia who *are* good Zionists, or at least want to be, and don't realize the game Ahad Ha'am is playing.

Ahad Ha'am's review in *Ha-Shiloah* had sent ripples running through the Zionist world. Now, Nordau's article caused a tidal wave. In newspapers, periodicals, letters to editors, and manifestos, in Hebrew, Yiddish, Russian, and German, Ahad Ha'am's supporters rallied around him. Nordau, they protested, had penned "a disgusting broadside." He had produced "a tirade full of hatred." His article was "an assault on freedom of thought" and on "a man and writer, admired by us all, in the vanguard of our national movement." His display of bile was all he had to offer. "Is it possible," asked Yosef Klausner, "for a snake not to bite?"

But Nordau had just as many defenders. "Herzl builds and you tear down," declared the Zionist intellectual Shmaryahu Levin in an open letter to Ahad Ha'am; "Altneuland" was a novel, not a political tract, and it was unfair to judge it as one. Ahad Ha'am, wrote the German rabbi Samuel Gronemann, was a habitual fault-finder who, "face to face with Achilles, would see only his heel"; he had written his review "to destroy political Zionism." Nordau, said a letter to *Ha-Melitz*, had spoken harshly only because "it takes heavy artillery to blow up a fortress of wrong ideas." It was Ahad Ha'am, not Herzl, who was "the dreamer of dreams," declared the Russian Zionist Hillel Zlatopolsky. Ahad Ha'am was deliberately splitting the Zionist movement and Nordau was right to denounce him.

There were dozens of published pros and cons. Not a few treated the clash as one between East and West-European Jewry. "How much Western insolence," wrote Klausner, "there is in Nordau's lies – insolence toward the Jews of the East and insolence toward Hebrew literature, its authors and readers alike!" One of these authors, Micha Yosef Berdichevsky, though himself a severe critic of Ahad Ha'am, declared: "It is not just the profanation of Ahad Ha'am's name that angers us [East-Europeans]....The disgraceful affront is to the bulk and mainstay of our people, we Hebrews [of the East]." On the other side of the ledger, Herzl's close associate Max Mandelstamm wrote to him: "Pay no attention to the howls of Ahad Ha'am and all the half-Asian yeshiva types.... The Russian swamp has come to life and its frogs are croaking."

Yet it was far from just an East-West battle. Mandelstamm was himself an East-European Jew, as were Levin, Zlatopolsky, and others who took Nordau's side, and Nordau received public declarations of support from Zionist societies in Minsk, Bialystok, Rovno, Lodz, Odessa, and elsewhere in Russia. Conversely, there were prominent West-European Zionists like Marcus Ehrenpreis, Benjamin Sagel, Martin Buber, Alfred Nossig, Davis Trietsch, and David Neumark who backed Ahad Ha'am and signed statements on his behalf. Ehrenpreis, who strove more than most participants in the debate to see both sides of it, rightly called it a case of "one [legitimate] point of view against another." Nor were the two sides necessarily irreconcilable. "Perhaps," he wrote, "victory will go in the end to a third, synthetic view that will unite cultural and political Zionism together." Meanwhile, however, "there are clearly different schools of thought within the Zionist movement, the proponents of each of which have the right to defend [their position] as best they can."

5

It was natural for Ahad Ha'am, in writing about "Altneuland," to deplore the absence of Hebrew in Herzl's Jewish state. Like every Jewishly educated East-European Jew, he had grown up with Hebrew as a second language – and as a first one when it came to the prayers and rituals of the Jewish day and year, the biblical and rabbinic texts he studied, the secular literature he first was exposed to, and his own choice of a medium to write in. Hebrew was an essential component of his Jewish identity. A Jewish renaissance in Palestine without it was inconceivable to him, as it was to many of his generation.

Ahad Ha'am did not, it is true, use Hebrew in his private conversations or public addresses, for which he was taken to task in a pro-Nordau article by Eliezer Ben-Yehuda. (Ben-Yehuda and his wife had raised their son, born in Jerusalem in 1882, entirely in Hebrew, making him the first native speaker of the language since ancient times.) Yet he clearly did expect Hebrew to be spoken in the "national spiritual center" in Palestine. In this he differed from writers like Lilienblum and Smolenskin, who did not believe that Hebrew's spoken revival was possible or necessary for Zionism's success. No purely literary language had ever before been brought back to full life from its extinction as a vernacular, and while Hebrew might serve as a lingua franca for Palestine's ethnically diverse Jews, it was unlikely, they thought, that it would ever replace Yiddish, Arabic, or Ladino in the homes of Palestine's Jews. At the time of the "Altneuland" affair, attempts to introduce Hebrew as a spoken medium were largely limited to the Yishuv's elementary and secondary school classrooms, from which it was unclear if and how far it would spread or whether it would be able to cast off the "artificial chains" that Ahad Ha'am had found it burdened by.

He had thought about language extensively. A man of great intellectual curiosity, he was familiar with the writings of linguists like the American William Dwight Whitney and the Frenchmen Ferdinand Brunot and had read widely in the social sciences, then dominated by the neo-Darwinism most famously represented by Herbert Spencer. Ahad Ha'am knew Spencer's work well; it held human societies to be the products of slow, generally unconscious developments, in the course of which, much as in the evolution of a biological species, their component parts grew more complex and mutually well-adapted. Every society was an interlocking system of such parts, none of which could be altered without affecting all the others – and there was no better example of this than a language, whose speakers, no matter how heterogeneous, shared a commonality of concepts and values.

Language functioned, Ahad Ha'am wrote in an essay on it, like a neurological system, processing experience on an unconscious level and making it available on a conscious one. It did so for peoples no less than for individuals, the difference being that "the individual mind has no choice but to submit to the linguistic usages of its times," so that, "even if it idiosyncratically strays from a [linguistic] norm, it will be called back to it by a multiplicity of counter-examples," whereas "the mind of a people, though also governed by inherited rules, is not so bound by them that it cannot frame new ones." A phonetic shift, new word, or altered grammatical form was comparable to a minor biological mutation. It originated with a single person and rarely went further; only if it served some collective need or purpose was it passed on and disseminated, often with a ripple effect on other parts of speech. The evolution of a language was the sum of such successful mutations, every language being a repository of a people's "national spirit" and a record of its growth. A people that lost its language did not necessarily lose its literature, which could survive in translation. It did, however, lose the living nerve cells of its memory. The Hebrew-less inhabitants of Herzl's New Society were in effect amnesiacs.

The anomaly of Hebrew, Ahad Ha'am argued, was that it had ceased to develop organically when it stopped being spoken in the first centuries of the Common Era. As a purely literary language it had gone on changing, just as did, say, medieval Latin, but its different phases continued to co-exist on the written page, thus blocking its "evolutionary path"; a linguistic atavism such as the reversion to biblical diction of a writer like Mapu could never have occurred in the presence of a naturally evolved spoken standard. Although Herzl was right about railroad tickets, this was a triviality. A word for "ticket" could easily be invented. (As indeed it was when *kartis*, an Aramaic term in the Talmud for a bill of entitlement, was given this meaning in the early twentieth century.) Haskalah Hebrew had many such neologisms. The real problem was that, quite apart from missing terminology, Hebrew had yet to become a truly modern language. It was still not flexible and supple enough; its grammar and lexicon were a confusion of different periods; it compulsively kept quoting its own past; its purists resisted the positive influence of more developed European tongues; it lacked the habits of simplicity and directness that were a feature of everyday speech.

As a writer and editor, Ahad Ha'am was determined to teach it such habits. He was not operating alone. Nineteenth-century Hebrew, particularly in its daily and weekly press, had performed much of the work before him, gradually adding new vocabulary, pruning away the dead wood of awkward or outmoded usages, and adopting a more European-like syntax. Gordon's editorials in *Ha-Melitz* were a good example of this; Ahad Ha'am went further in the same direction. The Hebrew of his later essays set a new standard of functional fluency. Take the opening paragraph of his essay "Moses," written in 1904:

> When I listen to scholars debate the effect of the "great men" of history on human life, some saying they are history's makers and the common people plastic material in their hands, and others saying, no, the people is the moving force and its great men in every generation the inevitable products of its circumstances; when I listen to such arguments, I think: how little do the savants see past the tips of their noses! Isn't it obvious that the true great men in history, those who have remained active influences throughout the ages, have not done so as real beings who existed in a specific time and place? No historical great man has not had his spiritual portrait painted by his people's imagination differently from the reality, and it is this imaginary composition, the work of a folk pursuing its needs and propensities rather than some actual person whose brief life was not at all what it was subsequently taken to be, that constitutes the true great man who continues to make himself felt – sometimes for thousands of years.

This is not simple prose. It is syntactically complex and expresses an intricate thought. There is not a word in it, however, that is inexact or redundant. It says what it has to say straightforwardly, without frills or rhetorical flourishes. It is purged of every trace of biblical diction and grammar and of the self-preening allusions to the classical texts of tradition that were an age-old feature of Hebrew literary style. It unselfconsciously borrows European words like *historiya*, "history," for which it was the Haskalah's practice to search for often clumsy Hebrew substitutes. Today's translator of it into English does not have to strain to make it sound modern. It *is* modern.

6

The disagreeing "savants" of "Moses" could be personified as Thomas Carlyle, who wrote in his 1840 "On Heroes, Hero-Worship, and The Heroic In History" that "In all epochs of the world's history we shall find the great man to have been the indispensable savior of his epoch," and Spencer, who stated in his 1860 "The Study of Sociology," with Carlyle in mind, that "the genesis of a great man depends on the long series of complex influences which has produced the race in which he appears.... Before he can remake his society, his society must make him."

Neither Carlyle nor Spencer put the matter in terms as starkly opposed as those Ahad Ha'am reduced it to. Each, presumably, would have agreed with William James's bridging judgment that great men and the societies they emerge from are interdependent, both being "essential to change; the community stagnates without the impulse of the individual; the impulse dies away without the sympathy of the community." But Ahad Ha'am's point was that the argument itself was misconceived, since historical heroes are indistinguishable from their communities. The great men of the past are remembered as the myths they have become, without which they would have faded into oblivion – and these myths are the work not of their generation alone but of all the generations that came after it. If archeologists were to unearth proof that the historical figure of Moses had never existed, this would not make the slightest difference, since Moses the folk-creation would be unaffected by it.

Who is this Moses? He is, Ahad Ha'am writes, the archetype and greatest example of the uniquely Jewish concept of the prophet. The prophet is not a hero in the ordinary sense. He takes up arms in no wars and wins no battles as do the heroes of other peoples. He fights not against specific enemies but rather for "truth and justice," which are ultimately one and the same, since "what is justice but truth in action?" When Moses, as a young man, kills an Egyptian beating a Hebrew slave, he does so not as an Israelite patriot but as someone with a passion for fairness who instinctively sides with the weak. This is also why, fleeing from Egypt, he comes to the aid of Jethro's daughters at the well upon arriving in Midian, even though they are not Hebrews. "Why should that matter?" Ahad Ha'am asks. "The prophet makes no distinction between persons apart from the distinction between right and wrong. [Moses] saw shepherds aggressively taking advantage of defenseless women and [as the Bible says] 'stood up and rescued them and watered their flock.'"

Moses's decision to return to Egypt and liberate his fellow Israelites after years of living quietly in Midian expresses the same impulse. Yes, he is commanded to do this by God in his vision of the burning bush. But were he not unconsciously looking for a moral cause – did not an inner voice tell him "Go! Fight! This is what you were created for!" – he would not have heard God's summons. For the first time, he knows where to find "the road that will take him on his life's quest." One thing alone deters him: he is, Ahad Ha'am writes, "a man of truth," and to get the Israelites in Egypt to believe in him, he will have to be, he fears, "a man of words" – that is, of rhetorical manipulations such as a truth-teller must avoid. As tempting as it would be to employ cheap oratory to achieve his end, "the prophet in him rebels against this offensive thought."

Luckily, there is a solution. Moses has a verbally facile brother, a priest, not a prophet, who will popularize his ideas. And so, with Aaron's help, he returns to Egypt and leads Israel forth from it. Pharaoh and his army are destroyed and Moses is now the leader of a free people that he will take to the Promised Land. Little does he realize that the most difficult part still lies ahead and that "while the masters have ceased to be masters, the slaves are still slaves." Satisfied that he has taught the people at Sinai that their God is a moral being whom they must painstakingly learn to emulate, he discovers on his descent from the mountain that Aaron has betrayed him by sacrificing to the golden calf of populist emotions that clamor for immediate gratification. For a moment, he is on the verge of giving up. Remembering, though, that "he is a prophet, a teacher and an educator," he comforts himself that the process will be a long one. If he perseveres, he will yet succeed.

But then comes the episode of the twelve spies. Sent to scout the Land of Israel, they return with the grim truth and it is more than anyone can bear. "A people sets outs to win a homeland and create a new national life there…. and a single negative report demoralizes it to the point of despair!" Now, Moses realizes that his hope of educating this people in his lifetime is a vain one. It will take a generation or more in the wilderness for such a development to take place. Haste can only lead to disaster, as it does when the Israelites, seeking to bolster their shattered spirits, press ahead in the desert against Moses's advice and are routed by the Amalekites. It is necessary to proceed step-by-step, even if this means that Moses himself will die before entering the Promised Land. Indeed, he *must* die, because once the people enters this land,

> a new time begins in which prophecy is no more – a time of compromises and concessions such as belong by the nature of things to the conflicts of life, whose reality can never match the prophet's vision….Let others come and make these compromises while doing the best and accomplishing the most that they can. Be this more or be it less, it will be neither what the prophet wished to achieve nor how he wished to achieve it.

7

"Moses" is one of Ahad Ha'am's finest essays. It exhibits him as Hebrew literature's first true master of the form, which he honed his skills at while editing *Ha-Shiloah*. The monthly was run by him with a firmer and more professional hand than Hebrew periodicals, thankful for whatever material they were able to scrape together, were guided by before him, and the standards he imposed on himself in the many pieces he published in it were even higher than those demanded of others. His essays had beginnings that stated general truths or posed clear questions; middles that developed and discussed their themes without repeating themselves or wandering off in digressions; ends that tied it all together. Such things were not taken for granted in the Hebrew press of his day.

Ahad Ha'am's essays were never personal in the sense of openly introducing his own life into them. One learns none of its details from them. Yet if one knows something about it, its traces are often visible. Any reader familiar with Ahad Ha'am's thought and career will realize that his "Moses" was an intended self-portrait. The founder of B'nei Moshe clearly thought he was writing about himself. He, the courageous truth teller who would not pander to the public he hoped others would win over in his name; the lonely campaigner for ideals too lofty to be popular; the realist who warned against exaggerated expectations from the Land of Israel; the Zionist who insisted that generations of Jews would remain in the Diaspora while Zionism did its slow, incremental work – he was the Moses of his time. He, not the charismatic Herzl, was the true prophet.

Reticent about his own religious beliefs, Ahad Ha'am was loathe to embroil himself in disputes with either the upholders or detractors of tradition. Yet not without justification did Nordau bitingly refer to him in his *Die Welt* attack as a "secular rabbi," and his secularism lies close to the surface of "Moses." The essay's rarely mentioned God is but an exteriorization of Moses's conscience in the same way that the entirety of Judaism was for Ahad Ha'am a projection of the Jewish "national spirit." It was, one might say, this spirit's phylogenetically evolved form, just as its predatory habits and tawny camouflage are the lion's and its ruminant stomach and swiftness in flight are the antelope's. And just as the lion and the antelope become endangered species when their environment is encroached on, so the Jews, the religious and social walls separating them from European society having been breached, were threatened with the loss of their identity. They needed their own habitat in which to survive and continue to evolve.

What Ahad Ha'am envisaged for Palestine was a Jewish society in which the "national spirit" assumed new forms while conserving many of the old ones. The Sabbath, for example, would remain a day of rest, though not necessarily one of worship. "Whoever feels truly connected to the life of the [Jewish] people over the centuries," he wrote, "cannot possibly imagine it existing without its 'Sabbath Queen'....One can say without exaggeration that even more than the Jews have maintained the Sabbath, the Sabbath has maintained the Jews. There is no need to be a Zionist to be aware of its sacred historical significance."

The Sabbath is hallowed by Jewish history, not by God or the Torah, but this makes it no less incumbent on Jews to honor it. When Nordau publicly attacked Reform Jews who observed their Sabbath on Sunday for being shameless assimilators who might as well "convert to Christianity and be done with it," while at the same time emphasizing that freethinkers like himself had no need for a religiously sanctioned day off from work and took one whenever it suited them, Ahad Ha'am fell on him with a fury. "And that's all?!" he asked scathingly. "Not one word from our esteemed Zionist intellectual about the Sabbath's historic and national value? ... The whole question for him is a religious one and has nothing to do with him personally, since he is a freethinker and will rest when he wants to."

Whatever form it took, the Sabbath would be one of the Yishuv's central institutions. And by the same token, Ahad Ha'am envisioned, the Jewish festivals would be celebrated by the Jews of Palestine as their national holidays. The great Jewish books would be read and taught as their national literature. The Land of Israel's historical sites would be visited as their national monuments. Hebrew would be spoken as their national language. And all this would be informed by the "national spirit," which would put its stamp on every aspect of life.

The national spirit! It would be manifest in all things. And yet one can search Ahad Ha'am's essays in vain for any meaningful description of this spirit or explanation of what makes it distinct. His discussions of the subject remain on the level of generalizations that sometimes descend to out-and-out tautologies. Thus, in an 1899 essay on "National Morality," he observed that

> In distinguishing between right and wrong, we find many differences among peoples: what one considers good another considers evil, and what is a moral duty worth sacrificing one's life for in one case is a matter of indifference in another... And if this is true of all advanced nations, which are not that removed from each other in circumstance, experience, and character, how much truer it must be of the Jews, who have always been [as stated by the Bible] "a people that dwelleth apart," different from all others in the remarkable course of their development. It would be impossible for them not to have a national morality of their own based on their spiritual inclinations, past history, and present condition.

The Jews, in other words, have their own national morality because....they must have their own national morality. Of what this morality consists, Ahad Ha'am's writings give only one concrete example. This, too, involved Herzl and Nordau – each of whom, curiously, had written a play (Herzl "The New Ghetto" in 1895, Nordau "Dr. Kuhn" in 1898) ending with the death in a duel of a sympathetically portrayed Jewish protagonist. Both Herzl's Jacob Samuel and Nordau's Leo Kuhn are assimilated Jews who nonetheless have a strong sense of Jewish pride, and both are killed when they bravely but rashly challenge an anti-Semitic insulter. "I hardly need say," Ahad Ha'am wrote,

> how opposed such behavior is to the basics of our national morality – not just to the commandments of Judaism, but to our core sense of right and wrong. Apart from a few writers and intellectuals, the peoples of Europe have yet to free themselves of the crude concept that a slight to one's honor must be expunged with blood. Yet the true Jew....knows very well that a culture that is thousands of years old elevates him far above such primitivism, which is a remnant of more ignorant and cruel ages....He will answer [his insulter] with a single contemptuous look and go his way.

Although dueling with swords or pistols was certainly not a traditional Jewish way of settling disagreements, Ahad Ha'am was missing the point. Neither Herzl nor Nordau was holding his character up as an example for other Jews to follow; both were depicting the tragic situation of a Jew who feels compelled by an anti-Semitic Christian society to win its acceptance by risking his life. If their plays had a moral, it was that Samuel and Kuhn died pointlessly, since they stood no chance of being accepted in any case.

Ahad Ha'am, however, had little appreciation of imaginative writing, which he rarely published in *Ha-Shiloah*, and no aptitude for reading it. He saw only what he took to be its bottom line, which was in this case that Herzl and Nordau had no inkling of what true Jewishness was. He was convinced of this before the "Altneuland affair"; convinced even more in its wake; and convinced most of all by the Uganda debate at the Sixth Zionist Congress in Basel in the summer of 1903.

8

A sense of impending crisis hung over the congress long before it convened. In April, 1903, two decades after the pogroms of 1881–82, anti-Jewish rioting of a far more savage nature had broken out in the Bessarabian city of Kishinev, not far from Odessa. Killing dozens of Jews, the Kishinev massacre demonstrated more powerfully than its forerunners the lethalness of European anti-Semitism and the urgency of finding a more reliable refuge from it than America, whose gates would clearly not stay open forever.

It was no secret that Herzl, having gotten nowhere in his negotiations with the Turks, had also been conducting talks with the British for a territory on the northern coast of the Sinai Peninsula, in the vicinity of El-Arish. If successful, this would have confronted the Zionist movement with a difficult choice. On the one hand, Sinai was not Palestine; opting for a Jewish state in it, the El-Arish plan's opponents argued, would mean taking the "Zion" out of Zionism. On the other hand, British Sinai bordered on Turkish Palestine. Any Jewish colonization undertaken there, countered the plan's supporters, would eventually spread across the frontier, making El-Arish a foothold next-door to Zion that it would be unconscionable not to take advantage of. The debate between the two camps stood to be stormy one.

As it turned out, however, the debate was not about El-Arish. Herzl's opening address stunned the delegates. The Sinai plan, he told them, had fallen through. Yet the British colonial office, which was looking for settlers for its territories in East Africa, had made the unexpected counter-offer of a large area near Lake Victoria (while actually in northwest Kenya, Herzl seemed to think it was in Uganda), where it was prepared to establish a Zionist-administered British protectorate. Although he had yet to form a firm opinion of the matter, Herzl said, it was worth considering. No such opportunity had ever been presented to the Jewish people before. He proposed sending an official Zionist delegation to East Africa to investigate its suitability and would introduce a draft resolution to that effect.

The congress was thrown into a turmoil. East Africa was thousands of miles from Palestine; there could be no spillover from one to the other. Even if Herzl's proposal was merely for a preliminary inquiry, a yea vote meant conceding that under the right circumstances Zion would be abandoned, while a nay vote would be defying Herzl and probably bringing about his resignation. The delegates were acrimoniously split. Most of the East Europeans, led by the Democratic Faction, were staunchly against the resolution. It constituted a betrayal, they argued, not only of Zionism but of the entirety of Jewish history. The Westerners were largely for it.

Surprised by the intensity of the opposition, Herzl spoke to the congress a second time, assuring it that East Africa was "merely an expedient for settlement purposes" and not a substitute for Palestine, which he would continue to fight for. Nordau, too, spoke twice, passionately asking the delegates to support Herzl. The Jewish people, he said, was being offered a *Nachtasyl*, a shelter for the night, by the greatest power on earth. It would be irresponsible to reject it out of hand. One delegate (Nordau was referring to Meir Dizengoff, the future mayor of Tel Aviv) had declared in the language of Ahad Ha'am that the problem was not the Jews, which Uganda could perhaps accommodate, but Jewishness, which it could not. Yet Jewishness without Jews, Nordau mocked, was "spiritualism." Another delegate had dismissed the fear that a negative vote would cause the British to lose interest in Zionism with the reassurance that "our wonderful Herzl will find a way to deal with it." Yes, Nordau retorted sarcastically: "First smash the dishes and then let our wonderful Herzl put them back together." It couldn't be done.

The Uganda resolution was put to a vote on the fourth day of the congress: 295 delegates voted in favor, 176 voted against, and 143 abstained. The "nay-sayers" walked out of the congress hall and assembled in a separate room, where they sat on the floor like mourners on Tisha b'Av. Some wept. Sentiment was for seceding from the Zionist Organization. Only a last-minute intervention by Herzl, who rushed to the scene from the hotel room he had adjourned to, could persuade the group to return for the congress's final sessions.

Ahad Ha'am was not present at the congress, the fifth in a row he had declined to attend. His response to it came in a bitter essay entitled "The Weepers," published in December 1903. There he asserted that Herzl, having never really cared about Palestine to begin with, had now shown his true colors. It was not on Herzl, however, that Ahad Ha'am vented his greatest wrath. This he reserved for his own disciples, who had failed him, so he felt, as Aaron had failed Moses. In Basel, they had sat and wept. But why hadn't they heeded his warnings about Herzl before then? Why had they allowed themselves to be used by him? And why, above all, had they rejoined the congress after the vote? "From the very first," Ahad Ha'am wrote, "they shut their eyes to avoid seeing where they were going....What else but weep can they do now – weep for the havoc they have wreaked on themselves and for their incapacity ever to repair it?"

But though Herzl's Zionist Organization was finished, Ahad Ha'am wrote, "historical Zionism" was not. "For it there is no need to worry. It can wait." One day new forces would appear to fly "the eternal Zionist banner" again. And if "some political wise man then arrives and suggests a shortcut to Zion, they will open the chronicles of our times to the page on Uganda in the chapter on 'Political Zionism' and tell him, 'Read!'...The way is long and the end must not be hastened."

9

Herzl, shaken by the intensity of the debate and his failure to command an absolute majority, died of heart failure within a year and the Uganda plan died with him. Whether he really thought it possible to make the enormous investment of time, money, and human lives needed to develop a Jewish colony in East Africa while continuing to press efforts to obtain Palestine is unclear. Ahad Ha'am and the nay-sayers at Basel were surely right in insisting that any serious East African project would have pushed Palestine aside, just as they were right in predicting that such a project would never get off the ground. A Jewish colony in Africa would have meant no more to the Jewish public than did Baron de Hirsch's empty spaces in Argentina. Palestine alone had the historical and emotional resonance capable of galvanizing Jewish emotions. Uganda was a straw Herzl clutched at, not a well-thought-out idea.

Ahad Ha'am was right, too, when he declared in his "Altneuland" review that not even Palestine could be attractive to Jews without Hebrew. Hebrew alone could unite Jews from all over the world, cause them to feel the Jewish past was speaking through them, connect them to their people's deepest self. A Yiddish, German, or English-speaking outpost in Palestine could do none of these things.

And yet a Jewish state *had* to be built quickly. This was what Ahad Ha'am failed to realize.

One can't say he had no sense of time. If anything, he had too much of it. He thought in terms of time's slow processes. He lacked an awareness of how time had speeded up in the nineteenth century and would accelerate even more in the twentieth, so that the Jewish people, running to keep up with it, would not be able to run fast enough. Zionism, he thought, was in no hurry. In his criticisms of Herzl, he repeated this again and again. He was wrong.

Herzl, with his fascination with modern technology, understood how quickly everything was changing. Nordau understood it, too. In his best-selling 1892 book "Degeneration," a critique of *fin de siècle* European decadence, he had written:

> One epoch of history is unmistakably in its decline, and another is announcing its approach. There is a sound of rending in every tradition, and it is as though the morrow would not link itself with today. Things as they are totter and plunge ... .Views that have hitherto governed minds are dead or driven hence like disenthroned kings, and for their inheritance, they that hold the titles and they that would usurp them are locked in struggle. Meanwhile, interregnum in all its terrors prevails; there is confusion among the powers that be; the millions, robbed of their leaders, know not where to turn; the strong work their will; false prophets arise, and dominion is divided among those whose rod is the heavier because their time is short.

And even Nordau, then a man of forty-three, could not have predicted that within his lifetime – he died in 1923 – Europe would be ravaged by a colossal war, most of its empires would be toppled, and Palestine would pass to British hands. The world was about to be transformed utterly.

It was true that Herzl, as Ahad Ha'am never tired of pointing out, had nothing to show for the seven years in which he led the Zionist movement apart from that movement itself. He had managed to create a political organization that masses of Jews identified with, but that was all. Had he not done so, others probably would have. It might have taken another decade or two, but it would have happened.

And yet those one or two decades were crucial. They made all the difference. Had Herzl not created political Zionism in 1897, it would not have been in place to carry on after his death in 1904; had it not been in place in 1904, it could not have obtained the Balfour Declaration from the British in 1917; without the Balfour Declaration, there would have been no flow of Jewish immigrants to Palestine in the 1920s and '30s; with no Jewish immigration in those years, Israel could not have been established in 1948; had it not been established then, Arab Palestine would have gained its independence and a Jewish state would no longer have been possible.

Even then, this happened too slowly to save the Jews of Europe. If Herzl had no idea of the centrality of Hebrew, Ahad Ha'am was blind to the menace of anti-Semitism. Precisely because it was more severe in Eastern Europe, East-European Jewish intellectuals of his generation, having little hope after 1881 for the liberalization of a Gentile society that had never opened its doors more than a crack to them, took anti-Semitism more for granted. Although its manifestations might rise and ebb, its essence, as they saw it, was immutable. Kishinev was frightful. Yet if truth be told, the seventeenth-century massacres of Jews in the Ukraine by Chmielnicki's Cossacks were far worse. What had been was what would be.

Thoroughly acculturated in the countries of their birth and careers, Western Jews like Herzl and Pinsker were more aware of changing anti-Semitic trends. They understood that the new form of racial Jew-hatred emerging in their age in France, Germany, Austria, and England was potentially more dangerous than what had come before because it was secular in nature and a product of modernity rather than a residue of the Middle Ages. If late nineteenth-century Europe might be compared to a shark-infested sea in which the Jewish people swam like a school of threatened fish, it was the swimmers on the school's outer edges, the Jacob Samuels and Leo Kuhns, who knew the sharks best and were most sensitive to every tremor caused by their fins. Those bunched protectively in the middle picked up only their own vibrations.

It was fortunate that Ahad Ha'am's followers did not heed his advice to walk out on the Sixth Congress's final sessions and on the organization that Herzl had founded. This would have spelled its disintegration, whereas remaining as a fighting opposition strengthened the democratic structure that Herzl had sought to give it. Democracy was not a concern of Ahad Ha'am's. Although he thought it the intellectual's job to lead, he never, following the dissolution of B'nei Moshe, grappled with the question of how ideas might be translated into realities. Herzl did. The Neudorf scene in "Altneuland," however simplistic, is a description of democratic leadership in action, and Herzl had sought from the beginning to conduct the Zionist Organization accordingly. While he counted on the strength of his personality to carry the day when necessary, he didn't shrink from putting his ideas to the test of the ballot and encouraged the Uganda plan to be debated and voted on. Never before in Jewish history had a decision of momentous national consequence been made in such a manner. This was the "national political life" that Lilienblum had called for.

The real winner of the Uganda debate was the precedent set for political process. It was one faithfully followed by Zionism in the decades to come, particularly after World War I, when the Zionist Organization became through its executive the de facto governing body of Jewish Palestine. Political parties, with mass followings in both Palestine and the Diaspora, competed within it; hotly contested elections were held throughout the Jewish world; ruling coalitions were cobbled together at Zionist congresses – all on the principle of majority rule. If Israel was one of the few new countries to emerge from World War II and its aftermath as a genuine, stable democracy, this was the result of the education provided by pre-1948 Zionist politics, which Herzl initiated and Ahad Ha'am disdained. This, too, belongs to the balance sheet between them.

10

In some respects, Marcus Ehrenpreis's hopes for a synthesis of Ahad Ha'am's and Herzl's Zionism came to pass. With Uganda forgotten, Herzl gone, and Ahad Ha'am's role in Zionist discourse diminished, especially after he ceased to be in close touch with his Zionist colleagues upon moving to London in 1908 (he was to remain there until 1922, when he settled in Tel Aviv, where he died in 1927), the polemical atmosphere vanished from Zionist life. Hopes for a Turkish-granted charter for Palestine died permanently when the nationalist Young Turks seized power from the Sultan in 1908, while at the same time, the Yishuv expanded as restrictions on Jewish immigration were eased. The Zionist Organization, both in Palestine and the Diaspora, concentrated on practical issues while putting

Herzlian diplomacy behind it. Although Herzl's dream of a Jewish state remained, and even loomed as a more realistic if still distant possibility, it no longer clashed in Zionist minds with Ahad Ha'am's gradualism.

Yet this truce – for it was no more than that – came to an end with World War I. Even while the war was underway, it was broken by an angry debate over Vladimir Jabotinsky's campaign for a Jewish Legion that would advance the Zionist claim to Palestine by fighting for it with the British against the German-backed Turks. Supported by some Zionists as a bold initiative in a Herzlian vein, it was denounced by others, including Ahad Ha'am, as a dangerous reversion to Herzl's adventurism.

And once the war was over and the period of the British Mandate commenced, the old differences flared up along a wide front, pitting the Zionist right against the Zionist left. Should the Zionist Organization's goals be quantitative and focus on bringing as many Jews to Palestine as quickly as possible, as Jabotinsky, presenting himself as Herzl's heir, demanded? Or should they be qualitative, as Chaim Weizmann and David Ben-Gurion thought, and directed toward the construction of a model Palestinian Jewish society – a "miniature of the Jewish people as it should be," in Ahad Ha'am's words? Should the Yishuv's economic policies appeal to the materialistic motives of the Jewish masses or to the Spartan values of an idealistic elite? Could Palestine realistically serve millions of Jews as a refuge from European anti-Semitism or was this too much to expect of it? Should Zionism press for an independent Jewish state in Palestine or be prepared to settle for a Hebrew-speaking autonomy? By the early 1920s, these and related issues were out in the open. By the mid-1930s, they had brought the Yishuv to the verge of civil war.

This was no longer, of course, a battle between Herzl and Ahad Ha'am. Yet it is striking how Ahad Ha'am set the agenda not only for many of the Jewish assumptions and debates of his times but for many of those of our own. His paradigm of a national center in the Land of Israel serving as a source of strength for Diaspora communities that choose not to live in it; his understanding of Judaism, or Jewishness (significantly, he never really distinguished between them), as an organically evolving body of thought and behavior selectively adapting to its environment throughout history; his view of tradition as the creation of a "national spirit" deserving of being preserved for its own sake even if not God-given; his belief in a secular Jewish moral mission – this interlocking conceptual framework, which, though not always intellectually rigorous, still shapes the outlook of many twenty-first-century Jews and their institutions in both Israel and the Diaspora, was given its first clear formulation by him.

And Herzl? If proof were needed that men who change the course of history exist, he would be it. Myths indeed formed around him. His life was turned into the folk-legend that Ahad Ha'am thought was the essence of all "great men." This legend portrayed him as the Moses-figure whose mantle of prophecy Ahad Ha'am had claimed for himself. Herzl had grown up, so it was believed, in the Pharaoh's court of European culture with next to no knowledge of his Jewishness; had become a prince of journalists and dramatists; and had been jolted from the cocoon of his success by an epiphany, its burning bush the Dreyfus affair, that convinced him to lead an exodus of his people to its promised land.

The reality was of course different. Herzl had received a Jewish education as a child; though he was a popular columnist and reporter, his career as a playwright had been a failure; he had wrestled with the subject of anti-Semitism long before the Dreyfus affair; his initial reaction to the latter was to imagine solving the Jewish problem by mass conversion to Christianity; and when he did think of a Jewish state, it was not necessarily of one in Palestine. Unlike the Moses of the Bible, he had no God to guide him – no clear religious beliefs of any kind. He had only his own daring. He was indeed an illusionist, half polished statesman and half reckless gambler, making wild wager after wager while never disclosing his pitifully low cards. He was everything that Ahad Ha'am – cautious, judicious, common-sensical – was not. His sanity was often questioned; he sometimes questioned it himself. A few days after the close of the First Zionist Congress, he wrote in his diary: "At Basel I founded the Jewish state. If I said this aloud today, I would be greeted with universal laughter. In five years perhaps, and certainly in fifty years, everyone will perceive it."

Fifty years and eight months later, the state of Israel was established. That settled, once and for all, the question of who was the prophet.

Chapter Six

Micha Yosef Berdichevsky, the Last Jew

1

A man sits writing in his diary in the German city of Breslau – today, Polish Wrocław – in the summer of 1903. His name is Micha Yosef Berdichevsky. Although he is writing in German, he is one of the best-known, and certainly the most controversial, of the Hebrew authors of his day. It is the end of July and he is summarizing the month's events in the kind of personal short-hand, fully understandable only to themselves, that diarists use. He writes:

> A grave and difficult question: should the baby be made to join the Covenant of Israel? It should never have happened but it did. There are historic forces to which individuals are subject. And still it shouldn't have happened.

Various matters come next:

> Our family physician, Dr. Cohn. "The Burden of Nemirov." Inquiries at the Russian consulate… "Between the Hammer and the Anvil" is finished. Malter was here. He hasn't changed much, he's just happy

no longer to be poor. We talked a lot and with little understanding between us. He's a shrewd fellow in his correspondence but overly tactful in conversation. And yet one is glad to have him.

And still other sundries:

The clinic has begun to operate. The competition: Hurwitz. The registry office. Rabbis regarding Emanuel... My father-in-law arrived for a surprise visit. The same conversation for three days. On his way to the Congress in Basel, where he expects to find a redeeming word.

The month's final entry is:

Ewa, who has been a true mother to the child and is able to calm its bawling with her love and devotion, is leaving. It's been a hard day.

A hard month! Its drama is barely hinted at even when the diary entry is decoded. Its nature is only revealed by a letter from Berdichevsky's friend Tsvi Malter, discovered in Berdichevsky's archives by his biographer, the Israeli literary critic and historian Avner Holtzmann.

Tsvi (Heinrich/Henry) Malter was a Galician-born scholar of medieval Jewish philosophy with a doctorate from the University of Heidelberg and a rabbinical degree from the Lehranstalt für die Wissenschaft des Judentums in Berlin, where he and Berdichevsky met during the latter's student years in the German capital in 1893–94; a fellow student there was David Neumark, later to become a prominent Reform rabbi in the United States. In 1900 Malter, too, moved to America to take a teaching position at Hebrew Union College in Cincinnati, and in 1903, shortly after the birth on June 18 of Berdichevsky's first and only child Emanuel, he visited him in Breslau, where they talked "with little understanding," while on a trip to see his ill mother. In early July, Malter sent Berdichevsky a Hebrew reply to a non-surviving letter from him. It reads in full:

Saatz [Czech Žatec], July 5, 1903

Greetings, my dear friend! I'm sorry to tell you that I am *not* sorry that I can't do anything in regard to the matter you write about, because I wouldn't do it even if I could. While I knew your views on Judaism, so little did I think you would have the "courage" to do such a thing that I had to read your letter twice to grasp the gist of it – namely (although you recoil from saying so in plain language), that you did not circumcise your son. I don't fear being suspected by you of false piety, because you know perfectly well what a freethinker I am, but I still must say that all this is far from me and completely alien. You don't need anyone's agreement or approval, and most of all, you don't need anyone's criticism. The very fact that you've found the strength to break with the thousands [*sic*] of generations of your forefathers gives you the license to do it. But this strength leaves you standing *alone* in our orb and you mustn't expect that I or Neumark will be as brave as you or your partners on your uncharted path. I've forwarded your letter to Neumark without stating my opinion. Let him do what he can. My mother died this week and I'm on my way home, and then to Berlin. With best wishes to your family from my wife and myself,

Your friend,
Tsvi

Malter's letter, with its combination of shock and qualified sympathy, spells out what the "grave and difficult question" referred to by Berdichevsky in his diary was. Even today the Hebrew reader feels something of the same shock at the thought of one of the great figures of modern Hebrew literature refusing to bestow on his own son the most basic distinguishing mark of Jewishness.

Just what it was that Berdichevsky wanted from Malter and Neumark is unclear. (Their support, obviously. But in what form?) And yet, as his diary tells us, his refusal did not last long. Emanuel, it is true, was not circumcised when he should have been, on June 25, the eighth day after his birth; so we learn from Malter, who may have discussed the question of circumcision with Berdichevsky without realizing the significance of their conversation. Sometime in the course of July, however, Berdichevsky changed his mind and agreed to have the circumcision performed, not by a *mohel*, a ritual circumciser, but by the family doctor – after which he castigated himself twice in the same paragraph for letting it happen, as if once were not enough to express his chagrin.

That same month, we also learn, Berdichevsky read in manuscript (it had not yet been published), or else heard about, "The Burden of Nemirov," Chaim Nachman Bialik's poem, later renamed "In the City of Slaughter," about the Kishinev pogrom. As a Russian citizen, born in the small town of Dubova in the Ukraine in 1865, he visited the Russian consulate in Breslau, presumably to clarify Emanuel's status. He finished writing his short story "Between the Hammer and the Anvil," which appeared in print in 1904. His wife Rahel, a native of Warsaw who had studied dentistry, opened a clinic that would vie with the nearby practice of a dentist named Hurwitz.

Berdichevsky registered Emanuel's birth with the German authorities. He consulted rabbis, or rabbinic literature, about Emanuel, perhaps to ascertain the validity of a non-ritually performed circumcision. Rahel's father, Yakov Romberg, passed through Breslau with his younger daughter Ewa on his way to the Sixth Zionist Congress in Basel, at which Herzl was to broach his fiercely debated "Uganda Plan"; for three days, apparently, Berdichevsky had to listen to him talk about Zionist politics. When Romberg left, Ewa stayed on to help take care of Emanuel, who was a cranky baby. Indeed, it was more likely the joint pleas of Berdichevsky's wife and sister-in-law rather than "historic forces" that broke down his resistance to circumcising his son. So I learned from the only conversation I ever had with Emanuel Berdichevsky, which took place in the 1970s in Tel Aviv. Recounting with a rueful smile the scandal of his near non-circumcision, he told me that "family pressure" had caused his father to relent.

2

"Between the Hammer and the Anvil," the story Berdichevsky finished writing in July 1903, contains clear autobiographical elements. Its narrator, Shimon Ben-Moshe (Moshe was the name of Berdichevsky's father, a small-town rabbi), is at the time of writing an assistant librarian in a city somewhere in central Europe. His account begins with a description of his early education in the Russian shtetl he grew up in as a child and of the vivid fantasies he wove from the biblical texts he studied in the heder. "I knew our father Abraham and mother Sarah as I knew my father's neighbors," he tells us. "When Miriam stood on the bank of the Nile to see what would happen to baby Moses, I stood by her side as she stroked my hair and asked me about my family. I crossed the Jordan with Joshua, carrying my own little stone [like the twelve stones carried into Canaan by representatives of the twelve tribes]."

When he is ten, Shimon's mother dies. (Berdichevsky lost his mother at the same age.) "Although all I felt," he relates, "was a kind of bafflement, my soul lived in shadow from then on." In the heder, the enthralling stories of the Bible make way for the rigorous logic of the Talmud. "I was torn from my heroic Samson, from the kings of Judah and Israel whose wars I fought and bore arms in, and went to study with Rabbi Tarfon and Rabbi Akiva." The first stirrings of rebellion take the form of semi-conscious anger at the strict world of paternal authority, untempered by a mother's love, that condemns Shimon to long days on a school bench when his young body and boyish spirits crave activity:

> Once, I imagined that my father had died, too. Freed from the yoke of the heder, I learned to wield a hammer at the forge from the village blacksmith, whom I had always liked stealing away from my studies to watch. The whole town pitied me for being an orphan, but I – I had the frightful thought of starting a fire in its streets and watching it rise to the sky.

The first stirrings of sexuality also. One time, Shimon recollects, when he was bar-mitzvah age,

> my father sent me to borrow ten rubles for the purchase of Sabbath provisions from a wealthy, attractive woman who lived by herself. There was no one else in her grand house, and she gave me a hug and a kiss. I felt a strange fire. I went about stunned all that day. I wanted to shout and caper in the streets .... Today this is just a memory, but I will say this of the soul's mysteries: a man is the sum of all the sin and fire in his bones.

The adolescent boy begins, surreptitiously, to read Haskalah literature and gradually loses his religious faith while continuing to practice it in public:

> The Haskalah told me, "Be strong, be a man, and acknowledge that you and your ancestors have lived foolishly." It taught me to study the sciences and give up my belief in God. At first I felt afraid and stripped of my most precious belonging. Soon, though, I made bold to think that I alone saw the truth and other Jews were blind.... My friends advised me to leave town for a city where I could pursue my studies. My father kept berating me.... I hated the Jews who prayed all the time, hated their long clothes, hated the Sabbath.... But though inwardly I, the enlightened Shimon Ben-Moshe, lived in a world apart, I still put on my tefillin, prayed in the synagogue, and washed my hands ritually before sitting down to each meal.

Ultimately, the narrator takes his friends' advice and leaves his native town and land:

> And so I went from Kiev to Brody, and from Brody to Königsberg, and from there to Leipzig, and on to Basel. I wandered from country to country. I sat in the lecture halls of universities without knowing the first thing about life or the world. I struggled not to starve while never planning for tomorrow. I had friends and knew nothing about people. I sought the secrets of the soul in the books of the poets and its laws in those of the philosophers.

Berdichevsky himself did not leave Russia so quickly. First came a year at the Lithuanian yeshiva of Volozhin, a vaunted center of talmudic learning that was also a notorious breeding grounds for the heresies of Haskalah thought; a return to the Ukraine, where he began his literary career as a journalist in the Hebrew press; two youthful marriages, both ending in divorce against the background of his religiously suspect views and behavior; and a stay in Odessa in 1889–90, where he worked as a Hebrew tutor while learning German. Only then did he set out for studies in the West, at first at the University of Breslau, and then at the Universities of Berlin and Bern, earning his doctoral degree from the latter in 1896 with a dissertation on the relationship between ethics and aesthetics.

Shimon Ben-Moshe does not get as far as a doctorate. His studies founder and he sinks into a sense of purposelessness. The student life he envisioned as a liberating adventure turns out to be a drab, lonely existence in rented lodgings and reading rooms. "I had thought I would be a valiant campaigner in the intellectual wars," he writes, "but all I did was fall by the wayside… My despair grew greater all the time. My soul yearned for a 'Yea' and could only say 'Nay.' I was in need of love and friendship and had nothing but my own doubts." Although he has ceased to practice Judaism and seeks to put it behind him, it refuses to stay there. "Each time I tried pressing on, I saw the wreckage of Sinai before me. It was wherever I went. Whenever I lay down to rest, the bad dreams of my people lay down with me." He is at a mental impasse. "I had heard it said that man does not live by bread alone, but I say unto you: the life of the spirit torments man, too. I had heard it said, 'Work and ye shall live,' but I worked and no life came."

If the last two sentences remind one of the vatic prose of "Thus Spoke Zarathustra," this is probably because Shimon has been reading it. Although there is no mention of Nietzsche in "Between the Hammer and the Anvil," his work, little known previously, became popular in Europe in the 1890s. The drastic if short-lived reversal of mood that Shimon now undergoes, as if he had been granted a sudden epiphany, is more suggestive of a literary than a real-life experience and hints again at the influence of "Zarathustra"'s dithyrambs:

> One clear morning all was alive. Resurrection! Let the sun shine! A thousand years count for nothing beside the light and purity of the morning!… Wrong is he who complains of the tedium of life. Listen to the day's song, seize the world with both hands, let us pray to the God of the thunderclouds!
>
> It was storming outside. The wind was howling. I thought, "I can't get out of bed." Yet lo, I did and I had something to live for.

But this euphoria passes quickly. Nietzsche is no match for the burden of Jewishness that Shimon can no more cast off than can the Jewish people. If there is indeed a God, he reflects bitterly, "He has chosen us among all peoples to torture us.... We want to repair the world and can't even repair ourselves." His depression returns until one day he learns of a new movement, his prior ignorance of which reflects how isolated he has been from Jewish life.

> Walking with a friend in the city park one day, I opened my heart to him. He had only one thing to say: We must return to the land of our fathers and make it our own!
>
> I looked at him in amazement. All my torment melted away....
>
> From then on, I, too, was one of the dreamers. Every time I saw a flag, I wanted it to be the flag of Zion. Every rally I attended made my heart rally for its people. What no single one of us could do for himself, we could all do together.

But Shimon's Zionist phrase fades as quickly as does his Nietzschean one. Zionism, he concludes once his initial enthusiasm for it has waned, is all empty talk. Waving flags and attending rallies in Europe is easier than settling in Palestine, and all Herzl's advent has done is replace the synagogue and prayer book with Zionist congresses and their speeches. "I dreamed one night," Shimon says sardonically, "that the Jews were still scattered over the face of the earth, and that they and their wives and children were chanting [in the words of the *Shmoneh Esreh* prayer], 'And may our eyes see Thee return to Zion in Thy mercy.'" Nothing has changed.

Shimon marries: if the Jews cannot build a home in Palestine, he will at least build one for himself. This, too, however, is a mistake. His marriage, like Berdichevsky's first two, soon falls apart. God's words to the serpent in the Garden of Eden, "I will put enmity between thee and the woman," should have been addressed, Shimon muses, to Adam. The whole episode, he tells the reader, "fills me with such shame that I can't say any more about it. You'll have to understand on your own."

We do and we don't. Although Shimon is only in his forties,

> I've grown old before my time. Life has stranded me in the job of an assistant librarian. I work every day from nine a.m. to two p.m. Then I return to my room on the outskirts of town. My bed is there, my books are there, my world is there.
>
> When I think of my old dreams and aspirations, I can't believe any of it. What is the past to me? What is the present? They're all the same graveyard, on their tombstones carved a language I don't even understand.

His life is for all purposes over. There is no fire left in his bones.

3

The loss of religious faith resulting from its encounter with modern critical thought, most often in the form of the writings of the Haskalah, is a major theme in the Hebrew literature of the late nineteenth century. Its protagonists are young Jews, generally yeshiva students, who are ejected by their own inquiring minds from the strict but warm world of tradition that has nurtured them since childhood. The sense of life's meaning and coherence that they lose is as great as the freedom that they gain. Such a fictional character is Nachman in Mordecai Ze'ev Feierberg's short novel "Whither?" that was published in installments in Ahad Ha'am's *Ha-Shilo'ah* in 1899 – the year its author, like Micha Yosef Lebensohn, died in his mid-twenties from tuberculosis. In a climactic scene, very different from the one that occurs on the same day of the year in Smolenskin's "A Pact of Vengeance," Nachman stands in a synagogue with the congregation of his father the rabbi on Tisha b'Av. Unlike the other worshipers, he is not grieving for the Temple. He is grieving for his own soul, laid waste by the books of philosophy he has been secretly reading. Kept by them from praying like the Jews around him, he thinks:

> Give me back my God, the God of the Jews! The God of Aristotle can do nothing for me. He is a figurehead, a king without a kingdom, not a God who lives.... Give me back the God who is near to

me and I to Him! The God of Abraham, Isaac, and Jacob, the God of Moses and the prophets, the God of all this holy congregation that is melting in its tears for the destruction of Jerusalem while its heart trusts and hopes that God will rebuild Zion!...Take what you want from me – heaven and hell, my share in the world to come – but give me back my light, my heart, my soul, my people, my God!

It can be asked why such spiritual anguish is rarely found in Haskalah writers themselves. Men like Mapu and Yehuda Leib Gordon were certainly conscious of having intellectually outgrown the faith of their fathers, too, yet they do not seem to have suffered emotionally from it. Even Smolenskin, who systematically blamed the Haskalah for the damage done by it to the Jewish psyche, never did so from a place of personal bereavement. A rare exception was Moshe Leib Lilienblum, who wrote in his autobiography of the final collapse, at the age of twenty-seven, of the religious beliefs he had struggled for years to prop up:

> My entire mental treasury, all the property I had accumulated in a lifetime, had been plundered all at once.... I was like a philosopher who has lost his system, a business whose account books have been burned.
>
> The God who had always been my shepherd was now the God of Spinoza. I felt alone and abandoned in life. I had taken the final intellectual step and my heart sank. My mind was a blank. I was terrified.

But Lilienblum, too, quickly got over his crisis. Within a few months he had taken a new job as editor of the Odessa Yiddish weekly *Kol Mevaser* and thrown himself back into the hurly- burly of Russian Jewish life.

It is only starting with Berdichevsky, born two decades after Smolenskin and Lilienblum and one before Feierberg, that we find characters like Shimon Ben-Moshe in Hebrew literature. This was because it was only in the period of Berdichevsky's coming of age in the 1880s that East-European Jewish life began to change dramatically. Until then its institutions, despite the Haskalah's unrelenting critique of them, had remained fundamentally intact and the great majority of Jews, Hasidim and Misnagdim, Maskilim and anti-Maskilim, had continued to live within their framework as before. It was not until the '80s that worsening anti-Semitism, the industrialization of the Russian economy, mass emigration, growing assimilation, and the incipient movements of Zionism and Jewish socialism began seriously to affect the traditional world of Russian Jewry, threatening to tear and even shred its very fabric.

As adversarial toward this world as the Haskalah had been, it had hoped for its improvement, not its destruction. The prospect of its disappearance never occurred to men like Mapu or (at least until the end of his life) Gordon – and because it didn't, their own place in it seemed secure to them, too. Although anathematized by its conservatives, they remained snugly within the confines of the Jewish community, participating in its life, remaining – if only for appearance's sake – observant of its main religious rituals, and never contemplating leaving it; nor, short of the unthinkable act of religious conversion, was there anywhere they might have left it for. Precisely this is the tragic situation of Yakov-Hayim in Smolenskin's "A Donkey's Burial." Cast out by Jewish society with nowhere to go, he is forced to live in a lonely shack outside of town with his child and wife, who becomes a Christian after he is murdered.

Such was no longer the case when Berdichevsky was reaching adulthood. Jews were now leaving Russia in droves; many more had begun to move from the small towns of the Pale of Settlement to its cities, where Russification was rapid and Jewish communal structures were weaker; for the first time, the possibility of living outside of these structures without renouncing one's Jewishness existed for a religiously disaffected young Jew. Yet choosing to do so, which often meant cutting one's ties with uncomprehending and unforgiving parents and everything one could call home, could well sweep one away, not only from the synagogue and study house, but from Jewish life entirely. Without its religious institutions, indeed, what remained of this life? Although secular or semi-secular Jewish coteries existed in the 1880s in East-European cities like Odessa and Warsaw, and even in some smaller towns, a fully functioning secular Jewish society did not. The very concept of it was nebulous. How could a people without a territory that had always defined itself by its religion turn its back on that religion and remain itself?

Shimon Ben-Moshe's short-lived enthusiasm for Zionism is great because he suddenly glimpses how such a thing might be possible; once he concludes that the Zionist movement is going nowhere, his last hopes perish. Not only does he have no answer to the question of why he should want to continue being a Jew, he has no context to be one in even if the question could be answered. And at the same time, he cannot help being one. As Berdichevsky relates of a similar but more fictionally developed character, Mikha'el, the protagonist of his story "Two Camps": "Nothing was left in him of his people – but he was still his people's son." Shimon Ben-Moshe's Jewishness cannot be rooted out. He cannot kill it by an act of will. He can only try starving it to death by living totally apart from his fellow Jews, which is what we see him doing at the story's end. Psychologically, however, this means starving himself to death, too.

4

When Berdichevsky left Russia in 1890 to study abroad, first in Germany and then in Switzerland, he was part of a growing trend. Unlike Russian universities, which admitted few Jews, German and Swiss ones accepted them on an equal basis and even allowed them to matriculate without a high school diploma. By 1900, an estimated 1,500 to 2,000 young Russian Jews were enrolled in German and Swiss higher institutions of learning with another several hundred in France. (Germany and Switzerland were preferred destinations because of the closeness of Yiddish to German, which made the latter an easy language for East-European Jews to master.) University cities like Zurich, Bern, Breslau, and Berlin had lively Jewish student bodies. A group of Berdichevsky's early stories, written in the late 1890s when he first turned to Hebrew fiction, consists of character sketches drawn from this milieu.

But the Mikha'el of "Two Camps" wants no part of it. A student of philosophy and history at the University of Breslau, he is lonely but wants friends who are German. Looking down from a bridge one winter day on a crowd of ice skaters below, one of them a dark-haired-and-complexioned girl he cannot take his eyes off, he laments that

Not one of the skaters knew him. Though he now spoke their language and was studying their thought, he was a stranger in their midst, an outlier.... And yet he felt that their thought was his own. The root of his soul was drawn to it; he sought their company, longed to be one of them.

Mikha'el is an internationalist. He believes in "complete equality between all people and nations," and feels that in leaving his Russian shtetl he has gone "from darkness to light." He prefers working mornings in a bookbindery to the better-paying job of giving Hebrew lessons to the children of Breslau's Jewish bourgeoisie because he thinks that Hebrew has no future. He has even managed to lose the tefillin and prayer book that he brought with him from Russia, so that he can be rid of "the baggage of Judaism." When a Jewish professor who knows his background hands him a generous sum with the request that he study a daily chapter of the Mishnah in memory of a dead relative, he is hurt to the quick: "He was in Germany, the land of freedom; he had sacrificed everything for his religious liberty – and here he was being asked to mutter words in some dark corner like a superstitious kabbalist!" Still, something of his Orthodox upbringing remains with him. So great is his scorn for the Reform Jews of Breslau that he draws the curtain on his window on Saturday mornings to avoid seeing them on their way to their temple.

Mikha'el lives in a rented room. One evening he finds himself locked out of the apartment by its absent owner and is invited in by his upstairs neighbors, the German tailor Markus and his Polish wife Maria-Jozefa – who, born to a family of déclassé nobility, looks down on her husband. Though the two quarrel in front of him, he feels comfortable with them because they respect him as a student and have nothing against Jews. As they are talking, their daughter Hedwig walks in: she is, he realizes at once, the same seventeen-or- eighteen-year-old he watched skating from the bridge. Mikha'el stares bashfully at the floor and hurries to take his leave as soon as he hears his landlord return. Yet from then on he begins to drop in on Hedwig and her parents and he and she fall shyly in love.

Hedwig is not, Mikha'el learns, Maria-Jozefa's biological daughter: she was adopted as a child when her real mother, a washerwoman who bore her out of wedlock, could not take care of her. Yet her illegitimacy, and the Catholic faith she was raised in, only stoke Mikha'el's ardor for her. They feed into an old fantasy:

> In his fights with the religious fanatics back in Russia, he had imagined marrying a Christian woman just to spite them. Now, no less scornful of the bourgeois conventions of Europe, he was entranced by the thought of linking his future to this child of foreign gods born in sin. He would cast off the bonds that still held him and be totally free! His was the last generation of its kind; let theirs be the first. ... He and she would go far away. He would write no more to his parents and old friends. He would never read another Hebrew book or take any interest in Jewish life. He would live with her in an unfettered paradise, liberated from patriarchal legacies and their punishments.

Winter passes. Then spring. Mikha'el's relationship with Hedwig grows stronger: they plan a civil marriage so that he need not be baptized. Meanwhile, however, his sexual energies have no release. A near-seduction by an older woman, a friend of Maria-Jozefa's, has ended awkwardly. It is summer, a Friday night, a time when Mikha'el still feels, despite himself, "something of the poetry of religious emotion." Walking the streets of the city, he encounters a woman sitting alone on a bench. He sits beside her; their hands touch; she invites him to come home with her and they have sex. When it is over,

> Mikha'el sat, embarrassed, on a stool, staring desolately ahead of him.
> He didn't understand what he was doing in this place.
> He didn't know what to do next and looked about in confusion. He rose to go.
> Softly, she asked him to stay for a while and have tea. She had never met anyone like him, she said, lighting the hob.

They talk. Mikha'el asks the woman about herself. She tells him she was an orphan raised by relatives until thrown by them into the street. The dialogue proceeds with the inexorability of a Greek tragedy:

"How old were you then?"

"Fourteen. For two years, I worked for a laundress. She worked me to the bone, so I began taking in wash on my own."

"And then?"

"But why should a young gentleman like you care?"

"Never mind. You can trust me."

"I gave birth. I was ill much of the time."

"Where was your husband?"

"I didn't have one.... It was just some damned Jew."

"What happened to him?"

"He ditched me."

"And the child died?"

"No."

"Where is it?"

"But why do you ask?"

"Trust me."

"I gave her away. I was weak and poor. I couldn't bring her up properly."

"Do you ever see her?"

"Rarely. From a distance."

"Where does she live?"

"Here. In Breslau."

"And you don't visit her?"

"I'm not allowed to. She doesn't even know who I am."

"That must be hard on you."

"What can I do? She comes from another people...It's God's punishment."

"And her parents, the ones she has now...are they well-off??"

"No. They're tailors."

"Tailors?"

"He is. She comes from nobility."

"And...her name...it's..."

"Maria-Jozefa. But what's wrong? You're shaking!"

It is hard to say at what point Mikha'el begins to suspect the worst; perhaps only upon hearing the word "tailors." A few seconds later, he rushes into the street with a cry of pain. He has fouled himself! He has fouled Hedwig, soiled her purity! He should throw himself into the river, be swallowed by the earth. He should poke out the eyes that do not deserve to see her again. He is a scoundrel. All his ideals are a façade. He is a damned Jew. "Yes, that's what she called him...her mother...*her* mother..."

For three days, Mikha'el shuts himself up in his room. Then he packs his things, goes to the railroad station, and buys a ticket for "somewhere far away." Wherever it is, it cannot be far enough.

His horror is understandable. He has not, like Oedipus (who actually blinded himself in self-punishment), unwittingly had sex with his mother, but having it with the mother of his fiancée is the symbolic equivalent of this. The Hebrew Bible he knows well considers it incest: "And the man who possesses a woman and her mother, this is lewdness. He shall be burned in the fire."

On second thought, though: is not Mikha'el overreacting? The Bible aside, he has committed no crime. A symbolic mother is not a real one, nor is it against the law to be picked up and taken to bed by a lonely woman. The chances of Hedwig's finding out about it are less than slim. She and the washerwoman, whom she would not recognize if she saw her, have no contact, and she and Mikha'el are planning to leave Breslau once wed. Why should he do something as devastating as disappear forever without telling her? By his own moral standards, this is far worse behavior than anything he did with her mother.

Mikha'el is in fact acting hysterically. And his hysteria is *Jewish*. It is the reaction of someone whose instinctive frame of reference is the punitive "patriarchal legacy" that he prides himself on having rejected, so that he takes Hedwig's mother's not necessarily anti-Semitic remark of "it was just some damned Jew" to apply literally to himself. (Ironically, of course, Hedwig, the "Christian woman" of Mikha'el's fantasies, now turns out to be half-Jewish herself, as has been foreshadowed by her dark complexion that Mikha'el notices from the bridge.) By deserting Hedwig as her biological father deserted her mother, he has earned the adjective. He *is* a damned Jew and will forever be one.

Most telling is the penance he now imagines:

Flog yourself! Lie on the ground where everyone can trample on you! Stretch out on the synagogue floor and be stepped on by the whole congregation!... Back to God, man!

Mikha'el, a student of history, must know that this was the fate of Uriel da Costa, the seventeenth-century son of Spanish conversos who returned to Judaism in Amsterdam, grew disillusioned with it, was excommunicated for expressing anti-rabbinic views, recanted because he could not endure his social isolation, and was readmitted to the Jewish community after being publicly flogged and trod on by its members. Mikha'el must know, too, that da Costa, unable to live with his humiliation, then shot and killed himself.

At the end of "Two Camps," its initial description of Mikha'el proves only half-true. Yes, he is still his people's son – and *everything* of his people is still in him. The only way for him to cease being a Jew would be, as it was for Uriel da Costa, to cease being entirely.

5

"Two Camps" was printed as a slim book in 1899, one of several volumes of Berdichevsky's fiction to come out that year. There were only two Hebrew periodicals at the time that might have accommodated its nearly 15,000 words, both managed from Odessa by Ahad Ha'am. One was the Warsaw-produced literary annual *Lu'ah Ahiasaf*. The other was *Ha-Shiloah*, printed in Berlin, where Berdichevsky had worked briefly as its assistant editor before resigning. The reason he left it was also the reason his story did not appear there.

Ahad Ha'am had made his position on literature clear in a statement of purpose that appeared in *Ha-Shiloah*'s first issue in 1896. There were, it asserted, four areas in which the review proposed to concentrate. The first three were Jewish historical scholarship, journalism dealing with the contemporary Jewish world, and reviews of books with Jewish content. The fourth was Hebrew belles-lettres – specifically, works of prose and poetry that "faithfully depict our [Jewish] situation in different times and places." Works of purely artistic merit that did not "enhance our national consciousness," Ahad Ha'am wrote, would not be considered for publication.

This statement, not shown to Berdichevsky in advance, surprised and dismayed him. Although he was aware of Ahad Ha'am's dislike of Hebrew fiction that failed to serve "positive" Jewish goals, he had not expected it to be made an editorial policy that would preclude publishing stories like "Two Camps" whose "enhancement of national consciousness" Ahad Ha'am would have questioned. Taking the unusual step of writing a letter of protest to the publication he worked for, he asked Ahad Ha'am to run it in *Ha-Shiloah*'s second issue. To his credit, Ahad Ha'am agreed to do so.

Berdichevsky's "Open Letter to Ahad Ha'am" was a call for a Hebrew literature that would deal with all aspects of life rather than be limited to subjects of supposed Jewish interest, and that would not have to answer to this or that notion of "enhancing national consciousness." "My dear Ahad Ha'am!" he wrote. "The minute we limit our scope to what is 'Jewish,' we acknowledge that everything else is not 'Jewish'.... We divide life into two realms, what is ours and what lies beyond it, and we widen the fissure in the minds and hearts of young Jews." This "fissure" or conflict between one's Jewish identity and the pull of the outside world could only be resolved, Berdichevsky argued, by expanding the frontiers of Jewishness until they were congruent with those of the world, a role best played by imaginative literature. "You are an intellectual," he wrote, "and so you make light of imaginative writing and fail to see its value for the individual and the nation.... We want the Jew and the human being in us to be nourished by a single source. We want the fissure to be healed."

Hebrew literature, Berdichevsky was arguing, should replace Y. L. Gordon's Haskalah adage of "Be a Jew at home and a citizen abroad" with "Be a Jew in all life has to offer." Ahad Ha'am responded to this in the third issue of *Ha-Shiloah*, in an essay entitled "Need and Capability." In theory, he stated there, he had no quarrel with Berdichevsky; he, too, was for a Hebrew literature that dealt with the totality of the human condition. At the present moment, however, Hebrew had neither the linguistic resources nor the literary talents required for such a task. "We want! We need! But can we?" Ahad Ha'am asked. "This is a question the younger generation doesn't pose and can't be expected to, since no one is posing it in regard to our national goals, either." Drawing a parallel between Hebrew literature and Zionism, he wrote: "We keep veering giddily from the slow but steady path. We either expect too much or too little of ourselves, and in the end all comes to nothing because the distance between high-minded ends and meager means proves too much for us." Until Hebrew writers were able to produce great poetry and fiction of universal value, Hebrew readers would have to seek these elsewhere. Meanwhile, let Hebrew specialize in what it did best by dealing with themes rooted in specific Jewish experience, for which it was an unparalleled vehicle.

Berdichevsky replied to this in turn. Now, though, picking up Ahad Ha'am's gauntlet of "national goals," he went further. He had been reading Nietzsche, and in a series of brief, aphoristic essays published during the next several years and collected under the title "Reevaluations," he called for a Nietzschean "transvaluation of values" in Jewish life that would not wait for literature to blaze the trail for it. What was needed, he proclaimed, was not, as the Haskalah had argued, a thorough reform of Judaism, but a radical break with it.

When it came to Judaism, indeed, the Berdichevsky of the late 1890s went a step beyond Nietzsche. Nietzsche, in blaming Christianity for declaring war on all the healthy, natural instincts of pre-Christian man in the name of a "slave morality" driven by guilt and a sense of sin, had included in his indictment the Judaism that Christianity grew out of. Yet he had distinguished, basing himself on the nineteenth-century Higher Criticism's judgment that the Priestly Code was a late addition to the Bible, between the life-affirming religion of the early biblical period, which he professed to admire, and a life-denying sacerdotal phase that followed. Berdichevsky made no such distinction. The problem with Judaism, he argued, developing an argument anticipated by Gordon's "Zedekiah in the Dungeon," was not that it had taken a wrong turn at some point in the past, not even one so distant as the rise to power of a cultic priesthood in the mid-first millennium BCE. The problem went back to Mount Sinai itself. It was already there that the heavy hand of the Law was imposed on all vital spontaneity:

God was buried beneath the Torah, the world beneath a book. Man stifled his senses and became a guardian of parchment....

> An entire people rebelled against nature. An ancient tribe went looking for a country and found a tome of commandments. Day turned to night; thunder and lightning boomed and flashed; signs and omens cowed the best in us.... When Moses descended the mountain, no prophet arose to snatch away the tablets of the Law and cry to the people in the wilderness: "Back to nature, back to your mother!"

Reflected in this passage is Berdichevsky's own resentment, writ large, of his early loss of a mother and subjection by a father to long years of dull study. Consciously or not, he was projecting his childhood experience onto a vast historical screen. But this was also the experience of his generation. Such rhetoric strongly appealed to many young Hebrew readers of the age because they, too, felt they had been snatched from the maternal warmth of the home when barely out of infancy and delivered to a harsh male regime of study and ritual observance that robbed them of childhood's joys. Berdichevsky's invocation of an ancient, idyllic, religiously matriarchal past that was also the lost childhood of the nation was both startling in its strangeness and instantly recognizable on a subliminal level:

> In the time when we worshiped many gods, burning our incense to them on the hills and mountains and building our altars to the Queen of Heaven [the prophet Jeremiah's term for the Canaanite goddess Astarte]; when we pranced like young rams and reveled in light and in the votaries of light; then came the one God from the desert to give us an eternal scripture into whose occult sinkholes we sank and have never stopped sinking.

Not even Gordon had dared launch such an all-out Hebrew assault on Judaism. Overnight, Berdichevsky became a cause célèbre. His polemical exchange with Ahad Ha'am was closely followed. The talk in Hebrew-reading circles in Eastern Europe, one Hebrew writer wrote from there, was "Berdichevsky, Berdichevsky, Berdichevsky!" And just as Nietzsche combined his critique of Christianity with a vision of a post-Christian future, so Berdichevsky now spoke of a future that would be post-Jewish. With Judaism no longer an intellectually viable faith among the young, the Jewish people would perish if it did not reinvent itself:

> The period we are now in has no parallel in anything previous. The fundamental conditions, internal and external, that have enabled us to survive for so many centuries have collapsed.... Not for nothing do we fear that we have left familiar territory and are faced with the collision of "to be" with "not to be." We will be either the last Jews or the first Hebrews.

Stirring language though this was, though, what did it mean? If a Jew and a Hebrew were two manifestations of a single identity, one associated with Sinai and the other with its repudiation, what could such an identity be based on? And if they weren't – if Hebrews and Jews were two different peoples – why should Jews care if they were followed by Hebrews or not? Peoples, like individuals, strive to survive as themselves. Survival as another is extinction.

This point was made by Ahad Ha'am in an 1898 essay on "Reevaluations" in *Ha-Shiloah*, from which Berdichevsky had by now resigned. Although, Ahad Ha'am wrote there, there were elements in Nietzsche's philosophy that were compatible with Judaism, such as the parallel between its *Übermensch* and the Jewish concept of the Chosen People, Nietzsche's belief that "the physical life needs to be liberated from the restraining power of the spirit" was not one of them. It was no wonder that Hebrew literature's self-proclaimed Nietzscheans

> feel an "inner fissure" when they exclaim: The transvaluation of values! New values for old! The sword in place of the book – instead of the Prophets, "the blond beast" [of Nietzsche's *On the Genealogy of Morals*]! This past year, especially, we have heard on a daily basis about the need to tear everything down from top to bottom and rebuild. What we don't hear is how you can simultaneously smash the national foundations of an ancient people and construct a new life for it after having denied its essential nature and killed its historical soul.

The question was a good one, even if Ahad Ha'am's understanding of Nietzsche was not. (The *Übermench*-Chosen People equation was far-fetched, and Nietzsche certainly never believed that the mental life mattered less than the physical.) But Berdichevsky was in any case never quite the Nietzschean he was made out to be. Nietzsche's thought had given him a crowbar with which to overturn Judaism; once wielded for that purpose, he let it go. If it had any relevance to the question of Jewish continuity posed by Ahad Ha'am, this was only insofar as Nietzsche considered thinking in terms of essences a lazily generalizing habit of mind.

This was precisely how Berdichevsky now answered Ahad Ha'am. Jewish life, he declared, did not have an "essential nature" and never had had one. It was simply the sum total of all the Jewish lives ever lived and of the innumerable contrasts and inconsistencies between them.

> Ahad Ha'am's Judaism is an abstraction, a conventional notion of what Jews are. But we are Jews pure and simple, with all the different thoughts and opinions that Jews have.
>
> You warn us that our views are incompatible with being Jewish. But the question is: What is Jewish? What is this eternal Jewishness in which we share?

Giving examples of how Jewish tradition was never unitary and often contradicted itself, Berdichevsky went on:

> We are told: observe Judaism! We reply: we are Jews and that's enough. You have chosen for yourselves a suitably high-minded Judaism by virtue of which we exist and alone have the right to exist. But we are not interested in an existence that is predicated on tradition-bound lives. The Jewish people is an ongoing process, not a cosmically predetermined formula. Although we are a people that has thought this, that, and the other thing, it is not thinking any of them that has made us a people.
>
> No abstract Judaism of any kind can be our guide. We are Hebrews and we will serve our own hearts.

Ivrim anahnu ve'et libeinu na'avod! Berdichevsky's readers would not have missed the defiant allusion to both the people of Israel's declaration in the book of Joshua, "The Lord our God we will serve!" and Jonah's confession of "I am a Hebrew and I fear the Lord, the God of heaven." It was not Jewishness, let alone the Jewish God, that produced Jews. It was Jews who produced Jewishness, and every Jew would help produce it in his way.

6

Roughly at the time of his marriage to Rahel Romberg in 1902, the subject matter of Berdichevsky's fiction changed. It ceased to be the uprooted lives of young Jews who had left the Russian shtetl for the cities and universities of Europe and became the shtetl itself. This may have owed something to his marriage and settling down: he was now a husband and father and no longer a wandering student. It also, however, expressed a desire to record a world that was, by the turn of the century, under severe stress and doomed, so Berdichevsky believed, to vanish or be fundamentally altered. Despite his physical and mental removal from the shtetl, his emotional ties to it had never been cut, and a successful visit to Dubova with his wife soon after their marriage, his first since leaving Russia a decade earlier, helped reconcile him to his memories of it.

The shtetl Berdichevsky wrote about was that of his childhood in which the old ways, relatively unaffected by modernity, still prevailed. Neither satirized in the manner of the Haskalah, nor romanticized as it sometimes was by post-Haskalah writers, its outward harmony is fraught with inner conflict. The most common motif in Berdichevsky's shtetl stories, with their wide variety of characters and situations, is that of disruption – of a person, action, or event that shatters an accepted mold of behavior and sends shock waves through a community that must struggle to contain it, often at a high price to those directly involved. A good example of this is his "A Generation Passes," set in a town called Lodozino.

Lodozino is undergoing a slow social transformation: its old class of wealthy Jews is on the decline and a new group of nouveaux riches has accumulated savings, opened shops and businesses, and become economically dominant. And yet while everyone in the town is aware of the change, the old social relationships persist. By a kind of undeclared compact, Lodozino's down-at-the-heels gentility continues to control the town's communal institutions, is accorded the show of respect it has always received, and refrains from mixing with those considered its inferiors – until one day a parvenu horse trader named Eizik-Hirsh, the crude and violent son of a blacksmith, persuades the once wealthy Menashe-Shlomo, now fallen on hard times, to marry off his well-bred daughter to his own, Eizik-Hirsh's, doltish son in return for rescue from financial ruin. It is the town's first "intermarriage" and Lodozino, to its surprise, accepts it with equanimity and even celebrates with relief the passing of a fictitious social order. Menashe-Shlomo alone, mortified for himself and his daughter, cannot come to terms with it. He withdraws into a world of unreality, convincing himself up to the day of the wedding that the betrothal is a bad dream.

> The day arrived. All day long Menashe went about unbelievingly. He only awoke when the musicians began to play. Yes, it was real ... it truly was. It was the first day of the Jewish month, on which the Hallel prayer is said, and he thought of its verse, "Dear unto the Lord is the death of His pious ones." Opening his tallis and tefillin bag, he took out his sash and his prayer book, in which he found the deathbed confession. Then he went up to the roof. Put your house in order, man!

It isn't clear if Menashe hangs himself with his sash, the Hasidic *gartel* worn in prayer, or jumps from the roof, just as it isn't clear if the story's last words are his own or the narrator's. Such ambiguity is common in Berdichevsky's fiction, in which the author slips in and out of the minds of his characters as if he were both their chronicler and alter ego, leaving us guessing whether a thought is his or theirs. In either case, Menashe-Shlomo has put his house in order as best he can. His daughter, whose wedding he is spared from having to attend, will be, though unhappy, well-provided for.

In some of Berdichevsky's best-known stories, the disruption takes the form of flagrantly non-normative behavior. One of these, "The Red Cow," takes place in the shtetl of Dashya. At first its narrator wonders whether he should relate its unsettling incident at all, but he decides to go ahead. "The fact of the matter is," he says,

> that our generation is dying out and the next one won't know who its ancestors were or how they lived in our world of Jewish exile. If it has the curiosity to read about them, let it know what their bright and dark sides were. Let it know that they were Jews, but also flesh-and-blood, with all that that implies.

In Dashya, many of whose inhabitants keep cows, lives a Jew named Ruvn who owns the handsomest and best milker in town, a rare red Holstein. One year in which meat is scarce, Dashya's Jewish butchers plot to steal and slaughter Ruvn's cow and divide it among themselves. In the middle of the night, they lead it from its barn, drag it to a cellar, wrestle it to the ground, and slit its throat.

> The cow let out a frightful, earth-rending bellow. Its blood spurted in a wide, fountain-like arc, glittering in the light of the lantern that hung from the ceiling. It spattered over the ceiling and the walls and the floor and the men's pants and faces and hands, and still the cow went on struggling with the last of its strength. The ground around it was a sea of blood. Its killers heaved it onto its side, and after a while the red Holstein gave up the ghost. Man conquers beast!
>
> One of the butchers took a sharp knife and plunged it into the dying cow's belly. As its guts spilled out, the others were already skinning it, all but tearing the hide from its flesh. They did it with a hidden strength and an obdurate passion they never knew they possessed.
>
> The cow was skinned. The butchers divided it up, cutting away the head and legs. One impatiently seized the fatty liver and threw it on some coals that had been lit in a corner. The men wolfed it down, blood and all, licking their fingers hungrily and drinking as they ate from a large bottle of vodka standing on the floor. They were like priests of the Ba'al ripping apart a sacrificial victim. And this wasn't at Beth-El or Dan. It was in the Jewish

town of Dashya. It didn't happen in the ancient kingdom of Israel before the exile of the ten tribes. The year was 5645.

The Jewish year 5645 was 1885, when Berdichevsky was a young man in the Ukraine, and it is possible that "The Red Cow" was based on an incident he knew of. The butchers' wild bacchanal, however, is entirely the work of his imagination. They themselves are surprised by it. It comes from a place deep within them that they have had no inkling of. The narrator, whether an ordinary Jew or an Ahad Ha'amist intellectual who believes in a "national morality," is embarrassed by the whole affair. Jews should not act this way. It is foreign to the essence of Judaism to indulge in orgiastic rites that evoke the worship of the forgotten gods of Canaan, the bitter foes of the biblical God who forbade blood-lust and the eating of blood. Yet the butchers of Dashya, who have their own synagogue and are every bit as "Jewish" as the town's respectable householders, couldn't care less about the essence of Judaism. They are who they are.

In "The Red Cow," something ancient and anarchic that appears to break into the life of the shtetl has in fact always been there. It dwells in the Jewish psyche even if its presence is denied; it is as old as the long-suppressed cult of the Ba'al itself. In others of Berdichevsky's stories, the intrusion of archaic forces into small-town Russian-Jewish life is less violent but more tragic. This is so in "In the Valley," which tells of the fate of Hulda, a Jewish girl from a Ukrainian hamlet whose beauty has about it "something of a folktale." Hulda is a strange, enchanted creature. Wherever she goes – and she likes, in an unheard-of fashion, to wander alone in the fields and hills, or by the river near her home – she is accompanied by "an echo of Eden before man sinned." When she is sixteen, she is betrothed by her father, the miller Shmaryahu-Avigdor, to a presentable young man from a good family in a nearby town. Here, too, the climax of the story is a wedding. Hulda's is held out-of-doors:

> Twilight! The setting sun, reflected with the fields in the river, reddened the sky. A grand wedding canopy had been erected. Men and women held torches; dark clothes gleamed in their glow; trumpets blared…. Wrapped in a long shawl, the bride

stood in the middle of it all like a Hindu goddess. The groom circled her the prescribed seven times. It was everything a wedding should be. The rabbi read the marriage contract and broke the glass. There were cries of "Mazel Tov!" Drums beat, cymbals clashed. A blaze flared up in the distance. Shmaryahu-Avigdor's peasant friends, seeking to please him, had lit a bonfire of dry branches. Its flames colored the night like the flames in which, in olden times, human beings were offered to the gods.

Waking the next morning, the bride and groom's families cannot find Hulda. She turns up that afternoon in the river, not a human being sacrificed to the gods, but a goddess sacrificed to human beings, drowned, perhaps of her own volition, for the violation of her sanctity. "And on the following day," the narrator relates, "Shmaryah-Avigdor and his wife harnessed two cows to a cart and put the drowned body on it and set out for town to bury it ... and the cows lowed all the way." The narrator's language is close to that of the book of Samuel's in telling of the return of the captured Ark of the Covenant by the Philistines after being punished for keeping it. ("And they took two milk cows and they tied them to a cart.... And they laid the Ark of the Lord upon the cart.... And the cows took the straight way and they lowed as they went.") Hulda, like the Ark, is a numinous presence, a manifestation of divinity in a world that fails, with grim consequences, to recognize it.

Playing off a contemporary scene against a biblical text is a time-honored Hebrew literary technique that Berdichevsky resorted to often, as did his contemporary, the great Yiddish and Hebrew story writer and novelist Mendele Mocher Sefarim. But while Mendele's work is set in the shtetl, too, his use of the technique is different. His biblical allusions are comic and serve to emphasize how pathetically far Jewish life has fallen from its ancient grandeur. In Berdichevsky, echoes of the Bible are meant to be taken seriously. Its myths erupt atavistically in his characters – who, unaware of acting them out, are defenseless before them. It is tempting to draw an analogy with the psychology of Jung, though Berdichevsky wrote nearly all of his shtetl stories prior to Jung's appearance as a psychoanalytic thinker and was certainly not influenced by him.

Not all of Berdichevsky's shtetl characters are unconscious of the claims of the past. One who isn't is Avram-Moshe in the story "The Lonely Ones." A young Talmud student in the town of Polna who dreams of a life of heroic action, Avram-Moshe is the opposite of his fellow townsman, a youth his own age with the symbolically reversed name of Moshe-Avram. Moshe-Avram is all action and no thought. The town brawler, admired for his courage and feared for his strength, he has no idea what to do with either of them. As the narrator observes dryly:

> He was not one of the biblical Judges. No one was asking him to assume the kingship or lead his countrymen against the enemy. He was a tailor and a tailor's son. He who could have done great things for his tribe sat sewing pants from fabric costing twenty kopecks a yard. The melancholy of a hero without a stage!

Meanwhile, the physically puny Avram-Moshe, under the influence of the Haskalah, has become a religious freethinker while continuing to feel born for the greatness that Moshe-Avram has no inkling of. But what greatness is possible in a town like Polna, whose Jews cannot think beyond "the several square feet of a store in the marketplace"? Avram-Moshe's high ambitions weigh him down. "What had he been put on earth for? Why had he come into a fortune that he couldn't spend a penny of?"

Moshe-Avram, chafing at his confinement to a tailor's shop, quits his job, falls in with bad company, and becomes a petty criminal whom no one in Polna dares challenge. "Who was going to tell him what to do? One might as well go and bind Samson!" Avram-Moshe, for his part, takes to airing his heretical views and is driven from the study house and ostracized. And so:

> When shadows fell and the sky grew dark in the east, Moshe-Avram sat listlessly by his window. What was he going to do tonight? Steal someone's chicken or duck? He needed bigger game to hunt, multitudes to make quake with his fists.

At the same time of day, Avram-Moshe languished in his room.... With whom was he going to do battle? Whom could he teach? Notions store owners, sellers of buttons and threads? How was he to rally the tribes from Dan to Beersheba and deliver his message, his great message, to them?

"The Lonely Ones," with its overly pat symmetries, is little more than an allegory. Great spiritual and physical powers, the powers of the people of the Prophets and the Judges, live on, it proclaims, in the Jews of the shtetl. Who, what, will unchain them?

7

Shimon Ben-Moshe, the protagonist of "Between the Hammer and the Anvil," goes through a Zionist phase that does not last. Autobiographically, this was prophetic, because at the time the story was written Berdichevsky's Zionist period was not over. It was in fact at its apogee, 1903 marking the height of his written involvement with Zionism. It was a year in which he contributed weekly columns of commentary on Jewish affairs to the Warsaw *Ha-Tsefira*, nearly half of them touching on Zionist issues.

It would be hard to think of another Hebrew writer of the age for whom Zionism was a more obvious cause to embrace. Everything in Berdichevsky's work called out for it as the one possible solution to the dilemmas of Jewish existence. His conviction that Judaism had repressed the natural man and woman in the Jew, who needed to reconnect to them; that its traditional structure in the Diaspora was disintegrating; that Jews were consequently forced to live in two worlds, an increasingly attenuated one of their own and an increasingly dominant one of the society around them; that this tore them psychologically in two; that growing assimilation was the inevitable outcome; that the Jewish people needed a new historical stage, commensurate with its innate potential, on which to remake itself; that this required a post-religious revolution in its life; that such a revolution, to be authentic and tap into the pent-up energies of the Jewish past, had to be a Hebrew one: who but Jews living as a free people in their own land could cope with such forces and be capable of such changes?

Yet when one reads Berdichevsky's *Ha-Tsefira* columns on Zionism, one is struck by his note of reserve. As an idea, he was for it; as a movement, he had little faith in it. In the great clash of 1903 between the supporters of Herzl and Ahad Ha'am, he was equally dismissive of both camps. Like Ahad Ha'am, he thought that Herzl was out of touch with reality and under the delusion that grand assemblies and gestures could accomplish for a people what it was unprepared to do for itself. Herzl, he wrote, acted like a philanthropist wishing to give Palestine to the Jews as an unearned gift. Had he been a profit-oriented entrepreneur instead – had he settled in Palestine himself as did, say, Cecil Rhodes in South Africa and developed like Rhodes farms, mines, and businesses to provide jobs and serve as economic models – he could have achieved far more. While the masses of Jews heading westward from Eastern Europe might applaud small numbers of other Jews for going to Palestine in the name of a national ideal, they knew ideals could not feed their families. "First give us the stones on which to lay our heads," Berdichevsky wrote, alluding to Jacob's sleep-vision in the book of Genesis, "and then we can dream."

But while agreeing with Ahad Ha'am that Palestine lacked the absorptive capacity for large-scale Jewish immigration and that Herzl erred in thinking that anti-Semitism rather than the inner crisis of Judaism was the Jews' main problem, Berdichevsky regarded Ahad Ha'am's "spiritual center" as no less of a fantasy than Herzl's Jewish state. The spiritual life of a people, he argued in *Ha-Tsefira*, had to grow out of material circumstances. Cultural and intellectual elites rested on broad social and economic bases; they needed a working society with all the occupations and activities of everyday life to nourish and support them and could create nothing of value unless interacting with it. "The upper spheres need to rest upon the lower ones," he wrote. Ahad Ha'am wished to construct a roof in Palestine without a building to hold it up.

Zionism was riven by internal dissent. Herzl had failed to obtain his charter from the Turks. The Yishuv was demographically stagnant, departures nearly equaling arrivals. "Every ship full of Jews that sails from Palestinian shores," Berdichevsky wrote in *Ha-Tsefira*, "gives the lie to the utopian visions of all the shiploads yet to dock." The "Gordian knot" would not be cut by resolutions passed at Zionist congresses. Only when Jews staked their futures on a life in Palestine forged with their own hands, with no expectation of outside aid, could anything be hoped for:

> However we think of our people's redemption, it will start with individuals and only with them. They may seem pitifully few in terms of the collective, but they will be the basis of anything real that the collective builds...We have committees and organizations. We have projects for the great national future we dream of. We lack only one thing – the main thing: a nation's work as performed by actual men and women *for themselves, for their families, for their own needs*.... Every culmination has its beginning. Show us each coin [of our assets] and we will tell you what we are worth.

Hebrew readers were not used to such language. Zionism had promised its supporters much and demanded little. Now, Berdichevsky was telling it to promise nothing and demand everything. For the Jewish youth of Eastern Europe, this had great resonance. The young, especially in times of inter-generational conflict in which they have cast off adult authority, suffer more often from too few demands on them than from too many. Berdichevsky's call for what soon became known in Zionist circles as *hagshama atsmit*, "self-actualization," spoke to them; it helped shape the ideal of the *halutz*, the Zionist pioneer committed unconditionally to a life of hard work in Palestine. Many of the young *halutzim* who founded the Labor Zionist movement in Palestine in the years after the failed Russian revolution of 1905 were motivated by their reading of Berdichevsky, even though his economic views were far from the utopian socialism they brought with them from Russia. One of them, by his own testimony, was David Ben-Gurion.

And here lies a puzzle. The writer who called on Jews to take personal responsibility for Zionism and scolded Herzl for not settling in Palestine never seems to have thought of settling there himself. Nor, in the years after his 1903 columns in *Ha-Tsefira*, did he encourage others to do so. When the Hebrew author Yosef Chaim Brenner consulted him about such a step in 1909, he advised Brenner to choose Germany instead. Not once until his death in 1921 did he even visit Palestine, although this was not a difficult thing to do in the early twentieth century. In a vituperative article, indeed, he mocked such a visit made by a colleague.

This was in 1913. The visitor was the Hebrew literary critic and historian Yosef Klausner, who had replaced Ahad Ha'am as editor of *Ha-Shiloah* in 1902. In 1912 Klausner spent time in Palestine, where he found a Jewish community markedly more upbeat than the one Berdichevsky had written about a decade previously in *Ha-Tsefira*. Its population was growing and had passed 80,000. Tel-Aviv, established in 1909 as "the first Hebrew city," already had 2,000 inhabitants. The old Rothschild farming colonies were beginning to prosper and had been joined by the first pioneering kibbutzim. Armed Jewish guards were patrolling and defending Jewish fields. Hebrew had left the classroom for the street, where it was winning its battle for everyday dominance. In a three-part series in *Ha-Shiloah* entitled "A World in Emergence," Klausner reported glowingly, although not uncritically, on what he saw. Among the things that impressed him most was the dedication of the young *halutzim*. "Their attitude toward physical labor," he wrote, "is as to something sacred. They engage in it in an ecstasy of purity and awe as Jews once engaged in study and prayer."

Berdichevsky had never liked Klausner. He thought him shallow and pompous and had declined to contribute to *Ha-Shiloah* because of him. Now, he published an attack on Klausner's articles from Palestine that was, for sheer venom, unmatched by anything he had ever written. Appearing in the Warsaw review *Netivot*, this was not a substantively weighty piece. For the most part, it made do with deriding Klausner's self-importance and penchant for hyperbole, as when he had stated that the intersection of the newly laid out Ahad Ha'am and Herzl Streets in Tel-Aviv symbolized the healing of a schism the equal of Peter and Paul's in early Christianity. In the piece's final paragraphs, however, Berdichevsky turned his guns on Tel-Aviv itself. Dwelling on Klausner's description of a festive reception, accompanied by singing and dancing, held for him at Tel-Aviv's new Herzliya High School, Berdichevsky wrote:

> Klausner is dancing! He spins in a circle and hundreds of adorable boys and girls who speak only Hebrew and obey the Hebrew instructions of their dance master sing and circle him merrily; their mood is infectious and he enters into it

and sings along. Indeed, he feels "a complete Hebrew," just like them. Yes, the Israelite hero Klausner... is dancing on historic ground with his own two historic feet while the whole Yishuv – the offspring of a supposed new generation, the bearers of our hopes – dances with him! Their forefathers placed an idol in the Temple and the Tel-Avivians are now dancing around it – and behold, the idol can speak, although it only speaks of itself....

Peter and Paul, Ahad Ha'am and Herzl! We cringe in shame for your doings, we cringe in shame for your Tel-Aviv!

One reads and cringes for Berdichevsky. What possessed him? What made him contemptuously compare the inhabitants of Tel-Aviv, innocently welcoming a distinguished guest from Europe with an evening of Hebrew entertainment – he, who had once celebrated a time "when we worshiped many gods, burning our incense to them on the hills and mountains" – to the ancient Israelites who danced around the Golden Calf and worshiped, according to a rabbinic legend, an idol in Solomon's Temple? What made him write "your doings" (*ma'aseikhem*) and "your Tel-Aviv" (*Tel-Avivkhem*), making it clear that he was disassociating himself not just from Klausner but from all of Zionist Palestine and its supporters? *What?*

8

Arguably, Berdichevsky's anger at Klausner was also envy. *He*, not Klausner, should have been the visitor to Palestine. It was *he* who should have been feted in Tel Aviv with Hebrew songs and dances. The *halutzim* in their tents and fields were responding to *his* call.

But what had kept him from visiting Palestine? Why wasn't he heartened by developments there? Why had he no interest in seeing them?

Clearly, he had none. When the Hebrew author Ya'akov Cohen requested in 1909 that he contribute to a Zionist anthology named, in a tribute to him, "The New Hebrew," he wrote back: "I'm sorry, but you've come too late. I feel nothing but despair [of Zionism] and have no desire to write about it, knowing as I do that we're only sowing weeds." Not only did he overlook the good news from Palestine, he exaggerated the bad. Reports of sexual misconduct in a Zionist institution in Jerusalem in 1911 caused him to note in his diary: "Although I never had much hope for the new Palestine, I didn't think it would turn out so disastrously." A minor scandal was a Zionist disaster!

Various explanations can be given for Berdichevsky's "despair" of Zionism, which was, for him, tantamount to despair of the Jewish future. He can be said to have doubted whether the Jewish people had the will to implement Zionism. To have disdained the Zionist movement's politics and politicians. To have feared, like Yehudah Leib Gordon, its being captured by religion and the rabbis. Yet none of this explains why his pessimism grew greater just as the Zionist project in Palestine was beginning to make headway.

Could it have been that, unconsciously, *he did not want Zionism to succeed*?

"We will either be the last Jews or the first Hebrews," he had declared in 1898–99. But to Ya'akov Cohen he wrote ten years later: "I may as well tell you that the name 'The New Hebrew' does not appeal to me. I never liked rhetorical titles." (As if his declaration had not been rhetorical, too! Had it been worded more carefully to read, "We will be the last Jews unless we are also the first Hebrews," it would have been a less dramatic but more logical expression of secular Zionism.)

Had he changed his mind about religion? Did he mock secular Tel-Aviv because he had come to perceive the shallowness of the post-religious Jew as much as he did the narrow-mindedness of the religious Jew? He could not stop wrestling with tradition. In a sequence of meditations on biblical and rabbinic texts published in 1910 as "Horev," a biblical synonym for Sinai, he had sought to extract from them a universal religion based on the power of direct moral and spiritual experience unmediated by the dos and don'ts of Jewish law. The book attracted little attention. Perhaps by then Berdichevsky's readers, wearied by all his twists and turns, had trouble following him – and indeed "Horev," if followed, led away, via its Jewish texts, from Judaism entirely.

Yet his identification with the Jewish people was total. Brenner, who wrote a long essay on Berdichevsky in 1912, stated there that his sense of Jewishness was so great that he felt that "he and the Jewish people were one" – that he contained in himself every contradiction and conflict of Jewish history, in which there was no period, prominent figure, or tendency that he did not feel to be part of himself. This meant, however, that if, Jewishly, he had reached the end of the road, so had the Jews. And like Mikha'el, like Shimon Ben-Moshe, he felt he had reached it. "Each time I tried pressing on," Shimon says, "I saw the wreckage of Sinai before me." Berdichevsky saw it, too. There was no going forward and no going back.

Such a man would not be the first Hebrew. He could only be the last Jew.

Which was what he wanted to be. He had already wanted to be it in 1903 when he had fought not to circumcise his son. At the time this may have seemed to him a mere matter of defying religious dictates. But circumcision was not necessarily a religious act. It could be considered a badge of secular Jewishness, too. This was how his friend Tsvi Malter chose to think of it. So did many Jews. Berdichevsky declined to.

He would be the last Jew. The Jewish people must not outlive him, not even in a Hebrew-speaking Palestine. Not even in his own son.

9

The last ten years of Berdichevsky's life, which were lived in Berlin, were devoted to scholarship. A man of immense Jewish erudition, he collected Jewish legends from a wide variety of sources and translated them into German in two anthologies, the six-volume *Der Born Judas* ("The Well-spring of Judah"), and the five-volume *Die Sagen der Juden* ("The Sayings of the Jews"). He also wrote several German works, all published posthumously, in which he made the case for some quirky historical theses. In one of these, *Sinai und Gerizim*, he argued that there had been two different biblical traditions of divine revelation, one associated with Moses and one with Joshua, and that the Bible's editors had concealed the rivalry between the two. In another, he looked for the Jewish roots of ancient Christianity. He was still pursuing his anti-essentialist polemic against Ahad Ha'am and the enchaining illusion, as he thought of it, of a monolithic tradition by which Jewishness was judged. Ironically, however, he who once had attacked Jewish life for putting the demands of the past before the needs of the present was now immersed entirely in the past himself.

The nineteenth-century German Jewish bibliographer Moritz Steinschneider had famously remarked that the task of the modern Jewish historian was to provide Judaism with a decent burial. Berdichevsky was now one of the pallbearers. To Brenner he wrote in 1912, explaining his refusal to meet the young Shmuel Yosef Agnon, then newly arrived in Germany and eager to be introduced to him, that he had not only stopped writing in Hebrew but had given up reading what was being written in it:

> I am in a state of absolute despair.... I know nothing at all about our younger Hebrew authors and feel at times that I don't want to know. I am like a man who has been buried alive. What am I supposed to say to those who still think they *are* alive and want to live? Any honest conversation would only be an obstacle in their way, and I have no wish to be one.

Only at the end of his life, as part of a contract for the publication of his collected works, did he return to Hebrew fiction. The result was several long stories and a short novel, "Miriam." All were again set in the shtetl, the historical passing of which took on a frightful personal dimension when the Jewish community of Dubova was annihilated in 1919 during the widespread massacres of Jews by anti-Bolshevik forces in the Ukraine. Of its eight hundred members, fifty survived the slaughter. Among the dead were Berdichevsky's father and one of his brothers.

Finished two days before Berdichevsky died of a worsening heart condition, "Miriam" can be read as a last will and testament. Like Hulda in "In the Valley," the heroine of its title is a dreamy, uncannily beautiful being. Simple yet mysterious, she comes as though from a distant realm that has not given her the words or thoughts to cope with the crude world she has been thrust into. Throughout much of the story, which follows her from childhood through late adolescence while often meandering away from her to other characters, she is not physically present. Even then, however, her magical effect on whoever comes in contact with her, or even glimpses her from afar, is lasting. Powerfully drawn to her, especially as she grows older, men are also confounded by her. Even as they desire her, they are neutered by a feeling of awe.

Miriam is a mystery also to herself, puzzled by her sense of unconnectedness to her surroundings. Orphaned at a young age and taken in by a kind uncle, she has been given, like most girls in the shtetl, no religious education, and she feels closer to the Russian literature she reads than to the Judaism she sees practiced. Turgenev and Dostoyevsky open worlds for her that lie far beyond the shtetl's horizons. Yet she is not, as some of her friends are, in rebellion against the shtetl. She is not by nature a rebel. She is an observer – quiet, self-contained, and yearning for something without knowing what it is.

Much in "Miriam" is familiar to the reader of Berdichevsky's previous fiction: the interweaving of the narrator's consciousness with that of his characters, who at times seem to be thinking the thoughts of a single, endlessly cogitating mind given to abrupt reveries and gnomic utterances; the sudden eruptions in their lives of mythic forces coming from no one knows where; the broad canvas of types ranging from wealthy merchants to poor laborers, pillars of the community to reprobates and outcasts, stern traditionalists to freethinking Maskilim – of one of whom, the tubercular Nachum Sharoni, the narrator says, "I must confess that I owe many of my thoughts to him." Nachum, shortly before dying, shares some of these thoughts with his friend Yerucham. "There is a reason," he says,

> that everyone hates us. The eternal hatred for an eternal people! It comes from our religion. Our prophets drew a line between nation and nation, tribe and tribe. All their preaching was destructive. It fostered hate. It will go down in infamy.

Yerucham protests. "But the prophets are sublime! There's no one like them. They're our pride among the nations."

> Nachum said nothing. He looked at his friend in despair and shook his head.

"Despair": the word occurs often in the late Berdichevsky. The dying Nachum Sharoni is his voice. The celebrated Hebrew author whose family had recently been murdered by a pogromist army was blaming the Jews for their murder! Their guilt went back to the Hebrew prophets – who, by distinguishing between Israel, God's chosen, and the rest of the world, set the stage for all the Jew-hatred to come.

Miriam's uncle dies suddenly. She does not know what to do or where to go. She has been reading the Christian ethical works of Tolstoy. Their words run through her mind – or through the narrator's – or through the universal consciousness that speaks through both:

> The day of God comes to pass through His son. Open wide the windows to the Kingdom of Heaven, cast off the idols you have made. Let each man know the next man's sorrow. Let him share his bread with the distant and lowly and put away all ties of blood and carnal pleasure. Every rich man is poor.

These exhortations cause Miriam to think of Dr. Koch, an elderly, unmarried physician who lives in her town. An ex-"Cantonist," a Jewish boy impressed into long years of military service in the days of Tsar Nikolai, Koch has long forgotten everything he once knew about Judaism and his only religion is now his medical calling. He works long hours in his clinic, where he charges his patients, Jews and Christians alike, no more than they can afford, which is often nothing at all. He is, without making an ideology of it, Tolstoyism in practice.

Miriam makes up her mind. "It happened toward evening," we are told.

> Miriam left her lodgings with a small bundle under her arm. She went to Dr. Koch's front yard, waited for the last patient to leave, and slipped into the waiting room, leaving her bundle in the vestibule. The old man rose from his long day's work and held out a compassionate hand. She lowered her eyes and said, "I'll be your servant. I'll help you with your patients and do all you ask." He kissed her on her forehead and said, "You'll be my daughter. Your kindness to me is great."

The novel ends with this scene. But what, exactly, has it ended with? Not with Christianity, despite its New Testament allusions. Koch has never become a Christian. But neither is he any longer a Jew. He is beyond all religions, beyond all "ties of blood," beyond all differences between men.

Has Miriam found what she is looking for? The answer, to the extent that the endings of novels have answers, is yes. At the very least, she has been redeemed, as Berdichevsky sought to be redeemed in "Horev," from the burden of Jewishness.

The Hebrew poet and critic Simon Halkin wrote of Berdichevsky that he was the most tragic Jewish writer of modern times. But not even my uncle, a great lover of Berdichevsky's work, dared notice – but how could he not have noticed? dared *say* – how far the tragedy in "Miriam" goes. Written at the end of a life that was one long and passionate struggle with his Jewishness, "Miriam" was Berdichevsky's last-minute declaration of surrender, his deathbed letter of resignation from the Jewish people.

And yet, as he wrote in his diary entry for July 1903, there are historic forces to which individuals are subject. Emanuel Berdichevsky, his father's only child, worked for many years as an editor at a Jewish encyclopedia whose termination by the Nazis before its completion led to his settling in Palestine with his mother in 1935. There he changed his family name to Bin-Gorion – the name, used by his father to sign his German books, of a leader of the great rebellion against Rome that ended with the destruction of the Temple. Emanuel translated several of these books into Hebrew and wrote some worshipful accounts of his father and his work. He died in Tel Aviv in 1987, a few years after my conversation with him.

Chapter Seven

The One and Several Mendeles

1

In 1928, the poet Chaim Nachman Bialik gave a talk to a Zionist youth group in Tel Aviv. Its subject was Mendele Mocher Sefarim, "Mendele the Book-seller," the pen-name of the Yiddish and Hebrew writer of fiction Shalom Yakov Abramovich. Bialik had known Mendele well in their years together in Odessa, and there was no Hebrew author whose style he admired more. He called it the *nusah* or "formulary," a norm-setting synthesis of Hebrew's different levels such as modern Hebrew prose fiction had been waiting for, and he never tired of pointing out how it had served him and others as a model. Before getting to it, however, he raised a preliminary issue:

> I find myself wondering how Mendele would have felt to be at this meeting of yours. He is said not to have been a Zionist and it has even been claimed...that he opposed the revival of spoken Hebrew here [in Palestine]. I won't waste your time refuting this absurd notion concerning an author whose life's work facilitated the use of Hebrew as a living tongue. How can one ask if such a man was or wasn't a lover of Hebrew and a Zionist? Whoever pays his annual dues to

the Zionist Organization and mouths some official credo is considered a Zionist ... and *he* has to bring proof of his Zionist credentials?

As an example of such "absurdity," Bialik alluded to the case of Mendele's having been denied honorary membership in the Hebrew Society of Odessa because of his alleged anti-Zionist views. In connection with this, Bialik said, Mendele once related to him an incident that took place when he was a young teacher in the Ukrainian town of Zhitomir. He was walking home with a colleague and their conversation grew so animated that they absent-mindedly entered the wrong house and lay down to rest there. The lady of the house, who knew them both, soon discovered them and asked in astonishment, "What are you doing in my home?" And Bialik went on:

> "That," Mendele said to me, "is how I feel about these people [the Zionists].... The Land of Israel is more mine than theirs. I was raised in it by the Bible from childhood on. It was in my thoughts all the time. And now I'm asked by them, 'What are you doing in our home?'"

This is a charming though in all likelihood imaginatively embellished tale (how absent-minded can even two Jewish intellectuals be?), but both Bialik and Mendele were dodging the question of Mendele's Zionism – Mendele by pretending to have answered it with a comic anecdote and Bialik by claiming that a Hebrew author of Mendele's stature could not have failed to be a Zionist. And yet this simply wasn't so. There were major Hebrew authors of the late nineteenth and early twentieth centuries who did not consider themselves Zionists. Yehuda Leib Gordon was one. Berdichevsky, in the latter part of his life, was another. Yosef Chaim Brenner, as we shall see, was yet another. Others could be mentioned, too. The question of Mendele's Zionism is not laid to rest so easily.

2

Not that Bialik didn't have a point. Zionism and early modern Hebrew literature were natural partners. Without Hebrew literature, Zionism would never have become a significant force in East-European Jewish life, nor could Hebrew have been revived as a spoken language in Palestine.

Without Zionism, Hebrew literature had no future readership to look forward to. Their relationship was symbiotic.

Zionism stemmed from two distinct historical situations, one Western and Central-European and one East-European, from which emerged a single movement in the late 1890s under the leadership of Herzl. Hebrew was of vital importance only to the "Easterners." Few of the "Westerners" had a functional knowledge of it or a visceral attachment to it or to the Jewish culture it embodied. They had been raised in non- or laxly observant Jewish homes, had been educated in German, French, or English, and felt thoroughly European. What convinced them of the need for a Jewish homeland was the impossibility, as they reluctantly came to perceive it, of even fully acculturated Jews like themselves being accepted by an irredeemably anti-Semitic European society. Though ultimately despairing of this hope, they did not think it had been an unworthy one. It had simply been unrealistic, and Zionism was the conclusion they drew from this.

Such was not the point of view of the Zionists of Eastern Europe. Nearly all of them grew up in Orthodox Jewish families, received an old-fashioned Jewish education with its strong Hebrew component, spoke Yiddish as their first language, and had entrenched Jewish identities. Assimilation was never their goal. Yet by the 1880s and '90s, the same process of Jewish acculturation that had been taking place in the West for the better part of the century was making marked inroads in the East, where the feared erosion of Jewish identity fueled Zionist thought as much as did anti-Semitism. In the modern European nation-state, the Easterners understood, there would be less and less room for a minority culture like their own.

These two differing perspectives formed the basis for the split between Ahad Ha'am and Herzl that reached its peak in the 1903 Uganda debate. Yet the two clashing forces were not equal. Prior to World War I, Zionism was a movement with a small following in the West, most of whose Jews still believed in the possibility of integration in their native countries. While Westerners like Herzl and Nordau were Zionism's generals, its army was in the East. There alone could be found hundreds of thousands of Jews ready to rally to its cause. And this was also the cause of Hebrew, because unless the Zionist project succeeded in creating a Hebrew-speaking, or at least Hebrew-reading-and-writing, society in

Palestine, the only Hebrew readers left in a generation or two would be the occasional scholar and, in Gordon's bitter words, "the Pharisees [who] expound the laws of the bathroom," Orthodox Jews with no interest in a secular Hebrew literature. Under such circumstances, one might indeed ask as Bialik did: How could a Hebrew writer not have been a Zionist?

And how, especially, could he not have been one when the East-European Jewish writer who wasn't but wished to write in a Jewish language now had the alternative of Yiddish, a spoken tongue with a far larger potential audience and seemingly brighter prospects for survival? Although it had always been the vernacular of Eastern Europe's Jews, Yiddish had seldom been used for serious literary purposes. Traditionally, literature had been the sole province of Hebrew, a facility in which was a mark of the educated Jew. Yiddish was commonly referred to throughout the period of the Haskalah as *zhargon*, a Judeo-German patois that had its rightful place as a tool of instruction or entertainment for the Hebraically illiterate (a category that included nearly all women and most men), but that was unsuited for anything higher. Its legitimation as a literary language in the last third of the nineteenth century resulted from a number of factors, such as a rejection, encouraged by the spread of revolutionary ideas in the Russian empire, of the Haskalah's elitist attitude toward the Jewish masses, and the cultural upgrading of other East-European vernaculars like Ukrainian and Lithuanian by their association with nationalist movements. By the century's end, the relationship between Yiddish and Hebrew, until then one of a mutually accepted division of labor between speech and writing, the Jewish home and the Jewish text, and the common and the cultivated life, had become one of competition – and this competition began, for all intents and purposes, not only with Mendele but within him.

Born in Lithuania, Shalom Yakov Abramovich lived his adult life in the Ukraine, first in Kamanetsk-Podolsk, then in Berdichev and Zhitomir, and finally in Odessa, to which he moved in 1881. He began his literary career in Hebrew in the 1860s, writing essays of social criticism, a book of popular science, and a work of fiction, "Fathers and Sons," that borrowed its title from Turgenev. Yet before the '60s were over, he switched to Yiddish and wrote his three major novels in it: *Dos Kleyne*

Menshele, "The Little Manikin"; *Fishke der Krummer*, "Fishke the Lame"; and *Dos Vinshfingerl*, "The Wishing Ring." In a Hebrew literary memoir penned long afterwards, he explained why he did this:

> It was then that I consulted with myself and thought: Here I am, doing my best to help my fellow Jews by giving them stories with Jewish content in the Holy Tongue – yet most of them don't understand this tongue and speak only Judeo-German. What good are all an author's thoughts and exertions if they are of no use to his own people? The question of whom I was laboring for gave me no peace and was a cause of great perplexity. Yiddish in those days was an empty receptacle. There was nothing in it of any worth – nothing but wordy trash penned by lisping nobodies. Women and poor folk read this matter without discernment while all others, even if knowing no other language, were embarrassed to be caught looking at it lest they be taken for simpletons.... Our Hebrew authors had a prideful contempt for Yiddish and looked down on it.... It disconcerted me to think that I would be disgracing myself with such a bastard child – and indeed, I was taken to task by the lovers of Hebrew for dishonoring myself by adopting it. Yet the desire to be useful overcame any supposition of honor and I decided, come what may, to have pity on Yiddish, the unwanted illegitimate daughter, and do something in it for my people.

This "something" was a body of work that marked the start of modern Yiddish literature and would remain one of its greatest achievements. Already in "The Little Manikin," Abramovich introduced the narrator who was to appear in his fiction again and again: Mendele the bookseller, an itinerant peddler of Yiddish and Hebrew chapbooks, prayer books, hymnals, penny dreadfuls, and works of Haskalah literature who drives his horse and wagon back and forth through the Ukrainian countryside between the hamlet of Tunayadevka, the town of Kabtsansk, and the city of Glupsk, the three imaginary locations in and between which his adventures take place. The novel begins:

"What's yer name?" That's the first thing one Jew asks another, even a total stranger, as soon as how-de-do's are exchanged.... And so I know that this Yiddish debut of my tales will be met before all else with a "What's yer name, friend?"

Well, then, it's Mendele! That, gentlemen, is how I was named for my great-grandfather on my mother's side, Reb Mendele Moskver, God rest his soul. He was called Moskver because he once went all the way to Moscow on some business, which won him great renown in his little neck of the woods. From then on he was thought so wise in the ways of the world that no one filled out an application or government form without first consulting him. But that's not what I was about to tell you.

The difference between such prose and Abramovich's stiff Haskalah Hebrew that preceded it is striking. Its Yiddish is casual, conversational, loquaciously off-hand. Although its speaker is not uneducated, he puts on no educated airs. He likes to ramble and digress, letting the natural flow of his language and its associations take him where it wants to go, as does the horse whose reins he sometimes drops. He is always ready to stop and gab with the first person he meets, to listen to his stories and swap them for his own. Yet he is also a keen observer whose jovial humor softens but never blurs the biting edges of his commentary. Yiddish brought Abramovich closer to the common Jews he wrote about; it made him more tolerant of them, even more loving; but it also led him to be more acutely aware of their shortcomings and comical traits than he was when looking down on them from the Haskalah's patronizing heights. The provincial Jews who think that a single trip to Moscow makes a man an expert in the world's affairs may be endearing yokels, but they pay a high price for their innocence in terms of the backwardness it condemns them to.

Yiddish freed Abramovich. It allowed him to speak in his own voice and at the same time in the voice of all East-European Jewry, which had never before been given such a hearing. All the bizarreness, the abjectness, the stubbornness, the suffering, and the powers of endurance of Jewish life in the Pale of Settlement as though spoke through him. For his readers he became Mendele, a Jew like themselves. The persona of the genial, sharp-witted bookseller merged in their minds with the figure of the author. Though the more sophisticated of them understood the distinction between the two well enough, some of them, too, might have been surprised to learn that S.Y. Abramovich had never peddled books in his life.

Mendele wrote exclusively in Yiddish for the next twenty years and enjoyed great popularity. Although there were other talented Yiddish novelists and dramatists of the period, such as Yisroel Aksenfeld, Yitzchok Yoyl Linetsky, Shloyme Ettinger, and Avrom Goldfaden, none were of Mendele's stature. Only when he was joined in the 1880s by Shalom Aleichem and Yehuda Leib Peretz did Yiddish have authors of the first rank beside him.

And precisely then, in 1887, Mendele returned to Hebrew, into which he eventually translated most of his major Yiddish works. His literary memoir stops short of this turning point and throws no light on it. Did it represent a sudden decision? The fulfillment of a commitment to a first love that he had known all along he would one day keep? The realization that only in Hebrew would his work be part of the classical corpus of Jewish literature? Although members of the next generation of Yiddish writers would challenge Hebrew's place in Jewish life, a gauntlet formally thrown down at the much-publicized Czernowitz conference of 1908 that asserted Yiddish's parity, if not supremacy, as a "national language" of the Jewish people, this had never been Mendele's view. His choice of Yiddish as a literary medium had not been an ideological one. As a matter of principle, Hebrew always came first for him.

Why did he return to it when he did? It has been suggested that he was influenced by his move to Odessa, with its vibrant Hebrew cultural scene, and by the first stirrings of Zionism in the early 1880s. Perhaps, too, he had foreseen by then that Yiddish, though on the verge of a great literary flowering, was itself living on borrowed time. Already in the 1880s, it was being deserted by speakers switching to Russian, Polish, and other languages. (A telltale case was that of Shalom Aleichem, who raised his children in Russian. And Mendele had bitterer evidence of Russian Jewish assimilation than that: his own son had converted to Christianity.) Zionism might give new life to Hebrew, but what, once acculturation in Eastern Europe ran its course, could perpetuate Yiddish?

The idea of an autonomous, Yiddish-speaking society in a multicultural post-Tsarist Eastern Europe, propagated by the Yiddisher Arbiter Bund, the Jewish revolutionary party founded in 1897, crystallized only a decade after Mendele went back to writing in Hebrew and could not have influenced him in the 1880s even had he taken it seriously.

The Hebrew that he now wrote, starting with his story *B'Seter Ra'am*, "In the Hidden Place of Thunder" (the title comes from the book of Psalms), was different from his Haskalah Hebrew of the 1860s. Without uprooting Hebrew from its classical matrix, he found ways of transferring to it the freedom he had gained from Yiddish. He made of it something folksier, more flexible, more imitative of the intonations and twists-and-turns of Jewish speech; while drawing on and integrating the entire gamut of Jewish sources, he built on the grid of the homier language of the rabbis rather than of the grander style of the Bible; in alluding to both, he did not so much invoke their authority or associational wealth as play them off ironically against the reality he was describing, contrasting a storied past with a fallen present in order to emphasize the rupture between them, the gulf behind their façade of linguistic and symbolic continuity. His Hebrew was, as he himself said of it, a "new creation."

Just as the opening paragraphs of "The Little Manikin" introduced Mendele the bookseller to the Yiddish reader, so those of "In the Hidden Place of Thunder" reintroduced him to the Hebrew one as the chronicler of Kislon or "Foolsville," the Hebrew Glupsk:

> Take Mendele's word: the city of Kislon, with which my tale begins, is second to none, since wherever Jews live in the land of the Tsar they are Kislonites after a fashion. Not without reason is Kislon renowned as a Hebrew cosmopolis; for who of us cannot, in one degree or another, trace his lineage back to it, and who does not possess a per centum at least of its virtues? If you, my friends, were not born there yourselves, your parents most certainly were, and if Kislonite blood does not flow in each lode of your veins, it is sure to be found in some lobe of your brains. Yea, I was young and now I am old, says the Psalmist, and never have I met a Jew who did not, in deed or demeanor, be his business

with man or with God, remind me of Kislon. Let him be rich or poor, a scholar or a bumpkin, the Kislonite in him sticks out as clearly as the head of a nail from a wall.

***

Let the word then go forth by land and by sea to our brothers near and far that Mother Kislon, praise be, is alive! Gather around me, dear readers, while I tell you about her Jews: of their coming and goings, their customs and costumes, their cogitations, cerebrations, and relations. Listen and do not spurn an old woman, for she is as spry as ever and her ways and manners live on among her children. Attend while I sketch of her so true a likeness that you will see her before your very eyes!

Despite its shedding of many Haskalah mannerisms (he was to discard still more of these as the second phase of his Hebrew career progressed), Mendele's "newly created" Hebrew remained in a higher register than his Yiddish. Yet it had a quality of spontaneously gener-ated narrative, and of that ambling storytelling style known in Russian literature as *skaz,* that had never been achieved in Hebrew before. Nor was it a Hebrew satirically translated from or corrupted by Yiddish like that of Perl's Hasidim. Rich and resourceful, it seemed to emerge from some deep structure in the Jewish mind that had produced Hebrew and Yiddish alike.

Whereas nineteenth-century literary Hebrew, both in the Haskalah and post-Haskalah periods, sought to avoid anything suggestive of Yiddish, Mendele's Hebrew put Yiddish to work. One simple example will have to suffice. When Mendele the bookseller says "Mother Kislon, praise be, is alive," the words translated as "praise be" are *barùkh ha-shem,* literally, "blessed is the Name." Pronounced *bórukhashem,* this was a Hebrew-derived phrase that Yiddish speakers used routinely in a wide variety of situations. (It was, for instance, their standard way of saying "Fine, thank you" in reply to the question "How are you?") Precisely because of this, it was shunned before Mendele as a Yiddishism by Hebrew literary prose, which stuck to "purer" Hebrew expressions like *ha-shevah la'el,* "praise be to God" – and

Mendele the bookseller's use of it helps give his introduction to "In the Hidden Place of Thunder" its familiar, just-between-me-and-you quality. It was Mendele's embrace of the symbiotic relationship of the two languages that made Bialik say, "Mendele worked a great miracle by knocking down the wall between Yiddish and Hebrew. He as though ran a siphon between them so that, like Siamese twins, or like Hebrew and Aramaic in antiquity, they shared a single life."

Kislon is an East-European Jewish microcosm. So, too, is the smaller shtetl of Kabtsiel or "Beggarsburg" in which the second half of "In the Hidden Place of Thunder" takes place. It is in the hideaway of Kabtsiel that the thunderbolt of the story's title strikes in the form of a pogrom, one of many to hit the Jews of the Ukraine in the outbreaks of 1881. And it is there, too, that the issue of Zionism first appears in Mendele's work. Dazed by the pogrom's destruction, a group of Kabtsielers meet in a synagogue to discuss what is to be done. One suggests that they try their luck elsewhere in the Pale of Settlement.

> "A lot of good that will do!" groaned some of the group. "There's such poverty now in the Pale that you can't earn a living anywhere, by hook or by crook. We have lots of room in our own graveyard. Why go off to die somewhere else?"
>
> "We need to get out of the Pale, out of Russia!" chimed in others.
>
> "'And the children shall return to their own border!'" came the cry.
>
> "Let's have some quiet!" shouted Leml. "Gimpl has the floor."

Gimpl is the group's acknowledged leader and reputedly its keenest mind. To the shouted verse from the prophet Jeremiah, he now adds another from Isaiah that has become a slogan of the new Lovers of Zion movement:

> A great whistle ran through the room, the sum of all the smaller ones with which everyone hushed his neighbor. "Yes, indeed," said Gimpl. "'O house of Jacob, come ye and let us go.' On the

one hand, I would say about that … shh, gentlemen, shh! Stop buzzing like flies! That's what I would say on the one hand. But on the other hand, to get up and go calls for get-go…. My point is that…"

"What's he saying?" the back benches asked those nearer to Gimpl. "Let us in on it."

"We don't know ourselves," answered the benches in front. "It isn't clear. He says one thing and then the other. He has one foot in the Pale and one out."

Gimpl has the ability to sound thoughtful while saying nothing and we are meant to laugh at him. When we are done laughing, however, we need to realize that he has expressed Mendele the author's position on Zionism rather well.

3

The subject of Zionism recurs more prominently in Mendele's stories "Those Assembled Below," "In the Time of the Quake," and "The Hair" – the former two written in the 1890s, the latter in 1905.

"Those Assembled Below," *B'yeshiva shel mata* in Hebrew, is the second half of a two-part work and follows "Those Assembled Above." The titles are a comic allusion to the prelude to the Kol Nidrei prayer on Yom Kippur in which the cantor asks permission from the powers in heaven and the congregation in the synagogue to proceed with the service. In our story, however, "Above" refers to the attic of an inn in which Mendele the bookseller and his fellow wayfarers have spent the night hiding from – once again – a pogrom, while "Below" is the ground floor to which they repair in the morning once the danger has passed.

When they descend to it, an argument breaks out between two of them: Ben-Tsiyon, a young Lover of Zion who announces that he is on his way to Palestine, and Yisrol, an elderly Jew who can't understand why he is going there. Ben-Tsiyon explains that Yisrol's generation has no comprehension of Zionism because it has no dreams of a better life. It is so downtrodden that its only ambition is to survive. His own generation, Ben-Tsiyon says, refuses to accept such passivity, and since life in Russia is intolerable, "My friends and I have gotten together.... We're off to the Land of Israel to till its soil and restore our people's former glory!"

Yisrol responds by accusing Ben-Tsiyon and his friends of wanting to preempt God's redemption. They are, he says, like "the children at a wedding who run to the wedding canopy ahead of the musicians, the bride, the groom, and all their families." Mendele the bookseller likes this comparison. He has just survived a pogrom himself; what is wrong, he wonders, with survival? "Listen here," he tells Ben-Tsiyon. "You and your friends can go where you want, but don't think so highly of yourselves.... Leave God's Jews alone. Don't mock them or their Judaism!"

Ben-Tsiyon protests that it isn't Judaism he is against but the "corrupted form of it that has become the Jewish religion" in the Diaspora. Yisrol is shocked. "Reb Mendele!" he cries. "How can you listen to such talk and not speak up?" Mendele, however, goes off to a corner to think – and as he does he wonders whether Ben-Tsiyon may not be right. Jewish life in exile has become so degraded that "there's no longer any telling the good from the bad in it." A moment later, however, feeling ashamed of such thoughts, Mendele wraps himself in his prayer shawl and turns to his morning prayers.

His confusion is only about to grow greater. He prays, lies down for a nap, and wakes to find that the debate has been joined by others. One of them sounds like Yehuda Leib Gordon. "Our spiritual liberation must precede our physical liberation!" he proclaims. For Zionism to succeed, Jewish life in the Diaspora must first be radically reformed. Otherwise, it will simply reduplicate itself in Palestine.

"That's so!" Mendele thinks.

"On the contrary!" retorts Ben-Tsiyon, as though speaking for Moshe Leib Lilienblum. "Physical redemption comes first! When the Jews dwell in their own land as they did in olden times, their spiritual level will rise."

"Truer words were never spoken," Mendele reflects.

Yisrol intervenes in the voice of anti-Zionist religious Orthodoxy. "There's no Redemption without a Redeemer!" he shouts. "And the Redeemer will come when God wills."

"You can't argue with that," Mendele tells himself. "The Talmud and the rabbis say as much."

Someone else takes a position like Ahad Ha'am's. "Political Zionism?" he asks. "Forget about it! It wants to achieve everything in one go and achieves nothing." Zionism must proceed slowly and build on the past so as to conserve "the national spirit."

"That fellow knows what he's talking about!" Mendele muses.

And so it goes. Mendele agrees with every opinion he hears, even if it contradicts what he has agreed with a minute ago. The question of Zionism, it appears, is so complicated that everything said about it is true.

The shock of the 1881 pogroms, and the Lover of Zion movement that grew out of it, provide the background for "In the Time of the Quake," too. To the figure of Mendele the bookseller is now added a second main character, Leib the schoolteacher, a fellow Kabtsieler. So many of Kabtsiel's residents have left town in the pogrom's wake that Leib has lost a large share of his pupils and can no longer make ends meet. Not, Mendele comments,

> that Jews aren't brainy enough to make a living from anything –
> but for that they need luck. As the saying goes: even a broom can
> shoot like a rifle if God wills it. The problem with Leib was that he
> and luck did not go together. And so, when the call went forth, "To
> the colonies [founded in Palestine], O Jews"... our schoolteacher
> said, "Amen! Count me in, every inch of me."

Mendele, whose book business is doing poorly too, is persuaded by Leib to join him and the two set out together for Odessa, where there is a committee to aid emigrants departing from there for Palestine. That two middle-aged Jews with no special skills might be ineligible for such assistance does not occur to Leib, who explains to Mendele what vast sums the committee must have at its disposal:

> "How many Jews are there in Russia?" Leib asked, looking at me
> while deep in thought…. "Let's say five or six million. If each of
> them pays a ruble a year in Zionist dues, that's six million rubles.
> In fifty years, that's three hundred million. Add the interest and

it's a billion! The numbers are simple. What Jew wouldn't give a ruble for such a grand idea? And that's not even counting the rich Jews who'll give a hundred times more…. What do you say, Reb Mendele? Won't we walk out of there flying high?"

Mendele's only reply is to cover himself with his blanket and fall asleep. He doesn't know what to think of Leib's arithmetic. There are times, he confesses, in which he feels that he is "not one Mendele but two, each a separate creature living with the other in a single body." One of the two gullibly believes all he is told about Zionism, while the other is of little faith.

In the days when troubles accrued and Kabtsiel was in dire straits, the believing Mendele had the upper hand…. Thinking of the colonies and imagining a new life there, he sold his horse, ditched his book business, became Leib the schoolteacher's partner, and set out with him to cross the sea…. No sooner had they reached Odessa, however, than the doubting Mendele got the better of it and gave the believing Mendele a good tongue-lashing for all his misprisions. "You old codger!" he scolded. "What on earth made you think you could accomplish something so far beyond your years and powers? How does an old man like you propose to give birth to himself and become young again?"

The doubting Mendele regards his situation as symbolic of the Jewish people's. To an acquaintance met by him on an Odessan street, he says:

The Jews are never on time. They gulp their food and drink too quickly, take too long to settle their debts and accounts, and marry, have children, and grow old prematurely. They're either too early or too late. At first they suffered insult and indignity because they were ahead of their times, and now they're hounded and harassed, so their enemies tell them, because they're behind their times. What fools we are to think we can set the clock back and return to what we outgrew long ago! Mind you, I'm simply explaining what got into me and made me think I could do what I'm too old for.

What he is too old for, the Jewish people is too. This the doubting Mendele does not doubt.

The believing Mendele doesn't give up. On his way with Leib to the committee to meet its chairman, a man named Karliner (the Odessa Committee was headed in the 1890s by Leon Pinsker, and the Belarussian village of Karlin was next to Pinsk), he rehearses a Zionist speech that he hopes will open purse strings. However, he relates, "the minute I entered Karliner's room, the believer was hushed by the doubter and forgot all he wanted to say."

It is the kindly Karliner who ends up giving the speech. The committee's means, he explains to Leib and Mendele, are limited and Zionism is a project in need of youthful energies, not of men like them. This doesn't mean, though, that they can't contribute to it. Just as individuals need to be educated, so do peoples – and if it is up to the young to build a new Jewish society in Palestine, it is up to the old to be their teachers. "Reb Mendele!" Karliner says. "I'll be frank. I'm told that all your life you've dealt in books…Why abandon your trade now, when we could use people like you to help spread useful knowledge?"

Mendele, relieved to renounce an adventure that he has come to realize is a size too big for him, is easily convinced. So is Leib, who has discovered to his delight that Odessa has an active Hebrew Society that wishes to hire him as an instructor. He has even begun to talk to Mendele, to the latter's great annoyance, in the stilted Hebrew of a heder teacher. ("I beg you, Reb Leib," Mendele pleads, "speak Yiddish! Why torture yourself and me with your weird palaver?") Tutoring young Zionists in Odessa is a step up from teaching children in Kabtsiel and certainly easier than going to Palestine.

Leib remains in Odessa and Mendele returns to Kabtsiel. "I felt the pleasure," he writes, "of a frog when, coming home exhausted from its escapades on dry land, it jumps into its native muck and sinks into it up to its ears." He even buys back his old horse, haggard from overwork and undernourishment, from the water carrier he sold her to.

I couldn't bear to see her wretched state, which was all because of me, and I pledged to redeem her on the spot.

And so I found peace, as did my horse. I reclaimed her from her harsh servitude and harnessed her once more to the wagon of learning, and now she pulls it as before, transporting my books from place to place for the enlightenment of all Israel.

4

Mendele the bookseller's aversion to speaking Hebrew was apparently shared by Mendele the author, to judge by his poor relations with the Hebrew Society of Odessa. He had labored to forge a literary language that, however talkative in tone, could hardly be improvised or reproduced off-the-cuff. To have to struggle to speak a crude version of it for the gratification of a club of Hebraists would have been painful.

Yet as readers, we are left as confused by the debate in "In the Time of the Quake" as Mendele the bookseller is by the argument in "Those Assembled Below." On the one hand, the naive enthusiasm of Leib and the "believing Mendele" for starting a new life in Palestine is ridiculed in the story, in which the "doubting Mendele" seems astute by comparison. On the other hand, the figure of Karliner is a sympathetically drawn one, and while Leib and Mendele are disabused by him of their Zionist fantasies, the roles they return to at the story's end are the ones in which, so he tells them, they can best serve Zionism's goals. Is the message we are to meant to come away with that these goals, if realistically set, are attainable? Or are we supposed to understand that Mendele's contented return to his "native muck" represents the inertia of a Jewish world that Zionism can never hope to transform?

Jewish stuckness is a central theme in the most idea-driven of Mendele's fictional works, his short novel "The Mare," published in Yiddish as *Di Klyatshe* in 1873 and, in a Hebrew reworking, as *Susati* in 1909. Zionism as a movement did not exist when *Di Klyatshe* was written, nor did Mendele update the novel by introducing it as a subject in *Susati,* to which he did add other material. Yet if one wishes better to understand his attitude toward Zionism, "The Mare" provides a valuable clue to it.

The novel (my summary of it draws on both its Yiddish and Hebrew versions) begins with a young man, named Yisrol like the character in "Those Assembled Below," who, constricted by the narrow confines of the shtetl he has grown up in, aspires to study at a university. Having received a traditional rabbinic education, he has subsequently read widely in the literature of the Haskalah, and he wants to get out into the world and do some good in it. He is also a member of his local chapter of the Society for the Prevention of Cruelty to Animals, and one day, spying a bony old nag being stoned and tormented by a gang of jeering boys and their dogs, he comes to her aid and rescues her. Great is his astonishment when she thanks him in human language and informs him that she is a transmogrified prince, a king's son imprisoned in a horse's body. This misfortune, she relates, befell the prince long ago while living in Egypt, whose ruler, jealous of his noble attributes, had the royal wizards bewitch him. Subsequently, an even greater magician came along and restored his human form, which he retained for as long as the magician's followers held sway. Upon their decline, however, he was made a horse again by his enemies, and ever since then, the mare tells Yisrol, he, or rather she, has wandered from land to land, driven by cruel taskmasters, exploited, maltreated, beaten, and finally, too feeble and decrepit to work, abandoned to her own devices and the taunts of urchins.

By now it is obvious that the great magician is Moses; that his followers are the prophets and early rabbis; and that the mare is an allegory of the Jewish people in exile – obvious, that is, to everyone but Yisrol, who has a real horse on his hands, if one with an unusual history. As a caring soul and animal rights supporter, he feels obligated to help her, and thus begins a relationship that, were it between two human beings, would have to be called neurotic. Yisrol becomes the mare's protector, leading her from place to place in the hope of finding her a safe haven while facing trying situations, as when he is caught with her in a violent thunderstorm in a forest. Determined to change her life, he seeks to convince her to take better care of herself, recover her health, attend to her grooming and appearance, behave like a thoroughbred, learn to make herself useful again, and present herself in a way that will earn the world's respect and cause it to treat her as an equal among horses. As unfair to her as it has been, she, too, bears some of the responsibility for her fate.

The mare, though happy to accept whatever food or shelter Yisrol can give her, shrugs off all his advice. For every one of his reasons why she needs to change, she has a reason why this won't do any good. It's too late; she's too old to learn new ways; she won't be treated any differently if she does; Yisrol is an innocent who doesn't understand that the world is an inherently cruel place in which there is no room for ideals of justice or equality. Not only does she fail to show him the least gratitude, she scoffs at the notion that she owes him any. He is only behaving as he is, she tells him, to satisfy his sense of duty and heighten his own self-esteem, so why feel indebted to him?

Frustrated by the mare's refusal to reform herself, or at least to acknowledge his nobility of purpose, yet unable to stop pitying her, Yisrol refuses to admit defeat, even though the futility of his efforts should have been evident to him from the start. Already in one of the novel's early scenes, the mare has annoyed him by sprawling contentedly on the ground and munching the hay he has brought her. How can she lie there with such equanimity, he wonders, "as if feeling nothing, without realizing the bitterness of her situation?" Suddenly, though, she lets out a sigh and he thinks:

> That's a good sign. Sigh, my mare, sigh! In your sighs I hear the unhappy prince wanting mightily to have his human face back. I hear him cry: "I'm still alive, I still feel all a man feels!"

But then,

> I took a look and saw that my mare had no hay left. She had eaten it all down to the last straw. Aha, I thought: so that's all her sigh was about! She sighed because her belly wasn't full yet.... Give her some more hay, a bit of grass or oats, and she'll be happy.

The mare notices Yisrol's distress.

> "You're upset," she said with a glance at me. "Don't you like my company?"

"I'm a human being," I answered pointedly. "I have feelings. I can reason. Maybe it pleases you to lie in the dirt, but it doesn't please me to see you there."

"It's easy for you to talk," she said with a toss of her head. "Anyone else forced to be a horse for so many years and to put up with so much – to be homeless, to suffer every misfortune, to be beaten within an inch of their life – would have lost their feelings and reason long ago. They would have lost their power of speech and become a dumb beast."

"Get to the point," I interrupted. "Do you like wallowing in dirt or don't you?"

"And what if I do? It's better than what came before. There was a time when I was so driven from place to place that I couldn't rest for a second. My enemies kept after me until I was on my last legs. Now, at least I can catch my breath. It's comfortable here in the dirt and I can rest my weary bones."

"And the blows you were given today by those boys? The dogs they set on you? Have you forgotten them? Did you like that, too?"

"I tell you, it's better than before."

The mare, we come to realize, is not the only allegorical figure in the novel. Yisrol is one, too. He is the Haskalah personified in its well-meaning striving to get the Jewish people to improve itself – and the Jewish people does not want to be improved. It wants, immobilized by the inertial force of centuries, to remain as it is. As long as it has enough to eat and a roof over its head, it is satisfied. Once it was a prince and now it's a horse? Fine, once it was a prince. But what good does it do to long for a past that is gone forever? It is the nineteenth century, and the nineteenth century, though far from perfect, is a lot better than the centuries that preceded it. Even its anti-Semitism is mild by comparison.

Indeed, as represented by Yisrol in "The Mare," the Haskalah is more deluded than the Jewish people it sets out to reform, for whereas this people, however benighted, at least knows who it is, its reformers do not. They think they can force the hand of history to move it to a place it can't be moved to.

Of course, nothing remains in one place forever. Once dislodged, however, there is no knowing where it will end up. This is a point made in the last part of the novel, which Mendele expanded in its Hebrew version. In it the mare is abruptly replaced as Yisrol's antagonist by the figure of Ashmodai, Jewish legend's ruler of the underworld. Like Goethe's Mephisto, who introduces himself to Faust as "the spirit that negates, / And rightly so, for all that comes to be / Itself deserves to die," Ashmodai is the principal of antithesis. He appears to Yisrol with the proclamation:

> "I am the power that always stands against my counterpart's. We defy each other, attract and repel, usher in what the other ushers out and oppose each other in all things, so that by our contending, all that is new comes into being. I am the Nothing from which, as though out of thin air, is born the Something. I am the Lord of Darkness – I am Satan – I am King of the Devils!"

History, Ashmodai explains, is diabolically dialectic. No undertaking produces its intended result. Everything is thwarted by a countervailing force, and the battle between them, which creates by destroying and destroys in creating, moves history forward in unpredictable ways.

Ashmodai illustrates this by soaring high into the air with Yisrol and showing him, far below, a bucolic vista of peaceful fields and villages. "O happy land!" Yisrol exclaims. "O happy folk who live in such sweet tranquility!"

> Ashmodai regarded me with a smile and said nothing. I looked silently back at him. Then yanking me by my beard, he forced me to look down again.
>
> I looked – and was aghast. "Oh, no!" I cried bitterly. How had such a beautiful paradise turned into a desert? Fire had scorched its green fields…. There wasn't a human sound, not a bleat of sheep or cattle. Not a bird, not a beast – nothing was left!
>
> "You can thank the Enlightenment for that," Ashmodai said in his sarcastic manner. "It came to this country unbidden with its weapons of war to educate the common people – and when

they didn't want its kind gift because they preferred the ways of their forefathers, it taught them the meaning of progress with guns and explosives."

Ashmodai is referring to the Napoleonic wars, fought in the name of the ideals of the French Revolution, the intellectual heritage of Montesquieu, Diderot, Voltaire, and Rousseau. And with them came a second, industrial revolution that, like the political one, promised a better future and delivered in some respects a worse one. Ashmodai continues:

"I'm thrilled to see the maw of the Enlightenment devour the world! There wasn't enough wood for it to burn, so it burrowed deep into the earth to exhume from their graves the bones of ancient plants, the coal that does its work for it. And when it has depleted the earth's womb it will look to the sun and sky and pillage the fire of God's chariot and the lightning of the clouds He rides, yoking them to its machines and driving them with electric whips to turn wheels and dynamos. All its thousands of factories with their chimneys will be the altars whose incense rises to the God of Mammon, Business, and the machinations of Commerce. Their smoke will desiccate every heart, consume every emotion, turn all into merchandise. Love, friendship, piety, religion, human charity – all goods to buy and sell…. One day, so I trust, the whole earth will be mine!"

This passage exists only in the Hebrew, not the Yiddish, version of "The Mare." Written when the optimism of the nineteenth century had yielded to a darker mood, it hinges on a pun not possible in Yiddish, for the Hebrew term used by Mendele for the European Enlightenment (*di oykflerung* in Yiddish) is the same as the term for its Jewish offshoot: *ha-haskala*.

Clearly, Mendele was not saying in *Susati* that the Hebrew Haskalah had anything to do with the wars of Europe or with the social and environmental destructiveness of nineteenth-century industrial capitalism. Rather, he wrote this passage to suggest that the same law of unintended consequences manifested in the Enlightenment's impact on European society also applied to the Haskalah's effects on Jewish life. The forces of modernity shaking the world of East-European Jewry at the start of the twentieth century were unforeseen by the would-be Maskilic benefactors of their people who had sounded the call for modernization fifty or one hundred years earlier. Worsening anti-Semitism, economic pauperization, mass emigration, quickening assimilation, the drastic weakening of Jewish tradition, the spread of Zionism and of revolutionary ideas – what Maskil in the days of Perl and Mapu could have predicted such things, let alone that some of them would be partly the Haskalah's doing?

Beware of the temptation to be a benefactor: this is the warning with which "The Mare" ends. As Ashmodai is conducting Yisrol on their aerial tour, word reaches them of the death of the *ba'al tova* of Yisrol's shtetl (literally, the "do-gooder"; the Yiddish and Hebrew word denotes any religious functionary, communal official, or wealthy patron who uses, or pretends to use, his power and authority to help others). A successor to the dead man must be found at once and Ashmodai nominates Yisrol. Yisrol is dismayed.

> "I don't want to be and can't be a *ba'al tova*!" I cried bitterly, shaking all over. "Have pity on me and choose someone else. There are so many Jews who would love to have the job – the town is bursting with them. Take one of them and not me!"
>
> "That's enough out of you, Yisrol! [Ashmodai says] I don't need your advice. I've made up my mind and it won't do any good to say no."
>
> "But what makes you think I'm your man?" I pleaded loudly. "I'm not a practical type and I'm not suited for the work you have in mind. I know much shrewder people than myself who could do it far better."

Yisra'el knows how busy feathering their own nests at the public's expense most of the *ba'al tovas* of the shtetl are and is horrified by the thought of becoming one of them. What he fails to realize is that he is getting his just deserts. He has wanted to be a social reformer, a *ba'al tova* himself, albeit an idealistic one – and who knows better than

Ashmodai how easily idealism is corrupted by power. Far from being arbitrary, Ashmodai's choice is fiendishly clever. "There's no time to waste," he tells Yisrol.

> "Without a *ba'al tova,* your town with all its Jews is like a widow. You'd better get there fast. I'll give you your mare to ride on."
>
> "No, no!" I cried hotly at his mention of my mare. "I don't know how to ride a horse…. I swear to you, I can't!"
>
> "Don't be foolish! Of course you can. Your mare is docile and obedient. You'll ride it easily!... You mustn't mind her looking like a bag of bones. She comes from noble stock and has many good points. I'm sure you'll enjoy her so much that you'll fight anyone trying to take her from you."
>
> With that, Ashmodai brought my mare. My heart sank when I saw the poor, wretched, mangy-coated creature…. I was on the verge of tears. Thinking of her having to bear me on her back, I couldn't look her in the eyes.

Yisrol is next dressed for his new station in life, that of an exploiter of his fellow Jews disguised as an altruist – Ashmodai is meticulous about getting him to look just right – and is given the mare to mount. Yet at the last moment, when Ashmodai demands a pledge of fealty, Yisrol balks and refuses to give it. Furious, Ashmodai seizes him by the hair and casts him down from the heights.

> "Aiyee, I'm done for!" I shouted bitterly, careening through space.
>
> "Don't give up,Yisrol!" called a voice behind me. It came from my mare, who was spinning like me through the vast ether. "I've been made to fall many times and have always risen again. We'll soon be back on our feet this time, too!"

Yisrol hits the ground with a thud and wakes up. It has all been (a good enough writer can get away with the most shopworn of tricks) a dream, one that ends with another pun found only in the Hebrew version of "The Mare." Yisrol is the East-European pronunciation of the name Israel, and the mare's exhortation of *al yovad Yisra'el*, translated here as "Don't give up, Yisrol," is a line in the morning prayer that means "May Israel never perish." And so Yisrol is brought down to earth with the words of the Jewish prayer book, which he has not opened in the course of the novel, ringing in his ears.

5

Herzl could claim, as he did after the First Zionist Congress, that he had laid the foundations for a state that would solve the Jewish people's problems, just as he could describe this state in detail in "Altneuland." Ashmodai could be permitted a smile – and Mendele, the thought that the Jews of Eastern Europe did not need benefactors like Herzl.

Mendele was no admirer of Herzl's. He lacked the faith that Zionism could succeed, or that if it did, the results would be anything like those hoped for. Zionism was not a reformist movement like the Haskalah. It was a revolutionary one. It was asking the Jewish people to change as it hadn't changed in thousands of years – and the Jews had survived for thousands of years by being resistant to change. Might this resistance not be the secret of their continued existence? "I've been made to fall many times and have always risen again," says the mare. She might have added: "And always as a mare. Now you want me to rise as a prince?"

Who could say what such a prince would be like? Or that he would not, out of sheer force of habit, revert to being a mare again? The mare has risen each time with the help of her faith in the God of the prayer book. Whom or what will Zionism turn to in adversity?

In "Those Assembled Below," there is a dreamed animal parable, too. In it Mendele the bookseller, tired of the argument that he has woken from his nap to find still raging around him, falls back asleep. In his dream he is a groundhog,

> a small creature, a furry thing, short-legged and stubby-tailed. I'm lying squat on the ground, as pleased as can be. There's not a thought in my head, not a worry on my mind, not a single pang of conscience. I'm nothing but a digestive system, a stomach, innards, and intestines, all working merrily away at the greens they've ingurgitated. It's enough for me that I am and that I exist

without questions, without doubts, without inquiries or explanations of why I am the odd being that I am and live the odd life
that I live. All is in conformity with my nature.

But then,

As I'm snuffling in my semi-sleep, I hear a hunter shout: "Look at
that little whistle-pig – let's bag him!" I jump up and run as fast
as I can to my burrow, suddenly aware that I'm a whistle-pig, a
member of a species of small, pusillanimous, whistling groundhogs. In the burrow are many others like myself, a large congregation of them, some blind, some lame, some with broken
limbs and cracked ribs, some missing a tail or half their fur….
I join them and fall asleep in sweet brotherly slumber until,
hearing the hunters outside, we wake and scatter every which
way, each looking for a new burrow. The group of groundhogs
I'm with is the best of the lot. "Let's go to the cave of our forefathers," I hear them say. "It's a fine place in the uplands where
we'll be safe." Excitedly, I enter a long tunnel and follow them
in the dark. Some stumble into crevices; some can't get out;
some do by the skin of their teeth. I'm bruised and scratched
all over, hungry, tired, and limping…. And yet we keep going
and near our destination, which has to be reached through a
narrow hole…. We plan to work our way through it by lining
up in a row, each with his nose in the rear end of the groundhog ahead of him. One by one we press forward, shoving and
gasping. Yet when my turn comes, my head gets stuck in the
hole and the groundhog behind me pushes so hard that I let
out a whistle of distress.

The whistle is a snore that wakes Mendele the bookseller's
neighbor, who in turn rouses him from his sleep. This is Zionism as a
nightmare, a parody of Herzl's scheme for an orderly, technocratically
administered exodus of Jews to Palestine in response to the menace
of anti-Semitism. (That Palestine is the groundhogs' destination we
know from the allusion to the biblical Cave of the Patriarchs and to

the Jewish folk-belief in *gilgul mehilot,* the magical transportation of the bones of the dead through secret tunnels to the Land of Israel for their resurrection there.) Like Yisrol's mare who wants to remain a horse, Mendele's groundhog wants only to be a groundhog. He would have been happier to have been left alone where he was, as lamentable as the state of his fellow groundhogs is, rather than undergo the trauma of relocation that Herzl thought could be managed like a holiday excursion. Now he is even more absurdly stuck than are the Jews of Eastern Europe.

And suppose Zionism were able to create Herzl's state in Palestine. Now Mendele the bookseller has a new worry. How, he asks the disputants in "Those Assembled Below," will this state cope with the Great Powers that seek to dominate the African-Asian land bridge that it straddles? Perhaps, he suggests, there is an advantage in Jewish dispersion. Without it the Jews

> would have forever lived in great danger and constant fear of the legions of powerful kingdoms taking shortcuts through their land, and would have met their doom in the end. What did God do? He acted aforethought and scattered them among the nations to be their neighbors and tenants.

Only in the days of the Messiah, Mendele muses, when nation no longer lifts up sword against nation, will it be safe for the Jews to live in their own land again. Yet told by one of the young Zionists in the inn, "You're talking about the days of the Messiah and we're down-to-earth people talking about work.... We want to farm our ancient land to keep body and soul together, because as neighbors we're flat broke, there's not a job to be had, and our landlord wants to throw us beggars out," he reverses himself once more:

> "Work? Well, now, that's a different story.... Body and soul, you say?" I replied in a plaintive singsong, my voice starting low and getting higher and higher before breaking off like a man's who has just heard such startling news that he changes his mind about everything he has thought about until now.

6

It has been said that, under the impact of events in Russia, the ambivalence toward Zionism in Mendele's fiction vanishes in his late story "The Hair." Ya'akov Fichman, who agreed with Bialik that Mendele's alleged non-Zionism was a "fiction" and that his work was "by its very nature Zionist" in its "powerful sense of revulsion at the degradation of Diaspora Jewry," pointed to "The Hair" as proof of this. Is it?

The story is certainly different from Mendele's other work. Not only is the figure of Mendele the bookseller gone from it, so is his narrative style. The Hebrew of the third-person narrator of "The Hair" is simple and direct. It has none of Mendele the bookseller's chatty meandering or folksy manner. Indeed, it has no "folk." Its main characters are two cultivated Odessa Jews, described soberly and without the hint of a smile.

One of the two is Gavriel Karpas, a professionally successful man of about forty who, raised in a religious home, has put his Jewish past behind him. Although it is Passover eve, when Jews everywhere are busy preparing for the Seder and the holiday, for Karpas it is just another day – or would be if his wife hadn't chosen to do her spring cleaning on it. While rearranging the house, she has decided to have an old bookcase inherited from Karpas's late father moved with its books to the basement, and Karpas, though unhappy about this, is too compliant a husband to protest. Taking an old Hebrew volume from one of its shelves, he opens it at random and finds a gray hair fallen long ago from his father's beard. Shaken by the sight, he begins to pace agitatedly up and down – and just then in walks his friend Zarchi, an old schoolmate who, like him, now lives the life of an assimilated Jew.

Zarchi notices his friend's distress and asks what is wrong. Karpas shows him the hair and explains that it has aroused long-forgotten memories of his religious upbringing, and that he is astonished to find himself suddenly yearning for the warmth and beauty of those years. He can all but hear his father's books crying out that he has abandoned them and see his father wringing his hands over the Jew his son has become. "I'm afraid," he tells Zarchi, "that you'll find me ridiculous. You must wonder what kind of person I am to let a single hair upend all I've stood for."

To Karpas's surprise, Zarchi does not think this at all. "Relax, old man," he tells him. "I've had a change of heart, too." Now it is Zarchi's turn to make a confession. His son Faddey, he tells Karpas, was raised in total ignorance of being Jewish. "I wanted," he says, "to develop the human being in him and expose him to life, not to the narrow creed of a people that divides the whole world into Jew and non-Jew, kosher and non-kosher." All went well until Faddey entered a Russian high school and encountered anti-Semitism for the first time. One day, Zarchi relates, he found his son lying depressed in bed.

> "'What's the matter?' I asked anxiously.
>
> "He sighed irritably. 'As if you don't know that I'm surrounded by boys who hate me! I've had to put up with a lot until now, and today I had to listen to them tell me that we Jews eat Christian blood.'"
>
> "I was too dumbfounded to know what to say. Odd waves of emotion – pity, shame, sorrow, contrition – swept over me one after another.
>
> "I stood looking at the anguish of the son I loved and I thought: this is all your doing! You tore him away from his people to make a universal man of him – and there is no such thing. Your universal man is simply the average of all the different peoples that exist … and you've uprooted your son from his own people for another that doesn't want him."

Zarchi doesn't know what to do. Faddey, however, does. Unbeknownst to his father, he begins to explore the Jewish identity that has been denied him. He reads books on Jewish history and religion, studies Hebrew on his own, and befriends Jewish youngsters like himself. All this comes to light when he invites his new friends to his home for a Hanukkah party. A festive meal is followed by a group discussion that begins with a talk given by him about the Messianic idea in Judaism. Behind the idea of an individual redeemer, he explains, lies a deeper concept: "We Jews must seek our redemption in our own powers and our national spirit …. This is why we have gotten together this evening to commemorate the Maccabees."

Zarchi, who has been led by his son's quest to re-experience his own Jewishness, is thrilled. "Who would have thought," he says to Karpas, "that my assimilated son who never knew the shape of a Hebrew letter would become such a Jewish patriot?" Faddey's friends at the party, on the other hand, are more critical. One protests:

> "Our friend Zarchi has said that our redemption lies in our national *spirit*. But a national spirit can exist anywhere, not just in Zion. This is nationalism but not Zionism!"

A second youngster is a religious anti-Zionist. Like Berdichevsky, but coming from the opposite pole, he is convinced that the first Hebrews will be the last Jews:

> "If we're to conserve the Jewish tradition that is the basis of our national identity, we Jews must avoid having a country of our own. No people running a modern state in Palestine can do so according to the laws of the Torah, most of which will not be observed there. They will end up being forgotten with all our other customs, prayers, and values.... Reviving the Jewish people in the Land of Israel means killing it! It will become a new people, without any of the objective or subjective elements that have characterized it until now."

The discussion goes on heatedly into the night. "Which of them was right," Zarchi proudly tells Karpas,

> "does not concern me right now. I welcomed everything they said because it came from the heart and was motivated by love for our people.... You were brought back by a hair. But what a single hair did to you in an instant took the anti-Semites long years to do to me. Hats off to it and to you!"
>
> "Hats off to your son!" answered Karpas enthusiastically. "Hats off to his young friends, the first swallows of our people's coming spring!"

The day is still young. It is not too late to organize a Seder, which the two men and their wives proceed to do in Karpas's home. That evening,

The Passover table was set as prescribed. Karpas presided over it in kingly fashion, leaning on the traditional pillow, his wife, the queen, to his right and Zarchi, his viceroy, to his left. The house brimmed with light and joy. The small children asked each other in wonderment "Why is this night different from all other nights?" and wished that all other nights were like it. The grown-ups read the Haggadah. They talked about the first Passover in Egypt and Passovers still to come and ended by chorusing, "Next year in Jerusalem!"

"The Hair" is not one of Mendele's better stories. In fact, it is one of his weakest. He wished to make a statement in it that he feared undercutting with his usual irony and humor, and the result was didactic and sentimental. He could not have written it without thinking of his own son, whose life took such a different turn from Faddey's. But was this statement a Zionist one?

Concluding with the declaration of "Next year in Jerusalem," it might appear to be so. And yet this is only at first glance. The declaration, after all, is not spontaneous. It is the Haggadah's final line, the closing flourish of a text that Jews have read aloud throughout the ages in a Diaspora they had no intention of leaving. In the context of the story, it means no more than what the Seder-goers want it to mean – and what this is, we aren't told.

Here, too, there is no intended irony. Mendele was not saying, as he does so often in his fiction, "Look at the Jews – what they say has nothing to do with what they do." He was providing us with two ways of reading the story's ending, a Zionist and a non-Zionist one, and letting us choose between them.

The whole of "The Hair" works by means of such complementarities. Karpas is restored to his Jewish self by guilt over a father, Zarchi by guilt over a son. The former is concerned with the loss of Jewish religious and cultural identity, the latter with anti-Semitism and Jewish vulnerability to it. One youngster at the Hanukkah party is a Zionist, another is an anti-Zionist.

Zarchi welcomes all these views because all express a sense of Jewish pride and self-assertion. But while Zionism and anti-Zionism can go together at a Hanukkah party, one can't really be in favor of both. And yet this is exactly what the story presents itself as being!

Was Mendele being ironic *here*? Was he saying, "Look how we Jews think, like Zarchi, with our hearts, not with our heads?" Once again, I think not. Read together with "In the Time of the Quake," "Those Assembled Below," and "The Mare," the ending of "The Hair" is telling us:

Yes, it is illogical to be a Zionist, a non-Zionist, and an anti-Zionist at one and the same time. But each of these positions has its own logic – and logic, in any case, never determined the course of history, which is beyond our control and predictive ability. As Jews we must do all we can to keep our people and culture alive and defend ourselves against our enemies, and every Jew joining the struggle should be cheered. Yet we can only guess what the best way to conduct it is. It is not foolish in such a situation to hedge one's bets.

Bialik, for all his closeness to Mendele, mistook his agnosticism regarding Zionism for a belief in it. From the vantage point of 1928, a decade after Mendele's death in Odessa, this was understandable, just as it was understandable for Fichman to see a Zionist in Mapu. Bialik was addressing a young audience of native Hebrew speakers living in a Hebrew-speaking city. Only Zionism had thought such a thing was possible; Mendele would have been delighted by it; ergo, Mendele was a Zionist, too. But this was the reasoning of hindsight. Mendele did not have the benefit of that. He had a believer and a doubter, and they fought each other to a draw.

Chapter Eight

He Who Could Have
Set the World on Fire:
Chaim Nachman Bialik

1

The pogrom that erupted in April 1903 in the city of Kishinev, today the Moldavan capital of Chişināu, dwarfing the damage of 1881 and resulting in the murder of forty-nine Jews, the injury of hundreds, and the looting and destruction of over a thousand Jewish homes and stores, was but a sign of things to come. Far worse anti-Jewish violence was to take place in Eastern Europe in the early twentieth century, well before the Holocaust. But there had been nothing on Kishinev's scale since the mass killings of Jews during Bohdan Chmielnicki's Cossack rebellion in the Ukraine in 1648–49, and the shock waves set off by it were great. One of the first Jewish responses was the sending of a commission of inquiry from Odessa to report on what had happened. Appointed to head it was Chaim Nachman Bialik.

The thirty-year-old Bialik, already a celebrated figure in the Hebrew literary world, arrived in Kishinev immediately after the pogrom and spent over a month interviewing survivors and witnesses and taking extensive notes. In the end, he never wrote his report. Instead, he composed a long poem that he finished in late summer. Called by him *B'ir ha-Harega,* generally translated as "In the City of Slaughter," its name was changed to "The Burden of Nemirov" at the insistence of the Tsarist censor, a baptized Jew named Israel Landau who wished it to appear that the poem concerned distant rather than contemporary events. (Modeled on such prophecies of Isaiah as "the Burden of Egypt" and "the Burden of Babylon," this title referred to the site of a notorious massacre by Chmielnicki's forces.) Subsequently, the original name was restored.

"In the City of Slaughter" did not need Landau to link it to biblical prophecy. Its opening line openly echoed such prophetic calls as the book of Jonah's "Arise, go to Nineveh, that great city, and cry against it" and the book of Ezekiel's "Arise, go to the valley and there I will talk with you":

> Arise, go to the city of slaughter, and come into its yards,
> And look, and see, and run your hands over the boards
> Of fences, and the stone of houses, and the plaster, and the wood,
> And the clotted brains of victims and their dried blood.

These words hit their reader with a gale force that he has had no time to prepare for and that does not abate until the poem's end. But who is speaking them? Is it God addressing the poet? Or is it the poet addressing us?

> From there proceed to the smashed kitchens and the battered walls
> Of the wrecked rooms with their gaping holes
> Bludgeoned and bashed by the sledgehammer's blows,
> Their blackened stones and bared flesh of charred bricks
> Screaming like mouths of dark, open wounds
> That no one can mend and no one can fix.
> Sink your feet into the feathers of torn pillows and the mounds
> And heaps and piles of broken things, of books and scrolls,
> The herculean labor of the ages –
> And then, leaving behind the ruins of their pages,
> Step outdoors and smell, against your will,
> The heathen incense of the acacias' perfumed bloom,

And while a thousand golden arrows of the sun
Pierce you to the quick and every glitter
Of shattered glass gloats at your doom,
Be not unpleased that spring has come,
For the Lord has summoned it and death together:
The sun, the blossoms, and the slaughterer.

Whoever the speaker is, it is a balmy day as the poet is taken,
or takes the reader, on a tour of the pogrom's devastation. How awful
to enjoy the spring sunshine! Already then Bialik must have known
that his report would have to wait. What was he to have written in it?
*There were bloodstains everywhere; the floors were littered with torn books
and ripped pillows; and the incongruously fine weather, which the writer is
ashamed to admit he enjoyed, only made things worse?* One can imagine
the frowns in Odessa.

A poet should write poems. This one goes on to describe a dog
and its owner, both with their heads chopped off, and then ascends to
an attic in which Jews sought unsuccessfully to hide: corpses swing in
it from a rafter, a man lies killed by nails driven through his nostrils into
his brain, a lifeless infant presses its mouth to its mother's cold breast.
From there we climb back down and descend deeper into the inferno,
to one more failed refuge:

And now go down to the dark cellar holes.
There, on each daughter of your people, amid junk and old tools,
Seven uncircumcised savages piled,
Despoiling child in front of mother, mother in front of child,
Before, and as, and after their throats were slit.
Touch the red-stained pillow and the gory sheet,
The satyr's cesspit and the wild pig's sty;
See the bloodied ax, and then espy,
Crouched behind barrels and moldy hides,
The husbands, the brothers, the betrothed of young brides,
Peering through peepholes at bodies that writhe
And choke, befouled on their blood,
Beneath rank donkeys, passed round like the food

> Shared by the brute goy workmen at their lunchbreaks;
> Ask how, too scared to move and cowering in shame,
> They managed to keep sane and failed to rake
> Their eyes out with their nails – yes, even prayed,
> "Dear God, just let me get through all this unscathed."

This is unbearable. Who would believe that Kishinev could have witnessed something more terrible than the bestiality of its pogromists? And yet, the poem tells us, it did: the cowardice of its male Jews, so great that they could think only of saving their own lives as they watched wives, daughters, and sisters raped and killed. How could any people breed such a contemptible race of men? There is no time to ponder this question, however, because we are now being led to a stable where, as though the Middle Ages had never ended, Jews have been lashed to wagon wheels, their limbs broken on them one by one until they died. From there, the voice drives us unsparingly on to the Jewish cemetery:

> And now leave the city and go, unseen and alone,
> To the graveyard and silently stand
> At the foot of each martyred child, woman, and man
> In the freshly dug, crumbly earth
> While you shrivel with shame and with pain.
> For I will strike you dumb;
> Though you would weep, no tear will come;
> And should you want to bellow like an ox
> Beneath the knife, you will not even groan,
> For I will harden you and turn your heart to stone.
> Here it lies, the butchered flock.
> You ask for restitution? What?
> Forgive me, you wretched of the earth!
> Your God is destitute like you,
> Poor in your life and poorer in your death,
> And if you knock upon my door to claim your due,
> I will open it and say: "Come, look about:
> There's nothing here – I've been cleaned out!"
> My heart goes out to you, my sons, it truly does.

You died in vain, and neither you nor I
Know what you perished for or why.
Your deaths were just as pointless as your lives.

At last we know who the relentless voice belongs to. It is God's –
and the poet's. Or rather, it is the poet's impersonating a God he does not
believe in – a God who promised Isaiah to make the deaf hear and the
blind see, who breathed life into the bones of the dead for Ezekiel and
raised Jonah from the belly of a whale, but who cannot save the Jews of
Kishinev because He no longer exists. Knock on His door and there is
no one there. We have been guided through Kishinev by a ventriloquist.

"In the City of Slaughter" ends with a memorial gathering. Prayers
are recited by the survivors for the dead. A cantor chants the *avinu mal-
kenu* prayer. "Our Father, our King! Act in the name of the slaughtered!
Act in the name of the infants! Act in the name of the beloved children!"
There are sniffles and sobs. For what have the Jews of Kishinev been
punished? Why is it always the Jews? God has no idea. "Why are they
pleading with me?" He asks the poet.

Speak to them! Get them to thunder at me!
Make them shake their fists at me for what I've done
To all their generations, from first to last,
And smash the heavens and my throne!

But the Jews of Kishinev do no such thing. A speaker gives a
trite speech. Someone yawns. It is getting late. Soon, the event over,
all disperse. The poet, the pretense of speaking in God's voice wearing
thin, thinks:

Let them go. The stars are out tonight.
Stricken, abased, they slink away like thieves,
Each to his home; each with his own griefs;
Each more bent of back and desolate
Than he was before; each to his own bed,
Bone-weary and his heart consumed by rot.
And should you take tomorrow to the road,

You will see, outside the doors and windows
Of the rich, a moaning, groaning crowd of Jews
Hawking their wounds like peddlers their wares –
Here a maimed hand, there a dented skull,
With outstretched arms, their bruises bared,
And eyes, the eyes of beaten slaves, that tell
Their benefactors: "See? My head's a bloody pulp.
You owe me for a martyred father too, so help!"
And our merciful rich Jew takes a long pole,
Ties to it provisions in a sack,
Holds it out the window for each soul,
And warns the solaced beggars, "Don't come back!"

In Hebrew, the entirety of "In the City of Slaughter" is rhymed. This is an implausible way for the God of the Bible, which knows nothing of rhyme, to express Himself – and yet were it not for the tight leash on which its rhymes hold the poem's metrically irregular lines, one feels they would fly apart from sheer fury at a people so shameless that it treats its own victimhood as so much merchandise to turn a profit on:

To the graveyard, beggars, to exhume
Your martyrs' bones and fill your sacks with them
And shoulder them and take them everywhere,
To every marketplace and country fair!
Find yourselves a roadside stop or shrine,
Spread them out on filthy rags in broad sunshine
For all to see, and wheedle till you're hoarse with wheedlery.
Pray for the pity of the goy! Cry for the world's sympathy!
Beggars you've always been – beggars you'll always be.

"Wheedlery?" There is no such English word. But neither is there any such Hebrew word as *shnorer*, which Bialik borrowed from Yiddish and turned into the phonetically awkward verb *l'shnorèr* in the caustic line *v'ka'asher shnorártem tishnorerú*, "And as you have schnored, so you will go on schnoring." With it, the poem's biblical God is openly exposed as an imposter from the shtetl.

Held up by additional problems with the censor, "In the City of Slaughter" appeared in print in December 1903. (Landau, despite having converted to advance his career, considered himself a loyal Jew, and the lines he most objected to, ironically, were not those describing the pogrom's savagery that the Russian authorities had failed to stop in time but those mocking Jewish religious faith.) Even before then, however, knowledge of the poem spread among Russian Jews and generated an excitement that grew greater after its publication, especially once a Russian translation by Vladimir Jabotinsky appeared in March 1904 and a Yiddish one by Bialik himself two years later.

There was nothing like it in Hebrew literature. Of dirges for Jewish suffering at Gentile hands and calls for God's vengeance, this literature was full; the prototype was the book of Lamentations. But "The City of Slaughter," though its opening lines might appear to place it in this tradition, was in fact a fierce attack on it. It was a diatribe, not a dirge; its fury was directed more at Jewish passivity than at Gentile brutality; and it blamed Jews for their misfortune not because they had sinned against a punitive God but because they had depended on a powerless one. Not even Gordon or Berdichevsky had gone as far in denouncing East-European Jewry's emasculation by its own religion and culture. The *j'accuse* of "In the City of Slaughter" was a *je nous accuse*, a pitiless Jewish self-indictment.

Was it justified? Some thought not. Bialik's poem, they protested, was unfair and inaccurate, scandalously insensitive to Jewish feelings and blind to the fact that many of Kishinev's Jews had behaved bravely and fought to defend themselves. The Hebrew author Y.D. Berkovitz, a son-in-law of Shalom Aleichem, relates a conversation held in Odessa in 1906 with Mendele Mocher Sefarim. In it, Mendele, who thought highly of Bialik and his poetry, said in the name of the pogrom's victims, of which he was not personally one:

> To this day, I can't forgive [Bialik] for that poem about the Kishinev pogrom that the whole world talked about.... Good grief! Wild beasts, the dregs of humanity, set upon me, my wife, and my children, kill and murder me in the most abominable ways, put me to every conceivable torture – and along comes

[Bialik] and berates me like a revival preacher, sowing salt in my wounds.

Indeed, Bialik's notes from his stay in Kishinev, which were finally published in 1991, make it clear that he knew that his descriptions of Jewish cowardice, though not untrue, were unbalanced. Recorded by him, too, were cases of Jews who armed themselves with guns and clubs, stood their ground in pitched battles, and repulsed the rioters in some places. If he refrained from mentioning them in "In the City of Slaughter," it was because this would have resulted in a different poem from the one he wanted to write. As a Zionist, he believed that Jewish life in Exile, and especially in the Eastern Europe that he was a product of, was incurably deformed. The pogrom in Kishinev was both a goad to stating this belief in the strongest terms and an opportunity for doing so. He could not have done this in an objective report.

Nor could any such report, however eloquent, have had "In the City of Slaughter"'s electrifying effect. The poem became required reading for young East-European Jews and helped spur them to form self-defense groups throughout Russia. Berkovitz was speaking for them when he wrote:

> Mendele's fierce reaction to "The Burden of Nemirov" surprised me. For me, as for all the members of my generation, Bialik's poem of protest was like a torch burning in the night, summoning us to a life of dignity and courage, of awakening, of rebellion.

"It was at this point," writes Avner Holtzman in his biography of Bialik, "that Bialik became a national poet in the eyes of large segments of the [East-European Jewish] public." He had already been called that prior to Kishinev. The first to do so, it would seem, was Yosef Chaim Brenner, who wrote to a friend as an eighteen-year-old in 1899 about "our national poet, Ch. N. Bialik." Bialik merited the epithet, Brenner thought, because, at a time "when tens of thousands of young Jews are thirsting for... answers to the terrible questions [confronting them], and when our people ... are either eternally spiritless slaves or wretched savages," he gave voice to "our feelings, our aspirations, [and] the throbbings of our hearts." Others agreed. When Bialik's first volume of verse appeared in 1902, it was hailed as the work of a "national poet" by two prominent reviewers, Yehoshua Ravnitzky and Yosef Klausner.

The term had been used by Hebrew literary critics before in regard to Yehuda Leib Gordon. It reflected the alliance of Hebrew literature with Jewish nationalism, and especially, with the Zionism that emerged in the late nineteenth century. If Russian had its Pushkin and Polish its Mickiewicz as supreme expressions of national consciousness, Hebrew deserved no less – and because poetry had a vatic status not accorded prose, it deserved it in the form of a poet. The objection to bestowing such a title on Gordon had centered less on his not being of sufficient poetic stature than on his not being a Zionist. But Gordon, for all his merits, fell far short of poetic greatness, as a later generation of critics acknowledged. Although he was the best nineteenth-century Hebrew verse had to offer, he remained bound to its stale neoclassical diction and prosody. Re'uven Brainin, in his introduction to an 1899 edition of the minor Hebrew poet Shimon Shmuel Frug, classed Gordon with Frug as representing the "old poetics." "The new poet," he wrote rhapsodically, "the prophet of the future, is on his way. I feel his breath, his approaching presence. Perhaps he is already walking among his people and we will soon hear his redeeming voice."

Such were the expectations when Bialik's first book of poems came out, soon to be followed by "In the City of Slaughter." The crown was already there, waiting for a head to be placed on. How heavily it would weigh on the head of a young poet with barely ten years of published verse behind him was not a question asked by anyone.

2

Mentally, Bialik had been preparing to write "In the City of Slaughter" well before Kishinev. In 1895, in a letter to Ravnitzky, he had said of the Jewish lamentatory tradition:

> Once, when our more innocent and "spiritual" ancestors believed in their God and lovingly accepted His decrees as atonement for their sins…every disaster was considered a divine reminder of God's ways and Jews responded by vindicating it with pleas and dirges and by praying for better times and Redemption. Now,

though, [Jewish youth] has had enough of this…. Let [today's poets] write about the despair, the absence of God, the rebellion against suffering, and the refusal to go on living the wretched life of dogs that characterize our generation.

Remarkably, the twenty-two-year-old writer of this letter was still outwardly a traditionally observant Jew who had just cast off the long gabardine of his ancestors for modern garb – a change facilitated by the fact that he was then living by himself in a forest, in charge of which he had been put by his new father-in-law, Shevach Averbuch, a lumber merchant. Bialik's childless marriage to Averbuch's daughter Manya was an arranged one, agreed to under family pressure, and although it lasted a lifetime on a foundation of mutual caring and respect, there was never any passion in it. His own father, Yitzhak Yosef Bialik, was in the lumber business, too, in the small Ukrainian village of Radi, Bialik's childhood in which was to be remembered by him as a period of never-to-recur happiness. Radi was, he wrote in an autobiographical sketch composed at the request of Klausner, then planning an article on him for *Ha-Shiloah,*

> a place of woods and meadows, an oasis of humble beauty where a simple and hale Nature was content to be itself and make do with its modest endowments – the brilliance of its sky, the expanse of its fields, the stillness of its forests, all posing a riddle that said "Solve me!"… To this day, the memory and vision of them are like morning dew on the grass.

When Bialik was six his father's business failed and the family moved to the nearby town of Zhitomir, where Yitzhak Yosef reluctantly opened a tavern in which Bialik recalled him serving his rowdy customers with an opened volume of the Mishnah on the counter, trying to shut out his surroundings with it. Soon afterwards he died, and Bialik's mother, burdened with three children and no means of supporting them, put Bialik in the care of his grandfather – "a stern, frightfully old man," he wrote Klausner, "who studied sacred books all day long. Obviously, he and I, a spirited, mischievous orphan given to emotional outbursts, didn't for the most part get along." In the heder that his grandfather sent him to, his teacher did not spare the rod. "If I shinnied up a telegraph pole – wham! If I went sliding on the ice – whack! If I climbed the teacher's roof at night and crowed like a rooster – drawing and quartering were too good for me." Yet eventually a more liberal schoolroom was found in which he proved to be an outstanding student in keeping with his grandfather's ambition for him that he become a rabbi and a scholar. Considered too young to leave home for a yeshiva at the time of his bar-mitzvah, the age at which a heder education ended, he was given a place in the local *bet midrash* or study house – in effect, a synagogue equipped with an extensive library of religious texts that all were free to avail themselves of.

By the 1880s, however, the study houses of Eastern Europe were languishing. The young rarely frequented them and their older occupants were dying off. "I was," Bialik wrote Klausner,

> the only boy in the study house. The one person apart from me was the local *dayan* [rabbinic judge], who spent half the day there praying and studying. Most of the inhabitants of the area were merchants who thought and lived for nothing but money and had sons like themselves …. I had no one to talk to or share my inner world with. Sometimes I felt that I was God's only child and the darling of his Shekhinah. She was with me, spreading her wings over me and guarding me like the apple of her eye.

In near total seclusion, he spent the next four years in this cloister "alone with my thoughts, my doubts, and the secret workings of my mind, sitting for days on end by the bookcase and pausing from time to time from my studies to fantasize and daydream." At the same time, like so many young students of rabbinic texts in his generation, he began surreptitiously to read Haskalah literature. Torn between a sense of religious duty and devotion on the one hand, and hunger for new experience on the other, he enrolled in the renowned yeshiva of Volozhin, where Berdichevsky, driven by similar emotions, had studied several years previously. His hopes of finding intellectual companionship there were disappointed. "There wasn't a trace of [interest in] the sciences or literature," he wrote in his autobiographical sketch. "There were only young yeshiva students like myself, some better and some worse, studying Talmud, Talmud, Talmud all day long. To hell with it, then! I would study Talmud, Talmud, Talmud, too, and become one more rabbi."

For a while, he kept it up while beginning to write his first poems, including his earliest published effort, "To A Bird" – a sentimental ode to a migrating songbird returning to Russia from Palestine for the summer. With such lines as "Do you bring me greetings from brothers in Zion, / My brothers so far yet so near? / Ah, happy are they! Can they possibly know / Of all of my suffering here?" the poem was no different from the sentimental Zionist verse of such now forgotten nineteenth-century Hebrew poets as Frug, Eliakim Zunser, and Menachem Mendel Dolitsky. Yet its appearance in a literary review in 1892 gave Bialik a sense of poetic vocation that heightened his alienation from his surroundings:

> I stood for hours on end at my lectern, surrounded by... hundreds of fervently chanting mouths. But though I chanted like them "Thus said Abaye" and "Thus said Rava," my mind was somewhere else. When spring came, I would slip away from the yeshiva and run like a madman through the streets, my soul beating against its bars like a caged bird. I had to get away, away!

He chose Odessa, the mecca of would-be Hebrew writers. Once again, his expectations were not lived up to:

> A shy, inarticulate half-savage with no knowledge of Russian or of city ways or manners, I arrived there without a penny, with nothing but my own feeble hopes – feeble because I sensed right away that nothing would come of them. The city was too big for a youngster like myself, who could only get lost in it without anyone to notice him. And so it was: for six months I wandered through Odessa like a stray lamb, hungry, wretched, living in tubercular cellars – and no one paid the least attention.

His stay there was cut short by word received from Zhitomir that his grandfather was dying. He arrived to find his older brother on his deathbed, too.

> There was a smell of death in every corner. I went to the study house. Again I found myself standing on the threshold of the place I had spent so many years in. It was empty; not a soul was there. After a while, some local residents began to arrive for the morning prayer and greeted me. "Hello there! *Sholem aleikhem*! How are you?" One of my uncles slapped me on the back and said with a laugh, "So, Chaim Nachman! You're back!"
> Which meant: "You're one of us now."
> Half a year later, I was indeed one of them – I had a wife. My brother was dead, my grandfather was dead, and I, at the age of nineteen, was a married man with a good and respectable life to look forward to.

Bialik's sketch ended here. To it he added a postscript that read in part:

> One thing I should mention is that my marriage did not put a sudden end to my development. On the contrary: in its aftermath, because of my solitude in the forest that I was put in charge of, I had time to read a great deal and continued to grow....
> And I'll say one last thing: all the events of my life have been like notes played by different instruments, each on its own. If they've added up to a single melody in spite of everything, this is nothing less than a miracle.

3

What were these "notes played by different instruments"? One can list some of them as they are found in Bialik's work and hinted at in his letter to Klausner:

- The bliss of a child's dawning consciousness of the world and of Nature. The struggle to recover or recreate it in later life.
- The loss of a father, and in effect a mother, at a young age. The permanent feeling of being an orphan in the world.
- The ecstasy of Jewish religious study and of its dedication to God. The disenchantment with it and the inner emptiness caused by its abandonment.
- The rebellion against one's surroundings and their conventional values. The sense of social responsibility that undermines this rebellion and the frustration and anger that ensue.
- The search for the love of a woman outside the marriage bond. The inability to integrate love with sexual passion in a relationship.
- The calling of poetry. The obstacles in its way.

Simply stating these themes is enough to suggest that they were interconnected. Some can be grouped together as dealing with loss and the dream of its restoration; some with deep ambivalences in social and sexual relationships; some with high ambition and its thwarting. Clusters of associations join group to group.

Consider Bialik's long poem "The Pond," written in 1904–5. An evocation of a pond in a forest at different times of the day and year, it is divided into unrhymed stanzas of varying length. In Stanza 3 the setting is a moonlit night, whose radiance makes it seem as if

Many-wiled, the forest bore the secret
Of an ancient kingdom, grand and courtly,
In which, on a bed of gold and hidden from all eyes
In the innermost of castle keeps,
A queen's daughter of a time gone by,
Forever young and of a beauty rare,
Innocently slept under a spell,
And it, the forest, was the castle's keeper,
Sworn to guard her every breath
And her sacred grail of maidenhood
Until a prince, her lover and redeemer, came to wake her.

With its sleeping beauty and primeval, Druidic forest, this scene taken from the world of the European fairy tale is un- and even pre-Jewish, suggestive of a stage of human consciousness, whether in the life of the individual or of the race, that has yet to awake from the magical spell of natural religion. Yet further on, in the poem's sixth stanza, we are told by the poet how, as a young adolescent,

> I, a boy in the fairest season of his life,
> When the Shekhinah's wings first beat above him
> And he longed and wondered wordlessly and sought
> A sanctuary somewhere for his prayers –
> I used to wander in the heat of day
> Through the mighty, peaceful kingdom
> Of the forest's depths.
> There, beneath God's trees that never heard an ax ring,
> On trails trod by none but wolves and hunters,
> I roamed for hours,
> Alone with God and my own self until I came,
> Stepping carefully between gold snares of light,
> To the Holy of the forest's Holies, its small, bright orb.

Now, we are in a world that is Jewish with its God of Creation by whom the forest was made, its Shekhinah, God's immanence in the world, depicted in rabbinic tradition as a tender female presence hovering like a mother bird over her nest and balancing the Creator's stern masculinity, and its Temple-like "Holy of Holies," the forest's inner sanctum in which lies the "small bright orb" of the pond. In Hasidic legend, especially the stories of Nachman of Bratslav, who was fond of fairy-tale motifs, the Shekhinah is often depicted as a *bat-melekh*, a "king's daughter" or princess, exiled from her father's celestial realm to the lowly world of humanity. Not that Stanza 6 seeks to Judaize the Sleeping Beauty motif of Stanza 3. The two sets of images remain separate, side by side. Yet a bridge has been thrown between them.

A bridge leads, too, from "The Pond" to Bialik's poem "Alone."
Written in 1902, "Alone" describes an adolescent's solitude in a study
house deserted for new horizons and opportunities by all but himself:

> All borne upon the wind, all swept up by the light –
> For all, life's morn new harmonies did sing.
> But I, a stripling of a lad, remained
> Under the Shekhinah's broken wing.
>
> Alone! And she, her limp throb of a wing
> Beating above me, also was alone.
> Our two hearts met. Mine knew the fear in hers
> For me, her only son.
>
> Driven from everywhere, she still had left
> One last, small, secret, forlorn room:
> The study house – and there I shared
> Her sorrow in the gloom.
>
> And when my soul yearned for the window's light
> And felt imprisoned by its servitude,
> She laid her head upon my shoulder and a tear
> Wet my Talmud.
>
> Silently she clung to me and wept
> While her lame wing shielding me shook,
> "All borne upon the wind, all gone far away,
> And me they forsook, they forsook…"
>
> And like the end of an ancient lament
> And an anxious, prayerful plea,
> I heard her hushed sobs and her tears
> Fell hotly now on me.

The same maternal spirit that protected the boy in the forest still
arches her wing over him, but now it is crippled and in need of protection

246

itself. This wing appears, too, in yet another poem, written in 1905, that was to become one of Bialik's best-known:

> Take me under your wing,
> Be mother and sister to me,
> Let my lost prayers rest on your breast,
> My head upon your knee.
>
> And at mercy time, in the dimming light,
> Let my lips sadly muse in your ear:
> "They say there is youth in this world.
> How did mine disappear?"
>
> And let me murmur this to you, too:
> "My soul burned away long ago.
> They say there is love in his world.
> Is it so?"
>
> The pale stars cheated me.
> I had a dream – it has flown
> And left me behind by myself,
> All alone.
>
> Take me under your wing,
> Be mother and sister to me,
> Let my lost prayers rest on your breast,
> My head upon your knee.

Is "Take Me Under Your Wing" a love poem? It is and it isn't, for it is spoken by a man to a woman he can only love and be loved by as a mother and sister – a Shekhinah-figure. His head on her knee, he kneels waiting for a tender caress. He does not reveal what his flown dream was. To be a prince awakening a sleeping princess in the sexually stirring depths of a dark forest?

We return to the image of the pond that faithfully but change-ably mirrors its surroundings – now those of a moonlit night, now of a sunny morning, now of a dark, flashing thunderstorm, now of the milky light of dawn. The oft-invoked image of art as a mirror, whether as a metaphor for art's mimetic powers or for the capacity of the artist's mind to register and erase endless impressions, is as old as Plato, though it is uncertain whether Bialik was aware of its place in the history of aesthetics when writing "The Pond." In his poem, at any rate, both aspects of the metaphor apply. Like mimetic art, the pond reflects endless moments that are the infinite fragments of the All – and like the consciousness of the poet, it is played on by each moment, each sounding its note that joins the others in the undifferentiated depths far below:

> There is a silent language of the gods, a secret tongue,
> Unspoken and unvoiced but endlessly expressive….
> In it God is known to his chosen,
> The World Spirit thinks its thoughts,
> And the artist crafts his realizations
> And unlocks his unarticulated dreams.
> Shall we call it the language of the mirror?
> It is spoken by each expanse and patch of the blue sky;
> By pure, silvery cloud puffs and black thunderheads;
> By the tremulous golden wheat and the proudly upright cedar;
> By the snow-white flapping of the dove's wings and the capacious
> beating of the eagle's;
> By the beauty of the human form, the brightness of a human
> look;
> By the sea's tantrums and the playful laughter of its wavelets;
> By night's plenitude, mute with falling stars;
> By the clamor of the light and the fiery oceans of its sunrises
> and sunsets.
> In this, the tongue of tongues, the pond, too,
> Spun its eternal riddle for me,
> Hidden in leaf-shade, clear, still, and tranquil.
> It was all-seeing, and all was seen in it and all kept changing.
> I thought of it as the wide-open eye
> Of the mysterious, long-ruminating Lord of the Forest.

"Lord of the Forest" is the Hebrew *sar ha-ya'ar*. A *sar* is a ruler subordinate to a higher one, and in rabbinic lore it is an angel empowered to preside over some feature of the world. The lord of Bialik's forest can be a pagan god or a Jewish God's plenipotentiary, as one wishes.

4

The stars once made you a promise and cheated you – and not just you, Chaim Yosipovich! And do you know why? They're taking revenge for being cheated by human beings.

Don't cheat the stars and you'll see how they twinkle at you! The most beautiful, the brightest stars! They'll give you the strength not to cheat.

"You're a strange woman," you said when we parted. That was said by a first-class poet.

Do you know what my strangeness consists of? Of not wanting to cheat the stars.

The woman who wrote these lines in a letter to Bialik as she was about to leave Russia for France was Ira Jan, the name by which the Kishinev-born Russian Jewish painter and illustrator Esphir Yoselevitch was known professionally and to her friends. Jan and Bialik first met when Bialik was in Kishinev to report on the pogrom. They struck up a friendship and a correspondence, and the relationship intensified when Jan contracted to illustrate Bialik's poem "The Dead of the Desert" and his prose poem "The Scroll of Fire." Although she could not read Hebrew, these and other poems of his were put into Russian for her. (A first Russian edition of Bialik's poetry, in Jabotinsky's translations, appeared only in 1911.) Among them, with its "cheating" stars, was "Take Me Under Your Wing," written like Jan's letter in 1905.

Separated from her husband, raising a small daughter, and frequently on the move, Jan was a cultured, witty, romantic, impulsive, and unconventionally minded woman. Although she never openly declared her love for Bialik, it is apparent in her letters to him, which were published after decades of being suppressed by his literary executors; his cautiously phrased replies, only a few of which have

survived, leave room for doubt whether the feeling was fully reciprocated. Certainly, he enjoyed Jan's company and their artistic col-
laboration; he had never before met a woman who was intellectually
and creatively his equal, and he was flattered by her enthusiasm for
his work. She was, he told others, "a great human being." But there is
no evidence of a sexual attraction to her on his part and it is always
she in their correspondence, never he, who asks for more – more
mail, more openness, more boldness in his life and poetry, perhaps
even (though this remains implicit) more of a willingness to leave
his wife for her.

As time went by, Jan's letters to Bialik grew frustrated and impa-
tient. He was not, she scolded him, a truly free spirit; he was a prisoner
of his surroundings, trapped by their mores; he was sacrificing his happiness and poetic genius to them. In February 1908, two days before
departing for Palestine in the hope of starting over there, she wrote him
from Switzerland, berating him for having chosen the "good little boy"
in himself over the childhood rebel he also had been. The letter was finished in Jerusalem. Alluding to "Take Me Under Your Wing," which she
may (perhaps correctly) have thought was written to her, and to "The
Scroll of Fire," which opens with an apocalyptic account of the destruction of the Temple in Jerusalem, Jan wrote:

> Chaim, when you'll be my guest on the rooftop [of her Jerusa-
> lem apartment], I'll let you be that little boy again. (You know
> which one: the good one.) I'll let you play on the rug and shout
> "Fire!" at night to the far ends of Jerusalem. All its inhabitants
> will come running to ask, "Where's the fire? Where's the fire?"
> And I'll step forward and tell them not to be afraid, because the
> man who shouted is a good person who has just had a little too
> much to drink and the fire was long, long ago. Yes, I'll tell them
> that once this grown man was a wonderful little boy with a fire
> in his breast, in his brain, in his whole world, because he had lit it
> himself in every corner of his fevered imagination. And now he's
> grown up and is a poet – a poet who wants a soft pillow. A "sister."
> A "mother." "Oh, just be good to me!" That's what he wants – he
> who could have set the world on fire!

Her teasing tone notwithstanding, Jan was writing in anger. She had never made the distinction in her own mind between the man who was not prepared to be her lover and the poet who, so she thought, had let die the furious energy of poems like "In the City of Slaughter." Yet she was not wrong about Bialik's poetry about women. Much of it consists of either wistful plaints to a woman related to as a comforter or fellow sufferer or harsh recoils from a woman with whom sexual intimacy or the thought of it has bred recrimination and remorse. To the first class belongs a lyric like "I Lay in Wait Outside Your Room," written in 1901:

> I lay in wait outside your room
> Last night and saw you sad and still.
> Perplexed, you searched for your lost soul
> As you sat by the window sill.
>
> You sought the promise of fled youth
> And did not see, my love,
> How at your window my soul throbbed,
> Timid as a dove.

A window both connects and separates a couple in "At Sunset Time," too. Joined by their shared isolation and longing, they gaze through it at a world they feel strangers in:

> Come to my window at sunset time,
> And gently face me;
> Lay your hand on my neck, rest your head against mine,
> And thus embrace me;
>
> And tightly clasped, let us lift our eyes
> To the gathering night;
> And sending forth our hearts' thoughts to rise
> On the ocean of light,
>
> Let us watch them soar like a throbbing of doves
> To the heavens' end,

Then wheel back once more o'er the red isles and coves,
And there descend.

Those are the isles, the faraway isles
We have dreamed of, whose spell
Has made of us outcasts under the skies
And our lives into hell.

Those are the fabled islands of gold
We are homesick for,
And have seen the beckoning beams of the cold
Stars tremble o'er.

And there shall we, twin flowers wind-tossed,
In the wilderness stand,
Two travelers looking for what they have lost
In an alien land.

"At Sunset Time" was probably written in 1898. The year before that Bialik wrote a poem, "Those Eyes That Hunger," that was one of his few to deal openly with sex – and that did so with a frankness, far greater than that of Berdichevsky's "Two Camps," that was unprecedented in the Hebrew literature of the century then ending. Nothing is known about the apparently older woman to whom it was addressed or whether she belonged to a time before or after Bialik's marriage. (Its third stanza can be read either way.) She is unlikely to have been purely imaginary.

Those eyes that hunger even as they eat;
Those thirsty lips that call out for more kisses;
Those tender roes, your breasts, that cry: caress us!
That hidden place, sweet and insatiate;

This carnal pleasure house from which you'd slake me –
All this rich muchness, all this copiousness,
Spoon-fed me from your secret springs of bliss:
If only you knew, my love, how tired they make me.

Yea, I was chaste, unsullied by the heat
Or storm of passion till you breathed on me.
And I, fool that I was, did wantonly
Cast all my young life's flowers at your feet.

For one brief fleeting moment did I bless
Your hand that meted out sweet pleasure's pain.
Ah, never can it be the same again:
How dear the price exacted by your flesh!

Is this the same woman spoken to in "A Single Ray of Sun," written in 1901, in which there is an even greater sense of sexual revulsion? Surely not, for now the poet is describing someone younger. Rather than appreciate her still innocent beauty, he can think only of the ravages that sexual experience will inflict on it:

A single ray of sun
And you were fully ripe
As on the laden vine
Is the lushly swelling grape.

A single night's fierce squall
Blasting bud and fruit
And the alley dogs will smell
From afar your beauty's rot.

As a poem, this is superb; as a sentiment, it is ugly. Bialik never again wrote anything quite so vicious about sex. It was to his credit that he did not shrink from including it in his 1902 collection of poems, from which he omitted others he had written. He must have known it was too good to leave out.

After Jan's move to Palestine, where she died in 1919, she and Bialik met again only once, during a visit of his there in 1909. It was a rushed and unsatisfying encounter, squeezed into the national poet's busy schedule. In her last letter to him, mailed from Tel Aviv in 1912 and addressed to "My dear, good friend," she wrote:

Tonight is Hoshanna Rabba [the last day of Sukkot]. It's a night on which [in Jewish folklore] an angel comes to each of us with the gift of something good for the coming year. We'll meet again, then – and since this will happen not in reality but only on the wings of the imagination, it will be a meeting so poetic and beautiful that we'll go on remembering it for the rest of the year. Can we agree on that?

You know, I sometimes sit by the sea and amuse myself by throwing a pebble onto the rim of sand by the water and watching what happens. A wave sweeps over it, moves it a tiny bit to the left or to the right, forward or backward, and retreats impotently. And so it goes, wave after wave, one after another. And then suddenly, a huge breaker crashes onto the shore and carries the pebble to a distance. That's your poetry. It's just waiting for that big wave. I know it will come….

[I've been told that] you're planning to come [to Palestine] for Passover. I don't know whether to be happy or not. To see you again as I did three years ago, entrapped by a whooping, tactless, intrusive, vulgar crowd of people? In such depressing circumstances? You seemed so helpless in them. Don't ever make your peace with them. You're more of a poet than even you imagine.

The Passover visit never took place. Two years previously, in the summer of 1907, Bialik, knowing of Jan's plans to settle in Palestine, had written a poem to her. Although it had themes and images found in other poems of his (the guardian star, the Shekhinah-like mother, the disgust with carnality), it sounded a note never heard from him before:

> You're going from me – then go and be well,
> And may what you want for yourself be your guide
> And help you find peace wherever you are.
> And I? Don't worry about me.
> As long as the sun still rises and sets in its splendor,
> And God's stars have not tired of speaking to me,
> I won't be alone….

***

And I have my pure angel – the thought of you,
Watching over me like a sign of God's love
And whispering its tremulously pent blessing
Like the secret tear shed by a mother
In the tranquil, holy hush of lighting Sabbath candles....

***

And this I know, too:
There will come summer nights
Draped over the earth like gold-spangled awnings of indigo –
Feverish, soundlessly sweet summer nights
Blackly swooning with stars,
Each star a gold pome, a gold pome;
And weary of wanting, its thoughts rife with sin,
The world will recline in their lap
Until suddenly swept by a shudder of lust
In the vast silence;
The stars will be shaken, whole clusters of them at a time,
From their place and fall bit by bit
Like golden leaves in the leaf-fall;
And burning with hunger and thirst,
Each concupiscent soul will grope the walls blindly,
And hug the rocks, and throw itself on the ground
To crawl in search of one gold crumb of love or happiness
From what its star cast down.
If then, faint with longing,
You wander, hopeless and befogged,
In your quest for happiness or God –
Gaze up as I do at the sky above you
And learn from it to calm your heart.
Look:
Every night it loses so many and so many of its stars
And still it's there – as peaceful and as plenteous as ever,
And as unaware of its own loss
As if it had been left with no less gold.

These are stars that no longer cheat because they no longer promise a thing. They shine and fall and are replaced by others, and they speak to their beholder not of dreams but of a stoic acceptance of what is. At this point in his poetic career, which stalled permanently toward the end of the first decade of the twentieth century, Bialik knew the great wave would never come.

5

He was still young then, head and shoulders above the other Hebrew poets of his age. There were good ones beside him: David Frischman, Sha'ul Tshernichovsky, Ya'akov Fichman, to mention but a few. Yet none had his emotional power or technical facility. None bared so much raw feeling or was better at giving poetic language a directness that made it sound convincingly addressed to a reader or imagined listener. None knew as well how to play harmonically on all the notes of late nineteenth-century Hebrew's keyboard. None was as adept at handling rhyme and meter, weaving changing patterns of them into a single poem, often by means of what Gerard Manley Hopkins called "sprung rhythm," lines whose stressed syllables avoided monotony by throwing off different numbers of unstressed ones. None had Bialik's variety of styles, which ranged from traditional quatrains to free verse. None was the national poet.

Bialik had attempted a major poem on a national theme once before "In the City of Slaughter," in his "The Dead of the Desert." The poem was not initially conceived of that way. In 1901, he had agreed to a request from a Hebrew magazine for teenagers to contribute a poem based on a Jewish legend and had chosen for his subject a talmudic tale attributed to the traveler and yarn spinner Rabba bar Bar-Hanna, who claimed to have seen in the Sinai desert the sleeping bodies of the six hundred thousand Israelite warriors who, according to the Bible, left Egypt in the exodus. They were of such huge stature, Rabba bar bar Hanna related, that he was able to pass under the arches formed by their raised knees while mounted on a camel.

Bialik had already alluded to this confabulation before, in a poem published in 1896, and now, having decided to return to it, he concluded that it deserved a more serious treatment than one intended for juvenile readers. The poem that he wrote was finished by early 1902. Its 230 lines, written in the long six-beat cadences (sometimes reduced to five or increased to seven in my translation) of heroic verse, begins with a description of the sleeping warriors:

> By dusky tents they lie sprawled in the sun, the giants,
> Couched for all time in the yellow sand of the desert
> That settled beneath the muscular brawn of their bodies –
> Titans bound to the earth, their weapons beside them:
> Flint swords by their heads, lances spanning broad shoulders,
> Belts hung with quivers, javelins thrust in the sand.
> Heavy, their heads loll; their hair, wild and savage,
> Bristles in coarse, tangled locks like the mane of a lion;
> Their faces are bronzed, the hue of dun copper,
> Pocked by the sun's game of darts and weathered by the wind's rages.

Rabba bar Bar-Hanna's tale was suggested by an account in the book of Numbers of how God, angered at the generation of the exodus for losing faith in His promises after hearing the ill report brought back by the spies sent by Moses to the Land of Israel, told it that it would "fall in the wilderness." When its warriors repent their loss of nerve and declare, "See, we are here, we will go to the place that the Lord has promised," Moses tell them that it is too late and that they will only make things worse by pressing forward against the enemies blocking their way. Nevertheless, the Bible tells us,

> They presumed to go up to into the hill country [of Sinai], although neither the ark of the covenant of the Lord, nor Moses, departed out of the camp. Then the Amelekites and the Canaanites who dwelt in that hill country came down and smote them.

Since the Israelites were told only that they would "fall" in the wilderness, not that they would die there, talmudic legend pictured them as having lapsed into a comatose sleep. Around them is never-ending stillness. "But sometimes," Bialik's poem relates,

a shadow falls on the sands of the desert
And glides toward the camp of the dead and circles above it.
Back and forth, back and forth, it wheels in a narrowing gyre,
Then hovers, suspended, over a motionless body.
Dark grows the body, half-darkened its neighbor, from the great
wingspread.
A flap of those wings – a shudder of air – a swift plummet!
A broad-pinioned eagle, a creature of crags, crooked of beak and
of talon,
Lands all at once on its prey, bearing heavily down,
Its claws, adamantine, poised to rake an obsidian breast,
Its pointed beak aimed at a brow that is harder than stone.
In a moment they'll clash, eagle and warrior, steel against steel....
Just then, though, the raptor rears back and retracts its sharp
tools of attack;
Awed by the fierce, imperturbable majesty of the slumbering
host,
It spreads its wings and ascends, soaring higher and higher
Until with a mighty clap of the ether, screeching at the proud sun,
It disappears at the zenith of the azure's bright gleam.

The warriors slumber on. The scene of the eagle repeats itself, first
with a glittering cobra, then with a fierce lion. Both approach the sleeping camp, prepare to strike, and retreat, deterred, at the last moment.
But the deathly calm is not unbroken forever, for

Sometimes, too, the desert, vexed by the eternal silence,
Strikes back in an instant at the creator of its desolation
And rises against Him in stormy columns of sand,
Stamping its feet at the throne on which He sits startled
By its daring to turn His world upside-down. As though
kicking over a pot,
It undoes all He labored to make and returns it to chaos.
The Creator recoils in a fury. The sky changes color
And, incandescent, is clamped like a lid on the insurgent wasteland,
Which seethes and froths in a haze of orange resentment

That fills the vastness of space all the way to the far, burning
mountains.
The desert roars wildly, boiling up from the depths;
Underworld and Above are a single jumbled confusion.

The sleepers stir:

At such a time,
Life surging through them,
The titans wake and reach for their swords,
Eyes flashing, cheeks aflame,
A valiant, battle-tested generation – six-hundred-thousand
strong!
Their voices, cutting through the storm
And contending with the desert's roar,
Sound their cry:
"We are the brave,
Last to be slaves and first to be redeemed!
Our hands alone, these mighty hands,
Tore subjugation's yoke from our proud necks!
The heavens, when we gazed upward,
Were too cramped for us,
And we decamped to the great wilderness
And said, 'Be you our mother!'
On mountain peaks,
Amid far-ranging clouds,
In the company of eagles,
We drank freedom's draft!
Who can be our master?
Even now
Though a vengeful God would pen us in this barren land,
We sing the song of courage and rebellion – and we stand!
To arms! Unite! Form ranks!
Despite the heavens' rage,
We are here and we will take
The heights by storm!

> We are here!
> Disowned by God,
> Whose Ark will not bestir itself to join us,
> We will storm the heights without Him!"

For a moment, roused by the violent sandstorm, the warriors prepare to take their destiny into their own hands. The moment, however, soon passes: the storm subsides; the desert returns to its silence, and the "sixty myriads of corpses" sink somnolently back into the sand. Only rarely does a Bedouin horseman, straying from his caravan, climb a ridge and glimpse them before galloping away, as awed by the sight as are the creatures of the desert. "Bless Allah, O thou believer!" the leader of the caravan tells him. "By the beard of the Prophet, thou hast seen the dead of the desert!" His companions

> hear and say nothing, the fear of Allah upon them.
> Unhurriedly, they walk by the side of their heavily burdened camels.
> For a while, their white headdresses still can be spied from afar
> Until they and the humps of the camels vanish in the clear distance
> As if bearing the burden of yet another old legend.
> Then the infertile desert grows silent again.

Apart from its commanding power, what first strikes one about "The Dead of the Desert" is – over a year before "In the City of Slaughter" – its note of radical rebellion. If the poem's sleeping Israelites are taken to be not just the picturesque figures of legend but a metaphor for the Jewish people of Bialik's time, there is in "The Dead of the Desert" the same call that one finds in the early writings of Berdichevsky for casting off the heavy weight of the past; the same revolt against the "slave morality" of a Jewish tradition that subjugates man to a supposed divine will; the same "un-Jewish" extolling of physical strength and courage; the same turning away from the tyrannical fatherhood of a heavenly God to the permissive motherhood of Nature, be it that of a wilderness; the same proposed conquest of the Land of Israel by an act of Jewish will, independent of, and even in defiance of, religious beliefs and values. "The Dead of the Desert" was widely read when it appeared as a manifesto of militant Zionism. Its battle cry of the risen warriors, especially its Berdichevskyan proclamation of "We are the brave, last to be slaves and first to be redeemed," became a Zionist slogan, declaimed at meetings and rallies.

But on a second reading, "The Dead of the Desert" is a more ambiguous poem than all this suggests. If Berdichevsky's early Zionism was soon to end in despair, the specter of despair hangs over Bialik's poem from the start. Its Israelites do not wake for long; they stir in the storm and quickly sink back into the slumber in which we first glimpse them. Their battle cry, moreover, is suspiciously bombastic and poetically inferior to the rest of the poem, as if its bravado were being subtly mocked. It is thus also possible to read the "The Dead of the Desert" in an anti-Berdichevskyan and – if one seeks in it an allusion to contemporary events – anti-Herzlian vein. Herzl had taken the Jewish world by storm when he appeared out of nowhere in the late 1890s. Yet by 1902, the Zionist movement he founded had accomplished little and much of the initial enthusiasm aroused by it had demoralizingly waned. Is "The Dead of the Desert" a criticism of this enthusiasm rather than an endorsement of it? Does it take a position closer to Ahad Ha'am's, who had warned all along of the dangers of an unrealistically overambitious Zionism?

Ahad Ha'am himself, who published the poem in *Ha-Shiloah*, did not quite know, it would seem, what to make of it. In the same year it was written, having retired from the review and passed its reins to Klausner, he published in it an open letter in which he reacted defensively to an editorial in Klausner's first issue that spoke of changing *Ha-Shiloah*'s policies. The editorial implied, Ahad Ha'am protested, that he had edited his contributors high-handedly and suppressed their originality. Yet true originality, as opposed to mere mimicry of it, was had by only a few authors, whose work "is the product of an individuality that, even if we don't always understand or like it, we have to respect." As examples of such authors, Ahad Ha'am gave Mendele and Bialik; no one, he wrote, could accuse him of editorially intervening in the work of either. Of all that Bialik had written up to that point, it must have been "The Dead of the Desert" that he felt least sure he understood.

6

Bialik was a lifelong Ahad Ha'amist. Already as a student in Volozhin, he had considered Ahad Ha'am his mentor. In 1899, on the occasion of a celebration in Ahad Ha'am's honor, he recalled the impression that the latter's early essays had made on the yeshiva's student body (an impression at odds, it must be said, with his description of Volozhin's intellectual torpor in his autobiographical sketch written for Klausner):

> Every article that [Ahad Ha'am] published was a revelation, a new teaching. Each word of his was grist for commentary and interpretation. Our vague, confused minds found in him their clear articulation…. We felt – we knew – that we now had a leader to follow and emulate.

What was so attractive about Ahad Ha'am's Zionism for young East-European Jews like the students at Volozhin was its attempted harmonization of Jewish tradition with secular modernity within an intellectually sophisticated framework. Transformative yet conservative, it won the confidence of readers who still felt close to a religious upbringing they had outgrown. As Bialik put it:

> only someone who came from our midst and was one of us in his entire being…only someone who was a Jew through and through in body and soul…only he could stand at the head of the movement of national renaissance that goes by the simple name of the Love of Zion.

When Bialik wrote these words, "the Love of Zion," *hibat tsiyon*, was in the process of being replaced in Hebrew discourse by the more programmatic-sounding *tsiyonut* or *tsiyoniyut*, the Hebrew version of the German *Zionismus* favored by Herzl – the Jewishly uncultivated parvenu, in Ahad Ha'am's eyes, at whom Bialik's remarks contained a jibe. If, as Bialik was to declare in a poem read at a dinner honoring Ahad Ha'am upon his retirement from *Ha-Shiloah*, the latter was Zionism's "true prophet," there was no need to spell out who the false one was. "In a time of chaos and blurred lines / Between beginnings and endings, building up and tearing down," the poem stated, Jewish youth

> Lingered at the crossroads to ask: "Where to?"
> It was then, our teacher, that your star rose,
> Its mild rays shining through the fog –
> And to it, we all rallied.

This was a mediocre poem and Klausner, while accepting it for publication, was justified in dismissing it as "occasional verse." But it was not in his poetry that Bialik's Ahad Ha'amism most came to the fore. Rather, it was in his work as an essayist, anthologist, editor, and publisher, all areas that came to occupy him more and more as his poetic productivity waned. Ahad Ha'am had written at length about the need to construct a post-religious Jewish and Hebrew culture on the foundations of the religious past, but he had done so in generalities. Bialik, more than any other Hebrew literary figure of the age, strove to translate these into specifics.

His first publishing venture dated to 1901, when he helped found a Hebrew press named Moriah in Odessa, in which he and Manya settled in 1900 and lived for the next two decades. Its goal was both to promote contemporary Hebrew letters and to edit and make available out-of-print and sometimes textually corrupt Hebrew classics, and its first major project was a midrashic anthology that Bialik worked on with Yehoshua Ravnitsky. Called *Sefer ha-Aggadah*, "The Book of Legends," it took ten years to complete.

The vast corpus of Midrash or Aggadah, two roughly equivalent terms designating everything non-halakhic in the rabbinic literature of the talmudic period, was at the time a jungle of texts and passages not easily accessible to the Hebrew-reading public. These consisted of many different kinds of material: biblical exegeses, often of an imaginative or fictionalizing nature; stories about talmudic rabbis; rabbinic maxims and teachings; accounts of Jewish customs, folk beliefs, and superstitions; tales about God and man, angels and demons, this world and the next, and so on. Moreover, all this was found in two different types of works: tractates of the Gemara, where it was interspersed with halakhic discussions to which it might or might not be thematically linked, and midrashic collections such as Genesis Rabba, Leviticus Rabba, Lamentations Rabba, and the like. These collections, however, were themselves miscellanies; though organized by means of a verse-to-verse progression through a biblical book, they worked by association, the same verse often evoking unrelated remarks or stories attributed to different rabbis. In addition, the identical story might be found in different versions in different places, or else in fragments, parts occurring in one place and parts in another. And while much of this material was in Hebrew, much was also in Aramaic, which even educated Jews had difficulty understanding unless they had had a lengthy talmudic training.

And yet in this unruly profusion there was, alongside much humdrum matter, a wealth of Jewish lore and wisdom, including some of the most magnificent short-short stories – a genre the Midrash excels in – in world literature. Jewish tradition, of course, had never thought of midrash, to which it accorded the same sacred status given the rest of the Talmud, as literature. Precisely here, however, lay the Ahad Ha'amist rationale for the undertaking. The Hebrew reader demanded a literary experience of the highest order, one that could be found in the literatures of Europe but not in the Hebrew writing of the day. The Midrash could provide such an experience, but only if removed from the realm of the sacred so that it could be sensitively edited. A valuable part of the Jewish religious past could thus be transmitted to the secular present with a minimum of violence to its content.

This involved prodigious labors. Bialik and Ravnitzky had to wade through tens of thousands of pages; separate the wheat in them from the chaff; locate bits and pieces of stories and homilies and fit them coherently together; establish editorial principles by which to arrange their selections; translate Aramaic passages into Hebrew, and append a glossary explaining unfamiliar words and concepts. For years, they worked together in their Odessa homes on a nearly daily basis, reading, collating, debating what and what not to include, puzzling over meanings and translations, and deciding where best to place each selection.

"The Book of Legends" was published in six volumes between 1908 and 1911. It was not the only midrashic anthology of its kind. Two others were being worked on in the same years, Louis Ginzberg's English

Legends of the Jews and Berdichevsky's German *Das Born Judas*. But only in "The Book of Legends" were the Midrash's own voice and language preserved (both Ginzberg and Berdichevsky resorted to paraphrase), and only it became a Jewish classic and an indispensable presence on the Jewish bookshelf. (An English translation of it was published in 1992.) Its influence has been even more pervasive than is often recognized.

For example: one of the best-known midrashic stories is one telling how, during the Roman siege of Jerusalem, Rabbi Yohanan ben Zakkai had himself smuggled out of the encircled city in order to found a center of learning in Yavneh, thus paving the way for the rabbinic institutions that enabled Judaism to survive the Temple's destruction. As everyone knows, Ben Zakkai left Jerusalem in a coffin – but as few know, this is not what the principle account of the episode, found in the talmudic tractate of Gittin, relates. There we are told that Ben Zakkai was wrapped in foul-smelling rags until he stank like a corpse and carried in burial shrouds to the city gate, whose guards, thinking he was dead, let him through. But while it is only in a skimpier version of the story in Lamentations Rabba that a coffin is mentioned, this detail, woven by Bialik and Ravnitzky into the fuller version in Gittin, is the one we all know. The two men compared and chose on the basis of their literary judgment, which has determined in no small measure how we read Midrash today.

7

In the same section of "The Book of Legends" dealing with the destruction of the Temple is a pithy midrash from the tractate of Hagigah that tells of four hundred Jewish youths, half boys and half girls, taken captive after the fall of Jerusalem and shipped to Rome to be sex slaves. Knowing this was to be their fate, the midrash relates, all leaped into the sea and drowned.

When Bialik, in the summer of 1905, wrote his prose poem "The Scroll of Fire," he adapted this midrash to his purposes. "The Scroll of Fire" was longer and more ambitious than anything previously attempted by him. Although its initial scene was inspired, so he confided, by the fires that broke out in Odessa after the city was shelled by the mutinous battleship *Potemkin* in 1905's revolutionary uprising, its grand themes had long been on his mind. Now, in deciding to tackle them, he was seeking to demonstrate that he indeed deserved the national poet's honors conferred on him.

This could only be done by a commensurate work. It would have to be less circumstantially bound than "In the City of Slaughter" and more deeply probing of the Jewish experience than "The Dead of the Desert." It would need to be sublime in style, panoramic in scope, and of a complexity equal to the sweep of Jewish history. And it would best be written not in ordinary verse but in the freer lines of a lyrical prose that had the stretch and reach to encompass all this.

"The Scroll of Fire" begins with a prologue. The walls of Jerusalem have been breached. The Temple has fallen. The Romans have put it to the torch.

> All night long oceans of fire surged on the Temple Mount and tongues of flame licked upward. Stars plunged from their place in the scorched sky and spattered hotly on earth. Had God kicked over his throne, had he smashed His crown to smithereens?...
>
> Only when dawn glimmered above the mountains and a pale mist lay over the valleys did the fire and flames abate in the gutted shrine. The holy choir of angels assembled to sing the day's matins flung open heaven's windows; it peered out as was its wont. Had the doors of the Temple been opened, too, were clouds of incense already wafting through them?
>
> They looked – and lo, there was the Ancient of Days, the Lord God of Hosts, sitting amid the ruins. He was cloaked in columns of smoke; a heap of cinders was His footstool. His head lay bowed on His arms; over him towered his anguish. Silent and desolate, He stared at the destruction.

This indeed had an elevated tone – and one that, a discerning reader might have feared at the outset, did not portend well. Its sublimity was forced. It harked back to the inflating effects of old Hebrew tropes and rhetorical devices. Its neo-biblical style was a regression to the age of Mapu.

Already in the prologue, the symbolic structure of "The Scroll of Fire" starts to unfold. The more it does as the story progresses, the more it, too, seems wrong. The symbolism is too dense, too unremitting. Each sentence staggers beneath its burden of meaning. The structure is top-heavy, unable to support its own weight.

The first light of day exposes the ruined Temple. The morning star – *ayelet ha-shahar*, "the gazelle of the dawn," in the rabbis' and the poem's language – looks down and sheds a tear. A young angel catches the tear in a cup and notices a last ember burning on the Temple Mount. He scoops up the ember, flies with it to a barren isle, and deposits it on a crag for safekeeping, beseeching God to keep it from ever being extinguished.

The scene shifts to the four hundred captives. They have not leaped into the sea as in the midrash. Yet neither have they been brought to Rome. Rather, the ship's crew has abandoned them on the island visited by the angel, the young men at one end of it, the young women at the other. Two of the young men stand out, "one a fair-eyed youth, gazing upward as if seeking his life's star, the other, eyes lidded with wrath, staring fearsomely at the ground as though searching for his soul's loss." The two vie for leadership of the male group as it roams the island, hungry and thirsty, and comes to a dark river. All slake their thirst from it, not knowing that they have drunk from "the river of perdition," except for the fair-eyed youth. His wrath-lidded rival enjoins them poetically:

> From perdition's depths raise the song of destruction,
> As black as the charred stumps of your hearts!
> Take it among the nations and spread it among the God-hated
> Until it is hot coals on their heads.

"My brothers," the fair-eyed youth remonstrates, "know you not the song of final consolation?" Unheeded, however, he falls silent – and just then the two hundred young women appear on a cliff across the river, sleepwalking toward the edge of it, "the birth pangs of the Messiah frozen on their faces, an eternal faith behind their shut eyes." Oblivious to their surroundings, they plunge off the cliff into the water. The young men dive into it to save them. All perish. The fair-eyed youth, not having joined them, buries his face in his hands and weeps.

But he is not alone. Looking up, he spies on the cliff, in the beams of the morning star, a young woman who has kept aloof from her companions like himself, "as fresh and pure as an angel of chaste modesty." "My sister, is that you?" he calls out. "In my childhood's dawn I glimpsed your beauty and craved its hidden light!" In a long monologue he tells her about himself, starting with his birth "under climbing grape vines in the mountains of Samaria," his cradle "woven from shoots and branches," his lullaby "the song of birds," his religion "the gods of the hills and valleys." One morning he is found by "an old man from Judea … a holy, awesome man of the Lord." The old man takes him home with him and adopts him, instructing him "in his ways and in the worship of his God, banishing my soul's delights and teaching me to look heavenward." And yet, the fair-eyed youth tells the angelic figure, he needed "love, so much love! It was then that your image was born from my thoughts, appearing as a woman and a goddess." She and the man of God contend for his soul. "Wherever I went, I looked for you … but I dreaded the old man, lest he see that my soul had been ravished and reduce it to cinders with the hot coals of his glance."

All at once the angelic figure vanishes, leaving behind the morning star. The fair-eyed youth follows it and is led to the ember on the crag. As he reaches it, the young woman reappears in the depths of the water. Clasping the ember to his heart, he cries, "Heaven! Perdition! You!" and plunges into them. Dawn breaks. "The candles of God" go out overhead, and with them, the morning star. "Like a discarded scythe," only a crescent moon is left in "the bare, God-harvested sky."

But the fair-eyed youth is not dead. "The Scroll of Fire" has an epilogue:

> Then the waters spewed up the youth on the shores of a most distant land, the Land of Exile. And he roamed through all its regions among the exiles, passing through them like a legend of yore and a vision of days to come, a strange riddle to all … Many came and bowed their heads in silence before his blessing and his curse, seeking the prayer and remonstrance of his lips and the hope and pity in his eyes …. Yet he hungered for the dawn alone, for its glow was a seal set upon his soul and the glimmering of its light was his life's song.

How is one to navigate this morass of symbols? Bialik's contemporaries did their best. The saved ember was Judaism – or else it was the Jewish soul – or perhaps it was the Jewish faith in Redemption. The four hundred young men and women were the masculine and feminine halves of the Jewish psyche – unless they were the natural erotic life that was disrupted when the Jewish people went into exile. Yet might not the sleepwalking young women also represent the blind Jewish trust in God, or in His purported Messiahs, which more than once had led to disaster in Jewish history? In which case, the fair-eyed and wrath-lidded youths might stand for Jewish hope and Jewish despair, or Jewish idealism and Jewish cynicism, or Zionist construction in Palestine and Jewish revolutionary nihilism in Russia. And couldn't they also represent Bialik the tender lyricist and Bialik the raging voice of "In the City of Slaughter?"

And still it didn't add up, not least because the fair-eyed youth was both half of Bialik and all of him. The mountains of Samaria were recognizably the fields of Radi. The old man from Judea was the poet's grandfather. The years of banished delights were his years in the study house. The gazelle of the dawn could be identified with the bright, guiding star of Bialik's poems and the Shekhinah-like mother or soul-sister who was a fixture in them. As for the wandering spirit of the epilogue – who could this be but one of the Jewish people's visionaries, the keepers of the ember through the dark night of exile in whose company Bialik now placed himself?

But the wrath-lidded youth was Bialik, too. Had *this* Bialik now been repudiated? Was his consignment to "perdition" a retreat from the denunciatory passion of "In the City of Slaughter?" in the face of reactions to it like Mendele's? Was the solitary survival of the fair-eyed youth the national poet's promise to speak more positively, more comfortingly, from now on? Did this make "The Scroll of Fire" the capitulation to the "good little boy" mocked by Ira Jan when accusing Bialik of letting "the fire in his breast" go out even as he shouted "Fire!" over the rooftops of Jerusalem?

Reactions to "The Scroll of Fire" were mixed. Many readers were taken by its lyrical intensity. Klausner thought highly of it. So did Fichman. Peretz translated it into Yiddish. Yet Ahad Ha'am sat stonily through a reading of it given by Bialik in Odessa and failed to say a word to him afterwards, while Brenner found it "contrived" and "chaotic." Berdichevsky wrote that Bialik had "drenched" his readers in "a sea of language brimming with every imaginable wave of pathos." "The Scroll of Fire," he said, was the work not of a poet but of "a rhetorician, albeit an inspired one, carried away by his own words."

Most scathing was an article of Frischman's. It started out on a complimentary note. "Bialik," it declared, "is our most important poet." Then, however, alluding to Klausner's article about Bialik in *Ha-Shiloah* in which he called him "more of a poetic prophet than a poetic artist," Frischman exclaimed: "They've taken our Bialik, the quintessential artist, and made a prophet of him!" The worst of it was that "in this flimsy age that believes all that it is told, our poet, too, has been flimflammed into believing in his prophetic role" and was now seeking to be "endlessly, immeasurably prophetic." And yet what Bialik wrote, Frischman declared, was a mere parody of prophecy. The rage of the biblical prophets was genuine, whereas that of "In the City of Slaughter," or of the wrath-lidded youth in "The Scroll of Fire," was the posturing of a "modern, sensitive soul that could not lose its temper at a fly on the wall." Both works were artificial, and "no work of mere artifice can truly impress us, least of all 'The Scroll of Fire,' whose artificiality is really a bit too much."

Bialik kept his feelings about such criticisms to himself. Still, he was badly hurt. Although "The Scroll of Fire" would be praised by most critics in the years to come, it was his only work that he ever felt called upon to defend publicly, which he did many years later in a talk given in Tel Aviv. There, denying that he had internalized Klausner's and others' grandiose view of him, he also denied that the fair-eyed youth was himself. There were thousands like him in Jewish history. He was a representative type, not an autobiographical projection.

And yet what must have hurt him most was the knowledge that, while the rage of "In the City of Slaughter" was no pose, Frischman was more right than wrong about him. Determined to live up to the role he had been cast in, he had tried in "The Scroll of Fire" to play the oracle he was not cut out to be. The result was an artistic failure and a psychological surrender. With this judgment he was to come to agree.

He never said so in so many words. Say so he did, however, in a poem called "Evening" that he published in 1908, a year after the appearance of Frischman's article:

> And again a sun rose and again a sun set
> That I saw nothing of.
> And again a day passed without even one note
> To me from above.
>
> Far in the west are the inchoate forms
> Of cloud piled on cloud.
> Tell me, my wise ones: are new worlds being born
> And old ones destroyed?
>
> No, nothing old ends and nothing will ever be new.
> Darkness will fall
> And the idiot evening will strew
> Its grey ash over all.
>
> I went looking for your farthing and I lost
> My sovereign.
> And Ashmodai stands at my back and guffaws
> With his hideous grin.

"Evening" tells us what it is like for a poet to feel his inspiration failing – and what, to his mind, caused it to fail. The "your" of "your farthing," *prutatkhem*, is in the plural, just as "my sovereign," *dinari*, belongs to the poet alone. The poem is a statement of what Bialik felt to be his betrayal of his talent by trying to be what was expected of him rather than who he was. At such a spectacle of being seduced by one's critics and readers, the Devil could only laugh. So great was the trauma of it that Bialik was never to recover.

8

Bialik kept writing poetry, although less and less of it, until 1911; then at the age of thirty-eight, he stopped almost entirely. The last poem he wrote before doing so expressed his awareness and fear of impending poetic sterility:

> Trailing on a fence, a small branch sleeps –
> And so sleep I.
> Its fruit is gone. What matters then the trunk
> And what the tree?
>
> The fruit is gone and who recalls the blossom?
> Left is the leaf –
> And soon the storm will bring that, too,
> To grief.
>
> And after that will come dread nights
> Of no sleep at all.
> Alone in darkness I will bash
> My head against the wall.
>
> And when spring comes again
> Still will I droop,
> A naked rod, with neither bud nor bloom,
> Nor leaf, nor fruit.

There may have been more than one reason for his falling poetically silent. Fichman, who was friendly with him in Odessa, recalled those years as a period in which Bialik "was buffeted by life. His publishing house had eaten up all his savings … and left him with a pile of debts and endless troubles. The harder he struggled to gain some sort of freedom, the greater grew his worries, and there wasn't a day that didn't bring new tribulations."

But Fichman, too, thought that the main cause of Bialik's paralysis was a public image he felt trapped by. His readers wanted "the word of God" from him, "but he felt far from God. He felt that something in him had been irreparably broken." Blocked poetically, "he turned to prose and wrote [his story] 'Beyond the Fence.'"

As far back as 1899, Bialik had published a lengthy short story, "Big Aryeh," a portrait of a swaggering, Falstaffian Jewish lumber dealer in a shtetl like Zhitomir. Now, he returned to the same milieu. Once again he chose an ebulliently physical type for a protagonist – this time a boy, Noyekh, a lumber dealer's son.

"Beyond the Fence" has a second main character: the orphan Marinka, a Russian girl Noyekh's age and his next-door neighbor. Marinka lives with her foster mother, a woman with the jaw-breaking name of Shkuripinshchikha, on the other side of a high fence separating the two houses. Shkuripinshchikha is the last Russian holdout in a neighborhood, known as Lumbertown, into which Jews, mostly wagon drivers and lumber dealers like Noyekh's father Khanina-Lipa, have been moving. Relations between her and Lumbertown's Jews are bad, and she and Khanina-Lipa periodically engage in aerial battles in which they hurl objects at each other over the fence. Nicknamed for her feared watchdog Shkuripin, she is a cantankerous woman. She periodically beats Marinka, requires her to do endless chores, makes her sleep in a shack in the yard, and forbids her to leave the property, a large one with an orchard full of fruit trees.

Noyekh and Marinka are five or six years old when they first meet. Marinka has no one to share her unhappy life with except Shkuripin – until one day she and Noyekh, whose family is new in Lumbertown, discover each other through a hole in the fence and become friends. Their relationship, kept secret by them because they know it will not be tolerated by the adults who govern their lives, starts out as one of childhood play, develops into an adolescent romance, and becomes fully sexual at the story's end. As it progresses, Noyekh turns into an increasingly rebellious child. A poor and unwilling heder student who hits his teachers back when they resort to corporal punishment, he eventually, after a perfunctory bar-mitzvah, is allowed to run free, and when not spending his time with Marinka, whom he now climbs the fence to get to, he spends it with the Russian boys in the adjacent neighborhood. From them he learns to ride horses and swim in the river, and their acceptance of him is complete when he fights on their side in a pitched brawl with the Jewish boys of Lumbertown. For this, Khanina-Lipa beats him senseless, but it is for the last time. From now on, he gives Noyekh up as an untamable lost cause.

Noyekh and Marinka's happiest hours together are spent in Shkuripinshchikha's orchard. The first time Noyekh enters it, he breaks into an exuberant run.

> Light daubs of sunshine skimmed his face, his head, his clothes, scampering up and down, up and down, like golden mice. Their pleasant warmth tickled his cheeks. The dog [Shkuripin] took the lead and ran ahead, tangled in twining nets of light and shadow in which he flopped and floundered. Low-bent boughs, burdened with large apples, knocked Noyekh's cap to the ground when he bumped into them. Apples, apples, apples! Apples above, apples below, apples scattered on the ground and in the grass ... From the tops of the cherry trees, a few stray, forgotten, glossy black fruits peered out with furtive, animal eyes while half-visible behind the green leaf of a bush humbly hid a single silky gooseberry.
>
> Noyekh felt drunk. The cool shadows, the smells of the fruit, the chatter of the birds – all overwhelmed him and made his head throb. He picked and ate, picked and threw away, picked and stuffed his pockets, picked and trampled underfoot. Far from protesting, Marinka showed him how to choose the ripest fruit, pointing out the best varieties and helping him to whole armfuls of it.

This is supple, fluid prose, worlds apart from that of "The Scroll of Fire." It makes one forget while reading it that its author spoke Yiddish in daily life. How far we have come from the struggles of writers like Smolenskin, a mere generation previously, to write a Hebrew that sounded natural! Bialik's prose owed much to Mendele, who had worked wonders creating a contemporary Hebrew narrative style. But his manner in "Beyond the Fence," though Mendelean, was his own. One can almost feel his relief in it at not having to strain any more to write poetry.

The pull of the orchard and Noyekh's sexual attraction to Marinka, which grows greater as he matures, are linked throughout the story, culminating on a summer night when, now in their late teens, the two finally make love. They have arranged their tryst in advance. Noyekh, having told his parents that he is going to sleep in the stable, climbs to its garret, where a window faces a large apple tree beyond the fence. He waits there for all to go to bed.

At last the neighborhood grew quiet. Noyekh listened carefully. The tree outside the window, so it seemed, was rubbing stealthily against it. He rose and stuck his head out. The tree held out a scepter with two ripe, red apples as if to say: "Take them, they're yours."

Noyekh leaps into Shkuripinshchikha's garden and finds Marinka waiting for him with Shkuripin. The shack is nearby. "In another minute," we are told, "the two neighbors' children were inside. Shkuripin stood guarding the door."

There is barely a page left to the end of the story. What will happen to Noyekh and Marinka now? What can happen in a page?

What happens is this:

And so Noyekh eloped one night with Marinka?

I see you don't know the Jews of Lumbertown. On the Sabbath of Hanukkah, Noyekh was wed to a good Jewish girl, the daughter of a tax collector. The match was an arranged one and the wedding was presided over by a rabbi with all the trimmings. In late spring, Noyekh came with his new wife to spend the holiday of Shavuos with his parents. A fine time was had by all and when, following the traditional dairy meal, the young couple lay down to rest on a wooden deck built for it in back of the house, Marinka stood beyond the fence, a baby in her arms, peeking through a hole.

It is a stunning (in both senses of the word), cynical, and bitter ending. Once we get over the shock of it, we feel betrayed like Marinka. How could Noyekh have done it?

And yet, putting Marinka aside, hadn't Bialik done it, too?

One of my uncles slapped me on the back and said with a laugh, "So, Chaim Nachman! You're back…"

Which meant: "You're one of us now."
Half a year later, I was indeed one of them – I had a wife....I,
at the age of nineteen, was a married man with a good and respect-
able life to look forward to.

Of course, Marinka cannot be put aside, even though she is not a character drawn from Bialik's own life. Touchingly innocent and the more sexually passive of the two youngsters, she is still the alluring Gentile who stands in the male Jewish imagination for sexual freedom and social emancipation from the burdensome restraints of being a Jew. "Beyond the Fence," like Berdichevsky's "Two Camps" (in which the social aspect is more important than the sexual), was one of the earliest works of modern Jewish fiction to explore this theme. And like "Two Camps," it ends with the young woman's abandonment and the hero's surrender to the chains he has sought to throw off – the difference being that for Berdichevsky's Mikha'el this is a mental and emotional debacle, whereas for Bialik's Noyekh it is a practical accommodation to social realities. As opposed to Mikha'el and Hedwig, who could have lived unhindered as a mixed couple in Germany, what future could Noyekh and Marinka have had in Russia? And yet far from making Noyekh's decision less shameful, this only makes it seem more so. He has been tamed.

There is a postscript to all this. Between the writing of "Beyond the Fence" and its publication, Bialik undertook his 1909 trip to Palestine. On the whole, his reactions to the country were favorable. He was impressed by its Zionist farming villages and their Hebrew-speaking youth, and when informed that the first building lots in the new city of Tel Aviv were soon to be raffled off, he requested, contemplating making his future home there, to be included in the lottery. But at the same time, lionized by the public and surrounded everywhere by the crowds that Ira Jan would mention in her letter, he felt oppressed. He had been presented with so many bouquets of flowers when arriving at places and departing from them, he wrote his wife Manya from Jaffa, that he had had to throw them out of train windows. The religious sights he had seen – Rachel's Tomb, the Western Wall – had left him cold. Perhaps this was because, he wrote, "there were always people with me. I'm not only embarrassed to cry in front of them, I'm embarrassed to feel anything at all."

Worse yet, wherever he, the national poet, went, he was asked when he would write the great poem about Zionism's heroic accomplishments that his readers in Palestine were eagerly awaiting; now that he had seen the country with his own eyes, there was no longer an excuse to put it off. Bialik was infuriated by the demand. What made anyone think he could be told what to write? At a farewell party given him at the end of his visit, he let his feelings show. He had agreed to read something new as the evening's main event, and when the time for it came, he read "Beyond the Fence." The dumbfounded audience, which had been expecting the long hoped-for tribute to the Yishuv, interrupted him with cries of indignation. Was this what it had come to hear – a story about a *shiksa* and her Jewish boyfriend in a Ukrainian shtetl?

It had a right to be indignant. Bialik was thumbing his nose at it. What it didn't realize was that he was being even harder on himself. *This is what I have let you do to me,* he was saying. *Yes, I'm one of you now – damn you all!*

The postscript had a postscript. In 1913, Ira Jan, then living in Tel Aviv, published a story in *Ha-Shiloah*, still edited at the time by Klausner, that was signed "Dina Dinar." Its heroine was a romantic-minded woman in a Palestinian farming village whose dull life with her husband, a pedantic schoolteacher, and with her three children who look and act like him, has led to a severe depression. If only, she thinks, she had at least one child who resembled herself! Advised by the village doctor to take a vacation, and hearing that the famous Hebrew poet Weiler is visiting Jerusalem, where festive events are being held in his honor, she decides to go there.

Dina travels to Jerusalem and rents a room. One night she finds herself at a gathering on the rooftop of the hotel at which Weiler is staying. All evening she steals glances at him; she can feel him looking at her, too. After the other guests have departed, she remains with him on the roof. The summer night is chilly; he offers her his jacket; she refuses, then agrees to share it with him. They huddle beneath it and talk; the conversation becomes personal; they feel a powerful rapport. "We're really old acquaintances, you and I, aren't we?" Weiler says. "Why, we've known each other for twenty years, since the day I dreamed my first dreams of life and love! Where have you been all this time? I've waited so long for you."

Dina feels she is in a dream herself. "I loved you the moment I saw you," Weiler goes on. Yet she can't respond as he would like her to. "I don't love anyone," she tells him. "I can't. That feeling has gone dead in me. It's been murdered forever." All she longs for is a child who is like her. Perhaps Weiler...

The poet stares at her, wondering if she is mad. Sexually aroused, however, he tells her he will go to his room to make sure no one is there and return for her. While she waits for him, she climbs onto the roof's parapet. He returns smiling. The room is indeed empty.

> He walked quickly toward her. Dina flailed her arms. Either she had lost her balance, or...
> With a terrible cry, she plummeted three floors to the street below.

This was all Jan's fantasy, of course, its final scene suggested by the letter in which she had imagined hosting Bialik on her Jerusalem roof. Was it her revenge on him? She had illustrated "The Scroll of Fire" and surely knew she was paraphrasing it. *My sister, is that you? In my childhood's dawn I glimpsed your beauty and craved its hidden light!* Had she thought at the time that these words were meant for her? Was she now mocking them? And perhaps she was telling Bialik, "Yes, you may have loved me, but you lacked the courage to say so and you killed my love for you. You killed *me.*"

Had she dreamed of having his child?

And the strange name Dina Dinar! No, not strange at all. *I went looking for your farthing and I lost my sovereign.* In Hebrew, we have said, Bialik's sovereign is a *dinar.*

In the end, it was all connected: Bialik's marriage, and his coronation as national poet, and the "The Scroll of Fire," and "Evening," and Noyekh and Marinka, and the man who averaged barely a poem a year between 1911 and his death in Tel Aviv in 1934, and the woman who wrote: *And now he's grown up and is a poet – a poet who wants a soft pillow... he who could have set the world on fire!*

9

"Beyond the Fence" is a modern Hebrew classic. So is Bialik's narrative
of a shtetl childhood "Aftergrowth," written in sections between 1908
and 1923. Though he did not produce a great deal of Hebrew fiction, he
was one of its modern masters.

As he was also of the modern Hebrew essay. Here, too, his out-
put was slim but outstanding: "The Pangs of Language," "Revealment
and Concealment in Speech," "Halakhah and Aggadah" – these and a
few other such pieces, dating to the 1910s and '20s, are gems of thought
and expression.

"Halakhah and Aggadah," for example. Published in 1917, it has not,
one hundred years later, lost its power to surprise. It begins:

> Halakhah frowns. Aggadah laughs. The first is strict, exacting,
> harder than steel – the principle of rigor. The second is mild,
> forbearing, more fluid than oil – the principle of leniency. The
> one lays down the law and knows no half-measures; its "yes" is
> yes and its "no" is no. The other suggests but no more; it mea-
> sures each man by his capacities; its "yes" and its "no" are both
> "maybe." On the one hand, the body, the deed, the outer shell; on
> the other, the soul, the intention, the inner core. Here – fossil-
> ized tradition, duty, enslavement; there – perpetual renewal, the
> right to choose, freedom.

This is a Bialik we have not seen before. It is not the poet of many
registers or the poised narrator of fiction. It is Bialik the intellectual. His
language is an aphorist's, cut and polished like a diamond. It is confident, assertive. It does not say, "Let us think about this together." It says,
"Trust me. I know."

But what does it know that we don't? Aggadah has always been
a place of freedom from Halakhah in rabbinic texts. This is its function
in the Talmud, where it alternates with passages of legal dialectics to
let the tired mind relax in the playground of the imagination. For the
serious Talmudist, like the ascetic burner of the midnight oil in Bialik's
early poem *Ha-Matmid*, "The Steadfast Student," Aggadah can seem
superfluous, a distraction. For the more casually minded, however, let

alone for the poet or dreamer, it is an oasis between one dry stretch of Halakhah and the next. When, in 1910, Bialik revisited the study house of his youth and its heavy volumes of the Talmud in their famous editions in his poem "Before the Bookshelf," it was Halakhah he was thinking of when he wrote:

> Now, my soul as creased by years as is my brow,
> Life's wheel returns me to you and I stand
> Once more before you, you shelf-dwellers from Lvov,
> Slavuta, Amsterdam, and Frankfurt.
> Again I turn your heavy vellum pages
> And my eye gropes wearily between their lines,
> Searching dumbly in their labyrinth of words
> For some traces of myself and of the path
> Taken by my soul when, in its native home,
> It set out haltingly with its first steps.
> And yet, you testimonials to my youth,
> I feel nothing and no tear trembles on my eye's rim.
> I look at you, you Ancient Ones, as if I didn't know you,
> Nor do your letters return my gaze
> With that clear-eyed sorrow of the Ages
> That once penetrated to my inner depths.
> Black beads spilled from a torn thread is all they are to me,
> Their pages mute and every word an orphan –
> And if they murmur in a grave that no one visits,
> Their whisper fails to reach me.
> Have I forgotten how to see and how to hear you –
> Or is it you, forever dead and rotted,
> Who no longer have a place among the living?

And so in reading the opening paragraphs of "Halakhah and Aggadah," we take its championing of Aggadah for granted. Why prefer enslavement to freedom? Yet by the time we have reached the essay's end, it has performed an astonishing about-face. How has it gotten from its first lines to its last ones?

Give us commandments!

Give us firm molds in which to mint our incontinent wills in hard, lasting coin. We thirst for the bodies of deeds. Let life train us in them more than in words, in Halakhah more than in Aggadah.

We bow our necks: where is the iron yoke? Why do not the mighty hand and outstretched arm appear?

In the biblical account of the exodus, the "mighty hand" and "outstretched arm" are God's. Was Bialik calling for a return to the lost faith of his youth?

He knew it could not be returned to. The same year "Halakhah and Aggadah" was published, he wrote a poem, his only one in all of 1917, based on the well-known midrash about four rabbis who ventured into the "orchard" of mystical experience – one of whom, Shimon ben Azzai, "peered and died." (At what or from what, the midrash does not say.) Ballad-like, Bialik's poem tells of a seeker for truth who sets out, torch in hand, to traverse the fifty gates that lead to Ultimate Reality. At long last, exhausted by his life's quest, he arrives at the fiftieth.

The gate swung open and his torch went out
As he peered in.
By its fag-end he collapsed and lay
On Nothing's rim.

The Void of the "There's nothing here" of "In the City of Slaughter" has remained a void. The argument of "Halakhah and Aggadah" is entirely secular. It conceptualizes the two genres not as merely literary ones but as categories of Jewish life, two different ways of apprehending and dealing with the world: one poetic and one practical, one free to soar and one earthbound, one expansive and one contractive. Together they are the systole and diastole of Jewish existence – or, in Bialik's own image, the water and the ice, two manifestations of a unity that is most apparent in the moments of transition between them. "Halakhah is the crystallization, the final and necessary reduction, of Aggadah. Aggadah is molten Halakhah."

As an example, Bialik gives the Jewish Sabbath. This originated in antiquity, he conjectures, as Aggadah – that is, as the visionary idea, at a time when no such concept existed, of a weekly day of rest. Gradually, this idea was given halakhic form by Judaism's numerous Sabbath laws, and the Sabbath, having developed into a central institution in Jewish life, was then re-aggadized in various ways, such as being imagined by Jewish folklore as a queen who arrives once a week to spend the seventh day with her subjects. This folk-belief, in turn, was re-halakhized by such customs as the *Lekha Dodi* prayer in the Sabbath-eve service, in which the Sabbath Queen is ritually welcomed, and so on and so forth.

Aggadah is given concrete form by Halakhah and Halakhah is revitalized by Aggadah. The Aggadist conceives of a cathedral; the Halakhist is the stonecutter, the mason, the glassmaker, and the sculptor who build it over time. These, too, are creative tasks. "When I think," Bialik writes, "of all the ancients who labored on formulating the Sabbath laws, I say: 'Here were artists of life!'... And what was the outcome of all this monumental [halakhic] work? A day that is all Aggadah!"

The problem of post-religious Jewish existence, Bialik's essay contends, is that it has lost the dynamic balance between Halakhah and Aggadah. For the Jew quit of his religious duties, freedom has become everything. "We live in times that are all Aggadah, Aggadah in literature and Aggadah in life." The subjective has triumphed over the objective; the inward over the outward; feeling over form; taste over its justification; self-expression over communication; individual wants and needs over social norms. Yet Aggadah that is not accompanied by Halakhah is "onanistic" and has no staying power.

> There has developed a Jewishness that is all choice. It may make demands on us in the name of Jewish nationalism, Jewish rebirth, Jewish literature, Jewish creativity, Jewish education, Jewish thought, Jewish activity, but all these hang on the thread of likes and dislikes – for the Land of Israel, for the Hebrew language, for Hebrew literature – and what is the price of failing to live up to such bloodless preferences? Where are the obligations? Whence will they come? From Aggadah? But Aggadah is by nature a matter of free choice. Its "yes" and its "no" are always "maybe."

A Jewish life that is all Aggadah is like iron from the forge that has not been tempered and hardened. Inner strivings, good intentions, mental stirrings, likes and dislikes: all are well and good as long as they lead in the end to deeds – cruelly obligatory, hard-as-steel deeds.

These are the reflections of a conservative. But Bialik's conservatism was, like Ahad Ha'am's, social and cultural rather than political. Politically, he was a supporter of Chaim Weizmann, which placed him closer to the Labor Zionist left than to Jabotinsky's Revisionist right. Politics as such did not interest him much. The one time he found himself at the center of them was largely unintentional.

This was in 1931, when, following an international Zionist congress at which the Revisionists had helped block Weizmann's re-election as head of the Zionist movement, Bialik published a poetic broadside entitled "I Have Seen You in Your Impotence Again" that was aimed at Weizmann's critics. Although he denied having had the Revisionists specifically in mind, the poem was taken as an attack on them and led to angry ripostes, one by Jabotinsky himself. The incident, however, blew over and dragged him no deeper into the political arena.

"Halakhah and Aggadah" does not speculate about what a secular Halakhah might consist of. It is not a programmatic essay, and it tells us more about Bialik's state of mind when he wrote it than about his conception of a new Jewish social order. He himself, after all, was a *ba'al aggadah*, an Aggadist. He had spent years researching and collecting Aggadah. His poetry alluded to it frequently and as a poet he identified with its imaginative processes. In "Before the Bookshelf" he had expressed his alienation from the literature of Halakhah. Whence his unexpected upholding of it?

Perhaps he was seeking to reestablish a sense of Halakhah in himself – not the Halakhah of ritual observance, which he never went back to, but the Halakhah of human duty, of the obligation to be or do what one does not necessarily want to be or do because it is one's responsibility to be or do it. He had always acted this way, but with a resentment that colored his emotions and work, frustrated by a life that was not the one he had dreamed of. The Aggadist had been living halakhically all along. In "Halakhah and Aggadah" he finally came to terms with this.

10

Bialik settled in Palestine, in Tel Aviv, in 1924. The national poet was now living in the national home – in his own home, too, a large house with a Moorish façade built on a street renamed Bialik Street. A small and informal town, Tel Aviv clasped him to its bosom, and Bialik, a convivial man who found it hard to say no, let it do so. As described by Fichman, who had taken up residence in Tel Aviv five years previously, "his home was open to all. There wasn't a day when it wasn't besieged by people from all walks of life, each with his requests and grievances: the novice author looking for a patron, the bankrupt merchant, the peddler unable to get a municipal license, the widow whose house had been foreclosed on by the bank –all asked for his help and took him away from his work." He was a one-man academy of language. "Whoever opened a shop or restaurant, a company or a pub, pestered him to give it a Hebrew name. Every workman demanded Hebrew terms for his tools."

He bore it gracefully. Besides entertaining with Manya at Bialik Street, he spoke and appeared at numerous cultural and literary events; managed the important publishing house of Dvir; worked on scholarly editions of the medieval Hebrew poets Shlomo ibn Gabirol and Moshe ibn Ezra; wrote more essays and parts of "Aftergrowth"; composed words for folk songs and children's songs, some of which remain popular to this day (there isn't an Israeli parent who hasn't sung Bialik's "Swing, swing, up and down" to a child on a swing or seesaw); and instituted and presided over the practice, called by him *oneg shabbat*, of public lectures, readings, and discussions that gave secular cultural enhancement to the Sabbath. When he died of an embolism following prostate surgery at the age of sixty-one, Tel Aviv gave him the largest funeral in its history.

Many of his activities were related to the project that he called *Kinus*, "Gathering." *Kinus* meant taking inventory of the Jewish literary and cultural heritage, much of it neglected or even forgotten over the ages and relegated, sometimes literally, to the nation's attics; combing through it, as he and Ravnitzky had done with Aggadah, for whatever was of enduring value; and issuing this in popular editions prepared by scholars. It was as if, in preparing for the great move from the Diaspora back to the Land of Israel, Zionism needed to sort out the Jewish people's accumulated possessions, from the biblical apocrypha to post-biblical Hebrew poetry and from medieval Jewish philosophy to the Hasidic folktale; pack whatever was worth keeping; and prepare available shelves for it in its new home. A patrimony that religious Jewry had largely lost interest in would thus be put at the service of a new, secular, Hebrew high culture. Although Bialik was never able to get a comprehensive plan for *Kinus* adopted and funded, much of what he envisioned has been implemented on a piecemeal basis over time.

In 1933–34, shortly before his death, he returned to the writing of poetry with a series of verse narratives about his childhood that never was completed. As if also going back to his childhood's first book, he wrote with the cadences and internal parallelism of biblical verse:

> I did not see much of my father. His days by my side were not many.
> I was but a slip of a boy who still had not had his fill of him.
> I still was in need of his kindness, of his sheltering hand on my head,
> When he was taken from me by death and separated from me forever.

Although such lines had their poignant moments, their language was tired. By now, Bialik had long been under critical attack by a fresh generation of young modernist poets. Two decades after being hailed as the voice of the new Hebrew poetry, he was being assailed as outmoded.

There are critics who have held that Bialik was never at his best in his longer, narrative verse and that his finest work is to be found entirely in his short lyrics. Frischman was the first of them. Bialik was truest to himself, he wrote, when being "the great poet of small things." He should never have sought to go beyond them.

This was the cavalier judgment of an aesthete. "In the City of Slaughter," "The Dead of the Desert," "The Pond" – these are powerful, lasting poems that had and still have an impact that no single short lyric can have. But Frischman, as usual, had put his finger on something. The signature Bialik, the Bialik whose music we would recognize from a single stanza even if we had never seen it before as we recognize certain composers from a single phrase, is the Bialik of poems like "Take Me Under Your Wing" and "At Sunset Time."

Or like the first two-and-a-half stanzas of "The Summer Is Dying." This was a poem that Bialik wrote in the early autumn of 1905, immediately after finishing "The Scroll of Fire."

> The summer is dying in orange and gold
> And the fiery flood
> Of fallen leaves and an evening sky
> Bathed in a sea of blood.
>
> The parks are empty. Only a few
> Lonely figures out for a walk
> Still cast a pensive glance at the last
> Lingering flight of a stork.
>
> The heart is an orphan. Soon a drizzly day
> Will knock on the window pane:
> "Have you patched your coats? Have you cobbled your shoes?
> It's time for potatoes again!"

One's first reaction to this poem's last two lines, which almost clownishly destroy the lyrical mood that has been created, is a feeling of letdown. Potatoes indeed! Why did Bialik deliberately mar something so lovely?

But the fall from peak experience to commonplace existence is precisely what the poem is about. After "The Scroll of Fire," Bialik took Frischman's advice. Never again until his last years did he attempt anything major. In his more self-pitying moments, he blamed the Hebrew-reading public for being unworthy, not only of him, but of the national rebirth whose poetic symbol it had made him:

> And if my strength happened to fail,
> The fault lies with you, not with me.
> Wherever it drove in a nail,
> My hammer hit on decay.

Written in 1920, these lines come from a poem called "Seer, Be Gone!" – words spoken in the Bible by the Judean king Amatsiah to the prophet Amos, who replies in Bialik's poem by defiantly declaring that he will stand his ground. Yet Bialik's reign as the national poet was already ending. If his prestige and authority were unaffected by this, it was because he now increasingly held sway as the nation's immensely versatile man of letters.

His Ahad Ha'amist faith in a Zionist-led Hebrew renaissance in Palestine as the one sure anchor of a modern Jewish identity never faltered; nor did his labors on its behalf, even as they shifted from poetry to other areas. Yet he had also become, so he felt, Zionism's captive. This is always a danger for the creative artist who is identified closely with a national or ideological cause. The private "I" becomes entangled in a public one. This gives it greater buoyancy but hinders it from diving deeper into itself. The greater the unexplored depths, the more is lost.

He composed what might have been intended to be his epitaph. People meeting him for the first time often commented on the fact that he did not look like their idea of a poet. His plain, simple face, it was said, was more like a businessman's. This pleased him. He had always been in business – first, when young, as a lumber dealer (he had also briefly traded in coal), and then, for the rest of his life, as a publisher. The cost and quality of paper, the choice of print, debating a graphic design, negotiating with authors and booksellers – he enjoyed the practicality, the solidity, of these things. In 1923, he wrote, resorting for one of the last times to the simple quatrains he always had favored:

You have crushed me
With the burden of your love.
You have made of me your rattle,
A tin kettle on your stove.

What made you poach on my grounds?
What wrong had I done or what good?
No poet or prophet was I,
But a simple cutter of wood.

A woodcutter, a man of the ax,
Performing my daily chore.
But the day is done, and my arms are weak,
And the dull-bladed ax cuts no more.

Chapter Nine

Oved Etsot Meets Aryeh Lapidot: Yosef Chaim Brenner and A. D. Gordon

1

How translate the title of Yosef Chaim Brenner's novel *Mikan u'Mikan*, the first major work of modern Hebrew fiction to be written in Palestine, where its story takes place at the end of the first decade of the twentieth century? Until now this has been done, more or less literally, as "From Here and From There." The Hebrew title alludes, among other things, to the seemingly casual structure of the novel, whose different parts may strike the reader as semi-independent vignettes, and "From Here and From There" conveys this impression well.

But the novel's tone is anything but casual. It is, like all of Brenner's fiction, dark and anguished. Modeled on its author, the story's narrator, a Hebrew-writing journalist who signs his columns of political and social commentary Oved Etsot or "Out of Advice," is a tormented soul living in Palestine despite the fact that he does not believe in the Zionist dream, does not believe in the Jewish future, and does not believe in the possibility of his own happiness. In all this he contrasts with another of the novel's characters, the laborer-intellectual Aryeh Lapidot, based by Brenner on the real-life figure of Aharon David or A. D. Gordon.

Brenner and Gordon, who was unrelated to Yehuda Leib Gordon, knew each other well. They were friends, mutual admirers, and public disputants, as are Oved Etsot and Lapidot. Gordon, indeed, might have been describing Oved Etsot's state of mind in *Mikan u'Mikan* when he wrote in his book "Man and Nature":

> The question is: Is there any point or meaning in life when in it are death, sorrow, boundless suffering of every kind, lies, hatred, evil, imbecility, cruelty, pettiness, vileness, ugliness, filth, pollution, and tedium without end? Is there any point in living life with all its contradictions and inconsistencies that tear the soul apart like a butchered goat?... As an "I" that has only myself in this world, whose vastness I contemplate as a detached, unnoticed, solitary, uncomprehending being buffeted from all sides like chaff on a threshing floor – what is it to me or I to it?

Let us then call *Mikan u'Mikan* "From All Sides." This is no less true to the Hebrew language and truer to the novel itself.

2

"From All Sides" was the last of seven short novels that Brenner, who was born in 1881, published between 1903 and 1911 – a highly creative period in which he also wrote two plays and many stories, sketches, articles, and essays. Because the novels and plays are heavily autobiographical, the outlines of his life can be traced in them, starting with his childhood and adolescence in a Ukrainian shtetl, where he grew up as the eldest child in a poor family. His first novel, "In Winter," serialized in 1903–4 in *Ha-Shiloah*, tells of this period. Its central drama is a protracted struggle with a father who desperately wants his intellectually gifted son to pursue his religious studies, become a rabbi, and thereby confer on their family the social prestige and financial security that it lacks. This conflict becomes increasingly exacerbated as the novel's young narrator, Yirmiya Feierman, loses his religious faith and willingness to go on lying about it to his parents, culminating in a bitter rupture with them.

Four passages mark the extreme swings of mood with which "In Winter," which established Brenner's reputation as an important Hebrew writer when he was still in his early twenties, concludes. The first of these takes place on the eve of Yirmiya's final break with his parents. He has been having bad dreams, and in one of them,

> I was in a filthy sack. Sand was piled on my head and heavy rocks pinned my arms and feet. I struggled free from the sack only to be knocked back down by my father standing over me… Then I was a fly sporting on Rakhil Moiseyevna's cheeks. She grabbed my wings and pulled them off.

Rakhil Moiseyevna, a young woman Yirmiya is too shy to declare his interest in, has none at all in him. His two dreams are complementary. The domineering father threatening to rebury him alive (it is obviously he who tied him in the sack and piled dirt on him in the first place) makes him feel as puny and helpless as a fly. The sexually rejecting woman (the Hebrew verb *m'tsaḥek*, translated here as "sporting," has clear erotic overtones) symbolically castrates him. The two are allied in crushing him.

In a second passage, Yirmiya's sense of worthlessness and humiliating injury lead him to contemplate the possibility of suicide:

> The good or ill of society – this world or another – liberty or servitude – pleasure and pain – free will and predestination – matter and spirit – the eternal and the transient – hunger and the life of luxury – knowledge and ignorance – faith and unbelief – what have I to do with any of these? If I were to listen to the voice of inner reason, I, Yirmiya Feierman, would not go on living for another minute. And yet I'm alive and will be alive tomorrow. I'll never free myself. I don't have the will to free myself. I'm not free enough to free myself.
>
> In my Bible is written: "Behold, before you are two paths. One you are commanded to follow. The other leads to the way out. And thou shalt choose death!"
>
> Yet how far I am from choosing it!

"Thou shalt choose life!" says the Bible that Yirmiya was raised on – and in the next passage, he emphatically does. From the Russian city of N., where he is temporarily staying after parting with his parents for the last time, he writes to a friend:

> Today the sun is out – not a wintry sun with its face of a pale, sickly woman but a hot, summery sun too strong for the naked eye. Light and warmth are everywhere – Ah, brother, how I love life! How I love it, how happy it makes me just to feel and to breathe!... I love all that is good, beautiful, pure, sublime, powerful, just.... Although I know that only more suffering awaits me in the future, I'm not afraid, not afraid at all.
> Tomorrow I'm off.

Tomorrow arrives:

> It was an overcast night.
> At a small train station between N. and A. I was dragged from my hiding place beneath a bench in a third-class carriage and taken to the stationhouse.
> I had no money or luggage. I sat there until told to go back to where I had come from.
> "But it's the middle of the night!"
> "There's a village near here."
> "How far?"
> "No more than two miles."
> "Are there any Jews there?"
> "No, no Moshkes."
> "Then...how..."
> "You're being told to go!"
> "You Jews," growled the red-capped stationmaster. "Don't think I don't know all your tricks!"
> I rose and walked off.
> A tall policeman with nothing better to do escorted me.

> I crossed the embankment with its bare piles. A lantern
> gave some light. Beyond it was a stack of wood on which I lay down
> A wet, sleety snow was falling.

It isn't clear what Yirmiya's destination is and perhaps he, too,
doesn't know. He can't go home, he can't pay for a steamship ticket to
America, and he feels such an outsider as a Jew that he can't imagine asking for a night's lodgings in a Russian village from anyone but another
Jew. Odessa, once headed for by young Jews with literary ambitions,
has lost its allure. His only option is to join other young drifters like
himself living on the fringes of Jewish society in the towns of the Pale
of Settlement as odd job holders, unmatriculated students, indigent
Hebrew tutors, unemployed intellectuals, and would-be revolutionaries.

Such is the milieu of Brenner's second novel, "Around the Point,"
serialized in *Ha-Shiloah* again in 1904–5. Its protagonist, Yakov Abramson,
an aspiring author with a background like Yirmiya's but a year or two
older, has acquired the good knowledge of Russian that Yirmiya lacked.
Yet he insists on writing in Hebrew, even though few of his friends can
read it or understand his commitment to it. The language of Jewish
observance and study, despite his having given these up, is too deeply
embedded in him to forgo it. When he tells his friend Yeva (*née* Chava)
Isakovna Blumin, a young revolutionary he is secretly in love with, that
he is writing an essay in it on the unrecognized contribution of Hasidism
to nineteenth-century Hebrew literature, she predicts he will switch to
writing in Russian one day. He answers "Never!" and she asks:

> "But why not? You can't deny you'd have more readers."
> "And what if I did?"
> "What do you mean, what if you did?"
> "Just what I said. What do I care how many there are if I
> have nothing to say to them?"
> "It's not true that you have nothing to say to them. You
> don't want to have anything."
> "It's all the same," Abramson said morosely. "I don't want
> to want. Look, Yeva Isakovna: let's say that I could write – only
> that isn't so – but let's say I could write something of value in

293

Russian and get it published in some monthly – there's happily no shortage of Jewish journalists in the Russian monthlies – or even that my article on Hebrew literature were written in Russian for a Russian Jewish magazine. You're right that I have no readers now at all. I admit it: none. Not that I would have any then, either – everyone knows that no one reads the Russian Jewish magazines – but at least in theory I might have. You, Yeva Isakovna, would certainly look for such an article and find it. But that's just it! That's just it! I won't pretend it wouldn't matter to me. It would. It certainly would. But the whole question has no relevance." Abramson suddenly grew angry. "I'm a Jew and I write in Hebrew for Hebrews!"

Yeva Isakovna doesn't suggest that Abramson write in Yiddish, as she would do if she belonged to the Yiddisher Arbiter Bund rather than to an all-Russian revolutionary organization. Although she presumably understands some Yiddish learned from parents or grandparents, she doesn't read it or its literature. She has no use for Jewish separatism of any kind, let alone for the Zionism that Abramson believes in.

And Abramson is a Zionist mainly because of his feelings about Hebrew. Convinced that, despite the "bright spot of Hasidism," as he calls it, the last several centuries of Jewish life in Eastern Europe have been "the most disastrous time in the history of Jewish exile," he dreams of a great Hebrew cultural revival in Palestine in which "the original, once fertile Hebrew spirit will awake and be renewed." Yet he disdains the pettiness of Zionist politics, and gradually persuaded that Zionism cannot speak to the Jewish masses, he takes Yeva Isakovna's advice, burns his Hebrew essay, and begins a new one in Russian that rejects all nationalism. In effect a call for Jewish assimilation made under the psychological pressure of his fear of losing the friendship of the woman he loves, this lands him in an emotional and psychological void. No longer recognizable to himself, he considers suicide like Yirmiya Feierman, comes close to committing it, pulls back from the brink at the last moment, and suffers a breakdown at the novel's end.

In an incipient form, "Around the Point" hinges on what was to be the central theme of "From All Sides": the relationship between two different struggles to survive, or more exactly, to retain the instinct of survival – that of the Jewish people and that of the Jew identified with his people but fearful it is doomed. Abramson is an heir of the Haskalah: he shares its view of Jewry as a sick body that must either be healed or die. But he is also a product of the revolt against the Haskalah that started with Smolenskin and his age and intensified with Berdichevsky and his. The Haskalah, it was argued, diagnosed the symptoms of the illness without realizing that it was one of them. It urged the Jewish people to transform its life while undermining the religion that justified its will to live. Its proposed solutions to the Jewish problem – religious and educational reform, modernization, economic progress, and so forth – were those of an enlightened rationalism. But the will to live is irrational. It has to do not with reason but with a healthy vitality.

And this, when Abramson looks at the Jewish world around him, is what it lacks. This is why, though a religious unbeliever, he regards Hasidism, for which the Haskalah had a special animus, as a "bright spot." Hasidism, as an early Maskil like Josef Perl understood intuitively when he let the Hasidic villains of "The Revealer of Secrets" run away with its story, was the most vital impulse in nineteenth-century Jewish life. Its essential optimism; its sense of God's everyday presence; the noisy hubbub of its prayer; the endlessly self-renewing rhythms of its song and dance; its limitless faith in its rebbes and the wonders they could perform: through all these coursed a powerful life-force that had no need of intellectual rationalizations. An anti-Hasidic joke told in Brenner's day in Maskilic circles expressed, like Perl's novel, an unintended appreciation of this. A Maskil comes to a town and posts an announcement that he will give a lecture that evening. A large audience turns out to hear him. "Tonight," he begins, "I will give three proofs of God's existence." The enraged Hasidim in the audience rise from their seats. "Atheist, get out!" they shout as one man and drive the Maskil from the stage.

3

"From All Sides" is set in 1909–10 in mixed Arab-Jewish Jaffa and the nearby Jewish village of Petach Tikva, then the largest and most prosperous of Palestine's Zionist colonies, with flashbacks to other times and places. In an apologetic preface, its editor explains that its Hebrew manuscript consisting of six notebooks was found by him in the knapsack of "a suffering wanderer in our far-flung Jewish world" and occasioned an argument with its publisher. The latter, short of material, was eager to publish it; the editor was opposed. The manuscript, he tells the publisher, has no aesthetic value, "neither lyric pathos, nor intellectual scope, nor an accomplished style, nor an architectural structure, nor the slightest manifestation of the world soul." The publisher, who may or may not know that art as a manifestation of the "world soul" is a doctrine of the fashionable Russian literary critic Vladimir Soloviev, concedes the truth of this while sticking to his guns. "But the content... the Palestinian content!" he counters. "That's what the public is looking for." On the contrary, protests the editor: it is precisely what the public is *not* looking for! "There's not a single description in it of the beauties of Mount Carmel or the Plain of Sharon, nothing about the fields walked in by the shepherd boy David, not a word about the bravery of our native youth or its mettle with a rifle or on horseback." The Hebrew reader wants edifying descriptions of Palestine such as the manuscript does not provide. Ultimately, however, so the editor informs the reader, he grudgingly agreed and prepared the six notebooks for publication.

Just how Oved Etsot's knapsack – for the "suffering wanderer" is he – was found by the editor is unclear. Was it lost? Did Oved Etsot die somewhere in "the far-flung Jewish world" and leave it behind? Did he and the editor know each other? We aren't told. What matters are two things, the importance of only one of which we grasp immediately – namely, that we are being asked to make allowances for the literary shortcomings of what we are about to read, since it was not intended to be read by others. What merits it possesses exist in spite of its unpolished style, not because of it.

The literary convention of the found manuscript, designed to inspire credence or forestall criticism, is ancient. (The oldest recorded case of it, indeed, is a Hebrew one – the "discovery," according to the Bible, of the book of Deuteronomy by the scribes of King Hezekiah in the seventh century BCE.) For Brenner, it was one of several fictional conceits employed in his novels to warn readers of the bumpy prose ahead. "In Winter" begins with Yirmiya Feierman telling us: "I've prepared a fresh notebook in which I intend to sketch a few scenes from my life…. I'm writing this strictly for myself." "One Year," which relates the story of its protagonist Hanina Mintz's (and Brenner's) year as a conscript in the Russian army, is prefaced by the disclosure that it is a record of Mintz's oral account to the narrator while walking the streets of a city one night. "Breakdown and Bereavement," the last of Brenner's novels, starts with a private journal come across in an abandoned traveling bag. Although such fictions do not fool us, they bear a message from the author. "Don't expect this book to be a work of art," it says, "because my purpose is not to be artful. It is to be truthful – as truthful as I would have been had I simply transcribed something told to me or found by me without changing it."

Such pretended artlessness, of course, is a fiction, too. Brenner belonged to the first generation of Eastern European Hebrew writers to be deeply influenced by Russian literature; his approach to the novel reflected not only his own belief in honesty as a supreme value but the preference of much nineteenth-century Russian literary criticism for a scrupulous and engaged social realism. "Realism and aesthetics," wrote this school's most radical representative, Dimitri Pisarev, "are in a state of irreconcilable hostility," which can only end with "realism's destruction of aesthetics" – and while no novelist can accept a formulation that would make of him a literary vandal slashing the canvas that he paints on, a skillful novelist knows that is possible to create the successful illusion of a slashed canvas. In one way or another, this is what all of Brenner's novels seek to do.

Feigning an indifference to art while writing artfully calls for a technique of its own, and Brenner's prose often has the same "deliberate clumsiness" that has been attributed to Dostoyevsky, the Russian author he was most influenced by. Like Dostoyevsky, he took pains to write dialogue and interior monologue that mimicked the awkwardness of actual thought and speech. Abramson's explanation to Yeva Isakovna of why he can't write in Russian is a case in point. A more economical writer might simply have had him say, "It's the same thing. I'm a Jew and I write in Hebrew for Hebrews." All the stumbling that takes him from his first sentence to his last doesn't advance the content of his remarks. It doesn't even show the workings of his mind in any way that is unique to itself. What it shows is the workings of *the* mind, the roundabout way in which most of us grope while trying to make some point or arrive at some conclusion. In doing so, it creates an impression of reality as opposed to art, just as a painter's *trompe l'oeil* tricks us into thinking that we are looking at an actual scene and not a painting.

Oved Etsot, like Abramson, often thinks aloud without first organizing his thoughts. The first of his six notebooks is begun in a hospital in Jaffa, where he is recovering from a bout of illness. Wondering whether it is true, as is commonly believed, that a man's entire life passes before him at the moment of his death, he writes:

> O Psychology, where art thou?
>
> But anyway, I'm not that ill. This isn't my last day, and right now – or so it seems – that is, as of four o'clock this afternoon – my end hasn't arrived. And yet my whole past is on view in my mind – my recent past, anyway – and it hasn't been so bad, this past of mine – not so insignificant – as Psychology is my witness!... No, really. I accept it gladly, this past of mine; there's nothing in it I regret. I'm sure that if I were nineteen again instead of twenty-nine and could decide to relive those ten years...yes, I'm sure...but of what?

Brenner wrote such passages at a time when the spoken Hebrew revival was gathering momentum in Palestine. From Smolenskin on, Hebrew literature had sought to make Hebrew seem a natural medium of communication even though its speakers were "really" talking in Yiddish or some other European language; in Brenner's novels we find the attempt to make it seem a natural medium of *consciousness* even though those now talking in it are not yet thinking in it. While Hebrew, A. D. Gordon wrote in 1916 in one of a series of "Letters to the Diaspora," was increasingly being used for everyday conversation in Palestine and not just in schools and at public events, it was "fully alive" only in the mouths of the still small number of children being raised in it.

Oved Etsot is capable of deploying a more conventionally literary prose style when he wants to. He does so in the next paragraph:

> Ah, my past, my past! It's always the same reckoning. In it are no royal honors, no annals of bravery; no revolutionary escapades

or daring jail breaks; not a single mass rally at which I was cheered by thousands; not one brush with death or miraculous escape from it. The sad reality is that I have never even been clasped in the arms of a dancing beauty; never gone big-game hunting in Africa; never, for that matter, been as far as Transjordan.

Though more sardonic, this is close to the opening of "In Winter":

My past! Anyone hearing me utter those words might think I had something frightful to disclose, some heart-wrenching tale. Not at all! My past is not of the slightest interest; in it are no gripping events, no terrible tragedies; no murders or romantic dramas; not even a winning lottery ticket or an unexpected inheritance.

Yirmiya Feierman is about nineteen when he writes these lines circa 1900 – that is, he is the same young man whom Oved Etsot, now twenty-nine, remembers being ten years earlier. Brenner, too, was twenty-nine when he wrote "From All Sides," and Yirmiya, Yakov Abramson, Hanina Mintz, and Oved Etsot are all essentially the identical person at different stages of his life. Although the warning against confusing authors with their characters is always worth heeding, doing so is difficult in Brenner's case. Thus, in his first notebook, Oved Etsot recalls the time spent by him in the city of "L." in Austrian Galicia; Brenner, after deserting the Russian army and making his way to London, where he worked for three years as a Hebrew and Yiddish typesetter while publishing a Hebrew literary review, resided in Lvov, the Austrian Lemberg. From L., Oved Etsot departs for Palestine; so, from Lvov, did Brenner. After an abortive attempt at being a farm hand in Petach Tikva, Oved Etsot moves to Jerusalem; Brenner did the same. Oved Etsot then returns to Petach Tikva, finds work writing for the Jaffa-based political and cultural biweekly *Ha-Mahreshah*, "The Plow," and serves on its editorial board; Brenner, now a contributing editor of the Labor Zionist organ *Ha-Po'el Ha-Tsa'ir*, "The Young Worker," was soon back in Petach Tikva, too. It's hard to tell the two men apart.

Oved Etsot looks back on the years before coming to Palestine as wasted ones:

> What did I have in them? Wearisome days of writing and tutoring; dry bread to eat and plain water to drink; or else days in which I did nothing but gnash my teeth; nights of loneliness...a young man's rage at the cry of his repressed male nature; long hours of crushing, habitual despair.

The worthlessness of his past, as he sees it, is analogous to that of the Jewish past: both are dismayingly hyper-cerebral, removed from a healthy physicality, and lack any accomplishment in the real world. His life is Jewish history recapitulated. Describing a scene in Lvov in which he looks up from a book he is reading to regard a lively group of youngsters on their way to the theater, he writes,

> With my bent back and the faded color of my distinctly unfashionable clothes (whose patches called to mind dead leaves blown under a park bench such as the backless one I was sitting on while reading Goethe's *Faust*), I felt like a hoary old Jew, an anchoritic Essene from ancient times who had wandered by mistake into a pagan hippodrome where half-naked women pranced on noble horses.

"What really do I want?" he asks himself, rising from the bench. To which he gives the Zionist answer: "Land under my feet... redemption...a revolution from the ground up...a fundamentally new life!" Although he has no faith in the Ahad Ha'amian Hebrew revival that Yakov Abramson, too, has given up on, he regards Palestine as his and the Jewish people's only hope of making a fresh start. He writes of his conversations with a friend, the symbolically named David Diasporin:

> I explained to him that I, as a Zionist, didn't dream of a rebirth of the spirit of the Hebrew nation but simply of getting away, away from the ghetto. "Renaissance," *risorgimento* – those were

charming words, but they had nothing to do with us; our world had no room for them; we weren't Italy. Zionism meant for me only that it was time for that part of the Jewish people that still had some life in it to stop clinging to others and blaming them for its faults. We Jews had to see ourselves, past and present, for what we were. The Hebrew spirit? It didn't amount to a thing. Our great national heritage? Not worth a damn. For hundreds of years we lived among Polish and Russian brutes who spat on us – and all we did was wipe the spittle from our faces and go on writing our imbecilic, text-twiddling books. That's your Hebrew spirit!... I knew, I said, one thing: the only way to restore our honor and stop living like fleas was to seize our last chance and make a place for ourselves somewhere by dint of our own physical labor. Yes, our own labor! Every other people had lived, worked, and created for itself and for the generations that came after it while we were doing the devil only knows what. Not working was the root of all evil; work, honest work, the only remedy for it.

Jews as *fleas*? Not even Berdichevsky, whose Nachum Sharoni thinks "there is a reason why everyone hates us," ever resorted to such language. Diasporin, who is staying with a well-off sister in Lvov after being turned down for admission by its institute of technology because he is a Jew, teasingly calls Oved Etsot a "positively lyrical anti-Semite." Having just referred to an attractive maid working in this sister's home as "a pure Polish gem cast before Jewish bourgeois swinishness," Oved Etsot, growing "serious, very serious," replies: "Yes, I am one, perhaps even more of one than those who barred you from the institute. At any rate, I understand them."

Nor is it just Over Etsot who understands the anti-Semites. Brenner did, too. In his essay "A Self-Critique in Three Volumes," written on the occasion of the publication of Mendele Mocher Sefarim's collected works in Hebrew, he wrote, addressing his readers:

Just between us, gentleman, I have a small question to ask – a small but difficult and even crucial one that I'd be surprised to be told you've never asked of yourselves. Suppose that another people were to find itself in our place and that we ourselves were Germans, Russians, or whatever – wouldn't we scorn it? Wouldn't we hate it? Wouldn't we instinctively accuse it of every fault and wrongdoing?

If there is a difference between Brenner and Oved Etsot, it is in their attitude not toward their fellow Jews but toward Palestine. Brenner's kept fluctuating. Hearing a rumor, while in London in 1906, that *Ha-Shiloah* was planning to move its offices to Jerusalem or Jaffa, he applied for work there as a typesetter and added, "To live in Palestine with a decent job has always, always been, for reasons I won't go into, my great desire." *Ha-Shiloah* never made the move, but several months later Brenner wrote to the Hebrew writer Binyamin Radler, then living in Palestine, "One way or another, I've decided to come." Nevertheless, he stressed in his next letter to Radler, he would not be coming as a Zionist. "My journey to Palestine is almost certain," he stated. "I want to get away from literature and everything 'sacred.' I want to work with my hands, to eat, drink, and die in some field when my time comes. I have no higher ideal."

A few weeks later, however, he wrote Radler a third time.

I'm not coming to Palestine after all. I hate the Chosen People and I hate the moribund, so-called "Land of Israel." Phooey!... I plan to bury myself in some hidden corner of London, work in a print shop, and never be heard from again.

To another Hebrew writer, his friend Asher Beilin, who was also thinking of a new life in Palestine, he wrote in September 1908 from Lvov: "What will you do there? I myself would go to New York if only I thought I could find literary work in Hebrew or Yiddish and earn a living." And in January 1909, a mere three weeks before leaving for Palestine, he urged Beilin to join him in Lvov so that they might "open some business together. I'll tell you what: if we see there's nothing to be done here, we can always go to Palestine later."

For Oved Etsot, Palestine is a "last chance." For Brenner, it was a default choice. When he finally set out for it he did so, or at least so he told himself, for lack of a better alternative.

4

It would seem that Brenner made Oved Etsot the Zionist in L. that he, Brenner, refused to call himself only so that Oved Etsot could renounce his Zionism once in Palestine. His disillusion begins as soon as he steps off the boat. To Diasporin, now living with a brother in Chicago, he writes:

> I disembarked in Haifa…. That first evening I went for a walk. What narrow, crooked, dirt-infested streets! And yet my belief that I had come home to my own land was great.
>
> Two Jewish workers from a nearby colony rode toward me on donkeys, white cloths wrapped around their heads in the exotic Arab style. The Orient! For a moment I thought: I'm really in a new world!
>
> But there was no time to savor it, because a band of jeering Arab urchins burst from a squalid alley with a familiar tune: "*Yahud!*" I turned to the two men. "Why don't I punch one of their noses for them, mates?" I said, feeling as brave and proud as a man should feel when the ground beneath him is his own. They quickly rid me of the notion. Didn't I know we were in a city full of goyim, most of them Christians?
>
> Now, too, then… now, too, the world was full of goyim one had to take abuse from… to take it even from filthy ragamuffins!

This is Oved Etsot's introduction to the Arab problem, which he has not bothered to think about until now. In the weeks that follow, he is made aware of how Zionism is arousing Arab nationalism. Far from putting an end to anti-Semitism, as Herzl and his followers were convinced it would, Zionism is providing the fuel for one more outbreak of it:

> The cry of "Palestine, watch out for the Jews!" is already heard all over the Arab world and gaining in volume. Right now its venom is skin-deep, as is everything in Arab public life. It can easily work itself deeper, though. And that's frightening.

Palestine has a Jewish problem, too. On his way to Petach Tikva, Oved Etsot stops at a Rothschild-supported Jewish farming village. (Although unnamed in "From All Sides," this is clearly Zichron Ya'akov, twenty miles south of Haifa.) "The whole place," Oved Etsot writes Diasporin,

> was like a fat, ugly beggar seated at a rich man's table and slurping his food from a bowl gripped by a gross, dirty, leprous hand.
> The colony's officials and administrators were like fattened hogs, too obese to take an unassisted step.... The half-naked, degenerate, groveling Arab farm hands outnumbered the Jews.

A second colony that Oved Etsot passes through does not have many Jewish workers, either:

> I came to an inn there. Neglect and apathy were everywhere. The room hadn't been swept, there was no hot water, and everyone in the innkeeper's family tried getting someone else to take care it.
> Three Jewish workers sat around mournfully, one with a bad leg, one an old man, and one a thirteen-year-old boy. When they had gone to work in the fields that morning, two Arabs had set upon them and given them a beating.
> The lamed man told me that the two others had run off and left him to fend for himself.

Oved Etsot reaches Petach Tikva:

> The place was like a perfectly preserved Lithuanian shtetl; all that was missing was the Polish country squire. Most of the work was done by Arabs here, too, as if that were the normal order of things. There were a few Jewish farm hands, idealists like myself. (Yes, I was one of them for a while – the self-delusion, the self-abasement of it!) ... We were living proof that the simple, healthy, natural life of physical labor wasn't for us. Fruit trees can't be grown in a flowerpot, period! On the likes of us, life could only choke.

He tries life in Jerusalem. There, a long scene takes place in front of a public library, where a group of Jews, having come to read the week's newspapers, congregates one Saturday morning while waiting for the doors to open. All but one of them, a young newcomer from Eastern Europe (Oved Etsot writes about himself here in the third person), belong to Jerusalem's Orthodox community, which forms the bulk of the city's Jewish population. Each a representative type, most are spongers of one kind or another. When the library finally admits them, the newcomer lingers outside with a one-eyed yeshiva student.

> Jerusalem! – The young man uttered the word half-aloud, his sight dimming. It was one big religious artifacts shop, every item on display. No, it was a butcher shop in which holiness was sold by the pound ….
>
> Jerusalem! – The young man swallowed his saliva. Palestine's only city with a Jewish majority – and what a majority!... Carnal Jews without a drop of real blood with which to satisfy their carnality – with which to satisfy even one basic need …. Sickeningly crafty, calculating Jews who didn't know the meaning of love for any place on the surface of the earth – lacking the slightest human skill or trade – as sunk in a dream-world as any savage and without a single ideal – living the life of trodden-on worms and as proud of it as a Hasid granted the honor of eating the leftovers from his rebbe's plate ….

"What … what will become of us in the end?" the young man asks the yeshiva student.

> "Eh?" The student gawked without interest. His two eyes, the good one and the blind one, were like the holes punched in clay by Jewish housewives to stick their Sabbath candles in.
> "We Jews … is there no cure for us? None at all?"
> "None," declared the other gloomily. "*Farfaln!*"

The Yiddish word for "it's all over with" falls like a judge's gavel.

In 1910, of course, there was no need to dislike Jews in order to see the deficiencies of the Zionist enterprise in Palestine. The country's Jewish population was barely ten percent of its Arab one and growing slowly. The colonies of what was now known as the "First Aliyah" were still dependent on the cheap Arab labor and financial subsidies for which Ahad Ha'am had lambasted them nearly twenty years earlier in his "The Truth from the Land of Israel." The young "Second Aliyah" *halutzim* who arrived in the first decade of the century, many with socialist ideals brought from Russia, had trouble finding work and suffered from unemployment, low pay, harsh living conditions, and malaria; morale among them was low, re-emigration high, and suicide not unknown. The Orthodox inhabitants of Jerusalem, Palestine's main urban Jewish center, lived partly or wholly on charity from abroad. All this painted a depressing picture.

But Oved Etsot could have seen other things, too, had he cared to. By 1910, there was a modern, secular Jewish community in Jerusalem alongside its Orthodox one. The first houses of Tel Aviv were being built on the sands north of Jaffa. The Rothschild colonies were closer to standing on their own feet; the actual Zichron Ya'akov was a lively village with a native-born generation that spoke Hebrew, worked in the fields, and was indeed skilled "on horseback and with a rifle." Degania, the agricultural commune that was to become the first kibbutz, was founded in 1910 by Second Aliyah pioneers on the shores of the Sea of Galilee. There was a new spirit in the Yishuv, a sense that a turning point had been reached. This was the Palestine that had impressed Bialik in 1909 and that Yosef Klausner was to enthuse about in 1912.

Klausner was mocked for his enthusiasm by Berdichevsky, and Oved Etsot is a mocker, too. Worse than one. "Gross, dirty, leprous hands," "fattened hogs," "carnal Jews without a drop of real blood," "sickeningly crafty, calculating Jews" – a positively lyrical anti-Semite indeed!

Whether for the purpose of attacking Brenner as a self-hating Jew or defending him as an uncompromising voice of integrity writing from a place of deep pain, the connection between his negative feelings toward Jewishness and his negative feelings toward himself, as exemplified by Yirmiya Feierman's dream of being a fly (or shall we say flea?) with its wings pulled off, has often been commented on by Hebrew literary critics. However viewed, he is the most extreme expression in modern Hebrew literature of what the Israeli critic Baruch Kurzweil called "auto-anti-Semitism." "All that seems revolutionary in the demand for a 'transvaluation of values' in Jewish life in the works of Mendele, Smolenskin, Lilienblum, Y. L. Gordon, Mapu, and even Berdichevsky," wrote Kurzweil, "is child's play compared to its unbridled ferocity in the fiction of Brenner." Brenner's case can be understood better, Kurzweil proposed, by placing it alongside a similar phenomenon in a number of European authors of the times, particularly the three German-writing Jews Franz Kafka, Otto Weininger, and Karl Kraus.

Although Brenner grew up in the religiously traditional and poverty-stricken world of Eastern Europe and Kafka, Weininger, and Kraus in wealthy or bourgeois, non-Jewishly-observant homes in Prague and Vienna, all were reacting, Kurzweil argued, to the same fundamental absurdity of modern Jewish life – that of a people that pretended to know, and to teach its children, why it should continue to exist when the reasons it gave made not the slightest sense. Whether taking the form of a hidebound Orthodoxy that had exhausted its creative potential, as it did in Europe's East, or of a liberal Judaism that paid lip service to a supposed Jewish ethical mission that it did nothing to shoulder, as was the case in the West, these reasons struck an honest mind as delusory if not hypocritical and led to a revulsion at one's Jewish roots and at oneself for being attached to them. Brenner, Kafka, Weininger, and Kraus, wrote Kurzweil, all internalized anti-Semitic Christian stereotypes of the Jew because all shared the view that Judaism had "ceased to be a living religion" and had even become "diametrically opposed to every religious faith worthy of its name." And while all saw the logic of a secular Zionism that sought, as a way out of this dilemma, to redefine Jewishness in purely national as opposed to religious terms, all saw its illogic too, since such a Zionism, as Weininger put it while conceding its "nobility" of purpose, was in fact "the negation of Judaism." To seek self-perpetuation in self-negation was but compounding the absurdity of Jewish existence.

There may be something to be said for associating Brenner with such figures, especially with Kafka – who, besides being personally attracted to Zionism and more Jewishly knowledgeable than either Weininger or Kraus, had a lifelong relationship with his parents that bore a resemblance to the young Brenner's with his. (The parallel between Yirmiya Feierman's dream of being crushed to death by his father and the end of Kafka's story "The Judgment," in which a son drowns himself at his father's behest, is striking.) Yet as Kurzweil was the first to admit, such an analogy is at best partial. A product of the shtetl like Brenner was incomparably more steeped in his Jewishness than was Kafka (who studied Hebrew as an adult and even read Brenner's "Breakdown and Bereavement" in it), let alone Kraus or Weininger. Despite his assault on it, his Jewishness was whole as theirs was not, nor was it possible for him to conceive, as did they, of his life as a struggle to overcome it, since he had no non-Jewish side, no external point of German or European identity, to conduct such a struggle from. Whatever love he felt for himself or for others came, no less than his hate, from *within* his Jewishness – and nowhere in his fiction is there greater love than there is for the character of Aryeh Lapidot in "From All Sides."

5

A. D. or Alef-Daled Gordon settled in Palestine in 1904, five years before Brenner did. He was forty-eight years old at the time, a part-time Hebrew educator and a rural administrator in the business empire of the wealthy Russian Jewish magnate and patron of the arts Baron David Ginzburg, and the most remarkable thing about his decision was its commitment to starting life all over again as a simple agricultural laborer. He had never before engaged in hard physical work, and as Yosef Aharonovitz, the editor of *Ha-Po'el Ha-Tsa'ir*, observed in a biographical memoir of him, he was suited to it neither by his constitution, his training, nor his previous regimen.

The decision did not come out of the blue. Gordon had lived his life in the Russian countryside. He felt close to nature and to the agrarian romanticism of Tolstoy and the Russian *pochvennichestvo* or "back to the soil" movement, and as a Zionist he was part of something larger, too. The year he left for Palestine marked the start of the Second Aliyah and the Labor Zionist movement, set in motion by events in Russia and by the call of such opposed Hebrew writers as Ahad Ha'am and Berdichevsky for a Zionism of self-actualization rather than of waiting for the fulfillment of Herzlian promises. Gordon's conviction that this meant a life of manual labor had been germinating in him for some time. "Deep down," wrote Aharonovitz,

> the perception had formed in him that bodily work was the vocation not only of the Jew in Palestine but of human beings everywhere; he judged it materially and spiritually beneficial, and he

thought the difficulty lay not with it but with the failure to grasp its profound nature, with the absence of conditions conducive to its practice, and with the prejudices of the generations.... National and personal regeneration had to begin with it, especially with agriculture – and since they did, it was incumbent on him to be in the forefront.

It was not easy for someone of Gordon's age and frail physique to find such work in Palestine. Yet when offered a desk job there, he refused to hear of it, and he finally obtained employment in the vineyards and orange groves of Petach Tikva. "Can you imagine your father a day laborer?" he wrote to his two grown children and wife, who had remained behind in Russia. "I feel like a newborn babe. The work is physically exhausting, but it gives so much, so much to the soul!"

The Palestinian landscape, Gordon wrote in a "Letter from the Land of Israel" published soon after his arrival there, filled him with a sense of strangeness and awe. He was unused to the "transparency of its air" that lent everything "a powerful clarity painful to the unaccustomed eye"; to its "single tonality, the unchangingness of its beauty, that never loses its sharp edge"; and to "its eternally undisrupted silence." In it he felt "like a guest – a welcome one, and if you will, even a dear next of kin who has been eagerly awaited, but a guest nonetheless." Nature in Palestine did not have the "simple innocence" that it did in Russia. It was "deeper and infinitely more exalted in its spiritual grandeur. It bears the impress of an idea on its brow and an unspoken sorrow in its glance." And yet the country's Jews, even those living on the land in the First Aliyah colonies, had little appreciation of it. They lived a "half-alive" existence that testified to "how little they have risen to Nature's heights."

"Man and Nature," written during Gordon's years in Palestine, is a philosophical formulation of his thoughts on the life lived apart from Nature and on the need to end this separation. Gordon worked on the book at night, since, first at En-Ganim, a workers' settlement on the outskirts of Petach Tikva where he was joined in 1909 by his wife and daughter, and later elsewhere (from 1915 until his death in 1922 he lived in Degania), he put in long days in the fields for as long as his health permitted. Some of the book's sixteen chapters appeared, as did most of

his articles, in *Ha-Po'el ha-Tsa'ir*, which was also the name of the socialist party that put out the publication. Ha-Po'el ha-Tsa'ir was both less
doctrinairely Marxist than its rival, Po'alei Tsiyon or "The Workers of
Zion," and more respectful of Jewish tradition, and Gordon, though he
eventually lapsed in the ritual observance that he had adhered to while
in Russia, never wavered in his positive attitude toward Judaism, just
as he never warmed to Marxism. Socialism was for him a doctrine of
human solidarity, not class warfare.

Gordon's home in En-Ganim, a wooden shack, became a Second
Aliyah gathering place. Considerably older than his fellow *halutzim*, who
sometimes had to help him finish a day's quota of work, he was looked
up to as a spiritual elder as well. Yet his struggle to live a life that taxed
his strength to the utmost was plagued by inner doubts – about himself, about his right to impose hardship on the wife and daughter who
had followed him to Palestine, and about the future of Zionism. Aharonovitz relates:

> He was highly introverted and led an intellectually intense life;
> there was in his eyes and expression a terrible, world-suffering
> sorrow. At the same time, however, at least for the first half of his
> years in Palestine, he was a joyous – or perhaps I should I say joy-
> radiating – man .... He would [at communal get-togethers] dance
> himself into an ecstasy to the point of collapse, so that the physical
> side of him as though fell away. Yet there was more religious devo-
> tion than joy in this; or if joy, it was, to use Hasidic terminology, a
> "joy of the upper spheres." Not only did the sorrow in his face not
> abate at such times, it grew greater with each movement. He was
> fond of the word *freylikh* [Yiddish for "joyful"], which he would
> utter with a snap of his fingers or clap of his hands while danc-
> ing with every part of himself as though to the verse [in Psalms]
> "All my bones say, O Lord, who is like Thee?" Coming from him,
> though, the word was as though bathed in whole oceans of despair.

There was indeed something of the saintly rebbe in the white-
bearded, ascetic figure bearing the world's suffering on his shoulders
while urging his "Hasidim," the *halutzim* he was surrounded by, to

rejoice in their threadbare lot. More than the settlers of the First Aliyah, who remained largely loyal to Jewish religious practice, the pioneers of the Second, who did not, demonstrated the hidden power of religion. Nearly all had grown up in traditional homes, and there was a secularized messianism in their goal of national redemption that they believed themselves to be the heralds of, just as there was a secularized devoutness in their fervor for the physical work that alone, so they held (in part under Gordon's influence), could bring this redemption about. Although the Hebrew word *avoda*'s double meaning of "work" and "worship" goes back to the Bible, it informed their consciousness as it did no other generation's in Jewish history. Moreover, *kibbush ha-avoda*, "the conquest of labor," their term for the creation of a Jewish working class in Palestine, echoed the rabbinic phrase for the biblical conquest of the Land of Israel, *kibbush ha-aretz*, and the word *kibbutz*, too, had religious origins and referred in Eastern Europe to a commune of young men banded together for the purpose of Torah study. The templates of Judaism, though often unacknowledged, were never far from the Second Aliyah's mind.

"Man and Nature" is constructed on such a template. Although there is little explicit mention of Judaism in its pages, there is hardly one of them on which it does not make itself felt. Behind Gordon's account of man's separation from Nature and his call to heal the breach, lies the Bible's great myth of Creation, primeval harmony, rupture, and repair as reinterpreted by Hasidism via the mediation of Kabbalah.

"Nature" for Gordon is all that exists apart from man and whatever is man-made – *is* but not *was*, for once man was part of Nature, too. Or rather, he was part of it before he was man, since the dawning of human consciousness spelled the beginning of a wedge driven between man and Nature that, a mere crack at first, widened as consciousness – and with it, civilization – grew in the form of an ever greater awareness of the internality of the self as opposed to the externality of the world. In the human race, as in every infant born to it, the sense of self evolves through a rift with Nature. The more deeply the self is experienced, the greater this rift becomes.

For Gordon, therefore, man's alienation from Nature began long before the urbanization of human society. Urbanization, with its loss of daily contact with Nature and its surrounding of man by his own handi-work, simply aggravates a prior condition. This condition is one of dual-ity and conflict. On the one hand, human consciousness, aware of "its absolute singularity and concentration in itself," strives to live its unique-ness to the maximum. On the other hand, yearning to reunite with the world from which it has been torn, it feels imprisoned by its isolation:

> The same consciousness that raised man from the lowliness of his animal state; that granted him, as it were, free will (at least when compared to the wills of other living beings); that illuminated all of life for him and opened up entirely new worlds – this same con-sciousness has enslaved him far more than it has any other creature: first and foremost, to his own drives (including the drive to rule others), but also to his fellow man, to human society, and even to the Nature he aspires to dominate – and most of all, to the petty, diminished nature of his own self. And thus we see that human life, when judged by a higher, cosmic standard, is more limited, more difficult, more lived in darkness, and above all, uglier and more polluted than all other life because of its self-concentration that, hidden and obscure to all else, is detached from all else.

The Hebrew words translated as "self-concentration" and "dimin-ished," the noun *tsimtsum* and the adjective *m'tsumtsam*, derive from Hasidic thought. In the theosophy of Lurianic Kabbalah, *tsimtsum* des-ignates God's contraction at the time of Creation to allow space for the world to come into existence; in Hasidism, in which this is known as the "first *tsimtsum*," the term also refers to the human soul's analogous contrac-tion to form an ego delimited from the world. This second *tsimstsum*, like the first, is necessary for individuation to take place; yet also like the first, which results in a world separate from God, it has tragic consequences, since it is the source of all human selfishness and self-centeredness. And though God remains apprehensible in the world of Creation, in which He exists, as it were, behind a veil, the ego-bound individual is severed from Him, just as Gordon's "diminished self" is from Nature.

The opposite of *tsimtsum* in Hasidism is *hitpashtut*, expansion, the soul's venturing beyond its self-made walls to apprehend God, whether through the veil of the phenomenological world or in its own divinely-created depths. *Hitpashtut* is a key concept in "Man and Nature," too, where its meaning is similar. In a reversal of contraction, the self can expand either outward toward Nature by perceiving that it is a part of it, or inward toward the unconscious or pre-conscious mind on which consciousness rests. This pre-consciousness is called by Gordon, using another kabbalistic term, *ha-sekhel ha-ne'elam*, "the Unknowable Mind"; although consciousness can grasp it but dimly, it is the Universal Intelligence dwelling in Nature of which consciousness is a manifestation, so that by being open to this Intelligence's influx – its *tsinorot shefa* or "channels of abundance" in kabbalistic language – consciousness is informed by a greater reality. *Tsimtsum* and *hitpashtut*, though opposites, are aspects of a single process. There must be a contraction for an expansion to take place and every expansion flows back into a contraction.

Although it is never quite clear whether "Man and Nature" is written by a pantheist for whom Nature and God are one, or by a deist for whom Nature proceeds from God, it is the insistence on a life lived in conjunction with Nature and having no substitute for it in religious practice, prayer, or meditation that keeps Gordon's book from being a mere restatement of Hasidic or general mystical themes. Yet its author is neither a "nature lover" nor a primitivist. He has no particular interest in the naturalist's study of Nature or in the nature lover's appreciation of it, both of which treat it as an object of consciousness, thus perpetuating the rift with it; nor does he wish to roll back civilization in its name. "When you return to Nature," Gordon writes, "return not to your starting point or empty-handed. Be like the traveler who has circled the globe and come home again wiser, more experienced, and purged of the superfluous, but also wealthier and enriched by all he has seen and felt, by his material no less than his spiritual acquisitions." Living with Nature does not calls for the abandonment of railroads and electricity. It demands participation rather than exploitation.

And this, says Gordon, means physical work. Nature itself is continually at work. It is always creating, always producing; the only way to be at one with it is to work alongside it. "In all your ways, in all your life," states "Man and Nature," rising to a prophetic pitch, "learn to be a partner in the labor of Creation.

On that day, O Man, you shall be given a new spirit. New, too, will be your emotions and your hunger – not for bread, nor for wealth, but for work. You shall joy in all the work that you perform, in all that you do… and you shall do it in Nature, sharing the world's exertion, its life, and its expanse. Thus shall you work in the field, and thus shall you work in your home, and thus shall you build your home. And as you work you shall think of the world as your workshop and of Nature and you as its workmen. On that day you shall say: "Beautiful is Nature in its form, but more beautiful yet in the spirit of its striving." When you pause to stretch your limbs and take a deep breath, you will be breathing more than air…. You will know the bliss of being in the Infinite.

Although the "you" of this passage is grammatically singular, it is not addressed to the isolated individual. "Man and Nature" stresses not only the social but also the national dimension in which the relationship to Nature must be revised. Gordon subscribed to the belief in the nation as a natural, organic form of association, the highest rung on a ladder rising from the family, the clan, and the tribe, and he held attacks on it in the name of internationalist ideals to be psychologically and sociologically naive. "The role played by collectivities in the formation of individuals is far greater and deeper than is generally acknowledged," he wrote. No individual, no matter how unique, is imaginable apart from the national life he partakes in. "All of his specialness – all of his independence of personality, emotional and intellectual makeup, verbal expression, opinion, and art – are variations on collective themes." It was wrong to think of nations as accidental or mechanical constructions that interposed themselves between the individual and humanity. Humanity was an abstraction that could not serve as a social framework for individual development. "In reality, there are only nations."

It is the Jewish nation, then, and specifically, Zionism, that "Man and Nature" summons to a life of labor in Nature. The Jews were the least and the most likely of all peoples to respond to such a call – the least because they were the world's most de-naturalized, the most because the new life they were starting in Palestine gave them a unique opportunity to remake themselves. They had an additional advantage, too: a religion that sanctified both life and the nation and forbad turning away from either. Gordon understood well the affinities not only between his own thought and Hasidism but between Hasidism and other mystical traditions – of which, however, he was critical. "Man and Nature" concludes:

> I don't know if anyone has ever grasped as profoundly as Buddha the inner longing of the human soul to be freed from the private straightjacket that bars it from a higher life. But he misconstrued the matter, wrongly assuming that this longing was to transcend life when in fact it was for life itself. The nirvana he sought is *in* life – life that is greater than consciousness, that is one with Creation....
>
> Back to Nature, then, back to life! Back, that is, to the nation! The life of Man begins with it and the life of the nation begins with Nature.

6

The reader of "From All Sides" first encounters Aryeh Lapidot (a Palestinianized form of the Ashkenazi name Lapides) through the eyes of his wife Hinde, a "small, thin, quiet, meek-tempered woman who had gained nothing in stature from this, the most recent period of her life." Hinde has just returned from her daily routine of carrying two heavy cans of milk bought from local Bedouin to the marketplace in Petach Tikva, where she ladles them out to customers to supplement her husband's meager income from his work as a farm hand. For a moment she stands dreamily thinking of the comfortable life the two of them led in Russia, only to be brought back to reality by her surroundings.

> What had happened to them? What?
>
> Well, it had. This was their life now. Every evening he came home with his straw lunch basket, at the bottom of which might be an orange or dry piece of bread. Sometimes, especially if there was a visitor in the house, he would break into a little jig, a kind of dance. It wasn't to warm himself from the cold; he was simply grateful for a day that hadn't gone by without work. She would give him his supper – bread, olives, tea with milk – it was

his main meal of the day – and he would remember to ask as a matter of course, "And you, have you eaten?" A heart of gold!... He would recite the evening prayer (lately, he wasn't so strict about this), finish his food in two minutes, and go outside to find someone to talk to.

There is a tenderness in this description of a man of such simple needs that he hasn't finished the bread and oranges that were his entire lunch – and a tweaking of the hidden vanity that makes him caper with gratitude mostly when he has an audience and of the concern for a wife that can't keep him by her side for more than two minutes before he has to look for a better conversation partner. A heart of gold! No doubt. But an ego, too.

Aryeh Lapidot's life, or what we are told of it, diverges more from the real A. D. Gordon's than does Oved Etsot's from the real Brenner's. In Russia Lapidot was a "crown rabbi," a graduate of a government-recognized seminary filling an official clerical post, and he came to Palestine hoping to find a job commensurate with his background, turning to farm work only when nothing else was available. His family is larger than was Gordon's, too. It includes, besides his wife, two sons, one of them married, a daughter-in-law, and two grandsons. Yet the older grandson, Herzl, a sweet, lovable child, succumbs to an illness, while his father, a helpless hunchback attacked by an Arab marauder, dies from his wounds in the hospital bed opposite Oved Etsot's as the latter begins writing his notebooks. This leaves the unmarried Tsvi, who works as a functionary in a Zionist office in Jaffa, and the murdered man's widow and her son Amram, who live with the Lapidots in En-Ganim.

Life in Palestine has not gone as Aryeh Lapidot hoped it would. He has reason to feel both guilt and shame. His grandson Herzl might have lived had he not been brought to a country with poor medical care, and the fatal attack on Herzl's father takes place when, after despairing of a future in Palestine, he is on his way back from Jaffa, to which he has gone to arrange his emigration papers; near Petach Tikva he and his brother Tsvi are waylaid by a lone, unarmed robber – and when Tsvi, who brags about the pistol he always carries, tries to use it, he fumbles with the safety catch, lets the weapon be snatched from him, runs off leaving his brother in the lurch, and lies about it afterwards to cover up his cowardice. Like Oved Etsot's encounter with the three set-upon workers in a Rothschild colony, the incident is a derisive comment on Zionism's ambition of creating a brave new Jew in Palestine. Tsvi's office job, far removed from the physical work that Aryeh Lapidot practices and preaches, is a disappointment to Lapidot too, and the dead man's widow is no help, either. Unhappy and confused, she has no idea what she is doing in a leaky shack with her in-laws in a country to which she never wanted to come. How much gratitude for his lot can Lapidot really feel?

His one comfort is his other grandson Amram. An irrepressible, mischief-loving boy of nine or ten, Amram has all the courage his father and uncle failed to show. When an Arab shepherd grazes his flock on En-Ganim's land, Amram hurls himself on him and drives him off. Yelled at for tossing a stone through the window of the Petach Tikva town council, he retorts: "But it was a perfect shot! Bull's-eye! Rothschild can buy a new window." "The rascal will grow up to be a man!" Hinde exults and Oved Etsot comments:

> No one knew where the little tyke, who grew up under the Hasidic tutelage of his grandfather, had learned to be so fearless. He came and went as freely as an Arab in the desert; a few raw vegetables were a meal for him; and he liked nothing better than to go around with a cattle prod, poking at cows or anything else attached to the ground whether it belonged to him or not. At night, especially if it was moonless and dark, he sometimes sat at the high point of the village, challenging whoever approached with "Who goes there?" in Arabic.

"If all of Zionism had existed only for the sake of bringing this one being into the world," Oved Etsot reflects, "it would have been worth it." Amram is indeed the promise of the new Jew that Zionism has dreamed of. But is he a harbinger or an anomaly, the first of a new race or a chance mutation that will fail to be passed on? This question hovers over "From All Sides". It is present on a Saturday afternoon before sunset in En-Ganim when Aryeh Lapidot and Oved Etsot clash. Oved Etsot has just remarked sarcastically that most of the *halutzim* he knows in Palestine would rather be in Europe looking at Rembrandts in a museum, and Lapidot replies:

> "Is that so? You want Rembrandt? Then look above you. Look at that bluer than blue up there. What can I tell you? Do you see those clouds? Those colors in the corner of the sky? There's your Rembrandt!"
>
> Lying propped on an elbow with his legs tucked beneath him, he launched expansively into his usual talk about Nature, the Prophets, the Hebrew spirit. Gradually, a small group assembled around him: full-time workers, part-time workers, workers without work who were supported by their families in Russia, even a few homeowners .... One by one they arrived, said "*Shabbat shalom*," and found a place on the straw mats the old man had laid out. The conversation went on into the night, long after the Sabbath was over.

Mostly, Lapidot talks and the group listens. The listener he cares about most is Oved Etsot:

> "Even from your point of view," he said, speaking mainly to me, "even from your point of view, which is that the Yishuv won't develop, that there's no hope of its developing, that there's no more land to buy... what can I tell you? I hardly need say I don't agree. I believe the Bible has it right: from the fields, from the smell of the fields that the Lord has blessed, all will grow! And as far as our history is concerned – here, too, my good man, it's not as you say. Our people's history – what can I tell you? – I'm proud of it! But why talk about our whole people? We in this land are the people! If you ask me, the only Zionists are the ones who are here. The thousands of them who are here are enough. If we had one hundred thousand Jews – but the right kind of Jews – Jews who worked – we'd have all that we needed .... What can I tell you? You can't deny that life here is special. Things are happening, there's a struggle. And I have to ask you – *you*! – isn't this struggle – isn't our life here with all its suffering – especially with its suffering, that's our greatest asset – isn't it material ...."

"For a Zionist novel with Zionist heroes?" I asked.
The old man blanched. That was my answer?

Passages like these were on Gordon's mind when he wrote
Brenner an open letter in *Ha-Po'el Ha-Tsa'ir* a year after the publication of "From All Sides." Its subject was an article of Brenner's that had
appeared there a month previously in support of Yosef Aharonovitz.
Aharonovitz had attacked, on the occasion of its thirtieth anniversary
celebrations, the First Aliyah village of Rishon l'Tsiyon for continuing
to embody the vices of the Rothschild colonies, and had been accused
in turn of besmirching the colonists and belittling their central role in
Jewish history. In fact, Brenner now wrote, Aharonovitz was right; he
simply had not gone far enough. He should also have said that Zionism
itself was not central to Jewish history. It was time to stop thinking that
Jewish hopes all over the world should focus on Palestine. Zionism could
not solve the problems of the world's Jews, who would have to fight for
their dignity and well-being wherever they were. The Jews of Palestine
mattered no less, but also no more, than did Jews anywhere else.

Gordon's letter took issue with Brenner's pessimistic appraisal
of Zionism. Even if Brenner, he stated, overlooked some of Zionism's
achievements, the most remarkable of which was the revival of spoken
Hebrew, the two of them did not fundamentally disagree about its present state. They disagreed about the future, about what was possible. He,
Gordon, hoped Brenner might understand him.

> I say "might" because I'm not sure. Not that I consider myself that
> profound and you that superficial, but we inhabit two different
> worlds. A "dreamer," a "true believer," a "fantasizer," etc. – that's
> what many people think of me and that's what they must think if
> they wish to be honest. But you, though not compelled by your
> inner nature to think of me that way, are compelled by the work-
> ings of your mind. You're too much of a "realist" not to be – or at
> least so you regard yourself.

When it came to Zionism, Brenner indeed thought that Gordon
was whistling in the dark. Yet his esteem for Gordon's character was great.

In another scene in "From All Sides," Oved Etsot and Diasporin (who, perpetually on the move, has now turned up in Palestine) are discussing Lapidot's religious beliefs. "What do you make of it?" Diasporin asks when Oved Etsot observes that Lapidot never goes to synagogue and prays only when he is alone, and Oved Etsot answers:

> "I … what I mean is … as far as prayer is concerned … do you follow me?" (I must say that I wasn't following myself very well at this point.) "His religiosity comes, on the one hand, from his being unable to believe in nothing, and on the other – and this is the main thing – from that special vitality of his. I mean … of course, you have to take into account his age, his education, his habits … although to tell the truth … do you know what? The man, in his quiet way, is a hero – a hero every hour of the day. The entire regiment has taken to its heels and he goes on storming the enemy by himself with the flag held high: I tell you, it's stupendous!... And say what you will about his praying, I think the world of it. Prayer like that could make me get down on my knees and pray, too.

Gordon, for his part, thought highly of Brenner. Brenner's problem with Zionism, he wrote in his letter in *Ha-Po'el Ha-Tsa'ir*, was not that he despaired of it but that his despair was not great enough. The "great despair" was the despair of "a great idea, a great belief, a great wanting, a great devotion." He who possessed it, "even if he has rejected the possibility of his own private redemption, has no choice but to go on seeking the redemption of all else – to go on seeking it to the point of madness, as only the greatest despairer can do."

7

And Aryeh Lapidot is close to despair. On top of everything, he is out of work. Whether because he has grown older and weaker, or because there is simply no demand for agricultural labor, no one will hire him anymore. His son Tsvi has left Palestine to try his luck elsewhere, his widowed daughter-in-law is bedridden with malaria, and his wife Hinde has been driven from the milk business by an undercutting competitor. A collection has been taken up in En-Ganim to keep hunger from the

Lapidots' door. The money is used to buy flour, which is given to Hinde to bake bread with. Aryeh, it is agreed, mustn't know about it.

The secret is kept, at least for a while. But at En-Ganim's annual party, no one is fooled by Lapidot's show of high spirits or pays attention to the speech he has been prevailed upon to give. "There was nothing worth listening to," we are told. "It wasn't the same Lapidot of four or five years ago. What had happened to all his songs, his Hasidic melodies, his jokes? Those times were gone."

Oved Etsot isn't at the party. As in the scene in front of the public library in Jerusalem, an omniscient narrator now steps in.

"Have you heard about Oved Etsot?"
"No. What?"
"Nothing. But there were some workers here yesterday from Jaffa. The word there is..."
"Is what?"
"He's taken to drink. He belts down two glasses of brandy and one of red wine, and then the other way around...."
"You don't say! A drunk?"
"He hasn't been seen at 'The Plow' for ages. He's not working there anymore."

Oved Etsot may be drinking, but he has also been thinking. He has been thinking, a bit tipsily, about Aryeh Lapidot, with whom his depression has something to do. The man reminds him of Job.

"There was a man in a land in Arabia," I chanted to myself. "And the man was innocent and upright and feared God and eschewed evil." He truly did. Truly, he did some good. And it came to pass that a hunchbacked son was born to him, and so on and so forth. And in all this the man did not sin with his lips or cast aspersion upon his God. Who did not answer him out of the whirlwind. Who did not answer. Who...

Oved Etsot is not grieving for a world without God. He got over that long ago. He is grieving for Aryeh Lapidot, who has lost *his* God and will not, like Job, get Him back. And in grieving, he realizes how much Lapidot means to him, not just as the "hero" of a Zionism that stands no chance of success but as the one person he loves.

But no, there is someone else, too – and Oved Etsot now has a perfectly mad idea: he will adopt Amram! He knows it is mad, not only because Amram is happy where he is (like most children his age, he is not particularly aware of, or troubled by, his family's financial worries), but because he, Oved Etsot, is the last person anyone would entrust with a child. Still, the thought makes him happy and helps pull him out of his depression, and he sits down one morning to write Aryeh Lapidot a letter proposing that Amram be put in his charge. Halfway through it, he stops.

> The pen dropped from my hands. Perhaps I shouldn't. Was I taking on too much? Mightn't it be better to leave things as they were? But a minute later, I thought:
>
> No, I'm not deluding myself. I'm not a self-deluder. Amram must come live with me. There's no delusion in that. And if there is, I'm aware of it. I know that my telling myself, "Don't worry, life will be good now" – that all the positive thoughts I'm about to express in my letter to Lapidot – that it's all *necessarily* self-deluding, that it comes from the irresistible desire to live and fill one's life with meaning. But since I know it's a delusion, I've overcome it – unless the belief that I've overcome it is a delusion, too…. How do I know, though, that I can devote my life to Amram? Am I capable of devoting it to anyone? And even if I devote myself to devoting it, how many Amrams are there? Can I take care of them all? Still, I'm ready. Amram will come and life will be good, better than it's ever been.

Oved Etsot lies down for an afternoon nap. When he rises from it, his state of infinitely self-regressing consciousness is gone.

> I was awake. I hadn't died in my sleep. That was good. I took a few steps around the room. I coughed. I spat. I took a bracing sip of the cold, sweet tea on the table (I'd given up liquor earlier that

winter), stood there for a minute or two, and then went to the window and opened it. Children were playing noisily outside. I went to the other window; it was open. There was a stormy sea in the distance. The Mediterranean. Walking on the beach that morning, I had come across the antlered corpse of a deer vomited up by the waves and I had thought: "It's not at all nice to be dead vomit. But how nice everything else is! How nice it is to be alive!"

Ah, brother, how I love life! How happy it makes me just to feel and breathe, thinks Yirmiya Feierman a short while after contemplating ending his life. And Oved Etsot, Yirmiya's final incarnation in Brenner's fiction, continues:

> Alive. Yes, to live. And a man must live – well, no, not *must*, but it's good if he does – in one place. Let him stay there and strike roots .... It may be – it may very well be – that it's impossible to live in this place, but one must live in it anyway. One must die in it. There's nowhere else.

The letter proposing to adopt Amram never gets written, because that same day Oved Etsot suffers a relapse of his illness and has to be re-hospitalized. His thoughts about living and dying in Palestine, in any case, have not made him a Zionist. Rather, as he explains in a letter that he does send to Aryeh Lapidot, which reads like a first draft of Brenner's 1912 article in *Ha-Po'el ha-Tsa'ir*, living "in one place" can mean living in Argentina or America, too: "Our Palestinian exile (yes, exile, because there will never be a Jewish majority here) may in some ways surpass other Jewish communities and in others fall short of them. Not everything, my dear Lapidot, is up to us. We have to do what we can where we are." His own "where we are," Oved Etsot has decided, will be Palestine. That is as far as he is willing to go.

It is still the wet Palestinian winter. "It rained and rained and on the fourth day it stopped," the ending of "From All Sides" relates. At dawn Hinde, who has regained her milk route by undercutting her under-cutters, sets out for the Bedouin encampment. Amram's mother drags herself from bed to knead dough for the day's baking. Aryeh Lapidot looks on and says nothing; there are things it is best to pretend not to know. Hinde comes home exhausted, drops the empty milk cans, rests for a second, and spells the sick woman at the kneading board. Aryeh Lapidot and Amram go to look for firewood with which to bake the pita bread that Hinde prepares.

The boy gathered armful after armful of thorny, woody-stemmed weeds left from the summer and loaded them onto his grandfather's back. Then he collected what had fallen, down to the last stem, and they brought it all to the yard.

Amram went to sit by his grandfather – who, momentarily lost in thought, had already put down his load – and laid his little head in his lap. There was a premonition of bread in the rain-rinsed air and, more faintly, inside the shack. The sick woman was asleep. The rain had stopped drumming on the windows and in her ears, though its last drops still dripped from the wooden planks of the walls. A single drop broke away from a wet patch and hung on the edge of a void.

On the void's edge.

Tongues of flame rose in the oven. Hinde carried out the pitas like an Arab peasant woman, a tin sheet of them balanced on her head. The folds of the tin suggested hopeful rows of sown sesame. And there was hope that the bread, enough to last for a week, would come out well, too. Amram's head still rested in Aryeh Lapidot's lap. There was something simple and sad in how they clung to each other, something worthy of compassion but also mysterious and infinitely precious. Thorny burrs stuck to their hair and loose clothes. When the old woman asked for help with the baking, they rose together. There was a great mystery in how they stood, too. At their posts. The old man and the boy, crowned with thorns, at the posts where life had placed them. The sun was out as before the rain. The world was full of thorns. The final reckoning was yet to come.

8

In his desire to end "From All Sides" on a poetically resonant note, Brenner underlined the symbolism of the thorns and the drop hanging over the void. The thorns' Christ-like crown must be seen against the background of what came to be known as the "Brenner Affair" – a dispute set off in the Hebrew literary world by a 1910 article in which, while making the case for a secular Jewish identity independent of Judaism, Brenner dismissed the Jewish "fear" of the New Testament. The Gospels' story of Jesus, he said, could legitimately strike "a religious chord" in a Jew just as it did, say, in a post-Christian artist of the Renaissance like Leonardo da Vinci.

In the furor that followed, in which he was accused of erasing a line between Judaism and Christianity that even a freethinking Jew like himself should have respected, Brenner had his detractors and supporters (of whom Gordon, who stood up for him on the grounds of freedom of expression, was one); now, in bringing his novel to a close with a pro-vocatively Christian image, he was having, as it were, the last word. Still, the point was not to portray Lapidot and Amram with Christian haloes but to cast their human steadfastness in a universally sacral light. The entire scene is posed like a Mannerist painting. Reading it, one imagines a shaft of radiance from above, illuminating, in the darkness of the world, the man and the boy at their posts.

Aryeh Lapidot emerges in "From All Sides" as an indomitable figure. And yet despite Oved Etsot's mention of Lapidot's "usual talk about Nature, the Prophets, [and] the Hebrew spirit," a reader knowing that Lapidot was modeled on A. D. Gordon would never have guessed from the novel that Gordon was one of the three original thinkers of his age to grapple with the relationship of secular Zionism to Judaism. The other two were Ahad Ha'am and Avraham Yitzhak Hacohen Kook, the chief rabbi of Palestine in the 1920s and early '30s, and each man took a different path. For Ahad Ha'am, secular Zionism was a natural evolu-tion of Jewish tradition, which was fated to shed its religious character in the modern age. For Kook, it was a historically necessary but tempo-rary break with tradition, of which it was a sublimated expression and to which it would return. For Gordon, it was a potential bridge from tradition to a new form of religiosity unlike any that had come before.

When considered today, all three men strike one as having grasped something essential while missing at least as much. If the Gor-don of "Man and Nature" still has something to say to us, this is not what he had to say to the Second Aliyah generation that found its inspiration in him. In the century since his death, the rift between man and Nature has widened far beyond anything he could have imagined. What is most striking about his thinking today is how overtaken it has been by history. He was not a forerunner of the environmentalism that is our contemporary reaction to Nature's destruction; this is about man saving Nature, whereas "Man and Nature" is about Nature saving man. Gordon's creed of physical labor, too, while it may still speak to some readers, seems dated in an age of robotics, as does his neo-Hasidism now that its context of Zionist pioneering has long ceased to exist. What most remains is the man himself. A figure who thought that a thought not lived in the life of its thinker is only half a thought, he chose not to live by halves.

It was this that Brenner esteemed in him. A declared atheist with a stated aversion to mysticism of any kind, Brenner considered "Man and Nature" to be simply one more rationalization, as Oved Etsot puts it to Diasporin, "of the inability to believe in nothing." But Brenner also thought that Gordon's philosophy expressed, as Oved Etsot states in the same passage, a "special vitality," a powerful life-force in search of a justification. Although the will to live needs no reasons, the willer to live demands to experience it as rational. Already in "In Winter," Yirmiya Feierman ponders the suicide he would commit if he were to listen to the "inner reason" that finds life senseless, and in all of Brenner's fiction the possibility of suicide, personal and national, keeps coming back to haunt its characters. Aryeh Lapidot – not the philosopher of "Nature, the Prophets, and the Hebrew spirit" but the man who rises on a cold, wet morning to bake the bread of life with his wife and grandson – is the only answer to "why live?" that Brenner has to give. This answer is: *because*. Or, to give it a subject and a predicate: *because the will to live wills to live.*

The Jewish will to live, for Brenner, meant the Jewish will to work and create life, and his thinking about this, which linked him to Gordon, can seem as dated as Gordon's. The concluding lines of his "A Self-Critique in Three Volumes" are surely the oddest of any major essay of literary criticism ever written:

> Ever since Mendele [who, according to Brenner, was the first Hebrew author to give an honest account of the pathology

of East-European Jewish life], our literature of self-criticism has outlined our duty to acknowledge the historic ignobility of our existence, our essentially flawed character – and to go beyond it and start all over....

And at the same time, our literature – our poor, bewildered Hebrew literature! – asks: by what logic can a we become a not-we?

But let logic ask what it asks. Our will to live, which is above all logic, tells us otherwise. It tells us that everything is possible. It whispers to us the hope: workers' communes, workers' communes.

Workers' communes: this is our revolution! The only one.

By what logic can a we become a not-we *that is still a we*? This was the question posed by Weininger and raised more gnomically by Berdichevsky when he wrote, "We will be either the last Jews or the first Hebrews." It is one that secular Zionism struggled with practically from its inception. To suggest resolving it by means of "workers' communes" – the kibbutzim and moshavim of Jewish agriculture in Palestine that barely existed when Brenner wrote these words – might be compared to trying to lift a steel ingot with a feather duster.

Brenner was not alone in this. The conviction that the future of Zionism depended on new forms of social and economic organization in Palestine was the essence of Labor Zionist ideology, and Brenner, who insisted on a life of monastic simplicity (this was one reason that his marriage in 1913 to a Jerusalem schoolteacher with whom he had a son broke up after a few years), was close to Labor Zionism in his views. He wrote for its publications, took part in its educational activities, and even, not long before his death, lived for several months in a tent in the Galilee, where he taught Hebrew to a "Workers Brigade" engaged in road construction.

His death was one of several dozen resulting from the Arab disturbances of May 1921, the first massive outbreak of anti-Jewish violence in Palestine in the period of the British Mandate. He was living at the time with a Jewish family in an isolated farmstead near Jaffa, and though warned to move to a safer place, he remained with it to protect the property and was murdered together with it. He had as though predicted such an end for himself in a eulogy for eight *halutzim* killed in a gun battle with superior Arab forces in April 1920 while defending the isolated commune of Tel-Hai in Palestine's far north. Led by the ex-Russian army officer Yosef Trumpeldor, the outnumbered group had refused to evacuate the settlement when it could have done so. Brenner said of it:

> A cold calculation would have left no room for doubt [that Tel-Hai should have been evacuated]. But the heart, the self-less heart, believed in miracles; it believed the normal laws would be suspended; that devotion was everything; that love for a piece of earth could move mountains. Besides, if we left every place in which there was danger, there would be no place we would not have to leave, no position we would not have to retreat from – *but to where?*... And what now? Danger is everywhere. And when, tomorrow or the day after, it overtakes us in this or that form, will we know, every one of us, that we have no choice? Will we realize the necessity of rising to the occasion? Will each one of us stand his ground, with the name of Trumpeldor and Trumpeldor's comrades on his lips, in the place chosen for him by destiny?

Brenner's death consummated his conversion into a Zionist legend that was already in the making in his lifetime. It made him a symbol of the pioneering ethos of *af-al-pi-khen*, "nevertheless": *nevertheless we will stand firm, nevertheless we will endure, even if the situation seems hopeless.* His decision to remain committedly in Palestine despite his belief that Zionism would fail was, paradoxically, held to be the ultimate Zionist act. He had become in the eyes of many the Great Despairer that A. D. Gordon had urged him to be.

9

And so "From All Sides" is Brenner's non-Zionist affirmation of Zionism as a supreme manifestation of the Jewish people's will to live in modern times?

Not quite. Brenner remained in Palestine. Oved Etsot, let us recall, did not. Wherever he was when his notebooks passed on to their editor, it was as "a suffering wanderer in our far-flung Jewish world." The man who wrote of Palestine "It's impossible to live in this place, but one must live in it anyway. One must die in it. There's nowhere else," went somewhere else.

This act of desertion – in the context of the novel, it is no less – is not stressed in "From All Sides." On the contrary: after its mention on the first page, indeed in the very first sentence, it is never referred to again, so that by the time we have reached the story's end, we are more than likely to have forgotten it. It is a detail disclosed to us when we cannot appreciate its significance and then buried beneath all that follows.

There is a literary underhandedness in this that is uncharacteristic of Brenner. What made him do it? There was no compelling fictional reason, after all, why Oved Etsot could not have died in Palestine and left his notebooks behind there. It wouldn't have changed a thing.

Nothing, that is, except the perspective in which the entire novel needs to be read. It is as if, having worked our way through a 150-page contract that we are satisfied we have understood, we are now told by our lawyer, "You had better take another look at Clause 1a."

But what does this new perspective reveal? That the "nevertheless" of "From All Sides" is not really nevertheless? That it is nullified by Oved Etsot's reneging on his words? That a people of suffering wanderers will always be a people of suffering wanderers?

Or does it tell us that Brenner and Oved Etsot, having kept company since Lvov, have finally parted ways, one sticking to his post while the other jumps ship, so that the authorial "nevertheless" is nevertheless nevertheless?

There is no answer to these questions in "From All Sides". There is one, however, in a letter that Brenner wrote in September 1911, scant months after finishing the novel, to the Yiddish author Avrom Reyzen, who had just left Warsaw for New York. Brenner's letter was written in Yiddish:

To my good friend, A. Reyzen,

You must remember asking me in a letter a while ago whether you should come to Palestine. I answered what I did, and now the shoe is on the other foot. I have to get away from Palestine. In the first place, I'm fed up with it. And secondly, even if I could live with that – after all, where would I not be fed up? – I quite simply have no way of making a living here, especially now that I have a brother and sister with me. [Brenner's younger brother Meir and younger sister Lyuba had arrived from Russia earlier that year.] But where should I go? I have no desire to return to England or Galicia. That leaves America.

Brenner went on to ask Reyzen for a favor. He wasn't planning to take his brother and sister with him and he would manage to scrape together the money for his passage, but he was worried about being turned back by the immigration authorities in New York if he arrived with no means of support and no relatives to vouch for him. Could Reyzen obtain a written job offer for him from one of the city's Yiddish newspapers that he could produce if questioned? The job could be a proofreader's, a translator's, a headline writer's, or anything else; the paper wouldn't actually have to hire him. "Don't delay doing it," he urged Reyzen, "because I want to start out before cold weather sets in."

And so the "far-flung" place Oved Etsot's notebooks were found in was New York – and Brenner was planning to join him there!

Did Brenner know all along while writing "From All Sides" that he intended to leave Palestine and abandon his newly arrived brother and sister, as Oved Etsot abandons Amram? Is Oved Etsot's desertion in the novel a reflection of this, a premeditated element of the plot meant to expose as a pathetic bluff all of its protagonist's brave talk about making his stand in Palestine? Is this hidden from the reader's eye because Brenner wished it to come as a surprise or shock at the novel's end and could think of no other way of accomplishing this than by planting it at the novel's beginning, where it would be revealed by a second reading?

Or did he have no such prior intention? His letters from Lvov show how mercurial his moods could be. He could have written "From All Sides" convinced that his commitment to life in Palestine was genuine only to change his mind at the novel's end. He has had enough! He wants to leave. And yet knowing that his readers will identify him with the character of Oved Etsot, he does not want to be accused of having written a dishonest book. What does he do? He writes a preface, or returns to an earlier draft of one, and inserts the fact, seemingly of little importance when we first encounter it, that Oved Etsot has left the country. Now, if he, Brenner, leaves it too, he will have told the painful autobiographical truth. The novel's readers can blame only themselves for not realizing they were tipped off.

In either case, this makes "From All Sides" in some ways a frightfully cynical novel. But it would be a mistake to let our reading of it be overly determined by its opening sentence. Oved Etsot is not its hero. This is Aryeh Lapidot. The Jewish will to live is his. In Oved Etsot, it falters and fails.

Though Brenner never left for New York, his prognosis for Zionism remained grim. In mid-1919, two years after the Balfour Declaration, he wrote to the Labor Zionist intellectual Berl Katznelson:

> From all I know about what's called the Jewish people, I don't believe it will ever build a thing in Palestine. It will continue to live off the dole (its Zionists as well as its old-time Orthodox). Every year a few Zionist big wigs will settle here along with several hundred more ordinary Jews. Sixty or seventy percent of them will re-emigrate. Fifty percent of the young people who are here would leave at the first opportunity.

It was Gordon, not Brenner, who proved to be the realist. This was not because Gordon was politically more astute but because he believed more in the Jewish people and thought it capable of more. Brenner's love-hate relationship with his Jewishness could take him only so far. It could make him desperately want the Jews to be cured but it could not persuade him that they were curable. In the end, Gordon might have said, his despair was still not great enough.

Chapter Ten
Rahel at the Well

1

Bearing a dedication to A. D. Gordon and entitled "State of Mind," it was Rahel[1] Bluvshtayn's first published Hebrew poem:

> The day grew dark
> And faded from on high.
> A dull gold ringed
> The mountains and the sky.
>
> Black stretched the fields around me,
> Black and still.
> Far ran my dreary,
> Solitary trail.
>
> And yet I would not challenge fate,
> Tyrant though it is.
> Whatever comes I'll greet with joy,
> With thankfulness.

---

1. The Hebrew form of the biblical name Rachel is accented on its second syllable, with the "h" pronounced as a *het*.

Appearing in *Ha-Shiloah* in the summer of 1920, this was not an exceptional piece of verse, although its simple language and Sephardi stress patterns in an age in which Bialik's architectonic, Ashkenazi-accented Hebrew was still the gold standard might have drawn some attention. (While Sephardi stress, with its favoring of final syllables, had been adopted by Palestinian Hebrew speech, most Hebrew poetry in the early twentieth century was still being written in penultimate-leaning Ashkenazi meters.) Rahel – she signed her poems with only her first name, and so she was known to her readers – was living at the time in Degania, and Gordon, a fellow member of the kibbutz, sent her a short poem of his own in response. "Follow your trail!" it encouraged her.

The two had known each other since 1909, when Rahel, then a nine-teen-year-old, came to Palestine from Russia with two sisters on a visit, was enchanted by what she saw, and decided to remain instead of continuing on a planned tour of Italy. For several months she lived in the First Aliyah colony of Rehovot, studying Hebrew; then she joined a group of Second Aliyah pioneers in the farming commune of Kinneret, which bore the Hebrew name of the nearby lake known in most languages as the Sea of Galilee. In 1913, convinced it was her best way of contributing to the kibbutz, she traveled to France to study agriculture at the University of Toulouse. From there she wrote Gordon that she couldn't wait to finish her planned two-and-a-half years of studies and return to Palestine. He wrote back:

> Why think of your stay in France as merely preparatory, a time of getting ready for life rather than of life itself? It's a mistake to look at things that way. We talked about this once when I said to you that a person should live as Jews are told to wor-ship: "Know Him in all thy ways!"... Yes, Rahel, *live*, live all you can! Don't be afraid of compromising your ideals or risking the hopes you have for the Land of Israel. More important than bringing back what you've studied in Europe is bringing back what you've lived here.

She took his advice. Besides excelling in her studies, she per-fected her French, read widely in its literature, enjoyed Toulouse's rich cultural life, hiked and toured the Occitan countryside, took art classes, spent summers in Italy, and had a romance with a Russian Jewish engineering student, Mikhail Bernstein – who, she later was to confide to her intimates, was the great love of her life. (Though they never saw each other again after Toulouse, she and Mikhail continued to write each other for years.) Yet after receiving her degree in agronomy, she found the way back to Turkish-ruled Palestine barred by war: Turkey was allied with Germany and its territories were off-limits to Russian nationals. She returned to Russia, lived for a while with a sister in Kremenchug, and found work in an orphanage in Berdyansk, on the Sea of Azov, where she spent most of the war years. When, in 1919, she finally made it back to Palestine, now in British hands, she brought with her, besides more years of her life than she had counted on, a lung condition contracted in the orphanage.

Instead of rejoining Kinneret, she chose to live in nearby Degania. Her health was too poor for the farm work she had trained for and she was assigned to the kibbutz kitchen. "For some reason, I've been feeling worse," she wrote her sister Shoshanna, the great-aunt of the Israeli military historian Uri Milstein, the author of a biographical sketch of her. "The doctor told me that if I had any sense I would understand how irresponsible it is not to have my own separate dishes and utensils. But obviously, Shoshana'le, this isn't possible in a commune!" From the kitchen, she was transferred to the children's home. (One of her small charges was the five-year-old Moshe Dayan, the future Israeli general and politician.) Examined again, she was diagnosed with active tuberculosis. The kibbutz members were warned that she mustn't spend another day with the children. Indeed, they were told, she was a danger to them all.

She had had a premonition that she would have to leave Degania. In "State of Mind," she had imagined herself a lonely outcast. Still, the shock was great when it happened. As described by Milstein:

> There was turmoil over how to inform Rahel [that she was being asked to leave]. A young kibbutz member, David Gil'ad, was

chosen to tell her. Although exactly what passed between them is unknown, she was devastated. She had yet to come to terms with her illness. She wanted to stay in the kibbutz; she loved her work with the children. It was a terrible blow…. [In a letter] she wrote how painful it was to be told by Gil'ad, "We're well and you're not. You have to go."

The event was traumatic for the members of Degania as well. They were a small group, living intimately together. Some delayed coming home from the fields that evening to avoid having to confront Rahel. In the kibbutz's work sheet, found in its archives, her name on the next day's list of assignments is followed by the terse entry: "Gone to Tel Aviv with her belongings."

There is no record of Gordon, then ill himself with the cancer that soon would kill him, having come to her defense. Gil'ad's visit to her room was later described by her in a poem.

> The messenger arrived at night
> And sat upon my bed,
> His fleshless bones protuberant,
> His eyes deep-socketed.
>
> At once I knew that the old bridge
> The hands of time had hung
> Between the future and the past
> Had snapped and been unslung.
>
> He shook a skinny fist and laughed
> With cruel mirth, "You're right.
> Of all the poems you might write,
> You'll write the last tonight."

In point of fact, nearly all of Rahel's poems were still to be written. But a life had indeed come to an end that night – not a whole one, certainly, but the one she had wanted to live.

2

Poems like "State of Mind" and "The Messenger Arrived at Night" have caused Rahel's verse to be compared to Emily Dickinson's. Although it is unlikely that Rahel had any knowledge of the American poet, who died in obscurity four years before she was born, there are points of resemblance between them. Both were minimalists who preferred short poems, short lines, and plain phrasing. Both had a conservative preference for the rhymed quatrain. Both were fond of little surprises – the unanticipated phrase or word, the perspective-changing final line or stanza.

It goes beyond that. In both, there is a similar wryness of tone. A ruefulness over life's caprices and missed opportunities. A fatalism and resignation to loss. A real or feigned modesty that says: *well, this is me – I know it's not much but it's what there is.* Rahel paints her self-portrait:

> As still as lake water:
> That's how I am.
> I like quiet days, babies' eyes,
> And the poems of Francis Jammes.
>
> Long ago my soul wore purple.
> On mountain peaks
> I walked with the wind
> And the great birds' shrieks.
>
> Long ago…but that was long ago
> And time goes by.
> It's different now.
> So am I.

Of Jammes, her favorite French poet, she once wrote, "He sits in his corner in his native mountains puffing on his pipe, reliving old memories, saddened by a passing cloud and rejoicing in a sun ray; not deep, not broad, not complicated, but evoking a mood like none other in which, all worry gone, you shelter and rest."

Dickinson tells God:

> Father, I bring thee not myself –
> That were the little load;
> I bring thee the imperial heart
> I had not strength to hold.

Purple is the color of emperors. Both poets speak of having surrendered whatever large claims on life they may have had, in part because they are women in a man's world. Though a source of regret, this is also one of strength. It frees them of the masculine drive to compete and control and allies them with all in life that is content to be merely itself. "I'm nobody!" declares Emily Dickinson.

> Who are you?
> Are you nobody, too?
> Then there's a pair of us – don't tell!
> They'd banish us, you know.

And Rahel, who said of Jammes that "like the animals and birds, [he] demands nothing of anyone," asks:

> Was I once a wild thing among other wild things
> In another, a far incarnation?
> Is that why I feel such a sister to them
> And a fear of man's domination?

Yet as personalities, Rahel and Dickinson were very different. Dickinson, the more quirky and original of the two, was a spinster and recluse who rarely ventured beyond the New England home she was born and died in. Rahel, though she too never married, was a fully social and sexual being. When she was forced into increasing isolation by her illness in the years before her death in 1931, it was not of her own choosing. In her poetry is a quiet anger at her fate not found in Dickinson.

She was born in 1890 in Saratov on the Volga and grew up in Poltava in the Ukraine. Her father, Isser-Leib Bluvshtayn, was a Cantonist in the reign of Nicholas I, one of thousands of Jewish boys, like Dr. Koch in Berdichevsky's "Miriam," who were snatched from their families by professional kidnapers and impressed into military training and the Russian army. Although these youngsters, some no more than eight or nine years old, were not forced to become Christians, they were denied all means of practicing Judaism, and few had the stubbornness and strength of character needed to retain their Jewish identities throughout their twenty-five years of military service. Isser-Leib was not only one of the exceptions, he was an outstanding soldier who served with distinction in the Crimean War, and the qualities that served him well in the army helped him to become a successful businessman after his discharge. When his first wife died and left him with four children, he married a younger woman, Rahel's mother Sophia Mandelstamm, and had eight more children with her.

The Mandelstamms were a distinguished Russian Jewish family. Sophia's father was a noted rabbi. Her uncle Leon was the first Jew to enroll, in 1840, in a Russian university, and her brother Max, Rahel's uncle, was a noted ophthalmologist and Zionist leader; in the "Altneuland" debate that rocked the Zionist world in 1902–3, he actively sided with Herzl. Less reputably, a cousin of Rahel's, Rosa Mandelstamm, was a revolutionary involved in the 1861 assassination of Tsar Alexander I, while a more distant relative was the Russian poet Osip Mandelstamm. Sophia herself, who died when Rahel was sixteen, was well-versed in Russian literature and corresponded with Tolstoy. She and Isser-Leib raised Rahel in a home that was both strongly Jewish and thoroughly Russianized, a combination less uncommon in the 1890s and early 1900s than it had been in the 1870s and '80s.

There were fewer young women than men in the Second Aliyah and Rahel was more of an attraction than most. One young *halutz* who was drawn to her was Zalman Rubashov, later to become, as Zalman Shazar, the third president of the state of Israel. In a memoir, he recalled setting eyes on her for the first time after a nighttime hike to Kinneret along the lakeshore:

> From a rise overlooking the lake, I caught sight of the commune's farmyard. Dawn was breaking. The Kinneret shone beneath me, peaceful and blue. The yard was surrounded by a fence. I hadn't yet reached the gate when I heard it unbolted from within, followed by an orchestra of lively quacks and flapping wings conducted by a wonderfully vibrant, commanding voice. I stopped in my tracks. The

gate swung open and through it, flouncing over the hillside, burst a noisy gaggle of white geese. Behind them, gazelle-like on her feet and as winsome as the waters of the lake, strode a tall, stately, blue-eyed gooseherd in a snow-white dress. In one hand, her lithe figure held the branch of a date tree, and with this wand, in strong, young, ringing tones, she took charge of the clamorous flock. Gently but firmly, in a lilting Hebrew, she led it to pasture at dawn from the farmyard.

I watched from beyond the fence, holding my breath, until the gleaming white procession had passed.

The gooseherd was the poetess Rahel.

Needless to say, Shazar could hardly have made out the color of Rahel's eyes from a distance in the dimness of dawn, nor was she likely to have been carrying a date branch, whose large fronds and nasty thorns would not have made it a suitable baton. When he wrote these words, Rahel was long dead and had become a legend that his description partook of. Nonetheless, one can credit the substance of it. By all accounts, Rahel was tall and striking. If photographs of her from this period fail to reveal a face of surpassing beauty, they do show one of a sensitive, finely-featured, brooding intelligence such as could easily have captivated a beholder. Shazar was not the only *halutz* to fall in love with her, nor the only one whose feelings were at least partly reciprocated.

"How did the days [in Kinneret] pass?" Rahel wrote in a recollection from 1929.

> Dawn would be breaking when we began work. There were fourteen of us – our hands callused, our legs barefoot, scratched, and sun-bronzed, our jaws set, our hearts aglow. The air rang with our singing, laughter, and talk. Our hoes kept rising and falling, stopping only long enough for us to wipe the sweat from our brows with a corner of our Arab *keffiyehs* while glancing lovingly at the lake. How good it all felt! So much blue, so much halcyon, restorative, inexpressible blue! Far out on the water, a fishing skiff rocked. Soon the little steamboat that ferried passengers from Tsemach to Tiberias would send up its plume of smoke.

It was, as it were, the fulfillment of Gordon's prophecy to those laboring in "the workshop of Nature" that "when you pause to stretch your limbs and take a deep breath, you will be breathing more than air... you will know the bliss of being in the Infinite."

In the late 1920s, when the Second Aliyah was already history, Rahel objected to the emphasis placed on the *halutzim*'s readiness for self-sacrifice. What had motivated them far more, she wrote in response to an article about them by the physician and Labor Zionist publicist Moshe Beilinson, was their spirit of youthful adventure. "They [put everything behind them] and started life anew," she quoted Beilinson as saying, as if this were the highest form of self-abnegation, and commented: "As if all young hearts (if they're truly young) don't hunger to start life anew, as if sleeping on a haystack or in a stable to the jingle of a mule's chain isn't a hundred times sweeter to them than a night spent in a featherbed!" Whereas Beilinson, she wrote, "saw heroism in the renunciation of the comforts of the Diaspora for a bitter subsistence in a desolate homeland, I see it in the courage to be happy in a homeland reborn and to stake one's life on this."

She looked back on that time with longing. A poem written in 1927 wondered:

> And perhaps it never happened that way?
> Perhaps
> I never set out for work on the garden path
> In the first light of day?
>
> Never once in the hot, long
> Harvest time,
> High on a wagon piled with hay,
> Broke into song?
>
> Never bathed until pure in the blue quietude
> Of my Kinneret?
> O my Kinneret!
> Was it only a dream, then, not you?

She had known happiness in Degania, too, even when already ill. She described it in a poem called "Sabbath," written while still there. Degania was situated at the Sea of Galilee's southern end, where the Jordan flows out of it, and the poem speaks of lolling by the river on the week's day of rest. Its last two lines, *kol dikhfin ye'ete, yitol*, echo the Passover Haggadah's *kol dikhfin yeitei veyeikhol*, "Let all the hungry come and eat."

> The Jordan's banks. I sprawl at ease.
> A fishing skiff.
> I drink my fill of peace.
>
> I look above me: how much light!
> And in my heart, as when I was a child,
> There is no cloud in sight.
>
> And now I know it: everything is here.
> Let all the needy come
> And take their share.

Was Rahel's being made to leave Degania avoidable? Moshe Dayan's mother Dvora thought it might have been. "There were many things we didn't know how to care for properly in those days," she told an inquiring journalist years later,

> the greatest of which was Rahel's desire to remain in spite of her illness. I'm not overlooking the difficulties we faced; it goes without saying that we had to be as practical-minded as possible in building our collective. But we'll never cast off the shadow of that terrible night when Rahel was told, "You're sick and can't live among the healthy." As obvious as this may have seemed to all of us, there was no real attempt to talk it over or look for a better solution.

Milstein judges the members of Degania even more harshly. They were guilty, he writes, of an injustice that presaged, at the kibbutz movement's very inception, utopian socialism's incapacity to construct a more moral society than the one it sought to replace. In thinking only of themselves, they were acting as selfishly as the institutions of capitalism denounced by them. The banishment of a single sick woman from a small settlement by the Sea of Galilee was, for Milstein, Labor Zionism's original sin, "a social and cultural tragedy." Not only Rahel was expelled from her paradise that night. The Labor Zionist dream itself – Brenner's "Workers communes: that is our only revolution!" – was exposed in all its nakedness.

Quite apart from its sweeping historical generalizations, however, Milstein's accusation hardly seems fair. Had Rahel been made to leave Degania solely because her illness kept her from pulling her share of the weight, it would indeed have been a betrayal of the kibbutz's principles. But what parents in even the most moral society would knowingly expose a child or themselves to a contagious and potentially fatal disease in order to accommodate a sick woman's needs? The members of Degania had to make a decision; one can legitimately fault the way they carried it out, but not the decision itself. It was not just to Rahel that they were capable of being insensitive. Their lives were hard; they had to be disciplined; too much emotion could be dangerously disruptive. In recalling her years in Degania, the Second Aliyah pioneer Aliza Shidlovsky wrote of "how afraid we were of being weak. This fear made us cruel, knowingly so, to ourselves and to others. No one thought that a companion's feelings of loneliness or isolation needed to be a reason for concern. No one thought that anyone's depression or despair demanded special consideration."

Would it have been a "better solution" for Rahel to have been allowed to remain in the kibbutz in a state of quarantine? She herself never appears to have thought so. Nor did she, like Milstein, regard Degania's treatment of her as proof of a fundamental flaw in the idea of kibbutz life, in which she never lost her belief. Two years before her death she went back to Degania, now a larger but still Spartan settlement, and wrote about revisiting its children's home.

> Evening. Autumn. A farm shack in the homeland.
> Thin, chinked walls. An earthen floor. A room.
> In one corner, a crib with white netting.
> In the window, distances loom.

> Guide me still, stubborn toil and hope of the tiller!
> I still am yours, life of pure, patient want!
> The children gather and silently wonder:
> Why is she sad, the visiting aunt?

3

The argument that Rahel's poetry, which has been called senti-mental and simplistic, is neither of these things might start with this poem.

On the face of it, the speaker of its first stanza expresses no feeling at all. She simply lists what she sees or is aware of, from the all-pervasive (evening, autumn) to the specific (an earthen floor, a crib). And yet even as she being merely enumerative, her voice is choked with feeling. This is conveyed to us by the pauses, dictated by the meter's caesuras, between one brief utterance and the next. We feel her eye linger on each thing that she names; the effort she puts into naming it; her need to rest from that effort before proceeding to the next thing; her fear that saying anything more might cause her to falter or break into tears.

Why? We cannot yet say. The little shack, the infant's crib with its mosquito netting, the gray evening gathering outside the window: in all this we sense a drama that has yet to be revealed. This is the very oppo-site of sentimentality: not an excess of emotion but a concealment of it.

In the second stanza, emotion bursts forth in a sudden release. Speech breaks through the barriers holding it back, as though it had been forming behind them all the time, in a pair of exclamations completely different from the halting words that have preceded them. *Guide me still, stubborn toil and hope of the tiller! I still am yours, life of pure, patient want!* Only now do we understand that the poet is stand-ing in a place that belongs to her past, though she still identifies with its idealism, its ascetic way of life, its ethic of hard work, its faith that it is building a better future for a people in its land. Resolutely, she declares that these values continue to be hers. Prayerfully, she hopes they always will.

So she tells herself and us. But the stanza has two more lines. There are small children in the shack and when they regard the visitor – the "aunt," as Hebrew-speaking boys and girls were taught to address a female stranger – they do not see resoluteness or hope. They see sadness. And although they say nothing, she sees in their eyes that they see it in hers. Is this a sadness she has been conscious of all along but has not wanted them to be? Or has she has been hiding it from herself, too, and is now forced to acknowledge it? It is the sadness of knowing, her brave words notwithstanding, that she can never again be part of what she sees.

A simple poem? Perhaps. But not simplistic.

Simplicity was Rahel's poetic creed. It came from her reading of the contemporary poets she admired most: Akhmatova and Yesenin among the Russians, Jammes, Paul Fort, and Charles Vildrac among the French. "I consider it evident," she stated in a short piece in the Labor Zionist newspaper *Davar*, in which she published her poetry and a bit of prose throughout the 1920s,

> that the signature of our times in poetry is simplicity of diction: language that expresses the first struggles of a lyric emotion to be born; that is immediate and has not had time to clothe its undress in satins and silks; that is free of all "literariness" and refreshingly unjaded, so that its human truth speaks to us directly.

Her being a woman had something to do with it. Although she had received a Jewish education in Russia, this was more elementary than that given boys, so that she arrived in Palestine with practically no knowledge of Hebrew. She learned it from speaking it and hearing it spoken, the way a child learns its native tongue, and while her poetry was not free of literary influences and mannerisms – what poetry is? – her desire to make it seem so was that of someone whose first, formative contact with the language she wrote in did not come from books, as it had for every major Hebrew poet before her. The knowledge of Hebrew literature that she eventually acquired was appreciable. But although she knew, as she wrote in a poem, "All kinds of fine words / That haughtily strut and parade," none spoke to her like "The innocent speech of a child / That is humble as dirt." She had taught and been taught by such children in Degania.

Rahel is the first modern Hebrew poet of note whose language is immediately recognizable to Israeli readers as their own. The two other leading young Hebrew poets of the 1920s, Uri Tsvi Grinberg and Avraham Shlonsky, were both characterized by the "literariness" she criticized. Although they broke with Bialik's poetics more sharply than she did, they retained his conception of the Hebrew poem as a text potentially interactive with the entire Hebrew literary corpus. Grinberg, raised in a Hasidic home in Galicia, came to Palestine in 1923; in his first years there, before veering politically to the Right, he, like Rahel, was associated with Labor Zionism and *Davar*. In the opening lines of his long poem "Heroica," which appeared in his first volume of verse, published in 1925, he addressed the *halutz* of the Third Aliyah, the wave of immigration that reached Palestine in the years after World War I:

> Like you I am poor on this holy earth the curse of whose beauty
> afflicts you and me by day and by night.
> Like you I know not why we left the house of our fathers and
> desertwards came, joyous and barefoot.
> For us did the sands glow, the clefts of the rocks to inherit.
> Words were like poems.
> Like you I know not wherefore the soil's clods were sweetened
> for us by the mercy of God and the moon
> and the wailing of jackals.
> Yet one is the well from which we have all slaked our thirst
> on the hashish of Hebrew.

Grinberg's long, sprawling lines of free verse were unique in the Hebrew of the times, as was their heavily cadenced, incantatory rhetoric whose sometimes archaizing language and obscurity (how is one, syntactically, to construe "the clefts of the rock to inherit"?) clash with brash modernisms like "the hashish of Hebrew." His scavenging of ancient sources went beyond anything that Bialik and his generation permitted themselves. The dative "us" of "For us did the sands glow," for instance, is, for rhythmic reasons, the Aramaic *lan* of the Talmud, a usage totally foreign to Hebrew, in which the word is *lanu*. It would be hard to think of a poetic style further removed from Rahel's.

Shlonsky, too, grew up in a Hasidic home, in the Ukraine. Arriving in Palestine in 1921, he briefly belonged to a pioneering work brigade and a kibbutz before moving to Tel Aviv. More tightly controlled than Grinberg's, his poetry was no less steeped in the imagery of a religious upbringing. In one of his own salutes to the Third Aliyah *halutz*, his poem "Work," Grinberg's "Like you I" becomes simply "I":

> Dress me, good Jewish mother, in a coat
> Of many-colored splendor and send me off to work at dawn.
>
> My land dons light like a prayer shawl.
> Its houses are boxes of phylacteries,
> their leather straps the blacktopped roads that muscled arms
> have paved.
>
> The comely city prays to its Creator.
> A creator, too, am I,
> your son Avraham,
> a poet-road paver in Israel,
>
> And at eventide, home from the day's toil,
> Father prays, whispering with pleasure:
> Is not Avraham my dear son?
> Skin, sinew, and bone.
> Hallelujah!

"Work" is an extended metaphor in which the Land of Israel is likened to a praying Jew whose tefillin are the handiwork of the Zionist pioneer, and the pioneer himself first to the biblical Joseph, who sets out to join his brothers in his coat of many colors; then to God's partner in creation, the builder of the "comely city" of Tel Aviv (Shlonsky's word for which, *kirya*, is taken from the 48th psalm, where it refers to Mount Zion and Jerusalem); and finally, to the wayward Ephraim of the book of Jeremiah, of whom God says, "Is not Ephraim my dear son? Is he not a pleasant child? For since I spoke against him, I do earnestly remember him still." As God is reconciled to Ephraim despite having been deserted by him for other gods, so the poet's father in Eastern Europe, though initially angry at his son for abandoning him for a pioneering life in

Palestine, is now pleased by him. He has added the sinew of muscle to the frail skin and bone of the exilic Jewish body.

Like Shlonsky's "Work," Grinberg's "Heroica" frames the *halutzim's* experience in religious terms. The coarse bread that is their supper is "more sacred than the shewbread on the golden table of the Temple." The smoke rising from their cheap cigarettes is like priestly incense. God himself knows how "holy is the hand that holds the hoe." Behind both poems, each a hymn to a new, physically robust type of Jew, stands a body of biblical and rabbinic literature; the sublimated religious emotion of the synagogue and the study house; and a century of Haskalah and Zionist thought, from Perl's imagined utopia of Jewish farmers to Ahad Ha'am's proposed secular recasting of the symbols and values of Judaism, and from Berdichevsky's call for a revolt against Jewish tradition in the name of Jewish existence to Gordon's neo-Hasidic "religion of labor."

Rahel's experience as a *halutz* was a sometimes ecstatic one, too. She recognized both Shlonsky and Grinberg's poetic stature. But this did not prevent her from expressing her reservations about poetry like theirs in a poem of her own, "To My Land," written in 1926:

> I have not sung to you, my land,
> Psalms of high praise,
> Nor glorified you
> With a hero's deeds;
> Only with a tree
> Planted by the Jordan's banks,
> Only with a path
> Trod through your fields.
>
> How little, mother,
> That has been, I know,
> How small
> Your daughter's gift:
> Just a cry of joy
> When dawn broke over you,
> Just, for your poverty,
> A tear of grief.

It says much for "To My Land" that it makes "Heroica" and "Work," however taken by them we may be, seem posturing and declamatory. It too, of course, strikes a pose. But though its self-belittlement is no less calculated than Grinberg and Shlonsky's grandiosity, it strikes us, paradoxically, as surer of itself and no less accomplished in its art. "The path of simplicity is a difficult one," Rahel wrote, and it is indeed harder to get away with being simple. Complexity leaves room for error: a wrong word or phrase can be outbalanced by others and go unnoticed, or at least, not given undue weight. Simplicity leaves none. It walks on a ledge: one false step and you have fallen.

There are no false steps in "To My Land." Its simplicity presupposes daring just as its humility presupposes pride. If Rahel had poems like "Heroica" and "Work" in mind when she wrote it, she was saying of them, "That's all very rousingly put, but don't expect me to compete with it." *She* had only planted a tree and walked through fields, and she knew how little that was. And how much.

4

The Bible was as important to Rahel as it was to Grinberg and Shlonsky, perhaps even more so, but in a different way. Although it was a book she kept by her side from the time of her first Hebrew lessons in Rehovot, she rarely drew on it linguistically. Rather, she did so thematically, often by means of an identification with a biblical character. Such is her poem about her namesake, the matriarch Rachel:

> Her voice sings in mine.
> In me her blood wells.
> Rahel who pastured the flock –
> The mother Rahel's.
>
> If all cities feel strange
> And all walls hem me in,
> It's because her scarf fluttered free,
> In the desert's hamseen.

> And if I go my own way
> With such confidence,
> It's because my feet know the path
> Ever since, ever since!

Rahel sees herself in the biblical Rachel, the future wife of Jacob and mother of Joseph glimpsed as a surefooted young Bedouin shepherdess, the scarf that covers her face when in company now blowing freely in the hot Arabian wind. But she also sees Rachel in herself. She is both the projector and the reflector. A bond that starts with a name ends in a deep sense of kinship.

This was new. It was far from the first time in Hebrew literature that biblical characters were portrayed in terms other than those of traditional rabbinic exegesis. Nineteenth-century works like Mapu's biblical novels, the biblical ballads of Micha Yosef Lebensohn, and Y. L. Gordon's "The Love of David and Michal" and "Zedekiah in Prison," though innovative in other ways, had their eighteenth-century predecessors in this respect. But for a sense of closeness to a biblical character so great that it erases all distance and transforms her or him from a literary or historical subject to an immediately felt human presence, Hebrew had to wait for Rahel.

When Rahel speaks in her poem "Yonatan" to Jonathan, King Saul's son and David's close companion who stands by him when Saul seeks to kill him, the thousands of years between them dissolve all at once. The poem bears a superscription referring the reader to the story in the book of Samuel about how Jonathan, having led his troops to victory against the Philistines, is condemned to death for tasting a morsel of honey in contravention of his father's command that no food be touched until the battle is over. Although he is ultimately granted a reprieve, this comes too late, as it were, for news of it to reach the poet in time:

> Through a haze he emerges – a delicate youth
> In princely finery,
> Too stout-hearted to abandon a friend
> Or flee an enemy.

And you must die, Yonatan? The path of a man
In this wrathful existence is sad.
Each of us pays with his life for the taste
Of what little honey he's had.

And you must die, Yonatan? Tender and sorrowful, the words have
the intimacy of a whisper. "Yonatan," like "Rahel," is about the poet no less
than the biblical figure. She, too, has fleetingly tasted the honey of happiness and been sentenced to die – not by a royal father but by her illness.

The Bible was as immediate for Rahel as was its landscape in
which she lived. In general, writes the Israeli historian Anita Shapira,

> the Bible had a special place in the life of the Second Aliyah.
> There was hardly a *halutz*'s room that didn't have a copy of it.
> The memory of the Land of Israel as the Jewish people's homeland was preserved in it. It made the tie to this land tangible. It
> served the pioneers as a geographical, zoological, and botanical
> guide. They commonly hiked about the country with it, using it
> as a Baedeker to the places they passed through.

Of course, the First Aliyah, too, was highly Bible-conscious. So
was all of Zionism. Ben-Gurion's much-quoted remark to the British Peel
Commission in 1936 that the Bible was the Jewish people's title deed to
Palestine said nothing that Zionism hadn't repeated endlessly from the
start. What distinguished Rahel's generation was its belief that it possessed, by virtue of its closeness to the land of the Bible, a key, held by
none before it, to the text of the Bible.

Rahel was a poet – *the* poet – of the Second Aliyah. No other
book, no poet she loved, meant to her what the Bible did. Although it
was not religious truth for her, neither was it fiction. It was a lived reality.
She makes us feel that she experiences Jonathan from within because
she has taken him into her. The same holds true of Rachel; the same of
Michal, Saul's daughter and David's first wife.

As opposed to Yehuda Leib Gordon's long narrative treatment
of David and Michal's relationship, Rahel's poem "Michal" focuses on
a single moment. In II Samuel we read how David, after recovering the

captured Ark of the Covenant from the Philistines, accompanies it back to Jerusalem with a throng of rejoicing Israelites, "leaping and dancing" with no thought of his royal dignity, and how Michal, observing the scene from the window of her palace, "despised him in her heart" for his commonness. (She is after all a king's daughter, whereas he comes from rustic stock.) In her poem Rahel speaks to Michal directly, as she does to Jonathan:

> Michal, my distant sister! Unbroken is the cord that binds the ages.
> In your rueful garden grow no weeds of time.
> Your silken mantle's purple stripes have never faded,
> Nor have your golden anklets ceased to chime.
>
> Ofttimes I've seen you standing by your window,
> Pride mixed with tenderness in your fair eyes.
> Michal, my sister! I am as sad as you are.
> The man I love I too, like you, despise.

5

To judge from her poetry, which is our main source of information about her in the absence of a full-length biography, Rahel's relationships with men were unsatisfying. As her health deteriorated in the 1920s, it ruled out a full sexual life. Her illness wasted her body and made physical contact with her a risk. Even before then, though, her romantic involvements did not live up to her expectations. She was easily disappointed; acquaintances ascribed to her high standards and a sarcastic wit deft at deflating mediocrity and pretension. High-born in Jewish terms on her mother's side, she was anything but a snob; but if there is such a thing as a natural aristocracy of souls in the world, she felt she belonged to it. Men who demonstrated by their speech or behavior that they did not, however attracted to them she might be, were in peril of arousing her scorn.

Except for Mikhail Bernstein, she never fully gave her heart to anyone. In his letters to her after his return to Russia from Toulouse, Mikhail stated his remorse at not having been more open and emotionally expressive with her; the thought haunted him that he had let slip an opportunity for happiness that would not recur. Rahel's letters to him have not survived. Yet her poems reveal that frustrating ties with men who could not or would not share their inner selves with her were a repetitive pattern. One of these poems she called "A Cloister":

> Who are you? Why, a hand held out,
> Is none returned?
> And those eyes that waver for a moment
> And are downturned!
>
> A cloister. No path leads up to it.
> A cloister of a man.
> Should I have gone away?
> Or hammered on the rock until blood ran?

The image in the last line is taken from the biblical story of the rock angrily struck for its water by Moses, though told by God simply to speak to it. Although the woman in the poem has tried speaking and gotten nowhere, she remains drawn to the man whose defenses she has been unable to break through. Why else think of laceratingly persisting in her efforts?

Only once did Rahel write a poem about physical sex. It, too, has a line from the Bible, the verse "Set me as a seal upon thine arm" from the Song of Songs.

> Lips meet but hearts stay apart.
> Each heart the other heart fears,
> Jerked on a chain by fate's hand
> Like two dancing bears.
>
> The rattle of the iron leash,
> The drunken dance, the blood's wild peal,
> Drown out the yearning voice that prays,
> "Set me as a seal...."

Not love but lovelessness is the subject of this poem, whose man and woman, yoked together by bodily arousal, remain on guard against the animal aggression each might set off in the other. Although the woman is as willing a participant in the "drunken dance" of sex as is the man, a part of her has not joined it and longs for something beyond it. In the Songs of Songs, too, Hebrew's great duet of sexual passion, it is the woman who pleads for a "seal," a pledge of permanency to anchor the precariousness of erotic emotion. In Rahel's poem, this plea goes unanswered.

It went unanswered in her life, too. From some men, she could not have hoped for it to be. Contemporary gossip linked her to several who were married. Such liaisons were humiliating for her; yet if she wanted meaningful male companionship, her choice was limited. The Yishuv of the 1920s was a small world, its population less than a middle-sized city's. Not many men were her equal, and by the time she was in her thirties, nearly all who were had wives. Leaving them for her, even had they wished to, was not an option; sexually permissive in some ways, the Yishuv looked askance at divorce. Rahel's poem "His Wife" describes such a relationship:

> When she calls him by name,
> Her voice doesn't tremble.
> I don't trust my own
> To dissemble.
>
> She walks down the street by his side
> In plain sight;
> I, in the dark of concealment
> At night.
>
> She wears – shiny, serene –
> A gold ring on her finger.
> But my iron chains
> Are seven times stronger!

The last two lines are ambiguous. Is the poet boasting that despite the disadvantage she is at, the husband is bound to her by an attachment more unbreakable than his marriage bond? Or is she

confessing an inability even greater than his wife's to sever her connection to him?

Rahel was not, in our sense of the word, a feminist. She did not
make a cause of being a woman, and women's rights were a marginal
issue in her environment. Precisely the fact that the Second Aliyah and
the Palestinian Jewish society it molded were, ideologically, outspokenly
in favor of sexual equality made it difficult to protest against, or at times
even to identify, the inequalities that existed. Rahel was accepted by
her male acquaintances as their peer and was well aware of their admiration for her. Millstein quotes an account by the author and journalist
Meri Yatsiv of a meeting of *Davar*'s editorial board that she and Rahel
attended. Presiding over it were the paper's three senior editors, all married men Rahel was rumored to have had affairs with: Shazar, Beilinson,
and Berl Katznelson.

> There were three desks in the room. At each sat one of the
> men, a trio of close and good friends. Rahel took her place
> among them, a starry twinkle in her large blue eyes. She was
> in high spirits and joked with an inimitable flair. All three
> men were her playthings. For one, she had a fond word; for
> another, a saucy jibe; for the third, a compliment…. Sud-
> denly, the three friends were three rivals. They didn't look
> at each other. Each strove to outshine the others. The atmo-
> sphere grew tense. There was a sense of excitement in the
> air mixed with jealousy and a wistfulness that such a woman
> [so different from their wives] existed. Rahel was scintillat-
> ing, beautiful with a no longer physical beauty – clever, witty,
> lively, casting a spell.

And yet *Davar*'s highest positions, like those of every other
major institution in the Yishuv, were reserved for men. Rahel had
no steady income from the newspaper and lived her last years in
poverty. Although her father, who had taken a third wife, settled
in Palestine too, she did not get along with her stepmother, quar-
reled with them both, and received little support from them and
no inheritance. Despite her power over men, she could not help

internalizing her dependence on them, even her gratitude for whatever crumbs fell to her from their table. Her poem "A Woman" is candid about this:

> And so,
> Seen crystal-clearly from below,
> The view is like this:
> The hand of a master on which,
> With the sad, selfless look
> Of a slave or intelligent dog,
> One has the indistinct wish
> To lavish in silence
> A kiss.

It is hard, nearly one hundred years later, to appreciate the courage it took to publish such poems in a Hebrew-speaking community in which everyone knew everyone and anything, let alone a poem in a widely read newspaper, could set off a round of prurient speculation. Whose lips had hers met? Who was "his" wife? There was no way to avoid such talk or to deflect it with the explanation that poetry, like fiction, need not reflect the personal life of its author. This would have been disingenuous in any case, because Rahel's poetry *was* intensely personal. She once wrote, "I know only to tell of myself. / My world is as small as an ant's." The first of those two lines was true.

In one of her last poems, something in her relations with men seems to change. Its Hebrew title of *Edná* is difficult to translate. The word occurs once in the Bible, in the barren Sarah's bitterly laughing remark when told by an angel that she will conceive and give birth: "Now that I am old [i.e., no longer of child-bearing age], am I to have an *edná*?" Biblical commentators connected the word with a restoration of sexual vitality; in post-biblical Hebrew, it has the more general sense of a rejuvenation or renewal. In Rahel's poem it refers, nearly standing the biblical meaning on its head, to a quiescence of sexual feeling and the possibility of true female-male friendship, or something even deeper, undisturbed by erotic tension.

How strange it is: all the anger
And all the words of harsh strife
Have fanned the tenderest embers
Wondrously back into life.

No longer are we man and woman
Locked in the old, deadly war.
You have become the brother I love,
The little son I adore.

A brother, a son: how uncomplicatedly they could be loved! She had always, like the biblical Sarah, wanted a child of her own. In a poem called "Barren," she dreamed of being the mother of "a wise little boy, / His hair curly and dark, / With a hand I can hold / When we stroll in the park." In another, written in the same month as *Edná*, the dream is of returning to the blissfully pre-sexual state of childhood:

O again to be rosy-souled children who pick
Their joys like wildflowers in fields that are thick
With them! No one's hands tire and at a thorn's scratch,
The sun with a smile wipes the teardrops from each.

"God would be kind," the poem continued, "if we could forget all / The griefs of the years and their journey in which / We grow up and grow sad with too much to recall."

She died two months later, at the age of forty.

6

At the editorial meeting described by Meri Yatsiv, Rahel was already severely ill. "The marvelous show she put on," Yatsiv wrote,

did not last long. When she felt her strength failing, she rose and asked me to see her home while declining each of the three men's offer to escort her. They walked her to the street and to a waiting hansom [automobiles were still uncommon in Palestine] while she threw off a few last sparks from the fire she had lit. Once in the cab, she fell back lifelessly with a deathly pallor. Her breathing was frightfully loud. She had to be carried to her room.

Her last years were spent in and out of hospitals. A poem written in the mid-1920s describes being in one of them:

> The chalk-white path runs up the hill and disappears.
> What good does that do in my prison?
> I stare out the window and for no reason
> Burst into tears.

> The examining doctor remarks, "Your eyes are red.
> Is it from straining to see past that hill?"
> "That's very well-said," I reply with a smile
> And a bow of my head.

The straightforward first stanza followed by the ironic twist of the second is typical Rahel. The irony is twofold. First comes the doctor's. Aware that his patient has been crying and that she knows he has noticed, he seeks to ease her embarrassment with a teasing remark. Then comes the poet's. The doctor has spoken, she says, more truly than he knows: she has indeed been trying to see past the hill, which hides the path of a future that is perhaps blocked forever. The bow of her head is both an acknowledgement of the doctor's kindness and a token of submission to her fate. Does he understand? Does he comprehend all that is in her smile?

In the rented rooms in Jerusalem and Tel Aviv that she lived in, she was bed-ridden much of the time, too. In her poem "At Night," her bed has become a desk at which she conducts her correspondence. The poem harks back once more to the Bible and its story of Saul's nighttime visit to the witch of En-Dor. Saul, who is about to die the next day in battle against the Philistines on Mount Gilboa, asks the old woman to raise the spirit of the dead Samuel so that he might inquire what fate is in store for him. When it appears, it angrily rebukes him with the words, "Wherefore dost thou ask of me, seeing the Lord is departed from thee and become thine enemy?" and informs him of his imminent death. Rahel wrote:

Around, on sheet and pillow,
Old letters lie galore.
Bent over them, I call to mind
The sorceress of En-Dor.

Yet apropos tomorrow,
I need no prophecy.
The oracle that is my heart
Knows God is far from me.

It knows Gilboa's sorrow.
My preparations made,
I stare all night at writing
That is about to fade.

God is rarely mentioned in Rahel's poems. Like A. D. Gordon, she experienced the sacred in Nature and she felt far from it because she was forced to live in cities. "The sidewalks spurn / The gift of the rain," she wrote of Tel Aviv. Her sense of exile from the Kinneret never left her.

Yet poetically, as if spurred by the knowledge that she had little time left, her last two or three years were her most productive. She knew she was dying more clearly than did the friends who helped care for her. One of them, the future newspaper columnist and translator Rivka Davidit, who was barely twenty at the time, related:

> One day she felt very poorly, and listening to her frightful cough, I thought to my horror for the first time, "She's not long for this world!" But I didn't dwell on it, and though her condition, if anything, grew worse, she was so alert and sometimes even merry that I regarded her coughing fits as temporary setbacks…. I was so blind that when she said to me one evening after a long silence, "You know, I'll be setting out soon," I gave her a joyful look. "Really? You're going abroad?" Right away I imagined her in some magical sanatorium from which she would return totally cured. I stared at her is if awaiting confirmation. She nodded slowly. She didn't have the heart to puncture my foolish happiness.

In the early spring of 1931, she was moved to a sanatorium in Gedera, near Rehovot. In mid-April, her condition worsened further. A horse-drawn carriage was summoned to take her to back to Tel Aviv for hospitalization. On the way, she asked to make a detour to Rehovot; she wanted to see her friend Nakdimon Altshuler, with whom she had been in touch since his courting of her in her first days in Palestine. The doctor accompanying her begged her not to waste precious time. She insisted. Altshuler recalled afterwards:

> I went out to her. She was lying in the carriage.... Before me was a human skeleton. Her magnificent hair had turned to dry straw. Her sensitive, high-spirited face with its enigmatically mocking smile that no man could fathom had shrunk and collapsed. I looked at her and started to cry. Her blue eyes the color of the spring sky looked back at me; there was a single tear on her cheek.... She said, "Shalom, Nakdimon." I said, "Shalom, Rahel." The doctor signaled the coachman, who reached for the reins. With a lurch, the carriage began to move slowly.

Her last poem was found in her room in Gedera after her funeral. She had given it the title of "My Dead":

> They alone are left me, they alone won't feel
> Death plunge in them its dagger of cold steel.
>
> Up ahead, where the road bends,
> They'll fall in wordlessly when the day ends.
>
> We have a pact that no one can unsign.
> Only what I've lost is always mine.

7

Two volumes of Rahel's poems were published in her lifetime, one in 1927 and one in 1930. A third appeared posthumously in 1932. Since then her collected verse has gone through numerous editions, some illustrated, some accompanied by photographs, memoirs, and essays. With the possible exception of Bialik, no Hebrew poet from the pre-State of Israel period continues to have so large a readership. Her books are given as gifts. Their poems have been set to music, some in songs that all know. They are part of every Israeli school curriculum. Her gravesite on the southern shore of the Kinneret draws a constant stream of visitors. Hers is now the face on Israel's twenty-shekel bill.

There are obvious reasons for her popularity. Her poetry is accessible in a way that much serious modern poetry is not. It conforms to the ordinary reader's notions of what poetry should be like. It deals with situations and emotions that are easily identified with. Rahel's longing for Kinneret and Degania strike a chord in a country that, too, feels nostalgic for a time when it was smaller and less materialistic. She has been embraced by a national narrative that has given her an iconic status. After her death, her story was turned by the cultural and educational organs of the Yishuv and the State of Israel into the heroic drama of a beautiful and gifted young woman from a privileged home who, a world of possibilities before her, sacrificed all on the altar of Zionism.

She would have made a wry face at this. Her tuberculosis, without which her life would have been unimaginably different and almost certainly happier, was contracted in circumstances having nothing to do with Zionism. Even had she been healthy, she might ultimately have left Degania of her own accord, just as Shlonsky left Ein-Harod, and looked back on her years as a *halutz* as a fondly remembered episode from her youth. One imagines her wincing at being called a Zionist heroine and cringing at the thought of being fingered by a nation on its currency. Her large eyes stare out from it as if asking, "What am I doing here?"

There have been attempts to revise the accepted view of her. The same Israeli ministry of education that once helped propagate what has been called the "passion play" version of Rahel's life has now adopted the opposite approach. A recent ministry handbook urges teachers of literature to discard "gender stereotypes" that treat Rahel as a suffering victim and to avoid "the myth that has formed around her and helped 'market' her as a popular poet." Her poems deserve to be studied, teachers are advised, "because of their great lyric power, which make them classic expressions of pain, solitude, yearning, and regret that are humanly relevant to everyone."

There can be no quarrel with this. Rahel was a Zionist and she bore her illness bravely, but it was not as a Zionist that she was brave. She never blamed Zionism for her misfortunes or sought to justify them as the price exacted by it. Although the 1920s were a tumultuous period in Palestine, one that witnessed the beginnings of large-scale Jewish immigration, the establishment of dozens of new Jewish settlements, the rise to power in the Yishuv of Labor Zionism, the emergence of a right-wing Zionist opposition to it, the first massive anti-Zionist violence by Arabs, and the first clashes between the Zionist movement and the British mandate administration, there is no reference to any of this in her poetry.

A single poem of hers touched on it at all. Written in 1927, it was called "Here, On This Earth!"

> Here, on this earth! Not in some cloud land – no,
> Here on this mothering earth that is near,
> With its sorrows and joys, however threadbare,
> That comfort us so.
>
> Not in some mist time! Now, with what is at hand;
> With this warm, fleeting, palpable day,
> This day that is seizable only today –
> Here, in our land.
>
> Come, come all who can, before night's knell!
> Can it be for a thousand arms too much
> To roll with one last rallying push
> The stone from the mouth of the well?

What is it that makes this poem different from nearly everything else that Rahel wrote? Its sense of urgency, one might say. This is conveyed by the meter's extreme irregularity in certain places, by a predominance in these same places of strongly stressed, hortatory syllables, and by the insistent repetition of key words and phrases. There is an almost agitated need to be heard, to convince us of something.

What is this something? It is the need "to roll with one last rallying push / The stone from the mouth of the well." Once more Rahel takes a key image from the Bible. Arriving at the home of his uncle Laban to which he has fled from the wrath of his brother Esau, Jacob encounters Rachel waiting by a well to water her flock, which she can only do when all the shepherds in the area have gathered, their collective strength being needed to move the well's covering stone. But "it came to pass," the Bible tells us, "that when Jacob saw Rachel...he went near and rolled the stone from the well's mouth and watered the flock of Laban his mother's brother."

Rahel is calling on her readers, then, to make a herculean effort... to do what? They are to do it *now... here, on this earth... not in some cloud land.* But what is it that they are to do?

It is a call for action, this poem. It demands that something humanly fantastical take place without the aid of utopian fantasies, with plain, ordinary means, with "what is at hand." Here. Now. Today.

What?

Nineteen-twenty-seven was a relatively undramatic year in Palestine. The country was quiet. Jewish immigration was down. Violent Arab resistance to Zionism was resting between its explosion in the riots of 1921 and its next eruption in 1929. What was Rahel thinking?

Perhaps it was simply: *I'm Rachel, I'm at the well, I can't wait for all the shepherds to gather. If we in the Land of Israel, in the Jewish world everywhere, live this moment with all the solidarity and intensity that we can, we may yet do something extraordinary before I – before all of us – die.*

This is one of Rahel's few poems written, as it were, in a major key, and it is as close to being a Zionist statement as is anything she wrote. One does not associate her with Zionist politics. Herzl had thought that Zionism would solve the problem of the Jews and Ahad Ha'am that it would solve that of Jewishness. By Rahel we are told only that it would not solve – as A. D. Gordon and the *halutzim* of the Second Aliyah dreamed it would – any of the problems of the human condition.

She was a minor-key poet, not a minor one. The bird at the window has a small but perfect voice. Why would we want it to roar like a lion?

Chapter Eleven

Agnon's Tale of Two Cities

1

Yakov Malkov was a Habad Hasid and a bit of a writer. A day on which an article of his appeared in *Havatselet* was a red-letter day for him, since having readers made him feel he was doing some good in the world. Because he had a sensitive throat, he had chosen to live in Jaffa rather than in Hebron or Jerusalem, the sea being a physic for throat conditions – and because a man must provide for his family, and Jaffa was not one of the Land of Israel's holy cities whose faithful received charity from abroad, he had opened a boarding house. In it were three rooms: a dining room, a sleeping room, and a room for his family. In summertime, when vacationers came from Jerusalem to bathe in the sea, he spread a mat in the backyard, moved his family to it, and rented out the third room, too.

***

At sundown, the boarders returned from their work covered with dust, sand, and plaster and put away their tools. One went to wash his hands and face; a second to wet his throat with a glass of soda; a third to see if there was mail for him on the window sill; a fourth to glance at the day's *Havatselet*. One noticed that Brenner was there and hurried to greet him. Brenner shook his hand warmly like a man who would like to give a friend a gift and has only his own warmth to give.

"You should get yourself a glass of tea," he said.

"I will, I will," said Brenner's greeter excitedly, as if made suddenly aware of what he had been missing. "I'll go get some tea right away."

But he didn't. Having run into Brenner, it was hard to let go of him.

Malkov donned his long, heavy gabardine that came to his feet and put on the special hat that he wore to synagogue and other such occasions. "If you people were in the habit of praying," he said, "we could have a minyan here. Since we're not that fortunate, you'll excuse me for being off to evening prayers."

Glad for the chance to be with Brenner, we told him, "Pray for us too, Reb Yakov."

Malkov turned to look at us. "You can pray for yourselves," he said.

***

Malkov strode in briskly and called cheerfully, "Good evening, lads! A good evening to you all!" He took off his gabardine, hung it on a peg, doffed his hat, and gave it a loving pat. Seeing his wife standing and talking in the dining room, he scolded, "A person might think you were a rabbi giving a sermon. Back to the kitchen, woman, and tend to your affairs! Yosef Chaim, you'll have a bite to eat with us."

"I'm afraid not," Brenner said.

"Don't tell me that woman has scared you into thinking there's nothing to eat here," said Malkov. "All the fancy dishes she ate at her parents' made her think no other fare is fit for a Jew. Sit down, brother, have a seat and dig in. Hemdat, here's a piece of fish for you. At the feasts in the World to Come, you'll long for the tail end of its tail. Mapku, you're a regular here: go ask Azulai for a few dozen eggs." (Mapku was Gurishkin, called that by Malkov because he wrote fiction like Avraham Mapu.)

"I'll go, Reb Yakov," said little Yankele.

"You stay here," Malkov said. "You're a *kohen* and I don't send priests on errands, especially if they can't even say kaddish for their own father. Don't you think he's worth at least one kaddish? You'll come to synagogue with me tomorrow and say it. I knew this fellow's father, may he rest in peace," he said to Brenner. "He served God and country. He farmed land in Hadera and caught yellow fever, but he wouldn't leave it even when he was sick. He said, 'It's leaving the Land of Israel that kills a man, not yellow fever.' When he was dying he pointed out the window and said, 'Great is our shame, for we have forsaken the land.' Polishkin, put down that *Havatselet*! If you're looking for something to laugh at, try one of Ben-Yehuda's rags. Or are you afraid that heathen's clowning will rub off on you? Yosef Chaim, you're new in this country. You don't know how wise its wise men are. Listen to a penny's worth of their wisdom."

Brenner didn't like to hear talk of Ben-Yehuda, neither for nor against. Out of respect for his host, though, he shut his eyes and listened.

"The year Professor Boris Schatz opened his school of arts in Jerusalem," Malkov said, "he decided to throw a Hanukkah party. They made a statue of Matityahu the high priest brandishing the sword with which he stabbed the Greek who sacrificed a pig on the altar, and they ate and drank and had a bash. The next day Ben-Yehuda published a favorable editorial. His only problem was the statue. Matityahu, he said, was a religious fanatic, not a Jewish nationalist. As long as the Greeks merely overran our country, plundering and killing and laying everything waste, he and his sons in Modi'in didn't lift a finger to stop them. Not until our religion was attacked did they rise up valiantly et cetera et cetera, in honor of which et cetera et cetera we commemorate them for eight days. What do you think would have happened, Ben-Yehuda asked, if that statue had come to life last night? It would have run every last party-goer through with its sword, that's what. The sacrifice on the altar would have been us."

All this while Brenner never opened his eyes, as if better to see what Malkov was describing. When Malkov was done, he opened them and rocked with laughter.

"That's a damned lie, Malkov!" Gurishkin shouted. "A damned lie!"

"That's enough out of you, Mapku," said Malkov, stroking his beard. "You're so used to being an unbeliever that you don't even believe Ben-Yehuda."

Brenner laughed so hard that he had to grip the table to keep from falling to the floor. He stopped to catch his breath, burst out laughing again, and said, "You'll have to forgive me, my friends, for carrying on like this. It's just my vulgarity."

***

It was a lovely night, as most nights are in Jaffa when a hot, dry wind isn't blowing from the desert. The same sea that keeps the desert's parching heat away gave off a sultry redolence in which the flat sand shone. The sand didn't bother the strollers. It was pleasant, as sand is in the dark. And as it was pleasant to walk on, so we were pleased with ourselves. Every one of us knew where his next meal was coming from. Gone were the hard times in which we never went out at night because we were weary or hungry, too poor to afford a crust of bread because all the jobs went to Arabs. Now, the Jewish politicians of Jaffa had been forced to give us the contract for the new school they were building, and even those who claimed we couldn't compete with Arab labor had to admit we knew how to work.... Soon the first houses north of Jaffa would be going up and Jewish workers would be the ones to build them.... For the time being, only sixty of them were planned. But although sixty houses weren't sixty cities, we who had no grand aspirations thought them grand enough.

***

Brenner was not among the celebrants. What was there to celebrate? Did building sixty houses mean you had caught the

Messiah's donkey by its tail? Jews built houses: a single money lender in Lodz owned more of them than all the homes due to rise north of Jaffa. Did that make him the Jews' savior? You might say, of course, that building a house in Palestine wasn't like building a house in Poland. But houses were going up in Jerusalem, too, whole neighborhoods of them, and what good did they do apart from adding to the sum total of loafing, good-for-nothing, fawning, quarrelsome hypocrites who lived off the dole sent them by their benefactors in the Diaspora, those philanthropists of God's chosen who guzzled from the fleshpots of Europe and threw their brethren in the Holy Land a bone for their rotting teeth to gnaw on, in payment for which they and their *gesheften* were prayed for at the Wailing Wall? One thing alone was worth doing: farming the land and living from its bounty. But a plow made no commotion, which was why so few cared to walk behind one. We were simply building a new exile, the exile of Palestine, while thinking we were the deputized redeemers of the Jewish people – a people that had no use for us and didn't know the first thing about us. Only a handful of dimwitted idlers were hypnotized by Zionism's dreams of a glorious past and of a future in which everything would be done for them by Arabs so that they could sit at home drinking tea. "Except for the farmers of Rehovot, my friends, except for the farmers, it's all humbug, humbug, humbug! Yankele, what was it your father said as he lay dying? 'Great is our shame, for we have forsaken our land.' Forsaking the land is the greatest shame of all. Jeremiah knew that. Tell us about your father, Yankele."

Yankele blushed and said nothing. Brenner put a hand on his shoulder and looked at him fondly. Yankele took heart and said, "I never knew my father, because when people began dying of yellow fever in Hadera, we children were sent to Zichron Ya'akov. I'll tell you something I heard about him, though. Once he was asked, 'Well, Reb Yisra'el, are you happy here in the Land of Israel?' My father answered, "I would be if not for one thing. When I walked the streets of my native town in Russia with its Jew-hating scoundrels and constables, they spat at my beard and gave me dirty looks and I knew I was in exile. When I prayed, I prayed with a broken heart. Here, we're in our own country. There's no Russian constabulary and no exile. I'm a man without worries, and I'm ashamed to stand before my Maker an unworried man."

Brenner gave Yankele a big hug and began to sing to a tune of Malkov's, "Come, ye children, hearken unto me, I will teach you the fear of the Lord."

***

The night was a fine one with a fine sea, and Brenner's words were fine words. Once, when we had no work and nothing to eat or do, most of us thought as he did. Now that there were plenty of jobs and you could make a good living, we were like Yankele's father who missed his broken heart. Each of us thought of his own affairs: one of the new clothes he was going to buy, a second of paying for his girlfriend's passage to Palestine, a third of saving up enough to study at a university abroad. Our friend Yitzhak was thinking of Shifra.

***

Midnight came and went. A cool breeze began to blow. The sea changed its tune and foamed with waves that made pockets of water in the sand. Brenner gazed at it as if struggling to grasp its grandeur. He flexed a hand and took Hemdat's as though reaching for a pen while trying to phrase an insufficiently clear thought. "It's time for sleep," he said.

"*Yoh*," said Podolsky. "*M'darf geyn aheym.*"

Podolsky stressed *aheym* and laughed, because none of us had a home to call his own.

"*Kinderlakh*," Brenner repeated in a singsong, "*m'darf geyn aheym.*"

Once Brenner departed, and a while later Hemdat, all felt how tired they were. Each said goodnight and went his own way, one to his room and another to his bed in a corner of a cheap hotel in Nevei Shalom.

2

These excerpts come from a section of Shmuel Yosef Agnon's long novel *T'mol Shilshom*, published in English as "Only Yesterday." Appearing in Hebrew in 1945 and set in 1908–1910 in Jaffa and Jerusalem, the novel tells the story of Yitzhak Kummer, a young Second Aliyah immigrant to Palestine from Austro-Hungarian-ruled Galicia, as was Agnon in those years. Unlike the Zionist ideal of the *halutz*, Yitzhak is not a tiller of the soil. Although it was his ambition to be one upon arriving in Palestine several years prior to the scene in Yakov Malkov's boarding house, things turned out differently. Ending up in Jaffa rather than in a pioneer commune like Degania or Kinneret, Yitzhak has become a housepainter, a profession he earns well from, especially now that an increase in Jewish immigration at the end of the first decade of the century has led to a construction boom. One of its signs is a plan to build, on the sands north of Jaffa's Jewish neighborhood of Nevei Shalom, the first houses of what will soon be known as Tel Aviv.

Yitzhak does not live in a cheap hotel like Malkov's. He can afford a rented room of his own, as most of his Second Aliyah friends cannot. Nearly all of them are, like him, relatively new arrivals in Palestine from Eastern Europe; most have grown up in religious homes and have put religious observance behind them; most are single and have little prospect of marriage. Few could support a family even if they found a partner, which is difficult because there are more men than women among them. To this, Yitzhak is an exception. While shy with women, he has had a romantic relationship with a fellow immigrant his age named Sonya Tsvayring, and he is, at the time of the evening at Malkov's, in love with Shifra, the only child of Reb Feysh, a religious zealot in the ultra-Orthodox Jerusalem neighborhood of Me'ah She'arim.

Although Yitzhak dreams of marrying Shifra, a match between him and a daughter of the Old Yishuv, as the anti-Zionist, ultra-Orthodox community of Palestine was called, is hardly imaginable. Only unlikely circumstances could have led to their even meeting. Knocking on a door one day to ask for a glass of water after he has moved from Jaffa to Jerusalem, Yitzhak finds it opened by an elderly couple he recognizes from the ship that brought him to Palestine. These are Shifra's grandparents, who are staying with their daughter Rivka, Reb Feysh's wife. Invited in by them, Yitzhak chats and returns a second time, when he is served refreshment by their granddaughter. At once he is as smitten by her as "Adam was when God set Eve before him."

None of this would have happened had Reb Feysh been at home, since while he might have tolerated Yitzhak's presence there once, he surely would not have welcomed it a second time. Soon afterwards, however, Feysh is felled by a sudden stroke that leaves him speechless and semi-comatose, thus enabling Yitzhak to continue his visits by offering his assistance to the now providerless women. The neighbors gossip. Rivka, though less extreme in her views than her husband and grateful to Yitzhak for his help, is uncomfortable with it. So is Shifra. Still in her teens, she cannot conceive, even while feeling attracted to Yitzhak, of anything developing between them. When once they meet by chance out-of-doors and Yitzhak, seeing they are alone, seeks to hold her hand as no young man from Me'ah She'arim would dare do, she runs away in a fright. Yet not only is he determined to marry her, he decides to pave the way for it by returning to Jaffa and asking Sonya to release him from whatever obligations he might have incurred to her. Amused that he should think he has any (their brief romance has meant less to her than to him), she assures him that he is free – and it is at this point that we encounter him at Malkov's.

In all this there is an irony that no one but the reader is aware of, namely, that Yitzhak himself has been the cause of Reb Feysh's condition. This is because, approached by a stray dog while standing in the street at the end of a day's work, he playfully painted the Hebrew words *kelev meshuga*, "Mad Dog," on the animal's side. Spreading through the city, news of a rabid dog on the loose creates panic. It is talked about everywhere; the newspapers are full of it; new sightings keep being reported. One is by the headmaster of a French-speaking school, who, ignorantly reading the vowelless Hebrew consonants of *kelev* from left to right instead of the other way, takes the dog's name to be Balak. This is the name of the Moabite king in the Bible who hires the sorcerer Balaam to put a curse on Israel, and it is Balak, as henceforth the dog is known, suddenly appearing in front of Reb Feysh in Me'ah She'arim, who gives him such a fright that he bursts a blood vessel in his brain.

3

Yitzhak is nineteen or twenty when, his family's eldest child, he leaves its Galician shtetl for Palestine, about which he is as naive as he is idealistic. Since childhood he has avidly read Hebrew and Zionist literature and accounts of First Aliyah farming colonies, which have imbued him with a romantic view of the Land of Israel. "Only Yesterday"'s opening paragraph is a medley of the clichés, going all the way back to Mapu's "The Love of Zion," that they have cluttered his mind with:

> Like our other comrades of the Second Aliyah, Yitzhak Kummer left his native town and country for the liberation of his people, setting out for the Land of Israel to rebuild it from its ruins and be rebuilt by it. As far back as he could remember, there wasn't a day he hadn't thought of it. He had pictured it as a blissful place whose inhabitants were graced by God. Its villages nestled amid vineyards and olive groves; its fields were laden with grain; its fruit-festooned valleys teemed with flowers and were ringed by forests that rose to a cloudless blue sky; joy reigned in every home. By day, all plowed and sowed and planted and reaped, harvesting their grapes and olives, threshing their wheat, and treading out their wine in their presses; when evening came, they sat beneath their vines and fig trees, each man surrounded by his wife, sons, and daughters. Gladdened by their labors and grateful to be where they were, they thought of their days outside the Land as one thinks of sorrowful times in happy ones and felt doubly blessed. Yitzhak was an imaginative type and his imagination was guided by his heart.

Although Yitzhak is disabused of his illusions only gradually, the process begins, as it did for Brenner's Oved Etsot, immediately with his arrival in Palestine. Rowed ashore from his ship in Jaffa port by bawling Arab longshoremen who overcharge him, he next has his luggage snatched by a Jew who commands him to follow.

> The man led him through marketplaces, side streets, alleyways, and back yards…. The sun blazed down from above and the sand steamed up from below. Yitzhak's skin was on fire; every fiber of

him was aflame. Although he was a barrel of sweat, his lips were dry, his throat was parched, and his tongue felt like toast …. His escort brought him to a yard and dark house crammed with gun-nysacks, baskets, boxes, crates, bundles, and ropes and said, "I'll have a table set and call you when your meal is ready." Yitzhak reached into his jacket pocket for the letters of recommenda-tion he had brought to let his host know he was a worthy guest.

It is a comic moment. Inappropriately dressed in a jacket and tie and stunned by the savage Middle-Eastern heat that no one has warned him about, Yitzhak, who has traveled with letters of recommendation from Zionist politicians in Galicia in the absurd belief that they will make an impression in Palestine, thinks he is being invited to a fellow Jew's home in a brotherly gesture of welcome. In fact,

> While his host had not misjudged Yitzhak's worth, Yitzhak had misjudged his host. The man was an innkeeper and cared only for exacting what he could for food and lodging. … Yitzhak bore it cheerfully. "Tomorrow," he thought, "I'll have a job working in the fields and won't need any of my money." What difference did it make how much he was made to pay now?

This, too, is an illusion that quickly bursts. The next day Yitzhak sets out for Petach Tikva and goes from door to door looking for work. None is to be had. The farmers hire mostly Arabs, and if there are any jobs for Jews, they have been snapped up long ago. Yet now, too, he puts the best possible face on things. Told by a farmer's wife to try the next-door neighbor and discovering that the latter's house has been abandoned, he fails to see that he has been cynically treated. Rather, he wonders, "How strange: a house whose neighbors don't even know that no one lives in it!"

His trusting nature, however, also works to his benefit. He is drowsing on a park bench one day in the German Templar neighborhood of Sarona, his money all but gone, when a Templar, mistaking him for a worker who has fallen asleep while taking a break, hands him a paint can and a brush and orders him to get to work on a nearby fence. Instead of replying "Go paint it yourself," Yitzhak obeys without questions, is paid for his labors at the day's end, and is told to return the next day. This is the start of a profession that gives him security and status in a world of semi- or unemployed young immigrants. Although at first a mere "smearer," as he is called by a fellow painter, he eventually masters his new trade and becomes skilled at it.

It is the combination of innocence and a steady job that piques Sonya's interest in him. Sexually experienced as he is not, she finds him a challenge – a virginal young man who must be made a creative conquest of but who is also well-mannered and well-dressed, can afford to take her out for coffee and ice cream, and can be counted on not to disappear on the next ship to leave Jaffa, as her previous boyfriend Yedidya Rabinovitz has just done. Yitzhak is Rabinovitz's friend, too, and it is in Jaffa's port, to which the two have come to see him off, that he and Sonya have their first conversation. The description of their meeting is a fine example of what the Israeli critic Nitza Ben-Dov has called Agnon's "art of indirection," his masterly ability to convey subtleties of character and situation in passing and without comment, leaving the reader to notice them or not. Yitzhak and Sonya have just returned to shore after parting from Rabinovitz aboard ship.

A chill cloaked the autumnal silence of a diminished world. The smell of the sea mingled with the smell of rotting oranges. Yitzhak and Sonya walked wordlessly until they left the sandy shore for a city street. Sonya plucked a sprig of jasmine from a bush and sniffed its flowers, tossing some over her shoulder. "I think I'll have my shoes shined," she said. Hiking her dress, she placed her foot on the box of an Arab shoeshine boy. He straightened her leg, buffed her shoe, spat on his brush, dipped it in polish, and set to work until the shoe gleamed like a mirror. Yitzhak thought of how she had stood on the tips of Rabinovitz's shoes to kiss him on the forehead. He rubbed his forehead and stared at his hand. Placing her other foot on the box, Sonya admonished the Arab to do a good job, as if valuing the second shoe more than the first. And then what had happened? Yitzhak tried to remember. Then Rabinovitz had dusted his shoes with a silk handkerchief. "Finis," Sonya said. She paid the Arab and turned to go. Yitzhak walked beside her, sometimes closer and sometimes further off.

In silence, they reached the boulevard. It was lined by consulates, offices, and shops, in one of which Rabinovitz had worked. Since it was closed for the Sabbath, it didn't know yet that he had left it to go abroad. Above it was a balcony over which hung the white, blue-lettered sign of the municipal information and employment bureau. Yitzhak had been there many times with friends as down-and-out as himself. A melancholy muteness brushed his lips.

Sonya glanced at the shut store's sign and said, "Rabinovitz won't be back anytime soon. He's like Yarkoni. They come like a house on fire and leave like thieves in the night. Now Gurishkin will think he's the center of the world. Do you know Ya'el Hayyut? Gurishkin is running after her friend Pnina. You don't? That's no great loss. Have you seen Gurishkin's mustache lately? It droops over his mouth like two bananas." She brought the jasmine to her nose and sniffed it.

Yitzhak walked unobtrusively by her side. He couldn't think of a single clever thing to say. All he could answer to her questions was "Yes" or "No." Not that he cared about her. Or if he cared, it was only because she was his friend's girlfriend. Being unused to female company, he stepped as carefully as if she were a countess or a duchess. This amused her more than it annoyed her. Or perhaps it annoyed her more than it amused her. She glanced at him and asked, "Is this how you behave with a woman in Galicia?"

Yitzhak blushed and looked down at the ground. "The only women I've ever talked with," he said, "are my mother and my sisters."

Sonya had encountered Yitzhak before and wondered what Rabinovitz saw in such a provincial. She threw him another look and shut her eyes. Then she straightened the tips of her collar and laid a hand on her heart. When they reached Nevei Shalom, she pointed to a side street with the jasmine sprig and said, "That's where I live." For a moment, she seemed about to say more.

She thought better of it, shook Yitzhak's hand, and turned into the street. Yitzhak headed home.

In a careful study of "Only Yesterday," Amos Oz points to some of the seemingly minor details in this passage that reveal more than they may appear to at first glance. The dust Rabinovitz wipes from his shoes, for instance, tells us all we need to know about the shallowness of his feelings for Sonya. What man who genuinely cares for a woman would rush to wipe away, even from his feet, her last traces? And is not Sonya, in deciding on a whim to polish her own shoes, making a parallel statement? (Perhaps, having noticed what Rabinovitz has done, she is paying him back tit for tat. Her needless bossiness toward the shoeshine boy, at any rate, shows her need to be in command.) And while she may or may not be fully conscious of the symbolism of her act, she is surely aware of the opportunity it affords to show off her legs to Yitzhak. Her disdainful conviction, expressed as though to a confidant, that Rabinovitz will not return, and her disparagement of Gurishkin, are signals, too, that she is already available for a new partner and considers Yitzhak an eligible candidate.

Does Yitzhak understand her signals? If he does, it is only subliminally. His hand travels to his forehead to ascertain what a woman's kiss there might feel like and is then stared at as if the kiss might have rubbed off on it; yet in first denying to himself that he is drawn to Sonya and then telling himself that he only is because of their shared friendship with Rabinovitz, he is struggling to suppress the sexual feelings she arouses. She, for her part, scarcely able to believe his naïveté, is uncertain how to proceed. Should she reassure him that she is a proper young lady who needn't be feared? She primly straightens the tips of her collar. Should she let him know she is an emotional being who will respond to any overtures he makes? She lays a hand on her heart. And what can it be that she refrains from saying at the last moment? Is it "Drop by some time" and does she change her mind because she realizes this might scare Yitzhak off?

Like Rabinovitz, Sonya's friends, some of whom we have met at Yakov Malkov's, are Yitzhak's as well. While most come from Russia and think of Galicia as a backwater, their stories are similar to his. They, too, came to Palestine dreaming of being pioneers, of "plowing and planting and sowing and reaping," and they, too, whether because the opportunity has not presented itself, or because they lacked the courage to face the hardship that seizing it would have entailed, have failed to live up to their dream. Construction work in Jaffa, although physical labor, leaves them feeling that they have not given themselves fully to the land as they have been told they must do by such idolized figures as Brenner and A. D. Gordon (who also makes a cameo appearance in the novel). And Yitzhak feels this even more keenly, since as a housepainter, it seems to him that he is simply coloring what others have made.

Yet life in Jewish Jaffa, when there is work, is not unpleasant. There is the sea. There are miles of empty beach. There is a small-town atmosphere in which everyone knows everyone, an informal, easy-going code of manners, and the carefree camaraderie of young people unburdened by adult responsibilities. Yitzhak and Sonya's friends rarely talk seriously; they prefer to banter and joke, for though having taken their place in Zionism's vanguard by coming to Palestine, they are uneasy with the role, as if its weight were too much for them. Many have left for greener pastures like Rabinovitz, who plans to make money abroad, and many who have remained have doubts whether they should have. They belong to a small minority of Jews in an Arab country and Zionism's progress is too slow for them to have confidence in its success or to derive from it the sense of purpose that might replace the religious faith they have lost. In respect of religion, Yitzhak is no different.

> He behaved like the rest of us. He didn't go to synagogue or put on tefillin or observe the Sabbath or the holidays. At first he tried making a distinction between not doing what he should do, such as praying regularly, and doing what he shouldn't, such as eating non-kosher food, but he didn't persist in this. In the end, he did what was forbidden without qualms.
>
> None of this involved thinking very hard about such things. It was a matter of being surrounded by people who had come to believe that religion was of no importance, and that having no need for it, they had none for its commandments.

On the contrary: because they sought to live honestly, it would have been hypocritical to perform rituals they were far removed from. If Yitzhak thought about it at all, he was vaguely guided by the notion that the Jews of Palestine were divided into an Old Yishuv and a New Yishuv, each with its customs. Since he belonged to the new one, why keep those of the old one? Even when he changed his opinion of other things, he didn't change it of this.

And yet if his opinions didn't change, he still missed the home, the Sabbaths, and the holidays that he no longer had. Although he never entered a synagogue at such times, he often sat silently communing or humming a Hasidic tune until he forgot his workaday woes. He was not the only one. Jaffa was full of ex-yeshiva students. Sometimes, when getting together, they waxed nostalgic over Hasidic tales and melodies or imitations of rabbinic sermons. The generation before theirs had sung songs of Zion. Their generation had had enough of these. When their souls overflowed with longing, they looked for what was lost where they had lost it.

If Yitzhak, a descendant of the renowned pietist Yudl Hasid, the fictional protagonist of Agnon's novel "The Bridal Canopy" who settles in the Land of Israel in old age, is unlike his friends in such matters, it is because he occasionally muses about returning to Jewish practice. Even when experimenting with this idea, however, "he threw himself the sop of doing only what demanded the least effort, such as saying his bedtime prayers – and then, too, he said them less as a matter of duty than as a nostrum to help him fall asleep."

There is an emptiness in the lives of the young Second Aliyah immigrants in Jaffa that they try to ignore. As long as Yitzhak is involved with Sonya, he, too, is hardly aware of it. Having never had such a relationship before, he has no way of knowing that the excitement he mistakes for love is simply sexual pride and a newfound sense of manliness. Fooled into thinking that Sonya is in love too, he contemplates marriage, only to be rudely awakened when, her conquest of him accomplished, she loses interest in him and lets him know that their affair is over. Once again he is painfully slow to read her behavior, taking as long to understand her desire to be done with him as he did her desire to take up with him. This only forces her to be more cruel:

> Once he ran into Sonya and insisted on accompanying her on her way. The talk came around to Jerusalem.
>
> "I've never been there," Yitzhak said.
>
> "Anyone with blood instead of paint in his veins," Sonya said, "goes to see it."
>
> She added:
>
> "I've seen everything in Jerusalem there is to see. What didn't I see there! I saw Bezalel and Professor Schatz, and Ben-Yehuda's workroom, and the desk he wrote his big dictionary on…. All that time, I never slept a wink. Every day I went to see the sights and every night I walked the Old City's walls with the art students and danced with them in the moonlight."
>
> A pale flush spread over her face as on the night she gave Yitzhak his first kiss. His heart trembled like the golden gossamers playing on her lips and he reached out to stroke her hair. She turned her head away and said, "Let's go." When they reached her street, she shook his hand and said goodbye. Before he could say it back, she was gone.

Dancing in the moonlight, Sonya makes clear to Yitzhak, is not for dullards like him. In the end, half comprehending that he is no longer wanted and half still hoping to please her, he takes her advice and leaves Jaffa for Jerusalem.

4

Jaffa and Jerusalem, pre-World War I Palestine's two major cities, are opposite poles between which "Only Yesterday" moves back and forth. Apart from a brief account of Yitzhak's travels to Palestine with which the novel begins, its four parts are divided equally between them, with Parts I and III (in which the scene in Malkov's boarding house takes place) set in Jaffa and Parts II and IV in Jerusalem. Jaffa is coastal, flat, sandy, and humid; Jerusalem, land-bound, mountainous, rocky, and dry. Jerusalem is central to Jewish history and sacred in Jewish tradition; Jaffa, never a hub of Jewish life, is marginal to both. In the one city live Jews, some with roots in it going back generations, who are predominantly religious, anti-Zionist, and Yiddish-speaking; in the other, secular Zionist newcomers who do their best to speak Hebrew.

There were exceptions, of course. There were traditionally observant Jews in Jaffa such as the religious Zionist Yakov Malkov (a historical figure like Brenner and Gordon) and Rabbi Avraham Yitzhak Hacohen Kook, mentioned in passing in "Only Yesterday," whose embrace of secular Zionism as a force unwittingly furthering the divine purpose in history greatly influenced religious Zionist thought. And there were militant secularists in Jerusalem such as the students and teachers (one of them Bialik's friend Ira Jan) at the Bezalel School of Arts, or the circle around Eliezer Ben-Yehuda, who edited the daily *Ha-Tsvi* and the weekly *Hashkafa,* both rivals of the pro-Orthodox *Havatselet.* But though geographically the two cities were only several hours apart by train, the journey between them was one between two worlds.

"Only Yesterday"'s description of Yitzhak's arrival in Jerusalem has a lyricism, not often found in Agnon's prose, that makes it very different from his arrival in Jaffa. At the train station, he finds a wagoner to take him to a hotel.

> A breeze stirred, brushing the rocks and sifting the dusty earth. The air had changed. Its brittle silence could have been the quiet weeping of the mountains. Yitzhak was overcome by a hushed sadness, as if tidings were on the way that might be either good or bad. Good being the stronger force, he hoped for it while faint-heartedly fearing the worst. The old wagoner steered his horses at an easy pace while humming the melody of a prayer under his breath.
>
> Yitzhak peered ahead. His heart began to pound like a man's nearing a long-awaited destination. Soothed by the strains of the wagoner's prayer, he felt his fears melt away. Before him, laced with gold and veined with red fire, were the walls of Jerusalem, washed by a drift of gray and blue cloud that etched in them tones of fine silver, of burnished bronze, of lustrous pewter, of rare electrum.

Yitzhak leaned forward, wanting to say something. His tongue mutely sang a soundless song. He sat back again, dancing in his seat.

Yitzhak feels he has come home as he never did in Jaffa. He quickly finds living quarters and a job, and since most of his neighbors and fellow workers are observant Jews, he gradually reverts to the Orthodoxy that he has merely fantasized returning to until now. Now, too, his behavior is more a matter of social conformism than of considered conviction, but the way of life it conforms to is that of the shtetl he grew up in. Often, he goes to the Wailing Wall on Friday nights to participate in Sabbath eve prayers, which he once knew by heart and has partially forgotten.

Yitzhak would stand praying, in part from memory and in part from his prayer book. Sometimes he felt more drawn to the simple, heartfelt chanting of the Misnagdim and sometimes to the tuneful crooning of the Hasidim; sometimes to melodies ecstatic with the awe of God and sometimes to ones that caught fire from their own rapture. And amid them all, his heart sang its own song, his native town singing in it. Transported, he felt purged of all guilt, once again a blameless child, as unstained by sin as he had been, a boy among boys, in those faraway days.

The guilt he would like to be purged of is multiple. It is for having abandoned his family in Galicia; for having failed to live like a *halutz* in the Land of Israel; for having betrayed his friend Rabinovitz with Sonya and compromised, so he thinks, her good name; for having forsaken religion. His Zionism is no longer what it was. One day as he is at work with two other housepainters who know nothing about his past, he starts to sing.

Yitzhak's companions turned to look at him wonderingly. They had never heard anyone sing while at work.
"Are you a cantor's assistant?" one asked.
"No," Yitzhak said. "Why?"
"On account of your singing."
"I just like to sing," Yitzhak said.

"Are you a Zionist?"

"What makes you ask?"

"I've heard the Zionists sing a song called Hatikvah."

"What else have you heard about them, my friend?"

"I've heard that they want to hasten the Redemption by committing all kinds of sins."

"Why would they want to sin?"

"Because it's written that the Messiah will come in a generation that's all righteous or all sinful. Since it's easier to be sinful, that's what they've chosen to be."

Yitzhak did not respond. Gone were the days in which he had sought to make converts to Zionism. Nowadays, he was happy if no one sought to make an anti-Zionist of him. Yet whether for good or for bad – who was to say? – such things had their effect. If outwardly he was beginning to resemble a Jerusalemite, he was becoming more like one inwardly, too. When his fellow workers took a break for the afternoon prayer, he prayed with them; when they shared their meager lunch, he joined them in the grace after meals. If not for Bloykop the artist, his Jerusalemization would have been complete.

Bloykop is one of two people Yitzhak gets to know in Jerusalem who fits no conventional mold. A former Bezalel student and fellow Galician, he is, though not an observant Jew, an artist with a Jewish sensibility. "There's not a moment in Jerusalem," he tells Yitzhak,

that isn't eternal. Not everyone can see that, though. Jerusalem only reveals herself to her lovers. We should hug ourselves, Yitzhak, for having the good fortune to live here. At first, when I kept comparing Jerusalem to other cities, I saw all its faults. In the end, my eyes were opened and I saw *it*. I saw it, brother, I saw it! What can I tell you, my friend? Words can't describe a fraction of a fraction of it. Pray for me, brother, that God give me a long enough life to show you with my brush all that I see and feel. I don't know if I believe in God, but I know that He believes enough in me to give me a glimpse what most people never see. If I'm also given the time, I'll paint it.

Bloykop, who is dying of tuberculosis, is not given the time and his death, which leaves behind a grieving widow, is a blow to Yitzhak. Although painting houses and painting pictures may have little in common, Yitzhak has not previously thought of paint as a medium for anything but covering things. That it can serve to uncover them is a revelation. Dimly, he conceives of himself and Bloykop as standing on the same ladder, he on its lowest rung and Bloykop on one of the highest. While he is only to rise one rung more, which happens when Bloykop teaches him to be an expert sign painter, thereby increasing his earning power and professional standing, being taken into Bloykop's confidence and shown his art gives him, too, a glimpse of what "most people never see."

The second uncategorizable person in the novel is Arzef. Arzef is a taxidermist and an even more eccentric character than Bloykop. Born into Jerusalem's Old Yishuv, he left the yeshiva studies he excelled in to go his own way.

What had made him choose the odd profession of stuffing the skins of walking, flying, and crawling creatures? No one knew. Like Adam in the Garden of Eden, he lived by himself without a wife, children, worries, or complications, surrounded by mammals, birds, reptiles, spiders, and scorpions with whom he got along in perfect harmony. None had the slightest cause for complaint, not even when he took its life, since this only led to its acquisition by one of the great museums of Europe. Professors and scientists beat a path to his door with offers of money and honors. Arzef was no more impressed by the honors than he gave a fig for the money.... It was enough for him to regard his handiwork and know that no animal in the world was any the worse off for it. On the contrary: more than one Palestinian bird considered extinct had been rescued by him for posterity. All he cared about was the fauna of the Land of Israel mentioned in the Bible and in the Jerusalem and Babylonian Talmuds. He hunted it, discarded its flesh, and stuffed it to give it lasting existence. This was on the first six days of God's week. On the seventh he rested like everyone, unrolling a mat outside his front door and reading a book on it.

As opposed to the visionary Bloykop, Arzef does not seek to see through or past the surface of things. He is fascinated by the surface itself and his only desire is to capture Nature, quite literally, as no artist or sculptor can do and make it live forever. He kills to immortalize, and the immortality he grants evokes the Garden of Eden before Death entered the world. He is a restorer working in God's atelier, and like God he labors six days a week and takes the Sabbath off.

Each in his own way, Bloykop and Arzef are religious personalities with a firm compass in life that is not oriented to either Jewish observance or pioneering Zionism. They remind both Yitzhak and the reader that there are other possibilities of personal and Jewish fulfillment in Palestine than those offered by the New and Old Yishuv. Precisely because they are such autonomous beings, however, they are not models for imitation. Yitzhak can admire both but he cannot hope to become like either. They make him feel that for him the choice *is* between the new and the old, Jaffa and Jerusalem – and the longer he lives in Jerusalem, the farther from Jaffa he drifts even before meeting Shifra and painting "Mad Dog" on Balak.

5

Although Balak is only the second most famous animal in Hebrew literature, his name links him to the first. This is Balaam's donkey, which, struck by its master for balking beneath him on a narrow path, complains, "What have I done unto thee, that thou has smitten me these three times?" *What have I done?* is Balak's complaint, too, but he never, unlike the donkey, gets an answer.

From the moment Yitzhak plays his prank on him, Balak, until then just another stray dog living in Jerusalem's Jewish neighborhoods, undergoes a drastic change of life. He is not averse to being painted. It is a hot day and the cool, wet stroke of Yitzhak's brush on his fur is pleasant, so much so that he begs for more and is driven away with a kick. This causes him to take off on the run and soon reach the streets of Me'ah She'arim, where, to his astonishment, pandemonium breaks out. Whoever sees him, flees; screaming mothers grab their children and dash home; merchants, before bolting from their stores, pelt him with their weights, scales, and measures. Being a Jewish dog, he puts a Jewish construction on things.

> He knew enough to realize that a rabbinical court must have been sent to check the merchants' weights and scales. "Arf, arf," he barked, which meant: 'Are you foolish enough to think I can swallow all your false weights and keep the court from impounding them?' And in fact, had the weights weighed what they should have, they would have killed him; it was God's mercy that they didn't. 'Heavens above!' he cried. 'Jews have sinned and I'm to blame?' Before he could get out the words, every last man, woman, and child had sped home and locked their doors. Me'ah She'arim was emptied of all but a single dog.

Only when such scenes recur wherever he appears does it dawn on Balak that something about him must be the cause of them. His adventures, which occupy long parts of "Only Yesterday," tell of his increasingly frantic attempts to discover what this is. At first, he takes refuge in Jerusalem's Christian and Muslim quarters, where nobody can read the writing on him and he lives and eats well, playing with the local dogs and nipping and being nipped by them. But,

> he found no solace there for his soul. The food he crunched with his jaws could not replace the ground snatched from under his paws. The whole world wasn't worth the small corner of it from which he had been exiled. By now he had lived so long among the Gentiles, swayed by their heathenish ways and filled with their heathenish swill, that his addled brain no longer knew a shofar from a church bell. Yet even now he disdained the revenge of apostasy and still woke to howl at midnight, it being written in the tractate of Berakhot that dogs howl in the night's middle watch.

Longing for Jewish cooking and company, Balak returns to Me'ah She'arim and is again driven from pillar to post. A glimpse of his reflection in a store window causes him to connect the marks he sees on himself with the sign painter, and his suspicion that these are related to his adversity is heightened when the French headmaster bends over him to read them. But what do they signify?

Balak wagged his tail and said to himself, 'It's just as I thought. This whole kettle of fish is someone's fault. It's all because of that scoundrel of a painter who made a signboard of me. Do I deserve to be hounded just because some good-for-nothing scribbled on my fur?'

It is in the nature of Truth's seekers to seek it in its entirety. Balak was no exception. Having set his heart on the truth, nothing but the whole truth would do. "Arf, arf," he barked, crouched at the headmaster's feet. 'Are you going to tell me what it says? Tell me everything!'

Just then the school janitor [whose Hebrew is better than the headmaster's] came along, saw the dog and the writing, and took to his heels. 'He knows the truth! He knows the truth!' Balak thought. 'Only what am I to do now that he's run off with it?'

Indeed, Balak was still far from the truth. Nevertheless, his pursuit of it helped him to live with his predicament. As the divine poet has said,

Blessed art thou, O Science, which doth console
When the waves of misfortune o'er me roll.

Although Balak may not know that the author of these Hebrew lines is the eighteenth-century philosopher and kabbalist Moshe Haim Luzzatto, he is something of a poet himself. One night as he is lolling peacefully while Me'ah She'arim is asleep and unable to harm him, letting the angry frustration that has been building up in him drain away, a poem comes to him. He is composing its final stanza,

Upon the earth
Walks no one now.

All is silent.
Bow wow wow,

when Reb Feysh emerges from the darkness. What is Feysh doing out-of-doors in the dead of night? He is posting writs of excommunication on the walls of Me'ah She'arim that he is afraid to put up by day, lest the neighbors he is excommunicating for being less pious than himself tear them down before they can be read. Balak, who "took no interest in politics or religious disputes and didn't know the difference between one faction of Jews and another," thinks Feysh is out to enjoy the quiet night and greets him with a friendly bark. Alarmed, Feysh drops his lantern and glue pot while his posters are borne away by the wind.

> Reb Feysh's soul was borne away with them. 'What is it, Feysh?' soothed the mission he was on with a reassuring hug. 'Never fear!' His soul cajoled into returning, he ran after the posters. They, however, reasoning quite logically, 'If a mere agent of the law is trying so hard to retrieve us, surely we who are the law should be trying even harder to be retrieved,' swerved in midair and flew straight at him, their anathemas flapping in his face. As white as shrouds, they were uncritically presumed by him to be the ghosts of the ancestors of the excommunicated men.
>
> Feysh shrieked, turned, and ran the other way, chased by the posters, and tripped over the dog. It let out a yelp. Terrified, he went sprawling. No agent of the law should have to go through what he did.
>
> Balak saw Feysh lying on the ground and was nonplussed. What was he to make of it? One minute a man was running on two feet and the next he was sprawled on all fours. 'I'd better smell him,' Balak thought. 'Either he's not really a man or else he is one and needs a helping hand.' Reb Feysh came to just in time to find the dog sniffing him and took off for dear life. Balak remained where he was, thoroughly mortified. No helping hand should have to feel what he felt.

Reb Feysh staggers off and collapses again in the street. Found by the neighbors in the morning, he is carried home and put to bed, never to rise from it again.

6

In Princeton University Press's published version of "Only Yesterday," translated by Barbara Harshav, this same passage begins:

> And Reb Fayesh's [*sic*] soul also flew away. That Commandment began clinging to him and said to him, What's wrong with you, don't be afraid. And it tempted him until his soul returned. He started running and gathering up the posters. Those scraps of paper made their own inference. If Reb Fayesh, an emissary of the Commandment, is running, we who are the Commandment itself should run even faster. They immediately began rolling away and striking him in the face. And every single note cackles with those words Reb Fayesh wrote on it. In his innocence, Reb Fayesh thought that the forefathers of the excommunicated rose up from their graves and came to take vengeance on him, for the notes were white as shrouds of the dead.

There are, it would seem, different ways of translating Agnon. However, I quote from Harshav's "Only Yesterday" not so much to illustrate this point as to explain why Agnon's Hebrew confronts a translator with unique and in part insoluble problems.

What happens in this passage? Feysh, shocked by the appearance of a dog he believes to be rabid, drops what he is holding and his posters blow away. As he struggles to master his fear and collect them, the wind shifts and blows them at him, causing him to panic and run the other way. Stumbling over Balak, he falls, passes out, regains consciousness, sees Balak smelling him, leaps to his feet, and vanishes in the darkness, leaving the dog to feel once again that it has done something wrong without knowing what it is.

All this borders on slapstick, and Agnon makes the most of it by relating it from Feysh's and Balak's perspectives. Lacking all self-awareness, Feysh projects his fear, his struggle to master it, and his unconscious self-recrimination for excommunicating blameless Jews onto the soul that deserts him, the task he has set out to perform, and the personified posters that physically attack him after he first thinks they are trying to help. (Not that he doesn't know that posters can't reason talmudically, but in true primitive fashion, he thinks of himself as the cause of all that happens to him.) Balak's mental processes are equally crude. Since human beings, in his experience, do not lie down in streets, seeing Feysh sprawled in one makes him wonder, in a parody of syllogistic thinking, whether Feysh is truly human.

Harshav's translation is more literal than mine. Her "commandment" is closer to Agnon's *mitzvah* than is my "mission" or "law," and her "clinging to him" to Agnon's *megafefto* than is my "soothed [him] with a reassuring hug." But literalism brings us no closer to Agnon's meaning if its literary associations are ignored. Whereas in modern colloquial Hebrew the verb *l'gafef*, rendered by Harshav as "to cling to," has the sense of pawing clumsily or intrusively, in the Hebrew of the rabbis that Agnon is evoking it means to embrace lovingly. Feysh's sense of duty is, so to speak, putting a comforting arm around him, not desperately clutching at him.

Actually, the association Agnon is playing on is more specific than this. In Shir ha-Shirim Rabba, an ancient collection of midrashim about the Song of Songs, we read:

> When God declared [on Mount Sinai], "I am the Lord thy God,"
> [Israel's] souls were immediately borne away [by fear]. Seeing that
> they [the Israelites] had died, the angels began to embrace and
> kiss them [*hithilu megafefin u'menashkin otam*] and said, "What
> is it? Never fear!"... And He [God] cajoled them [*haya mefateh
> otam*] until their souls returned.

Clearly, Agnon wrote his account of Feysh and Balak with this midrash in mind. Although he could not have expected most of his readers to be familiar with it, a learned Jew like Feysh certainly would have been, which is literary justification enough for its presence in the text. But rabbinic language pervades Agnon's prose even when his characters are not learned Jews. Take Yitzhak and Sonya's conversation about

Jerusalem. The following elocutions in its opening lines are characteristic of rabbinic as opposed to modern Hebrew:

Once he ran into Sonya. "Ran into [her]" is *metsa'a la,* a talmudic idiom not used in the Hebrew spoken in Jaffa in the early twentieth century.

The talk came around. The verb for "came around," *nitgalgel,* is in the passive Nitpa'el rather than the active Hitpa'el construction, another throwback to rabbinic diction.

"I've never been there," Yitzhak said. Literally, this reads, "Said Yitzhak, 'I've never been there.'" Whereas in modern Hebrew, as in English, identifying phrases like "he said" appear at the end or in the middle of a quotation, quotations in rabbinic literature always begin with speaker identification, the verb "said" coming first.

"Anyone with blood instead of paint in his veins," Sonya said, "goes to see it." This sentence, too, begins with "Said Sonya," and her word for "paint" is not the modern Hebrew *tseva* but the mishnaic *mei tsva'im,* literally, "colored water." Although one might argue that this is Sonya's way of sharpening her insult, the expression is not one she would have known or thought of inventing.

There is hardly a paragraph in Agnon's work that does not contain such usages. They are an integral part of his manner, and an untranslatable one, since English, having never passed through a rabbinic period, has no equivalents of rabbinic language. To hope to create them by parallel archaisms like "Upon a time he chauncéd upon Sonya," or "Quoth Yitzhak, 'Never have I been there,'" would be patently absurd. Chaucer and Sir Thomas Mallory do not evoke the rabbis. Nothing in English does. It is possible to translate Agnon well by transmitting other elements of his style – its careful symmetries, its back-and-forth, talmudic rhythms, its tongue-in-cheek slyness – but any attempt to imitate it more closely is doomed to fail.

One must distinguish between the pre-modern element in Agnon's Hebrew and the Hebrew of nineteenth-century novelists like Mapu, Smolenskin, Berdichevsky, and Mendele, who were struggling, each in his way, to forge a language suitable for fictional purposes. Mapu, in adopting biblical diction for "The Love of Zion," was not being deliberately archaic. In the absence of a spoken tongue to serve as an arbiter of what was contemporary and what was not, he chose one of several stylistic options offered by literary Hebrew, none of whose different stages of historical development had effaced any of its predecessors. Indeed, he could hardly have written archaically had he wanted to, there being practically nothing in the Hebrew of his day, from the biblical period on, that was too superannuated to be used. Although Hebrew underwent a steady process of modernization in the course of the nineteenth century, from which the spoken Hebrew of the early twentieth evolved, the doors to its past remained open.

They were rapidly closing when Agnon started writing Hebrew fiction in Jaffa in 1908, There was now a spoken language in Palestine to whose speakers some things sounded natural and some did not, some belonged to the present and some to the past alone – and that Agnon's Hebrew was suffused with the past was recognizable to every reader at once. It had in it more of "the dust of the study house" than of "the dirt of a homeland," wrote Brenner, though he thought Agnon a writer of great promise. Its archaizing, which was to remain a permanent feature of Agnon's prose, was intentional.

This is not to say that Agnon wrote in the rabbinic Hebrew of any specific time or place, or that he eschewed all new developments in the language. When Sonya says, "I've seen everything in Jerusalem there is to see. What didn't I see there! I saw Bezalel and Professor Schatz, and Ben-Yehuda's workroom, and the desk he wrote his big dictionary on," she is speaking, though her phrasing might not have startled Rabbi Akiva, the Hebrew of her day. It is not until the conclusion of her remarks, when the moon by whose light she has danced is the mishnaic *levana* instead of the twentieth-century (and biblical) *yare'ah*, that she is made to speak archaically again. Her Hebrew is a dialect all its own, as is Agnon's in general – an integration of twentieth-century and rabbinic language, from the Mishnah's to the Hasidic homily's, so seamlessly modulated that its components seem never to clash. The Israeli intellectual historian Eli Schweid has said of it that it stands

> halfway between the revolution of modern Hebrew literature and the conservatism of the Hebrew literature that preceded it. Uniquely among modern Hebrew authors, Agnon reverted

to an eclectic rabbinic style because such Hebrew, with all its limitations, facilitated a total engagement with Jewish culture throughout the ages rather than with that of his own age alone. He did not recycle [rabbinic Hebrew]. He developed it in two directions, first by layering it with contemporary spoken Hebrew, and second, by finding an artistic way of harmonizing its various aesthetic dissonances.

This is well-put. Yet it ignores an important point – namely, that in setting his prose on an alternative course to that taken by twentieth-century Hebrew, Agnon was also protesting the latter's direction.

Hebrew's spoken revival and rapid rise to dominance in everyday life in Palestine was a historically unprecedented success without which Zionism could never have achieved its goal of recasting Jewish identity in a new, national mold. As a success, however, it was adulterated from the start. It was heavily influenced by Yiddish, the native tongue of most of its adoptive speakers. Its grammar departed in many ways from that of biblical, rabbinic, and nineteenth-century secular Hebrew alike. It was peppered with loan words and calque idioms from Yiddish, Russian, German, Ladino, Arabic, English, and Turkish. Its vocabulary and expressive capacities, though they grew steadily, remained limited compared to those of European languages, in part because the establishment of spoken standards consigned to instant obsolescence whole strata of Hebrew's past that had previously been accessible. At the same time that it was rapidly expanding to meet the demands of modern life, therefore, Hebrew also shrank drastically, shedding overnight layers of usage and idiom that normal languages took centuries to outgrow.

This contraction was not compensated for by the kind of rich folk-language, inherited from parents and ancestors, that is spoken by native populations everywhere. Ordinary Jews had spoken this way, too, in Yiddish, Ladino, and Judeo-Arabic. But the Hebrew they learned to speak in Palestine was an immigrant tongue, acquired from fellow immigrants who had had no native population to learn it from. At its crudest, it resembled a Palestinian version of the Hebrew of Josef Perl's Hasidim. At its most educated, it had a bloodless cultivation. Although the contemporary authors its speakers read – Brenner, for example – knew their Jewish sources and made use of them, they could no longer do so as freely. Much of the language of these sources was now strange or comical to Hebrew speakers, especially to young secular Zionists like Yitzhak Kummer's friends in Jaffa. Much was hopelessly *passé*. What had never been archaic in Hebrew before now became so.

Agnon's Hebrew is a refusal to acquiesce in this. It poses and attempts to answer the question: what might modern Hebrew have been like had it not undergone so sudden and brutal a rupture with the past? How could it have kept in touch with its rabbinic heritage and exploited it better? How much of what has ostensibly been lost to it can be restored by a skillful author steeped in tradition?

There can be no such refusal, however, that is not by implication also a critique of the secular Zionism that, born to the nineteenth century's aristocratic Lady of Hebrew, fathered her déclassé twentieth-century offspring, the demotic speech of the Palestinian and Israeli street. And nowhere is this critique more in evidence in Agnon's work than in "Only Yesterday."

7

Balak does not remain in Me'ah She'arim for long. He is impelled to keep wandering by his search for the truth no less than by the way he is treated, and his fame spreads beyond Jerusalem. Scholars come from afar to investigate his case. An anthropologist publishes an article about an ancient custom among Jerusalem's Jews of casting out a dog to expiate their sins – a possible result, he speculates, of Islamic influence, dogs being regarded by Muslims as unclean. This leads to international protests by animal lovers and even to anti-Semitic broadsides against Jewish cruelty.

Throughout the second half of "Only Yesterday," in which Balak plays a lead role, Agnon has great fun with him. He has him break into the rhymed prose of Hebrew medieval narrative. ("The dog set out with a strut in its gait, preening itself as though of high estate, and with each step that it stepped and each leap that it leapt a recital of its future reward and the wicked's requital ran through its brain with this refrain: *Out, damned fleas and curséd mites! Afflicted be all parasites for their itches and their bites!*") He uses Balak's wanderings to satirize different elements of Jerusalem's Jewish and non-Jewish population. He comments by means of Balak on human credulity, on the genesis of folk beliefs, on the Hebrew spoken in Palestine. (Since a mad dog in rabbinic language is *kelev shoteh*, not *kelev meshuga*, Balak, we are told, cannot be mad in any traditional sense.) He parodies anthropomorphic religious thought with a cosmogonic myth of Balak's own making, according to which the earth and sky were created by a primeval dog and eagle born from the stomach of a camel. When the sky, frightened by the eagle's screeches, weeps endless tears, filling the seas and flooding the land, the great ancestor dog, perched on the eagle's wings, bites it in retribution, and the rents he makes in it become the moon and stars.

Biting is increasingly on Balak's mind. As his plight worsens, so does his physical condition. He doesn't feel well. His head hurts. He is thirsty all the time, and drinkable water is hard to find because the country is suffering from a drought. He drags his tail between his legs and drools. His timidity gives way to pent-up aggression.

'Ay!' cried Balak in his torment. 'Why am I persecuted everywhere? Why is everyone out to kill me? Whom have I harmed? Have I bitten anyone? Why can't I have some peace?' "Arf, arf," he barked, appealing to the heavens. 'Are you going to give me a place to rest? Are you going to give me justice?'

The more he barked, the more he was assailed with sticks and stones. Balak bit the sticks and the stones and went on barking. 'Why bite us?' they asked. 'Do we have any choice? Bad people grab us and do what they want with us. If you're looking for revenge, go bite them.'

'What am I, a mad dog, that I should go bite people?' Balak asked.

'Then go complain to them,' said the sticks and stones.

'Do you think they care about my complaints?' Balak asked. 'They themselves say, "Might makes right."'

'In that case,' the sticks and stones said, 'you had better show them your might.'

Balak is also closing in on the culprit responsible for his suffering. As he roams the city one night, his senses tell him to start digging and he finds one of Yitzhak's discarded paint brushes.

> He sniffed its bristles and his hide tingled as it had on that day when the painter dripped something wet on it. This time, though, it didn't tingle with pleasure. It tingled with fear. His eyes filled with blood and he let out a sound. It wasn't a yelp or a yowl or a moan, but something new. It was the sound of vengeance.

Meanwhile, Yitzhak returns to Jerusalem. Having achieved the closure he sought with Sonya, he now feels free to ask for Shifra's hand. The scene in which he does so, quite literally and without an explicit word, is a marvel of delicacy. Arriving in Jerusalem as evening is falling, he finds a hotel in which he leaves his belongings and hurries to Reb Feysh's. The small apartment is lit by a lantern.

> Shifra was standing by a basin of water, washing her father's undershirt. She tugged at her sleeves and raised her eyes to Yitzhak. They were not the golden, dreaming eyes he remembered. Or if they were, their gold was tarnished and their dream had no interpreter. But though not the same Shifra, she was even more beautiful.
>
> Rivka sat knitting in a corner. At Yitzhak's appearance, she threw him a wondering glance. "I'm coming from Jaffa," he said, looking at Shifra.
>
> Rivka nodded. "I heard you were there," she said.
>
> "I've just arrived," Yitzhak said, "and here I am. How is Reb Feysh?"
>
> Rivka shone the lantern on her husband and sighed.
>
> Reb Feysh lay in bed. The fleshy sacks beneath his sunken eyes twitched. Rivka looked at her husband and said, "All our enemies should be as well as he is."
>
> "So nothing has changed," Yitzhak said.
>
> "Thank God for that," Rivka said. "Any change could only have been for the worse."

Reb Feysh stirred and seemed to stare at Yitzhak. Rivka moved the lantern away. "Why don't you sit down?" she asked. "Sit, Yitzhak. So you're back in Jerusalem. Let me get you some tea."

"That's kind of you," Yitzhak said. "Jaffa is growing by leaps and bounds. A new neighborhood is going up with sixty houses. There's work for everyone – me, too."

"Will you be going back there?" Rivka asked.

"If you'd like me to," Yitzhak said, "I will."

Shifra blushed and stared at the floor. He rested pleading eyes on her and blushed too.

A dog barked outside. "Go be with your father," Rivka told Shifra. "Whenever Feysh hears a dog bark," she said to Yitzhak, "he's frightened."

***

The door opened. A neighbor entered, saw Yitzhak, and turned to leave. Holding a lump of sugar, Yitzhak said, "Good woman, there's no need to run from me."

He took a last sip of tea, set the sugar on the table, stroked his beard, said "It's time I was off," and got to his feet. "Good night," he said to Rivka with a nod. He went to Shifra, took her hand, and said good night to her too. Rivka looked on in wonder. "Is this the young man?" the neighbor asked. Yitzhak smiled at her. "It is, it is," he said, giving Shifra's hand a squeeze.

Shifra withdrew her hand. "Good night," she said. Yitzhak stroked his beard and departed. Rivka took the lantern and went to the doorway to light his way. Shifra stood and listened to his footsteps. When he was gone, Rivka returned and hung the lantern on its peg.

With which of the many understated details in this passage does one begin? With Shifra's obeying the code of modesty she has grown up with by instinctively lowering the sleeves she has raised to do the wash even before knowing who the unexpected visitor is? (If it is a woman, there is no need for her to do this.) With her leaving the conversation entirely to Rivka, guided by the same code and her trust in her mother? With her eyes that tell us, as they perhaps tell Yitzhak, that she has been suffering from his absence without acknowledging to herself that this has been the cause of her unhappiness? With Yitzhak's finding her "even more beautiful" because a woman one loves, no matter how wan, is always beautiful? With Rivka's first moving the lantern toward Feysh and then away from him because, while she wants Yitzhak to see him, she is worried that, even in his unconscious state, he might see Yitzhak? With Yitzhak's self-confidence, which he has never exhibited before and now has because he has matured and feels sure, for the first time since coming to Palestine, that he is doing the right thing? With Rivka's warmth toward him despite her fear of social disapproval? (She is under no obligation to be so friendly, much less to offer him the tea that she serves, East-European-style, with a lump of sugar to sip it through.) With his twice stroking his beard in a gesture typical of the observant Jew that he has become – a conscious or unconscious signal that, consciously or unconsciously, must register on Rivka and Shifra? (We have seen Yakov Malkov make this same gesture in his boarding house.) With the narrator's leaving us to guess what Rivka hopes or fears to hear when she asks Yitzhak if he plans to return to Jaffa?

Yitzhak's answer to this question is in effect a proposal of marriage, and Shifra's blush conveys that she understands this well. He does not get a response because the bark of a dog (is it Balak?) mercifully spares Rivka the need to give him one. Yet he has every reason to feel encouraged. When he boldly takes Shifra's hand before her astonished mother and neighbor with every awareness of what he is doing (neither he nor she have forgotten his previous attempt), she does not pull it away at once – and when she does, she returns his "Good night," watches as her mother goes out of her way to light the dark street for him, and gets up from her seat to listen to him walk off.

"Only Yesterday" makes Yitzhak and Shifra clear a few more hurdles before they are wed, but the outcome is no longer in doubt. Abetting it are Rivka's discovery that Yitzhak is a descendant of Yudl Hasid (ancestry counts for much in Me'ah She'arim) and the unexpected support of her wise neighbor, who, having discerned the young couple's feelings for each other, urges Rivka to promote the match. Even then,

Me'ah She'arim is about to boycott the wedding when an eminent rabbi decides to officiate at it in tribute to an old friendship with Rivka's father. This changes everything and at the last minute "so many neighbors, men, women, and children came to celebrate with the bride and groom that there wasn't a place left to stand in."

8

Yitzhak and Shifra are blissful. One evening after finishing his work,

> Yitzhak was preparing to return home to his wife. His need to be with her was still like a bridegroom's. Shifra sat alone with her thoughts, marveling at how since the wedding they had been only of Yitzhak. She looked around as if to detect whether anyone had noticed the change in her. What she saw in the mirror on the wall made her marvel even more. Apart from the married woman's kerchief on her head, nothing about her looked different. And yet she felt like another person…. Standing beneath the wedding canopy with Yitzhak, she had been sure there would never again be such a moment in her life. Now, every moment was its equal. She went to the stove to check the dinner she had cooked and wondered why, though it was ready, Yitzhak was not home yet.

> Yitzhak has been delayed. On his way home he has encountered a crowd gathered on a corner to listen to a street preacher inveigh against the sins of the age, for which the drought is God's punishment. Suddenly, Balak appears. The crowd scatters in all directions. Yitzhak, who has been in Jaffa and not known of the mad dog hysteria in Jerusalem, calmly stands his ground and explains when told to flee that there is nothing to be afraid of because – so he shamefacedly confesses – it was he who painted *kelev meshuga* on Balak's side. Incredulity is followed by a wave of relief.

> No one feared the dog any more. And since no one did, no one understood why anyone had. In their newfound courage, all mocked the cowards who had run from it. The cowards, in turn,

resolutely blamed the newspapers, which had stirred up panic. That was the press for you. It had nothing better to write about and so it wrote about that. One day it scared you with dogs and the next with mosquitoes.

The dog no longer frightened anyone, least of all Yitzhak, who had forgotten it the moment he painted it. But the dog had not forgotten him. It understood only too well that it owed all its troubles to the sign painter. It had looked for him everywhere, barking when it saw him and barking when it only thought it did…. Make sense of it if you can: as long as Balak was in his right mind, he was feared to be mad; now that he wondered if he wasn't going mad, all fear of him was gone.

Balak has indeed gone mad. He has contracted rabies while playing with the dogs in Jerusalem's Arab neighborhoods. Face-to-face with Yitzhak as the crowd begins to disperse,

he fixed weary eyes on the sign painter's feet and saw they hadn't moved. 'Whoever knows the truth,' he thought with a sigh, 'is afraid of nothing. But the truth is heavy and few can bear its weight – I could help him to bear it.'

Yitzhak stood there crestfallen, like a man awaiting sentence. He noticed the dog, snapped his fingers at it, and said, "Did you hear what they said about you? They said you were mad." He didn't mean to offend Balak. He just needed someone to talk to and was too ashamed to talk to anyone else. Balak, though, thought otherwise. He glanced up at Yitzhak in alarm, the whites of his eyes vanishing and their pupils turning black. His mouth foamed and his teeth shook in their sockets. Then he shook all over. He wanted to jump on Yitzhak. In the end, he looked back down and nuzzled the ground.

Yitzhak turns to go home.

Balak wagged his head and thought, 'He has somewhere to go – and I'm a homeless outcast, despised and downtrodden.' His tongue hung from his mouth as if about to fall out. He tried putting it back in place and couldn't. Something sweet trickled between his teeth. His other senses in abeyance, a craving bubbled up there like a spring. Every tooth stood on edge. His body stiffened. Before Yitzhak could walk off, the dog leaped on him and sank its teeth into him. Having bitten him, it took to its legs and ran off

Yitzhak returns home, falls ill, and dies after several weeks of frightful torment. "And we, dear friends," laments the narrator, "are left dumbfounded when we regard all that befell Yitzhak. Why was this man, who was no worse than any other, punished in such a fashion?"

But there is a silver lining in the clouds that form on the day of Yitzhak's funeral. Soon they begin to pour. The drought, as though ended by a human sacrifice to an angry God, is over. It rains and rains. When the rain finally stops,

Every bush and blade of grass gave off a good smell, most of all the orange trees. The entire country was a blessed garden of God's and blessed were all its inhabitants. And you, our stalwart brothers in Kinneret and Merhavia, in En-Ganim and Um-Guni, as Degania once was called, went to work in your fields and gardens, doing what our friend Yitzhak was not privileged to do. Our friend Yitzhak never got to plow, sow, and farm. And yet like his ancestor Reb Yudl and other pious Jews, he was granted a grave in the Holy Land. Let the mourners mourn this suffering soul who died badly. We prefer to tell of our brothers and sisters, the sons and daughters of God's people, who tilled the earth of Israel to their everlasting glory.

Yitzhak's adventures are done.
The annals of our other comrades will be told
in the book of "The Field That Was."

Such a book, needless to say, was never written.

9

Although not all have chosen to read it as such, "Only Yesterday"'s end-ing, with its sentimental description of a life of happy toil on "the earth of Israel," is pure parody. It matches the parody of the novel's beginning, the two framing the story between them like twin bookends. This may seem an odd thing for Agnon to have done with what is not, despite all its humor, a comedy. But Agnon was a writer who liked to toy with his readers and never shrank from the risk – indeed, enjoyed courting it – of being misunderstood by them. One might almost say that "Only Yesterday" was written to fool the bookstore browser who weighs the purchase of a book by its first and last paragraphs.

There is a difference between these paragraphs, however. "Only Yesterday"'s opening lines ridicule Yitzhak Kummer's rosy picture of conditions in Palestine at the time he sets out for it. Ultimately disap-pointed by a life in Jaffa that is not like the one he imagined, he moves to Jerusalem, returns to religion, and ends up in anti-Zionist Me'ah She'arim, where he perishes, as it were, by his own hands, having set in motion the events that lead to his death. One can analyze his character and motives from many angles, as Agnon's critics have done, but this remains the novel's bare synopsis.

"Only Yesterday"'s closing lines, on the other hand, come after Yitzhak's death and do not reflect his point of view. They express that of the nameless narrator, a shadowy representative of the Second Ali-yah who knows the novel's protagonist well and regularly refers to him as "our friend Yitzhak." What about him, or the "we" in whose name he speaks, is Agnon burlesquing?

It certainly isn't the Second Aliyah's *halutzim* themselves. Rather, it is the Labor Zionist ideology that romanticized and mythologized them, making of them a yardstick by which all other forms of Zionism were judged lacking. "Many a critic," writes Amos Oz, "has found ample grounds in 'Only Yesterday' for generalizations about the Second Ali-yah ... which seemingly broke with religion, family, and tradition only to break in the end [as did Yitzhak Kummer] with its own pioneering ideals" – "seemingly" because Oz's understanding of Yitzhak is of some-one who never really broke with his past at all. The values Yitzhak grew up with, Oz writes, remain *his* yardstick, so that "from the shtetl proceed all his fantasies of the shade-giving vines and fig trees of Palestine, and to the shtetl they return." He and his friends in Jaffa "will never be reborn or shake off the dust of exile. On the contrary: they will carry it with them wherever they go."

Unlike the pioneers of Kinneret and Degania, in other words, Yitzhak is unwilling or unable to remake himself radically and is thus sucked back into the world of religion in it most regressive form. He has tried to live by a "naive synthesis," as Oz puts it, of Jewish tradition with the revolutionary ideals of Labor Zionism, and when this synthesis breaks down as it must because of its internal contradictions, he reverts to where he has come from.

Such would indeed appear to be the narrator's judgment of Yitzhak at the conclusion of "Only Yesterday." Oz's seconding of it, however, is surprising given the astute reader that he is, because it is a judgment that we are meant to laugh at. The novel's closing clichés are as mawkish as its opening ones. Substitute the agricultural communes of the Second Aliyah for the First Aliyah farming colonies that Yitzhak Kummer read about as a boy and the two passages are highly similar.

Oz accepts at face value the narrator's insistence in "Only Yesterday" that Yitzhak's fateful mistake was not having become the pioneer that he dreamed of being. In this, he is faithful to the Labor Zionist narrative, never more widely accepted than it was in the 1940s when "Only Yesterday" was written, of the *halutz* as an unequaled paradigm of Zionist self-fulfillment in whom the trapped religious energies of Judaism were freed and rechanneled into Zionist fervor and construction.

But while this is the narrator's opinion in "Only Yesterday," it is not, the novel's ending makes clear, Agnon's. The entire issue of Yitzhak's failure to become a *halutz* turns out in fact to have been a false clue that Agnon has the narrator repeatedly drag through the novel in order to throw us off the trail. By any reasonable standard, after all, being a housepainter in Jaffa rather than a tiller of the soil in Degania is hardly a betrayal of Zionism. The Yishuv needed housepainters, too, and could no more have succeeded without Jewish workers in Palestine's cities than without Jewish farmers in its countryside; in reality, a very small percentage of Zionist immigrants to Palestine in the years in which "Only Yesterday" takes place ended up living in agricultural settlements. Yitzhak's feelings of guilt at not being one of them are real, but they tell us only about his failed expectations of himself, not about his failure from the perspective of Jewish history. In denying him his Zionist credentials and classing him with his ancestor Yudl Hasid, who came to Palestine in order to die and be buried there, the narrator simple-mindedly echoes Brenner's declaration of "Except for the farmers, my friends, except for the farmers, it's all humbug, humbug, humbug!"

And *that*, as affectionately as Brenner is portrayed in Agnon's novel, is, so we are being told, where the real humbug lies. If Yitzhak makes a mistake it is, like the narrator, to buy into this belief, which is mocked by "Only Yesterday"'s final page just as he himself is mocked by its initial one. Challenging us at the last moment to see through a narrator we have trusted until then is the sort of game Agnon delighted in playing. There are other examples of this in his work, such as the conclusion of his 1951 novel "To This Day," set during World War I in Berlin. Its story, too, is told by a sophisticated observer who, keenly aware of the foibles of others, ends his account with an unwitting exposure of his own lack of awareness that forces the perceptive reader to rethink everything he has read.

The statement made by the ending of "Only Yesterday" is in fact the opposite of the one Oz attributes to it. Yitzhak's regression to Me'ah She'arim does not come from his inability to "shake off the dust of exile." On the contrary: it comes from shaking off too much of it by throwing religion and its values overboard in a Jaffa in which his friends do not even say kaddish for their fathers. This undermines his Jewish and human equilibrium, and in his attempt to regain it, he lurches too far in the other direction.

Although Yitzhak's story is unique, he himself is portrayed in the novel as anything but that. "He made," the narrator tells us,

> no special impression on anyone. There were many young men like Yitzhak, none of whom drew the slightest attention. There was nothing unusual about his appearance or conversation. Talking with him left you with no great desire to do it again, and it was possible to encounter him in public and not recognize him. Unless you happened to be fond of him, you didn't notice he was there.

Yitzhak is a Zionist Everyman, even if what happens to him does not happen to every Zionist. His life is his own; his fate, if we are to regard it as more than just a curiosity that would hardly justify a six-hundred-page novel, must suggest something greater. But what? Agnon wrote "Only Yesterday" in Jerusalem during the years of World War II, when the Old Yishuv was a much smaller part of the city's population than it had been in 1910. Its battle with the New Yishuv had long been lost. In Palestine as elsewhere in the world, religion was assumed to be on the wane before the wave of a secular future. Non-observant Jews turning or returning like Yitzhak to a life of Jewish observance were rare. Although the irony of a young Zionist coming to Palestine in the early twentieth century only to swallowed up by an ultra-Orthodox quarter of Jerusalem would not have been lost on Agnon's readers, it wouldn't, in 1945, have corresponded to anything significant in the world they knew.

Indeed, these readers could only have been puzzled by the apparent absence in "Only Yesterday" of the great and terrible concerns of the day: the cataclysmic world war that had just been fought, its murder of European Jewry, the desperate struggle for a Jewish state that lay ahead. How could the greatest living Hebrew author, as Agnon was already regarded at the time, have spent the years in which all this was happening writing a lengthy work of fiction about a life as peripheral as Yitzhak Kummer's?

The answer may lie in Balak.

Balak has perplexed readers of "Only Yesterday" even more than Yitzhak has. What is he doing in the novel? Agnon, who had written an independent, shorter version of Balak's story in the early 1930s before greatly expanding it in "Only Yesterday," was well aware that this question would be asked. In a chapter of the novel that he wrote and then deleted, he addressed it and the reader directly:

> I know you're displeased with me for mixing one thing with another and confusing animals with human beings. In your opinion, dear reader, I should have kept Yitzhak and the dog apart and made of them two separate stories. Moreover, you're annoyed at me for letting a dog talk and giving him language in which to

think about things that no bird or beast has the slightest need to think of … [especially since] a shrewd critic has already established that horses do not speak like people.

Although the identity of this critic might be searched for without being found, the horse alluded to is clearly Mendele's mare. Most critics of "Only Yesterday" have rejected the view that Balak, like the afflicted beast of burden in "The Mare," stands for the Jewish people, and have offered other interpretations of him. He is Yitzhak's alter ego; he is Yitzhak's repressed erotic and aggressive self; he is a demonic force let loose on a helpless world; he is the eternal victim of inscrutable Fate; he is all of these things and still more; he is only a dog. And a marvelous dog he is, sniffing, scratching, squatting, trotting, barking and growling, yelping and yowling, and cocking his ears and wagging his tail as dogs do.

Still, Balak is, as has been said, a very Jewish dog, and nothing is more Jewish about him than the way the world fears him, reviles him, drives him into exile, hounds him from place to place, and seeks to kill him without any reason that he can discern. Can it be a coincidence that Agnon gave him such a prominent place in a novel written during World War II? Is it conceivable that he could have done so without having Europe's Jews in mind?

I think not. "Only Yesterday" is a book written in the shadow of the Holocaust.

Mistakenly thought by his persecutors to be mad, Balak becomes mad. The Jewish people, though it had every reason during and after the Holocaust to go mad too, remained remarkably sane. But madness, like rabies, incubates before it appears. If the first great fear expressed symbolically in "Only Yesterday" is that a Zionism that is too secular will one day swing like a pendulum to its opposite extreme, the second is that sooner or later, today or tomorrow, a madness contracted from Jewish history will claim the Jewish people as its victim. Not even love (for who can doubt Yitzhak and Shifra's?) will be able to save it then.

Agnon, the wiliest of all Hebrew authors, believed in the synthesis that Amos Oz called naive and was as apprehensive for a Zionism that rejected or failed to achieve it as he was for a modern Hebrew that was detached from its roots. In terms of the great debate between Ahad

Ha'am and Berdichevsky, he was an Ahad Ha'amist like Bialik as opposed to a Berdichevskyan like Brenner. Unlike either man, with both of whom he had close personal ties, he was an observant Jew, though one who had lapsed during his years in Jaffa. When he returned to religion, however, he did not do so like Yitzhak. The Orthodoxy he practiced until his death in Jerusalem in 1970 was a carefully modulated one. The more one reads him, the more impossible it becomes to determine whether his Judaism was a matter of faith, ancestral loyalty, cultural conviction, inborn conservatism, a deliberately chosen bulwark against disorder, or some combination of these things. He had no more qualms about turning his accomplished sense of irony against it than about turning it against anything else.

Irony, present in all his work, was a balancing act for Agnon, keeping him equidistant from everything he wrote about, and a sense of balance characterized everything he wrote, from his language and sentence structure to his delineations of character and fictional plots. "Only Yesterday" is a novel about the loss of balance in one young man and its feared loss in a people. It may strike its readers today as being more timely than it did in 1945.

Chapter Twelve

Closing Thoughts

1

Brenner, in his 1914 review of Mendele's collected work, called it "A Self-Critique in Three Volumes." One could, multiplying the volumes, characterize similarly much of the Hebrew literature of the nineteenth and early twentieth centuries.

But, you say, haven't Jews always been critical – haven't they been *hyper*critical – of just about everything, themselves included?

Of just about everything, no doubt. When you view the world as your adversary, as Jews always have done, you criticize it freely. But of themselves? Prior to the Hebrew literature of the nineteenth century, Jews criticized themselves only when that meant criticizing other Jews who were not themselves. The Prophets castigated Israel but never doubted (although they sometimes complained about it) their prophetic mission. The rabbis reproached Jews for not observing Judaism as they conceived of it; Judaism as they conceived of it remained beyond reproach. The Haskalah questioned many aspects of Jewish existence without questioning its own ideal of the Maskil.

One finds such criticism of the other Jew in the authors discussed in this book, too. In some of them, as in a Maskil like Josef Perl, it is mostly what one finds. Yet starting with Smolenskin and his Yosef in "Lost On

Life's Way" (and even with Perl if one reads "The Revealer of Secrets" as I suggest doing), there is a profound empathy with what is criticized never encountered before in Jewish writing. Smolenskin, Y. L. Gordon, Berdichevsky, Mendele, Bialik, Brenner – their questioning of Jewish life is genuinely *self*-critical, it says: *Yes, I too belong to this; it has shaped me and is part of who I am; that is what makes attacking it so painful.* There is in them a call for Jewish self-scrutiny and an end to the Jewish illusions they were so familiar with because they had had to fight them in themselves – and at the same time, a fierce sense of loyalty to the Jewish people. Even Berdichevsky, as convinced as he came to be that Jewish history had played itself out, couldn't leave that people behind him. He had to write – in Hebrew! – his novel "Miriam" so that its heroine could do it for him.

They had great Jewish knowledge, these men. Without a rabbinical education such as only a small minority of East-European Jews received, they could never have produced a secular Hebrew literature; without rebelling against the values of this education, they *would* never have produced it. When Max Nordau called Ahad Ha'am "a secular Jewish rabbi," he was being – unwittingly, perhaps – more than facetious. Nor was he describing just Ahad Ha'am. Every Hebrew writer of the age had something rabbinical about him; each had rebelled against an elite training in an ancient legacy while never losing the aristocratic sense of being its bearer; each was, in relation to Jewish tradition, an "apostate angel of monarchal pride," as Milton calls the fallen Lucifer of *Paradise Lost,* "conscious of highest worth." If the rabbinic Judaism of nineteenth-century Eastern Europe was a tottering kingdom, Hebrew literature was the government-in-exile formed by the only deserters from its ranks who could claim to be its legitimate heirs.

A government-in-exile that seemed unlikely, to say the least, ever to have a land or a people to rule!

2

"In the Time of the Quake" has two Mendeles, one a believer in Zionism and one not. Mendele's ambivalence toward Zionism was total. Yet apart from Perl and Mapu, who lived in pre-Zionist times, and Rahel, who experienced Zionism with an all-accepting immediacy, every one of the writers I have written about had in him, when it came to Zionism, a believer and a doubter, too.

Zionism, in the late nineteenth and early twentieth centuries, did not have a highly credible program. There were too many unanswered and seemingly unanswerable questions. How could enough Jews be mobilized to go to Palestine? How, even if they could be, would they manage economically? How would they cope with an Arab population that did not want them in its midst? What were the chances that Turkey, or any other country ruling Palestine, would tolerate a large and growing Jewish community whose goal was eventual autonomy or independence? Herzl's assurances that such obstacles could be overcome quickly through diplomacy and high finance, like Ahad Ha'am's insistence that, though they could not be, Zionism could afford to take its time, were convincing only to those eager to be convinced.

The Hebrew literature of the day did not dodge such questions. Yet these were not the questions that concerned it most. The questions that concerned it most were the ones that stood to arise only if the practical ones could be solved. They were questions of identity. They had to do not with how Zionism might be implemented by the Jews but with who the Jews were, who they wanted to be, who they were capable of being, and whether Zionism in any of its forms was compatible with these things.

These forms included the Love of Zion movement, the political Zionism of Herzl, the cultural Zionism of Ahad Ha'am, and the Labor Zionism of the Second Aliyah. The last three especially were beset by many of the same contradictions and paradoxes. They were simultaneously an affirmation of Jewish history and a repudiation of it. They based their claims to Palestine and Jewish nationhood on a religious tradition whose tenets and rituals they did not uphold. They aspired to remake the Jewish people and to preserve it at one and the same time. They sought to normalize it territorially and linguistically by means of an abnormal return to a land it had not lived in and a language it had not spoken for long centuries.

There were Hebrew writers like Ahad Ha'am who thought that such contradictions were resoluble and others like Berdichevsky who came to think that they were not. The argument was intense and intimate. By its very nature, early modern Hebrew literature was the work of a small and homogeneous group of authors. Many knew each other personally. Even when they didn't, it was as if they did. All came from the same shtetl, the same heder, the same yeshivas, the same traditional Jewish home left behind in sorrow or in anger. Their quarrels were fraternal.

In none of these was more at stake than in the quarrel over Zionism. To be a doubter was, for a Hebrew writer, to relinquish all hope for the future of Hebrew literature, let alone for the survival of his own work. Without a Hebrew-speaking-and-reading public in Palestine to sustain such a literature, Hebrew was a language that soon would be read, as Y. L. Gordon predicted, only for its sacred texts. And yet the doubters could not give Hebrew up. It was too much a part of them. There was a tortuous illogic in this.

But the believers, too, could not help doubting. Suppose they were wrong. Suppose the only difference between them and the doubters was that the doubters had the courage to see things as they were. An existential dread of Zionism's failure pervades the Hebrew literature of the late nineteenth and early twentieth centuries.

Zionism did not fail. It succeeded spectacularly, though tragically too late to save most of Europe's Jews. And because it did, the deeper questions asked by early modern Hebrew literature have now come to the fore. Who are the Jewish people? Who do they want to be? Who are they capable of being?

3

The controversy between Ahad Ha'am and the early Berdichevsky never ended, though it may appear to have done so with the dissolution of the "Canaanites," the movement of Tel Aviv writers and artists, most active in the 1950s and '60s, that proclaimed the birth in Israel of a new "Hebrew people" distinct from diaspora Jewry. With its rhetoric of being more connected to the myths and gods of the ancient Near East than to the Judaism of the rabbis and the synagogue, Canaanism was pure Berdichevskyanism, even if Berdichevsky himself was too diasporic a figure to be invoked as its founding father.

Never more than a small if intellectually provocative coterie, the Canaanites faded away, leaving little enduring behind. The protraction of the Israeli-Arab conflict; the 1962 Eichmann trial with its reawakening of the horrors of the Holocaust that a busy young state had pushed to the back of its mind; the 1967 Six Day War that ended with the historical core of biblical Palestine in Israel's hands and a large and hostile non-Jewish population within its gates; the trauma of the 1973 Yom Kippur War, soberingly named for the Jewish calendar's day of judgment; the shock of the General Assembly's 1975 "Zionism is Racism" resolution, opposed by only one-quarter of the world's nations – such things left even the least traditionally religious of Israelis with the understanding that their Jewishness and its thousands of years of history could not be casually exchanged for a newly minted identity.

But what kind of Jews were they, these secular Israelis? A still coalescing amalgam of the first Jews since antiquity to live as a sovereign majority in a country of their own, they were clearly different from the Iraqi Jews, Kurdish Jews, Persian Jews, Egyptian Jews, Yemenite Jews, Indian Jews, North African Jews, Italian Jews, Greek and Turkish Jews, French Jews, German Jews, East-European Jews, and North and South American Jews of whom or of whose descendants they were composed. Yet different *how*?

Was it in the Ahad-Ha'amian sense of being a new but organic branch on the evolutionary tree of the Jewish people? This was how Israel's secular establishment conceived of them and sought to mold them in the matrix of a shared Israeli identity. Their home was the Land of Israel. Their language was Hebrew. They sent their children to schools in which the Bible and Jewish history, literature, and religion were part of the core curriculum. Their official day of rest was the Jewish Sabbath. Their vacations were the days of the Jewish holidays. Their national symbols – the star-of-David on their flag, the seven-branched Menorah on their passports – were Jewish ones. The Jewish dietary laws were observed in the army they served and patriotically fought in. They circumcised their male children, were married under a Jewish wedding canopy, were buried in a Jewish grave. They encouraged diaspora Jews to join them by a "Law of Return" granting Jewish immigrants automatic citizenship and government aid. If Jewish history was the record of an interaction between the Jews and a world to which the Jews gave and from which they took, filling what they took with Jewish content; and if the modern age was the age of the secular nation-state; then surely the state of Israel was the most appropriate of all possible Jewish responses to modernity.

But secular Israel was also a radical break with the Jewish past. Its Jewish identity had little or nothing to do with religious beliefs, synagogue attendance, observance of Jewish ritual, or familiarity with Jewish texts. The Jewish knowledge its children took away from their schooling was skin-deep. Its Sabbaths were spent at the beach and the barbecue grill rather than at cultural events like Bialik's *oneg shabbat*. Its Jewish holidays were occasions for vacationing in nature or touring abroad. The kosher kitchens of its army fed a military machine like any other. The Jewish rites of passage it observed were administered by a rabbinate it fiercely resented. Its attitude toward Jewish immigrants was at times unwelcomingly nativist. Its model of the good life was to be found in the affluent societies of Europe and America, not in Jewish tradition. Its patriotism did not prevent the emigration of close to a million of its citizens in the first seventy years of its existence.

Hebrew and the Land of Israel, yes. But where in all this was Ahad Ha'am's "national spirit"? Was not this secular Israeli society more like that envisioned in the 1920s by Berdichevsky's disciple Ya'akov Klatzkin and adumbrated as far back as the 1880s by Eliezer Ben-Yehuda in *Ha-Shahar*? "Zionism," Klatzkin wrote, "has inaugurated a new era that will ... redefine Jewishness in secular terms. One day Jews will stake their lives on the national forms of territory and language as their ancestors did on Judaism's religious content."

Form versus content. Land and language versus the culture and values bounded by them. The debate touches on all aspects of Israeli life. Is Israel to be, as is called for by some, a "state of all its citizens" – a country of Jews, Arabs, and others natively born, such as the non-Jewish children of immigrants from the ex-Soviet Union and of foreign workers from Africa, Asia, and South America, all equal before a neutral law? Perhaps one day these groups will fuse into a single Hebrew-speaking people living in historic Palestine. Meanwhile, all distinctions between them drawn by such policies as the official adoption of the Jewish calendar, or the favoring of Jewish over non-Jewish immigrants, should be abolished.

Or is Israel to be, as promulgated by a 2018 law of the Knesset, "the nation state of the Jewish people," with a "national, cultural, religious and historical right to self-determination" belonging to its Jews alone? This state is empowered to "preserve the ties between [the Jews of Israel] and the members of the Jewish people…in the Diaspora," as well as the latter's "cultural, historical and religious heritage." Non-Jews can be citizens and enjoy all civil rights, but they will never be part of a new Israeli nation because no such nation will ever come into being. There will only be an ancient Jewish one, part living in and governing the Land of Israel, and part in the rest of the world.

Berdichevsky versus Ahad Ha'am!

4

Neither of these men gave more than passing thought to the persistence in Jewish life of traditional religion, which both considered a spent historical force. The one feature of contemporary Israel that might have surprised them most is the remarkable resurgence in it of religious Orthodoxy.

It was rabbinic Judaism that kept the Jewish yearning for Zion alive throughout the ages – and that fought Zionism tooth-and-nail when it appeared on the Jewish scene in the late nineteenth century. Zionism, it held, was a *d'hikat ha-ketz,* a "forcing of the End." It was the latest in a long series of attempts to usurp God's prerogative of terminating the Jews' exile when and how He saw fit, and it could only lead, like all such attempts before it, to disaster.

A minority of Orthodox rabbis disagreed. They gave their blessings to the religiously observant Jews of the First Aliyah and held that Zionism and Judaism were compatible as long as the former treated the latter with respect. Secular Zionism was viewed by them as both a friendly and a rival force, to be collaborated with and contested simultaneously. So, fondly approving and sternly disapproving at once, is the attitude of Agnon's Malkov toward the Second Aliyah *halutzim* in his boarding house.

As twentieth-century Orthodoxy split into its modern Orthodox and ultra-Orthodox wings, their positions on Zionism helped define the difference. Ultra-Orthodoxy was anti-Zionist. Modern Orthodoxy participated in the Zionist Organization founded by Herzl, formed political parties to compete in its elections, and was active in its institutions. But although its *dati le'umi* or "national religious" community, as it came to be known in Hebrew, contributed significantly to the establishment of

Israel, its role was ancillary. From the time of the Second Aliyah, secular Zionism took the lead. Religious Zionism followed, frustrated by not being in the vanguard.

All this changed in the years after 1967. Once the euphoria of the victory of the Six Day War had passed, secular Israel found itself an increasingly consumerist society. Its pioneering ethos was on the wane. A. D. Gordon's "religion of labor," that great current of devotional emotion diverted from the synagogue and the study house to the shores of the Kinneret and the fields of the Valley of Jezreel, had run its course. The flagship institutions of Israel's Labor Zionist establishment – its kibbutzim, its moshavim, its interlocking network of labor unions and economic, industrial, social, and cultural enterprises known as the Histadrut – were in a state of decline. So was the Labor Party itself. Defeated by Menachem Begin's right-wing Likud in 1977's national elections, it lost its dominant role and its confidence. The spent historical force turned out to be it.

Labor was of two minds about Jewish settlement in Judea and Samaria, the so-called "West Bank" of the Jordan conquered in 1967, which it had hopes of trading for peace with the Arab world. The Likud had no such reservations. It opened the entirety of the newly acquired territories to Jewish settlers, of whom a disproportionate number, and by far the most militant, came from the national religious camp. They viewed themselves as contemporary *halutzim* reclaiming the most treasured part of God's promised land, just as the pioneers of Labor Zionism had done for the Galilee, the Valley of Jezreel, and the Negev. As their numbers grew, so did their prominence and influence over government policies. At last, they and their rabbis, to whom they deferred, were at the forefront. The torch had passed to religious Zionism.

And at the same time, the place of ultra-Orthodox or *haredi* Jews in Israeli life was expanding, too. Once assumed to be a vanishing relic that would never recover from its decimation in the Holocaust, ultra-Orthodoxy made an extraordinary comeback. A phenomenally high birthrate swelled its numbers exponentially. A tiny fraction of Israel's Jewish population in 1948, it was five percent in 1990; 10 percent in 2010; projected to double that figure by 2030; to redouble it by 2060. Its rabbinically controlled parties, marginal players in Israeli politics before the late

1970s, now became pivotal in Israeli parliamentary coalitions. No Israeli government could rule without meeting at least some of their demands.

Agnon's Yitzhak Kummer regresses to ultra-Orthodox Jerusalem. So does Yehezkel Hefetz, the protagonist of Brenner's last novel "Breakdown and Bereavement." (A *halutz* from Eastern Europe like Yitzhak, Yehezkel's brief stint as a laborer in a Second Aliyah commune is cut short by an accident, followed by a retreat to one of Jerusalem's religious quarters.) Both novels disappointed their readers. They seemed detached from the Palestinian life that they knew. Today, they seem prescient.

Yitzhak and Yehezkel disappear into the streets of an Old Yishuv whose days were thought to be numbered. A century later, the rest of Jerusalem is following them. Everywhere, *haredi* Jews are moving into previously secular neighborhoods. Already they form more than a third of the city's Jewish population; their children comprise over half of its young. Their yeshivas have never had higher enrollments. As many of their men study in them, supported by public funds, as go to work. They are Jerusalem's poorest inhabitants and have helped to make it the poorest city in the country. They have spread to other cities they were never found in before, taking their way of life with them.

Blind in his dungeon, Yehuda Leib Gordon's Zedekiah, foresaw a time when all Judah,

> Young and old, would study Torah –
> From prince to peasant, all would be
> Scribes and devotés of prophecy.
> The plowman would put aside his plow;
> The soldier would no longer practice how
> To wield his spear and javelin;
> The potter's wheel would cease to spin;
> The smith would leave his forge, the shopkeeper his wares,
> To wear haircloth and be soothsayers;
> The carpenter's drills would be beaten into quills,
> His chisels into priestly codicils.

Was he thinking of 2060? Not even in the days when horse-drawn carriages journeyed between them has Jerusalem seemed so far from Tel Aviv. And meanwhile, the West Bank settlements go on growing. Any evacuation of them, as the small number of Israeli settlements in the Gaza Strip were evacuated in 2005, has long been untenable. Judea and Samaria are now zones of daily warfare in which Palestinians attack Jews and Jews attack Palestinians; the most zealous settlers and their rabbis set the tone; the police and army are helpless to rein them in; and the government, more often than not, lets them have their way. A rabid religious nationalism has invaded the Israeli bloodstream.

> Since our nation first began to be,
> The Law's upholders and the monarchy
> Have been at war. Always the visionaries
> Have sought to make the kings their tributaries ....

***

> So every prophet in his hour
> Has fought to get the king under his power.
> What Samuel did to Saul is what
> I met with from the man of Anatot,
> And what awaits each ruler of our nation
> Until the final generation.
> I see how on that distant day
> The son of Hilkiah will have his way.
> His dispensation will prevail;
> All governance will founder and then fail;
> Our people, erudite in chapter and in verse,
> Will go from woe to woe and bad to worse.
> I see ... alas, I see!

A Jewish state, Gordon feared, would ultimately fall into the hands of the same religious zealots who had once decried the thought of it. The Jews were an incorrigibly recidivist people. They never outgrew their past. History kept repeating on them. Yesterday's hopeless revolt against the Roman Empire would recur as tomorrow's doomed attempt to swallow an undivided Land of Israel with its indigestible Arab population. The battle between the limitations of reality and a faith-driven disdain for them would go on in Jewish life forever – and reality would not always win out.

5

Secular Zionism was a revolution in Jewish life, perhaps the greatest ever attempted. It sought to change the Jewish people fundamentally. To give it a home. To teach it to defend itself. To get it to take responsibility for itself. To be less bookish and more physical. To think honestly and critically about its situation. To give up the fantasies and delusions of grandeur with which it had sought to compensate for its lowly status. To rejoin the family of nations.

To be *like* the nations. So the Israelites tell Samuel they want to be when asking him for a king, because they wish to fight their enemies as a unified force rather than as the disjointed tribes they have been. Samuel grumbles. He warns them it's a bad idea, that they're better off under the sovereignty of God. In the end, he grudgingly accedes and crowns Saul. And then, as Zedekiah says, he proceeds to destroy him.

Are we now living through the counter-revolution? Was secular Zionism, as Rabbi Kook thought, no more than the temporary disguise behind which religious impulses were operating all along?

Did Zionism go too far? Did it not go far enough? Did it change the Jews too much or too little?

Did the pendulum overshoot its swing back because it overshot its first swing, as Agnon suggested in *Only Yesterday*? Or did the failure lie in the first swing's falling short, as Amos Oz argued in writing about that novel? Did Zionism get stuck halfway between a religious and a national definition of the Jews like the groundhog in Mendele's tunnel?

6

Historically, of course, Jews never thought of themselves as just a religion. This was the Berlin Haskalah's innovation. Nor did they think of themselves as just a nation. This was the invention of nineteenth-century Hebrew literature, starting with Smolenskin. They thought of themselves as a religion *and* a nation, "a kingdom of priests and a holy people," as the Bible puts it. The Berlin Haskalah sought to dissolve this bond. So, in a reverse fashion, did secular Zionism.

Was – is – the bond indissoluble?

There is at first glance no resemblance between the issues that tore apart the sixth Zionist Congress in 1903 and those tearing Israel apart today. Then, the argument was over British East Africa. Today it is over Judea and Samaria.

And yet it is essentially the same argument. What is the Jewish people's relationship to its past? How much should this past be allowed to define it? To what extent should its founding myths play a part in its policies? How far can it go in declaring these myths irrelevant without doing violence to itself?

Herzl was not particularly interested in Judaism or Jewish history. The Jews, as he saw it, had a problem – anti-Semitism – that needed to be solved. If it could be solved by means of Palestine, so much the better. If not, it would have to be solved elsewhere. To insist on an unattainable Land of Israel in the name of history and religion, however emotionally understandable, was self-destructive.

The largely secular opposition to Herzl protested bitterly. The Land of Israel was an inalienable part of the Jewish psyche. To renounce it was to mutilate this psyche. Palestine was not available? Better to wait until it was than to jump off the Ugandan cliff.

Putting the military and geopolitical aspects of the matter aside, is the case of Judea and Samaria any different?

7

Herzl was certain that anti-Semitism would vanish from the world once there was a Jewish state. That such a state might become a new focus of anti-Semitism never crossed his mind. And yet not only has this happened, the movement he led is now classed by much of the world with anti-Semitism's bedfellows.

"Zionism is a form of racism and racial discrimination": thus, Resolution 3379 of the United Nations General Assembly, passed by a vote of 72–35 with 32 abstentions on November 20, 1975.

Preposterous and obscene! Zionism has nothing to do with racism. It is no more racist to say that the Jews deserve their own country than it is to say that the French do.

Race has never been a criterion of Jewishness. Anyone visiting Israel is struck by all the shades and colors of humanity in which its Jews come. If the traditional rabbinic standard for belonging to the

Jewish people, matrilineal descent from a Jewish parent, is a biological one, so is the American law that a child of U.S. citizens born anywhere in the world is a citizen like them whereas other children are not. One can become a U.S. citizen by a process of naturalization? So can one become a Jew by a process of conversion. It's the same.

Except that it isn't. Naturalization is not conversion. Civil law is not religious law. A justice of the peace is not a rabbi. Other countries do not make the granting of citizenship dependent on the decisions of their clerics. As I write these words, fifty Filipino children born in Israel to guest-worker parents, their only language Hebrew, their greatest desire to be allowed to be Israelis, face deportation by the Israeli ministry of the interior because they are not Jews.

It would have been easier for them to become Jews, of course, if rabbinic Judaism hadn't stopped proselytizing after the first few centuries of the Christian era. It was then that the Jewish people became a closed club. In Israel, where Orthodox conversion alone is permitted, it still is one. The country's rabbinate does not welcome converts. It makes conversion as difficult as possible. It would have made it impossible for the Filipino children and their parents had they requested it.

Well, then, you say, the problem could be solved if Israel fully practiced religious pluralism, so that Reform and Conservative rabbis could perform conversions, too.

Suppose they could. Suppose conversion were an easy procedure, not only for Filipino children, but for every Colombian, Sri Lankan, Eritrean, or Sudanese – every inhabitant of any Second or Third World country – looking for a better life in Israel. It would then have to be ruled out as a way of acquiring citizenship in a Jewish state, for which only born Jews would henceforth be eligible. Then Zionism *would* be racist.

In the Diaspora, Jews fear assimilation because it means being absorbed by others. In Israel, they fear it because it means having to absorb them.

Paradoxes! Contradictions wherever one turns!

8

Like not a few other so-called secular Israelis, I sometimes say the Kiddush, the Sabbath blessing over wine, with my family on Friday nights. I like doing it. The Sabbath candles are lit. Our children and grandchildren sit around the table. The wine glows in its glasses. Even the phrase, in the singing of which I am joined, "For us have You chosen and by You are we hallowed from all the nations," doesn't bother me. Only afterwards do I think: *But that's it! That's the whole problem!*

We are told that anti-Semitism will always find a focus. Take one away from it and it will come up with another. The Jew as monotheist. The Jew as deicide. The Jew as parochial. The Jew as cosmopolitan. The Jew as capitalist. The Jew as Communist. The Jew as carnal. The Jew as brainy.

Blame the anti-Semite, not the Jew.

True.

But it is too easy to say that anti-Semitism has nothing to do with who the Jews are or have been. A people can't go on believing for thousands of years that it is chosen from all the nations and behaving as though it were without incurring resentment. It can't fully rejoin the family of nations without getting over it.

But how can it when its historical identity has been predicated on it?

By what logic can a we become a not-we that is still a we?

And how especially can it when its we goes so far back in time? "There is a reason," says Berdichevsky's character Nachum Sharoni, "that everyone hates us. The eternal hatred for an eternal people! It comes from our religion. Our prophets drew a line between nation and nation, tribe and tribe."

Sharoni's friend Yerucham is shocked. "'But the prophets are sublime!" he retorts. "There's no one like them. They're our pride among the nations.'"

And Berdichevsky writes:

"Nachum said nothing. He looked at his friend in despair and shook his head."

The despair was Berdichevsky's. And Berdichevsky understood, too, what Nachum may be silently thinking. The prophets not only laid the ground for anti-Semitism. They were the first anti-Semites. It was from them that Christianity learned to hate the Jews. "They taught Israel to believe," Berdichevsky declared in his "Reevaluations," "that its deeds were evil." They taught the world to believe it. Their denunciations of

Israel for not living up to its chosenness were unceasing. "Shall not my soul be avenged on such a nation as this?" asks the God of Jeremiah.

The world thought it was merely doing God's bidding.

9

If you are supposed to be better than everyone and you aren't, you may end up convincing yourself and others that you are worse. Hence the Prophets. Hence Brenner's Oved Etsot. Hence the moral groveling of the so-socially-just Jews of our times who think Israel's sins exceed all others.

Of such self-abasement, too, Zionism had hoped to cure the Jews.

10

I write these lines in the summer of 2019, between the indecisive Israeli elections of April of this year and their re-run that is scheduled for September. Rarely have elections in this country seemed so fateful.

However they turn out, though, they will not be quite as fateful as they seem. Some things can't be settled by a show of hands, as Herzl sought to settle the Uganda debate.

Think of Europe. There isn't a European nation that didn't come into being while grappling with many of the same problems faced by Israel today. Its ethnic composition. The relations between its majority and its minorities. Its languages. Its system of government. The struggle between its religious and secular authorities. Its independence from, or subjugation of, others. Its frontiers. Its relations with its neighbors. Its place in the world.

These things took centuries, often violent ones, for Europe to work out. It hasn't finished working them out yet. Why should we expect Israel to do so in our lifetimes?

And even if, in our impatience, we demand that it does, there's Mendele's Ashmodai to reflect on. The only thing we can definitely expect from the future is that it will be unlike anything we expected.

11

Yesterday, I went for a walk on the beach. It was a hot summer day with a gentle sea and a soft breeze, ideal for the beginning windsurfers practicing in the bay. Now and then they fell into the water, struggled back onto their boards, and stood again. There were five or six of them, boys and girls, slowly circling the bay.

Ordinary Israeli teenagers. They weren't worried about the future of their country or troubled by Jewish history. They didn't care what anyone thought of the Hebrew they spoke. They didn't know about Ahad Ha'am or Berdichevsky. They had never read a line by either of them and never would. A poem of Bialik's or Rahel's, a story of Agnon's, was all they would have to know of the authors discussed in this book for their high school matriculation exam in literature.

Few Israelis read these authors anymore. Their language is difficult and they wrote about times and places that today seem remote. Their names are known mostly from street signs. Mapu Street. Smolenskin Street. Gordon Street.

But Israelis do read contemporary Hebrew authors. When Amos Oz died this year, it was a national event. And Oz knew his Ahad Ha'am and Berdichevsky, just as he knew his Mapu and Smolenskin and Yehuda Leib Gordon and Agnon – and just as does his friend and literary colleague A. B. Yehoshua. When it comes to the attitudes expressed in their work toward Zionism, the Jewish people, and the state of Israel, it isn't going too far to call Oz an Ahad Ha'amist and Yehoshua a Berdichevskyan. Writers live on in other writers. They form a literary tradition. Where one exists, it is always there to be explored.

12

But not by the Jews of the Diaspora. Hebrew is no longer the international language of the Jewish people. It has ceased to be what Smolenskin called the cord that binds them. Far more Israeli Arabs can speak, read, and write it than all Diaspora-born Jews combined. Even the Orthodox who still learn it do so only for religious purposes. How did Yehuda Leib Gordon put it? The Sadducees will study Greek wisdom and the Pharisees will expound the laws of the bathroom.

Without Hebrew, does a Jewish people still exist?

13

I watch the windsurfers. They'll pass their exams. They'll graduate from high school and go to the army. If they're lucky, there will be no wars while they're in it. They'll finish their service and backpack in far parts of the world. They'll come home and study some more and marry and start careers. Perhaps one of them will leave the country to seek his or her fortune abroad. The others will stay. They'll settle down and raise children and live in what seems, to the casual tourist and most likely to themselves, a reasonably normal country.

And I ask myself: all this soul-searching – all this picking and picking at the Jewish soul – who needs it?

14

Still, the dread of failure persists.

15

Who are we? Who are we capable of being? Who do we want to be?

About the Author

Hillel Halkin was born in New York City in 1939 and has lived in Israel since 1970. A celebrated translator of Hebrew and Yiddish literature, he is also a well-known author whose books include *Letters to an American Jewish Friend* (1976), *Grand Things to Write a Poem On: A Verse Autobiography of Shmuel Hanagid* (2000), *A Strange Death* (2005), *Yehuda Halevi* (2010), and *Jabotinsky: A Life* (2014). His many essays have appeared in such magazines as *Commentary, Mosaic,* and *The Jewish Review of Books.*

The fonts used in this book are from the Arno family